RADICAL REVISIONS

RADICAL

EDITED BY BILL MULLEN AND SHERRY LEE LINKON

REVISIONS

REREADING 1930S CULTURE

UNIVERSITY OF ILLINOIS PRESS   URBANA AND CHICAGO

Library of Congress Cataloging-in-Publication Data
Radical revisions : rereading 1930s culture / edited by
Bill Mullen and Sherry Lee Linkon.
    p.   cm.
Includes bibliographical references and index.
ISBN 0-252-02206-8 (cloth : alk. paper). —
ISBN 0-252-06505-0 (pbk. : alk. paper)
    1. American literature—20th century—History and
criticism. 2. Radicalism in literature. 3. Politics and
literature—United States—History 20th century. 4.
Literature and society—United States—History—20th
century. 5. Women and literature—United States—
History—20th century. 6. Popular culture—United
States—History—20th century. 7. Radicalism—United
States—History—20th century. 8. United States—
Intellectual life—20th century. 9. Afro-Americans in
literature. 10. Proletariat in literature.
    I. Mullen, Bill, 1959– . II. Linkon, Sherry Lee, 1959– .
PS228.R34R33   1996
810.9'358—DC20   95-19533
                                                        CIP

CONTENTS

ACKNOWLEDGMENTS

Many people have helped bring this book to fruition. Its genesis was a conference on the thirties held at Youngstown State University in May of 1992. Among those who helped make that event extraordinary were Barbara Brothers, dean of the College of Arts and Sciences at Youngstown State; Morris Slavin, professor emeritus of history at Youngstown State, whose own experiences of the 1930s have been a constant inspiration; and other members of the conference planning committee: Taylor Alderman, William Greenway, Steve Reese, Susan Russo, John Russo, Martin Berger, and Lowell Satre. To our other colleagues of the English Department who either participated in or supported the conference, and who provided encouragement as we worked on this book, we offer our thanks and appreciation. Also a significant contributor to the 1992 conference was Tillie Olsen, whose reading from *Yonnondio* at Youngstown State galvanized those in attendance. Her political and creative spirit is also acknowledged in the text of *Radical Revisions*.

Others who helped in the preparation of the manuscript were Randy Abel, Michelle Donley, Robert Jakubovic, Anne Snellen, and Nicholas Veauthier. Funding for their activities was provided by the Youngstown State University Research Council. Bege Bowers has also been a patient source of editing wisdom throughout the process.

Finally, we acknowledge the faith and support of our own families. Elizabeth Petrasovic and Frank Bongen helped to guide us through the long process. Max Rudolph Petrasovic Mullen literally "came of age" during the production of this book. To them, for these things and others, it is dedicated.

INTRODUCTION:

REREADING 1930S

CULTURE

Literary history is never an innocent process of recovery. We recover what we are culturally and psychologically prepared to recover and what we "recover" we necessarily rewrite, giving it meanings that are inescapably contemporary, giving it a new discursive life in the present, a life it cannot have had before.
—Cary Nelson, *Repression and Recovery*

In 1974, Delacorte Books issued for the first time in book form Tillie Olsen's incomplete proletarian novel *Yonnondio: From the Thirties*. Olsen's book—like her writing career—interrupted by childbirth, the Great Depression, and the hard economic vicissitudes of being a woman writer on the Left, at once resurrected the reputation of a sadly forgotten author and cultural worker of the 1930s and created an instant "classic" of radical American writing. *Yonnondio's* lyrical protest of the silencing effects of economic dislocation on the bodies and minds of working-class women bridged at once the largely unsung story of women of the depression and emergent women's voices of the 1970s feminist movement. Seven years later, Deborah Rosenfelt's essay "From the Thirties: Tillie Olsen and the Radical Tradition" seized upon the overdue publication of Olsen's book and Olsen herself as a case study of how women on the Left and women of the 1930s had largely been ignored or excluded in literary histories of the radical tradition in U.S. literature.

The confluence of *Yonnondio's* republication and Rosenfelt's critical reevaluation of Olsen appears to be the beginning of a "recovery," in Cary Nelson's words, of the American literary 1930s. In the decades prior to this, critical attention to the literature of the 1930s had largely centered on variations on two critical questions that had assumed almost monolithic proportions: Did the writing on the Left, called variously proletarian, social-realist, or revolutionary during the 1930s, "succeed" as literature, and to what extent did its success or failure reflect the merits or failures of the American and Soviet communism that to one degree or another influenced its production?[1] Olsen's novel and Rosenfelt's essay helped reframe these questions to include consideration of the roles gender and sexuality played in the production of political and literary "discourse" of the 1930s. Put another way, the all-important question of class struggle in the 1930s met the gender struggle head on.

We begin with this anecdote because it symbolizes in several ways the issues underlying the appearance of this collection of essays. In the past ten years, a significant shift has occurred in the discursive direction of scholarship on American literature and culture of the 1930s. In many ways motivated by the feminist, New Left, and identity politics movements of the late 1960s and early 1970s, this challenge has taken the form of what Barbara Foley, in a slightly different context, defines as a "new textual perestroika" (214). Inspired by the canon revisions and pluralism of discourse in literary criticism since the 1960s, contemporary scholars have recently broadened the scope of inquiry on the literature and culture of the 1930s to include a variety of textual approaches: theories of feminism, popular culture, ethnicity, New Historicism, and various new formations of Marxism. Simultaneous with the application of these new approaches has come an appreciation that their intellectual roots lie in ways only recently recoverable in the political and theoretical debates *of* the 1930s. Debates within the Commmunist Left over the "Negro Question," the "Woman Question," and the role of popular culture in the formation of political consciousness have, as James D. Bloom and other contributors to this collection note, an uncanny resonance and significance for many of today's academic workers, whose critical (and political) consciousness may have been formed in parallel, albeit academic, debates over feminism, ethnicity, race, class, and mass culture. These critics have by and large situated their analysis of the 1930s in a way that openly and appreciatively acknowledges a debt to the material and idealistic gains of thirties intel-

lectuals and writers while conscientiously assuming the challenge of adding to, modifying, and refining discursive analysis of the intersection of
gender, race, class, and popular culture. "Just as our opinion of an individual is not based on what he thinks of himself, so we cannot judge . . . a
period of transformation by its own consciousness," wrote Marx and Engels (362–64). Contemporary scholarship on the 1930s as represented in
this collection adheres to this Marxian premise, and its "consciousness"
of the project of historical reconsideration is tempered by an understanding that its own judgments are mere steps in an ongoing evaluation of
history's meanings.

This general critical project, a "rereading" of the 1930s as it were, provides the collective critical drama of this collection. Its essays pose a new
set of questions about the 1930s by a generation of scholars actively reconsidering the critical and political legacy thirties literature and culture has left American letters, politics, and, more recently, textual theory. These questions include but are not limited to the following: What
are the possible responses to the existing paradigms of radical literary
studies as they pertain to literature of the 1930s? What has been the canon
of 1930s literature, and what are the assumptions behind its formulation
and existence? To what extent are women, writers of color, gay and lesbian writers, and other "marginalized" authors represented in the extant
literary histories of the 1930s, and how does our portrait of the decade
change when they are added? How has the important but at times narrow focus on class and communist influence in criticism of 1930s literature concealed or obscured nuances in political formulations of the
period and the accuracy of portrayals of positions attributed to Left writers? What are the "hierarchies" of literature of the 1930s—in genre, form,
and reception—and how have they aided or narrowed analysis of the
decade's overall literary production? Are the temporal boundaries implied by discussion of "the 1930s" sufficient to account for the influences and effects of the literature produced during that period? What may
be gained in understanding 1930s versions of communism inside and
outside the Communist Party U.S.A. by applying New Left, Neo-marx-
ist, and New Historicist modes of analysis? What political and historical
influences have determined the assumptions and directions of critical
evaluation of the 1930s? What affiliations may be sought and found between 1930s formulations of class, race, gender, and popular culture and
their intersection with and vital presence in contemporary literary and
cultural studies? What opportunities for new understanding of the radical tradition and Old Left and New Left Marxisms are afforded by alter-

ations in real world international communism, as witnessed in the break-up of the Soviet Union? Finally, what may be gained by a "cultural stud-ies" approach to the 1930s, one that perhaps best defines the cumulative meaning of the broad range of questions now being put to the decade's literature, culture, and history as represented in this collection?

In recent years, several outstanding studies of neglected or forgotten aspects of U.S. radical literary history, most of them focusing on the 1930s, have appeared to broaden the scope of inquiry into the period and raise some of these questions: Cary Nelson's *Repression and Recovery: Modern American Poetry and the Politics of Cultural Memory 1910–1945*, a study of left-wing poets largely bypassed or ignored in the formation of a largely modernist American poetry canon; Alan Wald's *New York Intellectuals: The Rise and Decline of the Anti-Stalinist Left from the 1930s to the 1980s*, a re-creation of the rise and fall of the Left, Trotskyist, and *Partisan Review* circles of the 1930s and 1940s; Paula Rabinowitz's *Labor and Desire: Women's Revolutionary Fiction in Depression America*, a reevaluation of female proletarian literature of the 1930s; James Bloom's *Left Letters: The Culture Wars of Mike Gold and Joseph Freeman*, a book that seeks to reclaim 1930s political debate as a source for contemporary academic discussions of political criticism; and Barbara Foley's *Radical Representations: Politics and Form in U.S. Proletarian Fiction, 1929–1941*, which diagnoses the legacy of anti-Stalinist bias in the critical tradition of scholarship on thirties pro-letarian literature. Cumulatively, these works have helped give urgency to a new direction in thirties scholarship that this collection is meant to mark and move forward, bringing together a cross section of its scholars and ideas in a kind of roundtable discussion about the causes and conse-quences of this moment in the intellectual history of the 1930s.

This partial list of titles also contours a new generation of scholars' unfolding discovery that the literary history of the U.S. Left, particularly in the 1930s, is an incomplete story, one fragmented or overwritten by larg-er prevailing cultural and political narratives.[2] In the opening essay of this collection, Alan M. Wald maintains that narrative began with the publi-cation of Walter B. Rideout's seminal study *The Radical Novel in the United States* (1956) and included such key works as Daniel Aaron's *Writers on the Left* (1961), David Madden's *Proletarian Writers of the 1930s* (1968), and Ralph Bogardus and Fred Hobson's *Literature at the Barricades: The American Writer in the 1930s* (1982). Collectively, these important texts have helped establish what Wald has aptly called elsewhere a "paradigm of U.S. radical literary studies" (xxiii). Its features include a central inter-action between "indigenous traditions of U.S. writers and Communism," both as ideal and in its so-called Stalinist manifestations; a concentration on the proletarian novel as the central literary form in the thirties and longer radical tradition; and, most important, discussion of radical writing "isolated from the development of contemporary Marxist theory" (xxiii-iv). Recent directions in thirties scholarship are beginning to supplement and challenge this indispensable literary paradigm because its New Critical perspective and at times narrowly class-based scholarship by and about white male writers have helped obscure the cultural diversity and the variety of militant traditions of radical writing in the United States. The outlines of that diversity begin to appear in *Radical Revisions*.

At the same time, the essays in this collection in no way constitute a *repudiation* of previous considerations of 1930s literature. Rather, they are an attempt to revise and reaffirm the essential depth of consideration already given to "marginal" writing in the United States in the 1930s. Significantly, and not coincidentally, this reconstructive approach to the U.S. Left and American literature of the 1930s also applies to larger currents of contemporary scholarship. If much of the literary academy today considers race, class, gender, sexual orientation, and popular culture its points of departure for reassessing U.S. literary history, it too is involved in a wholesale "recovery" of literary tradition. This "double" recovery of the 1930s and the larger U.S. radical tradition, as well as the critical codependence of these enterprises, is also in many ways the larger occasion for this book. It marks a kind of official consciousness on the part of a new generation of scholars that any honest and complete accounting of radical U.S. intellectual history—and the place of today's contemporary scholars in that history—demands a full-scale exploration of the 1930s as the decade when writers and intellectuals first articulated the often disabused and exploited but urgent issues of their time and ours. Thus we have chosen to title this book *Radical Revisions* to suggest both an engaged reconsideration of a historical period and the literal act of revising as providing a new discursive life, which is the communal impetus behind our collection. We also use the word *revision* in the sense of emending and improving. The goal of this collection is to broaden the literal and figurative parameters of critical understanding of "the 1930s" and the parameters of that decade's global influence on larger radical intellectual and literary traditions in the United States, including those driving the reconsideration of relations between politics and literature in the academy. As James Bloom notes in his introduction to *Left Letters: The Culture Wars of Mike Gold and Joseph Freeman*, it is perhaps only now, in the wake of a Soviet-style communism that once served as a straw figure for negative appraisal of much of the Left's writings in the 1930s, that a fair and accurate representation of the thirties and its intellectual and political legacy may begin with anything like fresh objectivity. The outlines of such a fresh perspective are also provided in *Radical Revisions*.

In gathering and arranging essays for *Radical Revisions*, we have looked for work that reflects both the tradition of thirties scholarship and recent developments in criticism. The essays included in this collection give a life to 1930s texts that they "cannot have had before." We begin with an essay that traces the evolution of thirties scholarship, and we close with an essay suggesting that nineties critics can learn much from the politically informed criticism of the 1930s. The remaining essays examine specific writers or texts. We have attempted to arrange them in an order that highlights the connections between the different categories of analysis and between specific essays. For example, while Cary Nelson and Fred L. Gardaphè use quite different texts in their essays on thirties poetry and on Italian-American writers, both raise questions about the development of the thirties canon and argue for new ways of reading the period. Similarly, Suzanne Sowinksa and Constance Coiner both discuss the work of white women writers who were active in the Communist Party, but Sowinska focuses on their representations of race, while Coiner emphasizes gender issues.

This boundary crossing typifies the best of recent cultural studies work, and as the essays here suggest, the eclectic, theoretically and politically informed approaches of this growing field work especially well for studying thirties culture. For a period so marked by contentious definitions of literature and literary genres, critical approaches that read across the boundaries between kinds of texts and use theories rooted in aesthetics, psychology, material reality, and politics yield especially rich results. Paula Rabinowitz, for example, combines literary texts with photography and journalism in her study of the relationships between working-class and middle-class women in the 1930s. Similarly, Lawrence F. Hanley ties together thirties essays, fiction, advertising, and film to explore the meanings of class. Individually and in combination, the essays in this volume suggest the importance of looking at the 1930s through the multiple lenses offered by cultural studies.

As Alan M. Wald argues in "The 1930s Left in U.S. Literature Reconsidered," we must begin by understanding and appreciating the history of thirties criticism. Wald provides a historical and critical context for the collection by examining past and current developments in the study of American literature of the 1930s. He reviews the "liberal paradigm" of

thirties scholarship from the 1960s and 1970s that emphasized the proletarian novel and the influence of the Communist Party, and he then
sketches the outlines of a new paradigm, influenced by feminist criticism,
multiculturalism, the ongoing "canon debates," and the more sophisticated
versions of Marxist criticism that have developed, in part, in response to
recent changes in Eastern Europe. Wald calls for a new methodology in
thirties criticism that would draw on previously neglected primary materials and contemporary theoretical work in the areas of gender, race, ethnicity, sexuality, mass culture, and national identities. He suggests that
thirties scholarship should reexamine the influence of thirties literature
on later writers as well as public responses to thirties radicalism in subsequent decades. Scholars should question traditional definitions and dichot-
omies often applied to thirties literature, he argues, including the opposition between realism and modernism. Its clear overview of the field makes
Wald's essay a particularly good starting point for this collection.

Cary Nelson also suggests that a reexamination of 1930s politics together with the application of 1990s critical practice can help us reread the
period in useful ways. Drawing on the Bakhtinian model of literature as
dialogue in his "Poetry Chorus: Dialogic Politics in 1930s Poetry," Nelson
suggests a rereading of 1930s poetry based on a new understanding of the
relationship between literature and political life. He argues that writing
poetry during the 1930s became a credible form of revolutionary action
and that reading poetry became a means of participating in social change.
Poets of the 1930s viewed writing as a collaborative, dialogic enterprise,
creating a chorus of assenting and dissenting voices, none heard entirely
on its own. Along with presenting a historically based argument for viewing 1930s poetry as a cultural dialogue, Nelson offers an extended example of the intertextuality of the poetry of the decade in a pastiche from the
works of many well-known and forgotten poets. His essay challenges the
established canon of 1930s poetry as well as our understanding of the politics of poetry.

Like Nelson, Fred L. Gardaphè critiques canonical approaches to 1930s
literature by considering the intersection of literary history, communist
political ideology, and the politics of ethnicity. "Left Out: Three Italian-
American Writers of the 1930s" examines the critical response to three
working-class Italian-American writers of the 1930s: Pietro di Donato, John
Fante, and Jerry Mangione. All three have been seen as marginal writers
in critical discussions of the proletarian novel, and Gardaphè argues this
is because of their ethnicity and religion. He also considers how their literary styles and the development of their careers may have kept them out

of the 1930s canon and proposes a revised literary history that includes their contribution.

James A. Miller's "African-American Writing of the 1930s: A Prologue" similarly challenges the accuracy of the existing paradigm of thirties literary history and offers a revision of the received history of African-American literature. He positions African-American writing of the 1930s in a larger historical context by reconsidering the relationship between the Harlem Renaissance and the development of "New Negro" writing in the 1920s. Miller focuses his discussion on the career of Claude McKay, one of the African-American writers most closely involved with "official" communism during the 1920s and 1930s. Instead of reading the works of African-American writers as marked first by political distortion and later by political disillusionment, Miller suggests that leftist politics nourished the work of African-American writers and provided an essential link between the 1920s and the 1930s.

William J. Maxwell's revisioning of the existing paradigms of 1930s literature extends this consideration of Claude McKay by examining the relationship between McKay and Mike Gold, who coedited the *Liberator* for several years during the 1920s. Like Miller, Maxwell considers the relationship between McKay and Gold to be central in the analysis of the connections between politics, literature, and race relations. Where Miller considers McKay's work with Gold in the context of McKay's relationship with the white Left and the Communist Party, Maxwell examines the relationship between McKay and Gold as part of a reevaluation of Gold's attitudes toward African-American literature and culture. In "The Proletarian as New Negro: Mike Gold's Harlem Renaissance," Maxwell draws on letters, literary histories, Gold's columns, and his little-known play *Hoboken Blues* to argue that Gold rightly saw himself as an intimate if critical supporter of the Harlem Renaissance. Gold's work with McKay on the *Liberator*, his play, and his attack on Carl Van Vechten's influence all show an author attempting to "Marxify" this Renaissance from within, linking class and race, the proletariat and the New Negro.

Suzanne Sowinska continues the discussion of how white proletarian writers responded to the issue of race in "Writing across the Color Line: White Women Writers and the 'Negro Question' in the Gastonia Novels." Sowinska highlights the Gastonia writers' efforts to incorporate African-American characters and perspectives in their work and explores how Mary Heaton Vorse, Fielding Burke, Myra Page, and Grace Lumpkin represented the roles of gender and race in the creation of working-class consciousness. These novels examine how the barrier of racial difference divided the working-class and suggest the importance of recognizing commonalities as well as respecting difference. Sowinska shows how these writers attempted to include the perspectives of black workers, especially black women, in proletarian literature, and while their explorations of African-American consciousness do not always succeed, their work represents a first important step toward crossing the color line.

Constance Coiner also considers the responses of proletarian writers to differences other than class in her examination of the relationships between Meridel Le Sueur, Tillie Olsen, and the Communist Party in "Literature of Resistance: The Intersection of Feminism and the Communist Left in Meridel Le Sueur and Tillie Olsen." She identifies the complex relationship between feminism and 1930s leftist politics in the writings of Olsen and Le Sueur. Although both were active in the Communist Party, which, Coiner argues, viewed "proletarian" and "masculine" as nearly synonymous, their fiction reveals their own growing feminist consciousness. Through close readings of Olsen's *Yonnondio* and Le Sueur's stories and reportage, Coiner argues that the two created a "literature of resistance" directed against both the dominant culture and the restrictive elements in the leftist subculture.

Jessica Kimball Printz argues that other women writers in the 1930s were also wrestling with feminist concerns in their work. In "Tracing the Fault Lines of the Radical Female Subject: Grace Lumpkin's *The Wedding*," she draws on the concept of female subjectivity as a means of understanding the success and limitations of women's resistance to traditional female roles. In her discussion of Lumpkin's 1939 novel, Printz argues that despite its middle-class setting and lack of overtly political material, the novel offers a strong critique of social constructions of gender and the limitations they place on female consciousness and women's resistance to patriarchy. In her examination of Lumpkin's story of two white, middle-class sisters, Printz traces the development of feminine identity and the conflict it engenders between desire and independence. She suggests that Lumpkin's novel both acknowledges women's resistance and critiques its limitations.

Paula Rabinowitz expands the discussion of women's subjectivity beyond "literary" texts to include journalism and photography as well as novels. In "Margaret Bourke-White's Red Coat; or, Slumming in the Thirties," Rabinowitz considers the use of the gaze in the writing of a number of middle-class white women of the 1930s and in the photography of Bourke-White. She argues that as creators of and characters in a variety of texts, middle-class white women were observers as well as objects of observation. Through their own observations, middle-class women critiqued the roles and behaviors of working-class women, while at the same time they were subject to the objectifying gaze of men and other women. Rabinowitz uses Bourke-White as a case study, exploring how the photographer used the camera's eye to define a subordinate subject position for the working-class women she featured in her pictures and how Bourke-White's contemporaries criticized her photos and her presentation of herself.

Colette A. Hyman similarly considers how popular texts operated in relation to thirties politics. In "Politics Meet Popular Entertainment: The Case of Workers' Theater of the 1930s," she examines theatrical productions staged by several labor organizations during the 1930s and suggests the importance of popular arts in the formation of the Left. In their efforts to dramatize the labor movement, she argues, playwrights and activists borrowed from the genres of commercial popular entertainment: melodrama, Tin-Pan Alley, and vaudeville. Such popular entertainment offered workers a new means of constructing class identity and presented a class-based analysis to theater audiences. Although adaptations of popular theater forms and styles risked distracting participants and audiences from the political concerns of the labor movement, Hyman shows how they allowed workers to create popular entertainment that reflected class-based views and to claim a place in mainstream culture as consumers of popular culture.

Morris Dickstein also suggests that the popular culture of the 1930s offered more than escape to its original consumers and that it offers substantive texts to 1990s critics. In "Depression Culture: The Dream of Mobility," he argues that 1930s popular films reflect conflicting ideas and desires about American culture, including contrary impulses toward mobility and stasis, freedom and captivity, autonomy and dependence. He looks not only at apparently "escapist" films, such as the Fred Astaire and Ginger Rogers dance musicals, but also at 1930s "problem" films, such as *I Am a Fugitive from a Chain Gang* and *The Grapes of Wrath*, suggesting that both genres illustrate American frustrations with the real difficulty of changing one's social position during a period of economic stagnation.

Like Dickstein, Lawrence F. Hanley considers film and other popular forms in examining the meaning of difference during the 1930s. Hanley draws on a variety of texts, including magazine ads; essays by Edmund Wilson; *Sanctuary*, William Faulkner's most popular novel of the time; and *King Kong*, to trace the development of the tension between dominant narratives of unity and the growing awareness of class differences. By constructing a constellation of literary and popular texts, Hanley challenges the categories of "high" and "low" culture and suggests we can gain a more complete understanding of the dynamics of class and difference in 1930s culture by considering the historical moment as a whole, through a variety of texts, instead of attempting to define an entire period through the narrow aperture of any one genre.

In "Political Incorrectness: The 1930s Legacy for Literary Studies," James D. Bloom considers what lessons critics can learn today from the intellectual politics of the 1930s. Bloom examines U.S. literary Marxism in the 1930s as a model for current academic literary studies and suggests that leftist scholars should embrace an egalitarian and inclusionary political agenda similar to that of the Left in the 1930s. Citing such writers as Mike Gold, Richard Wright, and Meridel Le Sueur, Bloom employs the perceptions and paradigms developed by contemporary theorists to support his conclusion that the contemporary academic literary Left often hobbles itself with rigid self-congratulatory proclamations instead of pursuing the diversity and inclusiveness we profess. If we could use the 1930s as a model for combining politics with criticism, we could offer more hope for political change as well as a truly engaged cultural criticism. Bloom's argument that we can learn from the 1930s seems a fitting ending for this collection.

NOTES

1. In *Radical Representations*, Barbara Foley argues for the necessity of recognizing the "anti-Stalinist legacy" of criticism of 1930s literature as a hindrance to clear analysis and appreciation of proletarian texts produced during the period.

2. See the text and notes of Alan Wald's introduction to the Morningside Books Edition of Daniel Aaron's *Writers on the Left* for a valuable list of recent works of criticism on the 1930s and Left literature as well as recent reprints of other primary source titles.

WORKS CITED

Bloom, James. *Left Letters: The Culture Wars of Mike Gold and Joseph Freeman.* New York: Columbia University Press, 1992.
Foley, Barbara. *Radical Representations: Politics and Form in U.S. Proletarian Fiction, 1929–1941.* Durham, N.C.: Duke University Press, 1993.
Marx, Karl, and Friedrich Engels. *"Preface* to a Contribution to a Critique of

Political Economy." *Selected Works.* Vol. 1. Moscow: Foreign Languages Publishing House, 1955.

Nelson, Cary. *Repression and Recovery: Modern American Poetry and the Politics of Cultural Memory.* Madison, Wisc.: University of Wisconsin Press, 1989.

Olsen, Tillie. *Yonnondio: From the Thirties.* New York: Delacorte, 1974.

Rabinowitz, Paula. *Labor and Desire: Women's Revolutionary Fiction in Depression America.* Chapel Hill: University of North Carolina Press, 1991.

Rosenfelt, Deborah. "From the Thirties: Tillie Olsen and the Radical Tradition." *Feminist Studies* 7 (Fall 1981): 370–406. Reprinted in *Feminist Criticism and Social Change.* Ed. Judith Newton and Deborah Rosenfelt. New York: Methuen, 1985.

Wald, Alan. Introduction. *Writers on the Left: Episodes in American Literary Communism.* By Daniel Aaron. 1961. New York: Columbia University Press, 1992.

———. *The New York Intellectuals: The Rise and Decline of the Anti-Stanlinist Left from the 1930s to the 1980s.* Chapel Hill: University of North Carolina Press, 1987.

1

THE 1930S
LEFT IN U.S.
LITERATURE
RECONSIDERED

On January 7, 1968, a fifty-six-year-old man, over six feet tall, heavy, and dark featured, collapsed and died of a heart attack in a laundromat near St. Nicholas Place in New York City. The ensuing investigation revealed that the man who died had several identities. One was that of a famous mystery writer, "Ed Lacy," whose works sold over twenty-eight million copies and were printed in twelve countries. Books by Lacy first appeared during the Cold War era, with such raunchy pulp fiction titles as *The Woman Aroused* (1951), *Sin in Their Blood* (1952), *Strip for Violence* (1953), *Enter without Desire* (1954), and *Go for the Body* (1954). However, in 1957 Lacy made literary history with *Room to Swing*, winner of the Mystery Writers of America's Edgar Award for the best novel of the year.

Room to Swing is noteworthy for introducing the African-American detective Toussaint Marcus Moore, declared by the *New York Times* to be "the first Negro private eye" ("Leonard Zinberg" 35). The entry on Lacy in John Reilly's authoritative reference book *Twentieth-Century Crime and Mystery Writers* states, "Before the civil rights movement made it fashionable, Ed Lacy made blacks a part of mystery fiction" (547). In fact, some readers and editors thought Lacy himself was black. His work appears in *Best Short Stories by Afro-American Writers (1925–1950)*, a collection of fiction from the *Baltimore Afro-*

American depicting African-American characters that go beyond conventional stereotypes.[1]

But the man who died had been known in an earlier time, in the pre-McCarthy years, by another name—his birth name, Leonard S. (or "Len") Zinberg. Zinberg was not African-American but Jewish-American. He was not in those years a detective pulp writer but spent the late 1930s writing a powerful antiracist novel about the boxing profession, *Walk Hard—Talk Loud* (1940). The book cover reads, "A Negro prizefighter in a SAVAGE white world!" When Zinberg returned from military service, it was produced as the play *Walk Hard* for the American Negro Theater Company in Harlem in 1944. The script was by the African-American playwright Abram Hill, a veteran of the Federal Theater Project of the 1930s.

Four novels appeared before Zinberg became Lacy. One of these, *Hold with the Hares*, was specifically about 1930s radicalism and the struggle to reconcile political ideals with economic survival. Although published in 1948, the work was regarded as so much a part of the 1930s culture that the *New York Times* reviewer protested: "Mr. Zinberg's book is well-observed and well-recorded. It is interesting and intelligent. But there is a curiously archaic quality about its idealism. Even the most enthusiastic reader would feel that he would like to take this author by the arm at times and say, 'Look, by all means, you may be absolutely right. But it is much, much later than you think'" ("Conscience" 22). The reviewer spoke more truthfully than he knew; for Len Zinberg, who was and tried to remain a Communist, the time *was* much later than he thought. Although Zinberg's views never changed, dramatic alterations in the political climate in the United States forced him to mask that early identity forever, and he was hardly the only one to do so.

In the 1940s, Zinberg had been a public activist in the Writers and Publishers Division of the ASP (the Committee of the Arts, Sciences and Professions, organized to support Henry Wallace's Progressive Party campaign). Throughout the Cold War era, as Lacy, he remained a part of a private Marxist discussion circle meeting monthly at the home of the blacklisted high school principal Annette T. Rubinstein. Rubinstein's salons were attended largely by the circle around *Masses and Mainstream*. This small publication was the vestige of what was once the powerful Communist intellectual magazine of the 1930s, the *New Masses*. According to Rubinstein, Zinberg was obsessed with keeping the truth about his identity as Ed Lacy a secret, even from his literary agents, and he related to the discussion group in an increasingly clandestine manner. Zinberg's wife was an African-American writer, who was for a period employed as a secretary for the Yiddish Communist newspaper *Morgen Freiheit*. In addition to the danger of literary blacklisting, the Zinbergs were seeking to adopt a child. This was hard enough in those years for an interracial couple, let alone one with allegedly subversive political associations.

To raise the issue of the cultural significance of Lacy/Zinberg is to raise the specter of an "Other" 1930s—of components of that era and its legacy that we are just now beginning to discover. We confront two names, two careers, two literary genres, and two political periods (pre- and post-McCarthy). These dualisms have a unique relevance to what I see as the "moment" of scholarship on the 1930s we are now entering in the 1990s, a moment well captured by this new collection of scholarly essays, *Radical Revisions*. This aspect is especially pronounced in relation to the central strand of 1930s culture on which I have been conducting research for the past two decades—the fiction, poetry, and literary criticism expressive of the radical critique and utopian vision of the left-wing social movements of the time, to which the democratizing social and cultural movements of our own day are very much indebted.

Moreover, it is telling that I can feel comfortable raising in an essay in this volume the name and career of Ed Lacy/Len Zinberg. Why not start with the names of John Dos Passos and John Steinbeck, which would have been de rigueur before the 1960s? Or the names of Henry Roth, Richard Wright, and Mike Gold, who were so widely discussed in the 1970s? Or the names of Josephine Herbst or Meridel Le Sueur, who were significantly reinscribed into the 1930s tradition in the 1980s? The choice of Zinberg shows the great distance I myself have come, with the help of so many others, in rethinking the decade.

After all, my project as a graduate student from 1969 to 1974 was much closer to canonical 1930s concerns, even though the intervention was conceived as building a bridge back from the New Left to the Old Left. The object was to reclaim the 1930s and 1940s legacy of James T. Farrell as expressing a coherent and usable independent Marxist tradition within U.S. literary radicalism. In the 1970s and early 1980s, this expanded to an attempted rescue of U.S. Marxist modernism as a hidden tradition within the cultural Left. The latter half of my *New York Intellectuals* (1987) seeks to document, among other things, the bankruptcy of politico-cultural anti-Stalinism divorced from anticapitalist premises and social values. The framework, seen in retrospect, was of augmenting, correcting, and developing the contours of a field for which the main lines had by and large been established.

In the 1990s, many scholars no longer feel that way. The more we have dug, the less we know for certain. We are far less confident than ever about what constitutes a decade, a period, a movement; about parameters of a cultural practice; and about the interconnections between literature and politics.

If I had not invoked Ed Lacy/Len Zinberg as an entree to this topic, it would have been just as easy to substitute John Stanford, Frank Marshall Davis, Martha Dodd, Ben Appel, Grace Lumpkin, or H. T. Tsiang. These and many other craft-conscious, as well as class-conscious, writers linked to the 1930s are still awaiting rehabilitation. There hardly could be a more auspicious time for doing so, now that our own "Berlin Wall" of the U.S. literary canon is in the process of crumbling under the blows of yearnings for cultural democracy.

The invocation of an "Other" 1930s, however, is in no sense an effort to *cast out* Dos Passos, Gold, and Herbst, as if we were engaged in a one-on-one competition for "America's Greatest Hits of the 1930s." Rather, we are seeking to complicate and contextualize all dimensions, the known and the unknown, of that stunning, mystifying, and semimythical decade in U.S. cultural life. Our goal is not to displace, according to the hierarchical model of literary scholarship. Nor is it to totally counterpose new discoveries and caricatures of older research, in the sordid tradition of academic one-upping.

Factoring in the "Other" 1930s means, first, to add to the growing list of traditional questions and to promote new angles of approach. Later, when the qualitative leap to a whole different notion of the 1930s actually occurs, such a new synthesis will be the result of a collective process. It will be the product, first of all, of the *many* scholars and cultural workers who have tilled the vineyards of the tradition over the decades. Behind them lie the social movements of women, people of color, workers, and students who have created space in academe and U.S. cultural life for such new perspectives through their material struggles, often in the streets, for a better world. This is a continuation in a later stage of the same efforts promoted by our thirties ancestors.

For example, a consideration of Lacy/Zinberg prompts us to ask if the literature of the 1930s is limited to texts that saw publication only between 1930 and 1939? After all, many of the works of the early 1930s were actually written during the late 1920s, before the crash, and refer back to previous times. *Jews without Money* and *The Disinherited*, to take two canonical Left novels of the decade, were largely published in literary journals during the 1920s, and they focus on pre– and post–World War I years. *Daughter of Earth* was printed in 1929. The famous Gastonia strike novels—the subject of a fresh interpretation in this volume—were based on an event that novelists either witnessed or read about before the 1930s. At least three of the authors—Fielding Burke, Grace Lumpkin, and Myra Page—were drawn to communism in the 1920s, not the 1930s.

Likewise, many important texts of later decades could not have been conceived without the 1930s experience behind them. K. B. Gilden's *Between the Hills and the Sea* (1971), a sophisticated, "Lukácsian," historical novel of the labor movement, is inconceivable without the thirties in the background, although the events occur between the post–World War II strike wave and the 1956 Khrushchev revelations. John Sanford's extraordinary *A Very Good Land to Fall With* (1987) is in large part a brilliant rumination on reproduced documents and remembered moments of the Great Depression.

From another angle, the question raised by Ed Lacy's interpolation of African-American characters, culture, and street life into his popular fiction in a central way is actually, in a 1930s context, no surprise at all. White radical writers of that generation, especially Jewish writers, made a *convention* of creating a figure of cultural resistance around a black rebel.

Zinberg named his detective Toussaint Marcus Moore—suggesting Toussaint L'Ouverture, the Haitian revolutionary; Marcus Garvey, the most successful black nationalist of the African Diaspora; and Richard B. Moore, the West Indian Communist who lived in New York. That he should choose this name during the repressive, McCarthyite witch-hunt era was, as we Marxists never tire of saying, no accident. Zinberg had been preceded by Guy Endore's *Babouk* (named for Haiti's legendary Boukman), John Sanford's America Smith (in *People from Heaven*), Aaron Kramer's *Denmark Vesey*, and many others.

Moreover, Lacy's decision to combine this convention of Red Jewish authors' cross-dressing as rebellious black protagonists in fiction and poetry with the detective mystery genre was also no accident. When the 1930s Left experience is resurrected in all its fullness, such a move may be recognized as *typical* of Zinberg's generation. Dashiell Hammett, of course, had been a major figure in the Left of the 1930s and after. But there were other Left writers out of the *Black Mask* school of hard-boiled detectives, such as William Rollins Jr. In 1934 Rollins published *The Shadow Before*, one of the most widely discussed of the early 1930s proletarian novels. Earlier he wrote *Midnight Treasure* (1929) and *Murder in Cypress Hall* (1933). Later he alternated between the Spanish Civil War novel *Wall of Men* (1938) and the thriller *Ring and the Lamp* (1947). Another example is Mike Quin, a prolific West Coast Communist, whose 1930s poetry and sketches were collected in *Dangerous Thoughts* (1941). He also wrote *The Big Strike* (1947), about the 1934 San Francisco general strike. Quin, whose real name was Paul William Ryan, had a second, pseudonymous career as a mass market pulp writer, under the name of Robert Finnegan. As Finnegan, he published *The Bandaged Nude* (1946), *The Lying Ladies* (1946), and *Many a Monster* (1948) before his premature death of cancer. These examples suggest that the majority of writers produced by the 1930s radical upheaval did *not* follow the trajectory of Steinbeck or Dos Passos in their literary *or* political careers. They entered the arena of what we choose to call "mass culture." Here, they produced literature along the full spectrum of possibility—from landmarks to formula work—in science fiction, children's literature, romance, horror, detective, pulp, popular science, adventure, and so on.

Of course, many followed the trajectory of Zinberg or, to take another example, the master pulp writer Jim Thompson, who was of 1930s Red origin as well. First they tried their hand at writing that was closer to canonical radical fiction in the 1930s. Then economic survival, political witch-hunts, and personal factors propelled them more directly into the production of mass culture. Chester Himes's evolution was similar. So was Frank Yerby's.

To declare that the time is right in the 1990s to turn our attention to these kinds of issues and the host of problems they raise is not to drive out of 1930s scholarship such mainstream figures as Dos Passos or Steinbeck. Nor is it to disparage those more conventionally promoted on the Marxist Left, such as Gold, Le Sueur, and Granville Hicks (all of whom had second careers writing children's literature).

But we must refuse to cut short the 1930s at 1939 and to limit our generic focus only to the kinds of texts traditionally seen as the site of literary value or as the kind usually generating radical and resistance cultural practice. If we do *not* refuse, we will be recycling the very elitism anathema to what was the most exciting in the 1930s cultural upheaval. Moreover, that refusal will take something very large, complex, and various, with extraordinary implications for enlightening our view of U.S. culture, and reduce it to something relatively small—something perhaps not completely without merit but something close to an "episode" that may have been well-intentioned but is ultimately judged to be an "artistic mediocrity."

Now that I have marked out the terrain where I think we stand in the 1990s, let us step back a minute to review how we got where we are. Understanding the evolution of a critical approach in relation to the general social trends is an important part of the self-consciousness necessary for developing scholarship in fresh ways that genuinely assimilate the strengths and rectify the limitations of previous efforts.

RISE AND DECLINE OF THE LIBERAL PARADIGM

The title *Radical Revisions* suggests that we are on the verge of a qualitatively new departure from all previous efforts to theorize and analyze thirties culture. Reconsideration of U.S. literature of the 1930s, particularly its relation to the Left, is proceeding faster in the 1990s than at any other point since the tail end of the McCarthyite antiradical witch-hunt of the 1950s. At the same time, Walter B. Rideout's *Radical Novel in the United States, 1900–1954* (1956) and Daniel Aaron's *Writers on the Left: Episodes in American Literary Communism* (1961) broke with red-baiting conspiracy theories of left-wing cultural influence to establish a "liberal paradigm" for the study of Great Depression literary radicalism. The two professors' views of literary radicalism as a well-meaning but modest tradition within U.S. literature that is mainly time bound to the 1930s more or less set the parameters of the field for the next two decades.

In brief, Rideout's and Aaron's books fostered a two-fold paradigm. First, the most important genre for left-wing writing was established as the novel (more by default than by rigorous comparison), which in the 1930s was strongly influenced by documentary techniques. Second, the most dynamic political force on the cultural Left was acknowledged to be the Communist Party, although critics simultaneously suggested that the closer the writer was to the Party, the less authentic the literary achievement was likely to be because of the internal compulsions to subordinate craft to political ideology.

Thus, within this paradigm, it was possible for students and scholars to agree with Rideout that there were some exceptional achievements among radical writers of the 1930s. His top ten were Nelson Algren's *Somebody in Boots*, Thomas Bell's *All Brides Are Beautiful*, Robert Cantwell's *Land of Plenty*, James T. Farrell's Studs Lonigan Trilogy, Josephine Herbst's Texler Trilogy, and Henry Roth's *Call It Sleep*—all books by pro-Communist enthusiasts at various points in the 1930s (Rideout 287).

At the same time, the paradigm did not challenge the overriding opinion that "the strongest writers of the thirties" were John Dos Passos, Ernest Hemingway, Sinclair Lewis, Theodore Dreiser, John Steinbeck, and Thomas Wolfe (Aaron 392). All of *these* writers were more erratic in their thirties relations to communism. Moreover, if we look closely, the thirties writings of Hemingway, Dreiser, and Lewis are fairly undistinguished, suggesting that *prior* reputation often played a decisive part in one's stature as a major thirties writer.

For the next decades, apart from new biographies and memoirs of veterans, the most influential of the fresh studies of 1930s radical literary culture mainly augmented the work of Rideout and Aaron. James B. Gilbert in *Writers and Partisans: History of Literary Radicalism in America* (1968), William Stott in *Documentary Expression and Thirties America* (1973), and Richard Pells in *Radical Visions and American Dreams: Cultural and Social Thought in the Depression Years* (1973) filled in details about the anti-Stalinist Left, the documentary form, and the shifts in cultural climate beyond the Marxist literary Left during the Great Depression.[2]

Surprisingly, most of the dissertations written then and through the 1970s — including a plethora about the "proletarian novel" and a number about such individuals as Mike Gold, John Howard Lawson, and Joseph Freeman — were never published. It is difficult to determine whether this was solely because of knee-jerk political prejudice, which certainly existed, or weaknesses in the quality of the scholarship itself. Starting in the 1980s, however, we began to witness the appearance of an impressive number of new kinds of reprints of 1930s novels, poetry, and anthologies from the Feminist Press, Monthly Review, West End Press, and various university publishing houses.

The original staple of 1930s texts included John Dos Passos, James T. Farrell, Mike Gold, Granville Hicks, and John Steinbeck, all of whom were in print in the 1960s. The new publications since the 1980s include Carlos Bulosan's *If You Want to Know What We Are* (1983), Fielding Burke's *Call Home the Heart* (1983), Meridel Le Sueur's *I Hear Men Talking* (1984), Mary Heaton Vorse's *Rebel Pen* (1985), Josephine Johnson's *Now in November* (1985), Joseph Kalar's *Poet of Protest* (1985), William Attaway's *Blood on the Forge* (1987), Joseph Vogel's *Man's Courage* (1989), Clara Weatherwax's *Marching! Marching!* (1991), Albert Halper's *Union Square* (1991), Guy Endore's *Babouk* (1991), Mary Heaton Vorse's *Strike!* (1992), and Ruth McKenney's *Industrial Valley* (1992). There also appear such rich new anthologies as Jack Salzman and Leo Zanderer's *Social Poetry of the Thirties* (1978), resurrecting Sol Funaroff, Edwin Rolfe, Joy Davidman, Kenneth Fearing, and others, and Charlotte Nekola and Paula Rabinowitz's *Writing Red: An Anthology of Women Writers, 1930–1940* (1987).

In retrospect, I think we can see that the qualitatively new and improved study of the epoch began in earnest with the consolidation of feminism in the academy in the 1980s, to which several essays in *Radical Revisions* offer strong testimony. Today it seems clear that Deborah Rosenfelt's 1981 essay "From the Thirties: Tillie Olsen and the Radical Tradition" was a landmark publication.

After this came the now famous "canon debates," raising challenges to the way in which the regnant literary models came to have sway. At first, the explicit tradition of the thirties literary Left played no part in these controversies. They concerned mainly the reinscription of neglected texts by women and writers of color, many from the nineteenth century, as well as reinterpretations of classic works and moments in the light of their darker and female "others."

However, a major study toward the end of the decade, Vincent B. Leitch's *American Literary Criticism from the 30s to the 80s* (1988), took note of certain patterns of continuity in cultural debate between the Great Depression and the 1980s Left critical trends. Since then, it has become clear that the thirties cultural Left is returning as part of the canon debate in ways far outdistancing the understanding of the tradition's original proponents in the 1960s and 1970s. It may be worth observing that the major reconsideration of the 1930s Left that began in the late 1980s evolved largely independent of, and occurs mainly in coincidence with, the recent crisis in the former Soviet Union and Eastern Bloc countries. Much more decisive for the views and values of the new "revisionist" scholars of the thirties literary Left has been the multifaceted impact of the 1960s, which is almost as far from us now as the 1930s was from the era of the New Left at its inception.

In the past few years, these fresh and hitherto neglected primary sources of reprinted fiction and poetry have been joined by a genuine renaissance of critical studies of the 1930s applying the new methodologies that grew out of the 1960s, especially feminist literary theory and a more sophisticated Marxism. Among the most exciting of such works are Cary Nelson's *Repression and Recovery: Modern American Poetry and the Politics of Cultural Memory, 1910–45* (1989), Paula Rabinowitz's *Labor and Desire: Women's Revolutionary Fiction in Depression America* (1991), and James Bloom's *Left Letters: The Culture Wars of Mike Gold and Joseph Freeman* (1992). Douglas Wixson, Barbara Foley, Constance Coiner, Harvey Teres, Morris Dickstein, Robert Shulman, and others are completing other book-length works.

Such a dramatic appearance of recent radical, Marxist-influenced methodology, along with texts by previously neglected writers, suggests that the late date of this renaissance may be understood partly as a consequence of a necessary time lag. Most of the new crop of vanguard scholars mentioned here are in their forties and have been following cultural debates for several decades.

One must recall the boom in Marxist literary theory of the 1960s was mostly European-oriented, due to such inspirers as Georg Lukács, Antonio Gramsci, and the Frankfurt School. Decades later, those trends have blended with the British Birmingham School cultural studies, Third World post-colonial theory, and feminism to create, perhaps for the first time, sufficiently rigorous and comprehensive methods and perspectives to carry out the complex task of replacing the liberal paradigm of the 1930s with one that will more fully allow the return of the repressed tradition.

The recent books by Nelson, Rabinowitz, and Bloom are more aggressively sympathetic than their prominent predecessors to issues of race, ethnicity, and gender and to popular literature. They also offer less elitist perspectives on modernism. Moreover, these scholars are ready to reopen the question of literary "value" (quality) in relation to the radical 1930s achievement.

It is worth noting, however, that there are some lines of continuity between the liberal paradigm and the more radical (methodologically as well as politically) considerations of the cultural Left. Both, for example, operate on the assumption that the Communist Party legacy is mixed in fairly precise ways, a liberating as well as delimiting force. In the early 1930s, Communists produced organizations and publications that gave voice to a broad range of writers, often from classes, races, and a gender that encountered considerable constraints in the institutions of the dominant culture.

However, the functionaries in the Communist Party, especially Alexander Trachtenberg and V. J. Jerome, believed Party cadres and institutions could lead and provide direction to such efforts. Moreover, not only such leaders but also most Left writers shared an understandable respect for the state-sponsored literary policies of the Soviet Union. This was a country where they (mistakenly) believed a healthy and enduring socialism was in progress. Although the idea of "leading" a literary movement has shown itself perennially and widely attractive, in the case of the literary Left it resulted in "functionalistic" pressures in literary evaluation. What too frequently prevailed among the *New Masses* and *Daily Worker* critics was the view that since all literature obviously has political dimensions and implications, cultural practice should be ultimately evaluated in relation to the more immediate concerns of the working class—that is, the Communist Party and the Soviet Union.

The difference in emphasis among the scholars of the 1930s literary Left, from the construction of the liberal paradigm to the present, has therefore not been about whether such problematic constraints existed. Rather, their inquiry has concerned the degree of balance between positive and negative aspects. What is often in dispute is in the tensive area of art and formal ideology. On the one hand, there is the issue of the autonomy of the writer as agent, complicated particularly if the writer is female or of color. On the other hand, there is the real weight of the impact of political guidance as manifest in reviews and the fate of publications, usually under the direction of full-time Party literary-critical functionaries who had the confidence of the top political leaders.

Aaron and Rideout, because of the breadth of their empirical research, were actually less mechanical than others in correlating Party policy and literary practice. The most notorious of the simplifiers of the relation between Communist political and literary practice was Philip Rahv in his 1939 essay, "Proletarian Literature: A Political Autopsy": "It is clear that proletarian literature is the literature of a party disguised as the literature of a class" (293). This is a view that contradicts not only the informed understanding of the complexities of the creative process but also much of Rahv's own excellent criticism of previous years. Regrettably, this sentiment and perspective were embraced and endorsed much too uncritically by such outstanding literary figures as Alfred Kazin and Irving Howe.[3]

Fortunately, in recent years we have seen the development of a "new history of American communism," expressed perhaps in its most admirable form by Robin Kelley's *Hammer and Hoe: Alabama Communists during the Great Depression* (1991). Kelley not only establishes greater agency among activists but also asserts the ability of such activists to appropriate and transform Party institutions to give voice in many instances to local expression. What Kelley theorizes for nonliterary, and in some cases nonliterate, militants seems equally apt for cultural workers, who conducted most of their writing in isolation and often came to the Left with much prior training in other literary traditions, ideas, and ideologies.

WHAT IS TO BE DONE?

These new perspectives do not mean that the elements of truth in the traditional critiques of the Old Left politico-cultural experiences are to be jettisoned or forgotten. This would only result in having to relearn the critique, probably the hard way, by repeating mistakes. Rather, the kind of arguments recounted above, along with others for which I lack either the time or expertise to consider, need to be reconciled with the traditional scholarship on 1930s culture.

As we know, much of this has centered on demonstrating the correlations between the political orientations of the Left movements and changes in the styles, themes, and organizational forms of cultural workers. The most famous correlation concerned the differentiation between the pre– and post–Popular Front era in the 1930s. In the first half of the decade (actually, starting in 1928), the emphasis was on working-class literature, revolutionary ideology, and the creation of venues to give voice to unknown cultural workers from the disenfranchised classes. In the second half of the decade, the emphasis was on the creation of a people's democratic literature, antifascist ideology, and the development of organizations and conferences with well-known and successful writers. Another familiar division is between the Communist Party–led cultural movement and non–Communist Party tendencies, which were allegedly less directly "political" and more open to modernism.

A new method is required to engage and transcend the binary of such analyses that would be based partly on fresh primary research — interviews with veterans of the cultural Left, examination of new archival deposits, and the reading of neglected texts and journals. This effort must be in tandem with a deepening of contemporary theoretical work in the areas of gender, race, ethnicity, mass cultures, utopias (including unacknowledged and acknowledged religious impulses), and national identities.

One feature of the new method would be to contextualize 1930s experiences within the decades of the 1940s, 1950s, and 1960s, when many of these same cultural workers continued to produce under new conditions and to interact with younger writers. Studies of U.S. radical writers' responses to World War II, the McCarthyite witch-hunts, the blacklist, the Korean Conflict, the advent of television, and the rise of the New Left would enable us to gain a more complex view of the traditions of cultural resistance largely beginning in the 1930s.

A second feature, one that is especially emphasized in *Radical Revisions*, would be to invoke the categories of gender, race, sexuality, and ethnicity to produce new areas of knowledge. Whatever the political paradigms promoted by left-wing organizations, and whatever the general features of the national cultural atmosphere, women writers, writers of color, and gay, lesbian, and bisexual writers deal with unique issues in their lives and literature. These do not lend themselves to the immediate political correlations of much earlier scholarship — a scholarship based mostly on the studies of the lives and writings of white males, very often from a few select regions.

In addition to the works of radical women and writers in most areas of mass culture, among the most neglected texts have been writings by left-wing Latinos educated in the 1930s tradition (for example, Jose Yglesias, Angel Flores, Alvaro Cardona-Hine, Bernardo Vega, and Jesus Colon) and by Asian-Pacific Americans (for example, H. T. Tsiang and Carlos Bulosan); writings depicting Native American Indian struggles (by, for instance, Mari Sandoz, Robert Gessner, and Howard Fast); and radical writings within certain ethnic traditions (by such Italian-Americans as Carl Marzani, Pietro di Donato, John Fante, Frances Winwar, and Vincent Ferrini).

In regard to the last category, so-called white ethnics, it is worth observing how central the radical 1930s working-class tradition is to the authentic literary history of most of these groups, especially Italian-American, Jewish-American, and Irish-American. Yet many of us have unpleasant recollections of the upsurge of interest in white ethnicity that occurred in the 1970s, because this incarnation had some features of a racist backlash against gains that had been made by people of color during the 1960s. Perhaps now is the time to rethink these ethnic cultures. After all, if the Euro-American ethnic culture were reintroduced in a way that centers on the class-conscious, antichauvinist, antiparticularist, and antiracist traditions of Farrell, di Donato, and Gold, such a cultural revival might have a salutary and unifying, rather than retrograde and divisive, impact on the general drive toward cultural democracy that we are witnessing in scholarship today.

Of course, African-American radical writers *have* received considerable attention. But many crucial figures linked to the 1930s tradition have fallen into neglect—such as Gwendolyn Bennett, Arna Bontemps, John O. Killens, Julian Mayfield, Alice Childress, Shirley Graham DuBois, Owen Dodson, Lloyd Brown, William Attaway, Willard Motley, Frank Marshall Davis, and Lance Jeffers.

Gay, lesbian, and bisexual writers of the 1930s—such as Newton Arvin, Harold Norse, Gale Wihelm, Richard Meeker, T. C. Wilson, Langston Hughes, William Rollins, F. O. Matthiessen, and Chester Kallman—have yet to receive serious attention. Other unique subcategories might be theorized as well—for example, the many British, Canadian, and Australian sojourners in the U.S. literary Left. This would include the novelists Cedric Belfrage, Christina Stead, Harry Carlisle, and James Aldridge, along with the better-known European literary-political exiles.

A third methodological move (in addition to contextualization and new categories) would be to abandon traditional hierarchies and opposition between realism and modernism (usually based on select formal features), highbrow and lowbrow culture, and avant-garde and mass culture. Even such controversial left-wing categories as "working class" and "revolutionary literature" must be retheorized in the light of their expansion and complication by writers of color; women; gay, lesbian, and bisexual authors; and writers in different regions and workplaces.

Moreover, many writers on the Left moved freely among poetry, drama, reportage, fiction, screenwriting, and other literary forms. Alfred Hayes's literary achievement in combing and crossing genres is not that unusual. He wrote the song "Joe Hill," three volumes of poetry, *The Girl on the Via Flaminia* (1949) and six other volumes of prose fiction, as well as plays, screenplays, and television shows. This is not to say that distinctions of genre, period, and quality cannot be made but only that we should interrogate from a dialogical perspective the ways in which traditional categories silence and repress many areas of cultural practice and see what new generic and valuative terms may be more effective.

Still, in the end, for all the exciting innovations of our own time, we must not succumb to arrogance. We must be conscious in *our* work of something of which those who have previously constructed versions of the 1930s were perhaps insufficiently aware in *their* work. Rethinking, retheorizing, and revisioning the thirties in the 1990s is a task that cannot escape the influence of debates that drive and animate intellectual, cultural, and political life at the present. We know the liberal paradigm of the 1930s was based on selections of authors and issues that were intimately bound up in the "moment" at which such scholarship appeared. It is thus obligatory that *we* not forget that our own selections of authors and issues are linked to the contradictory and complex location of intellectual and cultural workers in current national and international history.

Clearly, many of the issues that I and others are seeing in relation to the 1930s are partly out of fascination for what they might tell us about cultural practice today. I know this is the case in regard to identity politics; the cynical attack on alleged "political correctness" in U.S. culture; the defense of multiculturalism; the development of feminism; the need to combat homophobia; the sickening advance of the "new racism"; and other issues confronting contemporary cultural workers. There is no harm in this relationship. To the contrary, such feelings of continuity and kinship between issues in our time and those of the 1930s are necessary for deepening our critical understanding of its significance as a living legacy.

We must remain fully conscious of that aspect of our work. At the same time, we must realize that each reinvention of the 1930s is not equal to the other. There *can* be progress. If we see the evolution of 1930s scholarship as a whole and treat it with circumspection (by which I mean critically but not by caricaturing our predecessors), the present generation of scholars can re-create the decade more richly and meaningfully than any previous one did. Such an advance is the greatest tribute we contemporary scholars and cultural workers devoted to the 1930s can pay to those who lived in that decade as writers and activists, who fought its great battles against racism and fascism and for the rights of working people, and who suffered the brutal backlash of McCarthyism's attempt to destroy their achievements. What is vital and humane in so much of our work today is possible because of what they lived, wrote, and endured, including the painful recognition of their own mistakes.

In a memorable phrase, Leon Trotsky, who knew more than a few things about literature and social revolution, once recalled, "In my eyes, authors, journalists and artists always stood for a world that was more attractive than any other" (quoted in Howe 118). Many radical cultural workers of the 1930s did not read and did not think they had any use for the ideas of Trotsky and other heretical leftists of various persuasions. Of course, the contemporary world situation suggests that they were mistaken in this narrowness in ways that we must never emulate.

Still, regardless of formal ideological "position," the literary leftists in the 1930s lived out Trotsky's words far better than they knew. Their unfinished project of humanizing and democratizing U.S. culture is among the most attractive moments in our intellectual heritage. Placing ourselves in solidarity with and critically advancing that honorable legacy of cultural commitment is precisely what contemporary scholarship on the 1930s is all about.

NOTES

1. See "The Right Thing" in Ford and Faggett.

2. To see other ways in which studies that followed Aaron and Rideout expanded the terrain a bit, one might examine the anthologies edited by Madden and by Bogardus and Hobson. These collections present a range of essays that make the case for more recognition of previously neglected regions (the South, Midwest, and Northwest), genres (poetry, documentary), and political traditions (Trotskyism, anarchism).

3. For a sharp dissent from Kazin's treatment of the 1930s in his otherwise admirable On Native Grounds, see my essay "In Retrospect."

WORKS CITED

Aaron, Daniel. *Writers on the Left: Episodes in American Literary Communism.*
New York: Harcourt, Brace and World, 1961.
Bogardus, Ralph, and Fred Hobson, eds. *Literature at the Barricades: The American Writer in the 1930s.* Birmingham: University of Alabama Press, 1982.
"Conscience — or Ambition?" *New York Times,* October 3, 1948, 22.
Ford, Nick Aaron, and H. L. Faggett, eds. *Best Short Stories by Afro-American Writers (1925–1950).* Boston: Meader Publishing, 1950.
Howe, Irving. *Steady Work.* New York: Harcourt, Brace and World, 1966.
"Leonard Zinberg, Wrote as Ed Lacy." *New York Times,* January 8, 1968, 35.
Madden, David, ed. *Proletarian Writers of the Thirties.* Cabondale: Southern Illinois University Press, 1968.
Rahv, Philip. *Essays on Literature and Politics, 1932–1972.* Boston: Houghton Mifflin, 1978.
Reilly, John. *Twentieth-Century Crime and Mystery Writers.* New York: St. Martin's Press, 1980.
Rideout, Walter B. *The Radical Novel in the United States, 1900–1954: Some Interrelations of Literature and Society.* Cambridge, Mass.: Harvard University Press, 1956.
Rosenfelt, Deborah. "From the Thirties: Tillie Olsen and the Radical Tradition." *Feminist Studies* 7 (Fall 1981): 370–406.
Rubinstein, Annette. Interview, New York City, March 1990.
Wald, Alan. "In Retrospect: *On Native Grounds.*" *Reviews in American History* 20 (1992): 276–88.
———. *The New York Intellectuals: The Rise and Decline of the Anti-Stalinist Left from the 1930s to the 1980s.* Chapel Hill: University of North Carolina Press, 1987.

2

POETRY CHORUS:

DIALOGIC POLITICS

IN 1930S POETRY

As the depression deepened in the early 1930s, large numbers of Americans, including many writers, were drawn to the Left or to the Communist Party. There was a widespread conviction that capitalism had failed, that the old order could not be restored, and that only the most thoroughgoing social and political change could bring about social and economic justice. A number of active poets had already been writing from that perspective in the 1920s. For one thing, the much-heralded "roaring twenties" had not brought economic health to everyone. The entire rural economy had remained depressed throughout the decade, and several major industries were already in recession before the stock market crash of 1929. Especially in the South and in depressed areas in the North, working-class and labor poets, along with socialist poets, had been writing about economic inequities for years. Subcultural traditions of protest poetry stretched back into the nineteenth century, and some of the poets in those traditions felt themselves to be not only individual voices but also participants in movements for social change.

In some cases anthologies and other collaborative work helped reinforce a sense that poets writing on public themes were not so much working to silence or dominate one another by competing to write the best poem on a given subject but were contributing to a common cultural enterprise. A more successful, more eloquent, or more deeply moving poem might thereby seem less a personal triumph than a victory for the cause at issue. The sense of accomplishment could thus be partly focused on poetry's success at winning the moral ground in a cultural struggle, in establishing that authentic literary idealization belonged to one side and not the other. Recognizing that poetry had a historically constructed authority to speak with (and for) metaphorized idealization in the culture—an authority long recognized and reinforced by both the political Right and Left—poets understood that ground to be worth the struggle.

In the decades leading up to the Great Depression, poetry anthologies sometimes show progressive social movements working to establish a plausible textual history for their key commitments and beliefs. Especially with more ambitiously historical anthologies, a considerable effort was made to draw out of older texts the semantic elements that could link them to an emerging contemporary consensus. Particularly notable is the 1916 anthology *Socialism in Verse*, compiled by William J. Ghent as the twelfth volume in his New Appeal Socialist Classics series. The other volumes in the series are all prose, and the texts they print—whether individually or collectively authored—are mostly contemporary and are frequently devoted to extended argument. The eleventh volume, however, *The Socialist Appeal: Prose Passages Which Voice the Call for a New Social Order*, is composed of recent one- to four-page editorials and excepts from longer works and aims for a collective evocation of first principles. The final volume, on poetry, takes that impulse one step further, reaching back through the nineteenth century and beyond for evidence of explicit or implicit socialist vision. It is in the volume of poetry, crucially, that authors who were not socialists find a place; as the form of writing most fully secured as a site of idealization, poetry, it appears, can lend its passions to socialism, even if its authors would not have imagined that possible. If the project is successful, the long poetic history of protests against social injustice and visions of utopian futures will seem to culminate in the Socialist Party's present aims. Collectively, the poems offer a historical ground for current aspirations and work.

What is most interesting about the anthology, however, is its explicit reflection on the work of rearticulation such a project entails. A series of notes at the back of the book makes it clear some of the texts are excerpts because only those passages that can contribute to an authentic socialism are printed. When an author's beliefs leaned in other directions, that too is made clear rather than hidden. Lord Byron is thus credited with having "many quotable passages in celebration of liberty and in denunciation

of tyrants," but Ghent adds that "his notion of tyranny did not . . . go beyond the unregulated power of kings and dictators" (58). One would not,
therefore, look to Byron for poems about how class relations are played
out in the workplace. Similarly, he tells us that Henry Wadsworth Long-
fellow "wrote some notable verse in behalf of freedom and against slavery,
but either had no knowledge of, or no sympathy with, the cause of the
workers" (60). Thirteen years later, in the midst of the hourglass economy of the 1920s and on the eve of the stock market crash, Marcus Graham's more ambitious historical collection, *An Anthology of Revolutionary Poetry*, brings that project to the present day, even going so far as to
include T. S. Eliot's "The Hollow Men" and Ezra Pound's "Commission."
In effect, Eliot and Pound are allowed to testify to historical conditions that
they would interpret rather differently. Such an anthology is an effort to
construct a collective form of testimony so powerful, even inexorable, that
it can take up and transform some of the texts it includes. The anthologies themselves, however, demonstrate that the common threads they want
to emphasize will not quite be self-evident to all readers of poetry; they
are devoted not simply to reporting the existence of a progressive and revolutionary tradition but also to creating one—by rereading history and its
present implications—and thus creating a usable past with which poets
and readers of poetry can thereafter identify.

Collections of contemporary poetry and songs grouped around a more
focused issue or set of cultural commitments did, however, not only reflect
and define but also help call into being shared social and literary aims. A
list of such texts in the modern period, some still famous, some nearly forgotten, might begin with the IWW's *Songs of the Workers*, first issued in 1909,
and move on through Countee Cullen's celebrated Harlem Renaissance
anthology *Caroling Dusk* (1927) and the collaborative revolutionary poetry
collection *We Gather Strength* (1933). Collections on specific causes or problems perhaps best foreshadow the kind of multivocal dialogue and consensus one finds in the 1930s. Of these, the most suggestive may be Lucia Trent
and Ralph Cheyney's *America Arraigned*, a collection honoring Nicola Sacco and Bartolomeo Vanzetti published in 1928, the year after they were executed for robbery and murder in Massachusetts. Although many were persuaded they had been framed, they were nonetheless convicted in 1921; it
was a victory not only for reactionary politics but also for American xenophobia, since the men were immigrant anarchists. By the time they were
executed, the case had radicalized large numbers of Americans, many of
whom came to believe that the country's institutions were hopelessly corrupt and thus impossible to reform by ordinary means. Some sixty poets

contributed pieces to the anthology, which followed *The Sacco-Vanzetti Anthology of Verse*, a pamphlet anthology published by Henry Harrison a year earlier. Tied carefully to the development of the case, *America Arraigned* is divided into three sections: "Before Governor Fuller and His Advisory Commission Refused to Interfere," "After Intercession Was Refused but before the Crucifixion," and "After the Crucifixion." Purchasing the collection was also a political act, since profits went to defray the expenses of the Sacco-Vanzetti Relief Committee.

With the onset of the Great Depression the following year and the rise of a genuine mass movement on the Left, these traditions received more than a new or expanded life. Within a few years, the sense of a common political and poetic project no longer had to be cobbled together out of a sometimes resistant history; it was everywhere apparent. In some cases, to be sure, a new and different life was granted poets who now suddenly had a wider national audience. Some poets—such as George Henry Weiss— saw their work of the 1920s reprinted and given fresh meanings and new cultural purpose; in effect, some of the political poetry of the 1920s became new protest poetry of the 1930s when it was reissued in the midst of the depression. The changes in the practice and the social meaning of poetry went much deeper than that, though.

For a brief moment in American literary history, writing poetry became a credible form of revolutionary action. Reading poetry, in turn, became a way of positioning one's self in relation to the possibility of basic social change. Earlier, the IWW's poems set to music had been among the IWW's most successful recruitment devices. Now, to read a poem like Langston Hughes's "Let America Be America Again" was to find more than an echo of one's own sense of cultural crisis and necessity. It was to find a place to stand ideologically, a concise discursive perspective on America's history and engagement with its contemporary culture. It was also to find a voice one could temporarily take up as one's own. Poetry at once gave people a radical critique and visionary aspiration, and it did so in language fit for the speaking voice. It strengthened the beliefs of those already radicalized and helped to persuade some not yet decided. It was thus a notable force in articulating and cementing what was a significant cultural and political shift toward the Left. To write poetry under these conditions of readership was therefore to ask not only what one wanted to say but also what other people wanted to read; the sense of audience was pressing, immediate. A revolutionary poem in a magazine or newspaper could be taken up and used by an audience only days or weeks after it was written. Thus when Angelo Herndon, a black Communist unconstitutionally charged with "attempting to incite insurrection" for helping to organize a Georgia hunger march, was released on bail in 1934, poems celebrating his August 7 arrival in New York were written and published within days. Alfred Hayes's "Welcome to Angelo Herndon" appeared in the *Daily Worker* on August 9; Michael Blankfort's "Angelo Herndon's Bail" was published in the same newspaper on August 15; and Edwin Rolfe's "Homecoming" was in the August 21 issue of the *New Masses*. When such poems offered readers politically committed speaking voices with which they could identify, the poems were in a sense a gift to prospective readers, a text whose authorship was inherently transferable. To publish a poem that might prove politically persuasive was, in effect, to ask readers to live by way of these words as if they were their own.

The sense of rapid use—of poetry written to play an immediate role in public life—was not unique to the depression; it hearkened back to the abolitionist poetry of the nineteenth century and to broadside poems issued in the United States and Europe over a period of centuries. For readers in the 1990s it may recall some of the poetry read at antiwar rallies in the 1960s. Part of what distinguishes this phenomenon in the modern period are simply the means of circulation, the possibility of mass participation in the reading of poetry, and poetry's empowering integration with a wide range of other cultural activities. Long considered by academics a debased form of publication, mass circulation newspapers from the *Appeal to Reason* to the *New York Call* and the *Daily Worker* played a key role here.[1] Given poetry's history of identification with transcendentalizing (or at least transhistorical) idealization, there is, of course, a real tension built into its publication in the transitory medium of newsprint. Newspapers themselves sometimes marked poetry's difference by placing it in a special box, but that difference was also complicated by poetry's multiple relations with other items in the paper. When the *Daily Worker* put poems on its features page—along with letters to the editor, notices of events, and recipes—poetry's difference did not prevent it from being seen as an object designed for practical use in everyday life. For poets publishing in newspapers these ambiguities could be appealing rather than troubling. Mass readership reinforced the shift in emphasis from the production to the consumption of poems, shifting ownership from author to audience. What mattered to the audience, moreover, was not an effort to capture what an author meant but to take responsibility for how poems could change their own lives. Publishing poems in newspapers suggested not so much that poems were utterly expendable and transitory—the same poems, after all, might later be collected in books—but rather that their claims to transhistorical values mattered only if they were taken up in people's daily lives. For poets, therefore, a wide popular readership demonstrated that poetry mattered; compromising its elite status was a gain, not a loss. The mass audience for poetry in the depression was, paradoxically, one of the triumphs of a time of widespread suffering.

To begin to understand what it meant to be a poet on the Left in the depression, it is necessary to extend that recognition to the whole cultural field and accept it as a general paradox that typifies life in that period. Hand in hand with hunger and unemployment and the many difficulties of everyday life went a sense of impending revolutionary change. For those poets who participated in the mass movement of the 1930s the period combined sometimes desperate hardship with something like utopian exhilaration. Writing poetry often meant helping to articulate and dramatize both the period's suffering and its characteristic yearnings for change. To write poetry was not only to comment on these cultural processes but also to help shape them. And you were not alone. Down the street, across town, and in towns and cities across the country other poets were contributing to the cultural climate in much the same way.

If you were writing in New York, you might participate in revolutionary poetry readings or join the John Reed Club, where you could share drafts of your work or debate the social function of literature. John Reed clubs were started in other cities as well, and some issued their own magazines. The John Reed Club of Milwaukee published *War*, whose inaugural issue (see figure 2–1) included poems by Paul Romaine, Patrick Archer, and Erich Weinert, along with an anonymous poem "Did You Get Yours Today?" that satirized the menu at a lunch of "bankers, politicians, and 'charity' dispensers." Even at some distance from a metropolitan center, the post could bring some of the dozens of new or newly radicalized magazines that were publishing the political poetry of the times. As early as 1931 the third annual volume of Jack Conroy and Ralph Cheyney's *Unrest*, the "rebel poets anthology," lists thirty magazines and newspapers from which poems were selected, along with their place of publication, including the *Banner* (Tokyo, Japan), *Contemporary Vision* (Philadelphia), the *Crisis* (New York), *Driftwind* (Montpelier, Vermont), the *Daily Worker* (New York), *Earth* (Wheaton, Illinois), *Front* (Baarn, Holland), *Labor's News* (New York), the *Left* (Davenport, Iowa), *Letters* (Lexington, Kentucky), *Morada* (Cagnes-sur-Mer, France), the *Nation* (New York), the *New Leader* (New York), *New Masses* (New York), the *Northern Light* (Holt, Minnesota), the *Rebel Poet* (Moberly, Missouri), and the *World Tomorrow* (New York). Within three years, numerous other outlets for rad-

Published by The John Reed Club of Milwaukee

WAR

MILWAUKEE MILLIONAIRES in FAVOR of ANOTHER WORLD WAR to MAKE the WORLD SAFE for PLUTOCRACY!

Against imperialist war! For the defense of the Chinese people and the Soviet Union!

Against capitalist terror and forced labor which are part of the war preparations!

Let's make the rich bankers pay the back wages (bonus) to the ex-service men!

Let's stop the shipment of munitions to Japan!

Let's fight against wage cuts and the reduction of unemployment relief!

Work for the unity of all workers; negro and white, native and foreign-born, and against imperialist war!

Not another cent for war! All war funds for unemployment relief and insurance.

AUGUST 1, 1932 — 10¢

Volume 1   Number 1

FIGURE 2-1. *The cover to the inaugural issue of* War, *published by the John Reed Club of Milwaukee (author's collection)*

ical poetry would appear, including *Contempo* (Chapel Hill, North Carolina), *Dynamo* (New York), *Hinterland* (Cedar Rapids, Iowa), *International Literature* (Moscow), *Left Front* (Chicago), *Leftward* (Boston), *Masses* (Toronto), *Midland Left* (Indianapolis), the *Partisan* (Hollywood), *Partisan Review* (New York), and the *Symposium* (Concord, New Hampshire). As these abbreviated lists make clear, New York had a strong presence among the most visible publications on the Left, but there was also a diverse national and international range of magazines and newspapers. *Unrest 1931* also published each publication's address, thereby encouraging readers of the anthology to seek out the original publications. Larger circulation publications, such as the *Daily Worker*, regularly reviewed new radical journals, which helped publicize their existence and encourage the sense of a national movement. A correspondence among poets and between poets and editors not only focused differences but also further strengthened the sense of contributing to a common enterprise. In New York vast May Day parades would bring together writers, graphic artists, and musicians to march with radical labor union members and give material visibility to what seemed a decisive historical coalition. As with *Unrest 1931* and *We Gather Strength*, the covers to books of poetry sometimes made that sense of a unified cultural front explicit. Hugo Gellert's cover to the 1931 rebel poets' anthology uses two workers' tools, a pitch fork and a hand-held pick axe, as a symbol of both the solidarity that unites Americans across different occupations and the practical work revolutionary poetry can do (see figure 2–2). *We Gather Strength* takes that image two steps further, adding the image of a book to the tools that stretch diagonally across the cover and including a hammer and sickle among the tools, thereby invoking solidarity with the Soviet Union and expressing the collection's politics (see figure 2–3).

The part of the romantic heritage we have chosen to remember—with its image of the poet as a solitary creative figure—was still strong, but for a time in the 1930s it gave way to something else: an image of poetry as a collaborative, dialogic enterprise, a form of writing carried out by individuals responding to one another's work and in the service of shared but contested cultural aims.[2] There was a chorus of assenting and dissenting voices in poetry, and none was heard entirely on its own. That is not to say that individual poets did not bring to this conversation distinctive styles or formal and thematic inflections that mark their voice as their own. Nor is it to say that readers and reviewers failed to ask what particular poets were contributing to the common culture of the period. Indeed there was no lack of intense disagreement about the strengths and weaknesses and class

FIGURE 2-2. *Hugo Gellert's jacket for the rebel poets' anthology* Unrest 1931, *edited by Ralph Cheyney and Jack Conroy (University of Tulsa)*

FIGURE 2-3. *The cover to the 1933 anthology* We Gather Strength, *which included poems by Herman Spector, Joseph Kalar, Edwin Rolfe, and Sol Funaroff (author's collection)*

commitments of 1930s political poetry. But there was also an underlying and omnipresent sense of a common mission that pervaded much of the conversation about poetry during the height of the depression.

If the postwar values of the English profession have tended primarily to honor one poetic epistemology—that of expressive subjectivity—the largely forgotten political poetry of the 1930s went in another direction. One of the recurrent issues in 1930s poetry is the necessity of disavowing certain forms of subjectivity. "To welcome multitudes—the miracle of deeds / performed in unison," Rolfe wrote in the opening lines of his 1936 *To My Contemporaries*, "the mind must first renounce the fiction of the self" (59). It was as if, to clear the ground in poetry for a different kind of agency, one less self-absorbed and more directed toward the social text, it was in poetry itself that the ego had to be challenged. That is not to say that all forms of subjectivity were abandoned; both poetry and fiction became important sites for narratives of awakening political awareness and narratives of individual transformation.

The shift in the epistemology of composition meant more than the adoption of new subject matter, though. Poetry became a form of social conversation and a way of participating in collaborative political action. Poetry was thus in the immediate materiality of its signs dialogic—engaged in a continuing dialogue with other poetry and the other discourses and institutions of its day. Even now, to read the political poetry of that period is potentially to recognize the continual play of similarity and difference in other contemporary poems.

The points of comparison are most obviously thematic, rhetorical, and metaphoric—how poets represent the unemployed or the owners of industry, how they give voice to the period's suffering or its hope for revolutionary change—but the presence of potential dialogic relations extends also to formal choices and to the informing sense of poetic function and the vocation of poetry. There is thus a continual dialogue taking place in the effort both to describe social conditions and to invent ways for poetry to intervene in them. One relatively minor but indicative textual sign of changing notions of poetry's social role and its relation to individual expression is many poets' inclusion of political slogans in their work, sometimes printing them like banner headlines in capital letters.

This intertextual social conversation obviously cannot confine itself to poems in their entirety, though it certainly operates at that level as well. The pattern of verbal echoes, reinforcements, extensions, and disputes actually permeates poems at the level of individual stanzas, lines, images, and narrative units. To shut one's ears to that conversation is to silence the material conditions of poetry at that time. To hear that conversation is to witness poems in a constant state of disassemblage and reassemblage, as pieces of other poems are woven into any given text and pieces of every text are disseminated into related texts and discourses as we read. Moreover, these are not fixed intertextual structures—references and allusions to be identified, certified, and annotated—but potential relations to be effected in the work of reading. Part of the cultural work of reading—the semiotics of reading—was to confirm a poem's participation in the mass movement of the Left by enacting it. To *read* 1930s political poetry is thus in part to personify—to act out in one's person—a version of the intertextuality of that time. A proper reader of this poetry comes to occupy the cultural field in somewhat the same way the poetry itself did.

This kind of reading requires that we give up at least temporarily the strong bias toward thinking only in terms of self-sufficient, formally contained poems. There are many political poems from the 1930s with formal coherence and metaphoric inventiveness and many poems for that matter whose relative formal autonomy contributed to their success, but that is not the only historically relevant way to read them. For some decades the academy has so fetishized its own investment in individual poems that it has ignored the possibility that the poem as an object has meant different things to different audiences at various moments in history. In the case of poems published in songbooks, for example, it was considered quite appropriate to revise them to fit new political functions. Indeed, it is highly unlikely that people were always as invested in finished, sacralized, independent poems as we are. It is thus potentially quite disabling to write literary history under the sign of a transcendentalized and ahistorical notion of poetic form, for that limits us to our own interested notion of what we want poems to be and blocks any effort, however problematic, to try to understand what poems meant to people in their own time. At least in the 1930s, the many hundreds of poems taking up the major social and political issues of the moment also participate in the cultural dialogue that supports, complicates, extends, or resists what were the increasingly influential Left perspectives on current conditions. That dialogue can operate at all discursive levels, not just those dependent on an overarching sense of form.

Reading poems this way does mean coming to value their relational power and effectivity. It also means valuing individual lines and images for their capacity to reinforce or differ from the existing patterns in the discursive field. This does not, however, mean that we have to collapse poetry and rhetoric, for the special social functions attributed to poetry can operate through the echoing and counterpointing of lines and images as

readily as they can through entire poems. Yet we do have to begin to admire poems for their capacity to participate in history, not for their supposed capacity to transcend it. At that point something like a political
aesthetic of the poetic fragment becomes possible.

Of course poetry was only part of the dialogic cultural conversation taking place at the time. Narratives of economic injustice and political conversion were so prevalent—in fiction, journalism, and critical analysis—
that poetry could easily rely for its contextual intelligibility not only on
preexisting political images in its own genre but also on a growing body
of related texts in the surrounding culture. But poetry also had a degree
of relative autonomy and a distinct, though not exclusive, series of social
functions. It played a variety of social roles, each partially shared and in
competition with other discourses embedded in a variety of social institutions. Poets thus saw themselves as having a distinctive though contested
mission, and we have good reason to try to recover some approximation
of that mission if we want to keep that portion of our past alive in our
cultural memory.

One of the more interesting changes brought about by the culture's
redefinition of poetry's mission was in the concept of authorship, a corollary to the shift away from an emphasis on self-expressive subjectivity. Many
poets were concerned about establishing their careers, getting reviewed,
and selling books, though even these conventional personal interests sometimes had a different inflection. Reviews potentially represented not just
a source of personal pride but a confirmation that the poetry was meeting
the social needs it was written to serve. Sales too could confirm that an
audience was being reached. That Sol Funaroff's 1938 collection of poems *The Spider and the Clock* could sell five thousand copies at a dollar
each—when money was still not easy to come by—says a great deal about
the importance people placed on radical poetry during the depression.
There were, moreover, a number of poets who for years remained deeply
committed to writing and publishing poetry without much caring about
their careers or their fame as poets. Poetry was a major part of their engagement with the world, a way of intervening in history, a way of alter-
ing the hierarchization of values in the United States, but not primarily a
means of promoting their personal prestige. Among others, Joe Freeman
and Mike Gold, both of whom established reputations on the Left in the
1920s, thus wrote poetry more as a form of political action than as a mechanism for personal advancement.

It was, however, the worker's correspondence poem of the 1930s, the
found poem of that era, that most clearly displaced notions of authorship
and originality. In 1927 Gold published a poem, he was pleased to note,

drawn entirely from Vanzetti's published speeches and letters. In the 1930s a number of poets, including Gold and Freeman, published poems based on workers' correspondence, and some wrote poems of their own that imitated workers' letters. In most cases the original sources for these poems have not survived, though it is clear the level of intervention and manipulation varied. Some poets no doubt wrote original poems and called them worker's correspondence. Others clearly did turn workers' letters into poems, though with different degrees of revision.

Tillie Olsen, who was then writing under her maiden name, Lerner, wrote a poem based on a letter that had been published in the January 9, 1934, issue of the *New Masses*, so both texts are available. The *New Masses* published the letter under the heading "Where the Sun Spends the Winter," a version of the slogan adopted by a Texas Chamber of Commerce as the motto for a tourist campaign. The letter describes the impossible lives of four women who survive by embroidering children's dresses for a few pennies each. The author of the letter, Felipe Ibarro, may well have been a journalist or a social worker or perhaps simply an activist, so the letter is not the direct testimony of the workers described but reported testimony that is already self-consciously rhetorical. Nonetheless, it offers one interesting version of this distinctive 1930s genre. It is worth comparing the opening two paragraphs of the letter with the first three stanzas of the poem:

I want the women of New York, Chicago and Boston who buy at Macy's, Wannamaker's, Gimbel's and Marshall Field to know that when they buy embroidered children's dresses labeled "hand made" they are getting dresses made in San Antonio, Texas, by women and girls with trembling fingers and broken backs.

These are bloody facts and I know, because I've spoken to the women who make them. Catalina Rodriguez is a 24-year-old Mexican girl but she looks like 12. She's in the last stages of consumption and works from six in the morning till midnight. She says she never makes more than three dollars a week. I don't wonder any more why in our city with a population of 250,000 the Board of Health has registered 800 professional "daughters of joy" and in addition, about 2,00 *Mujeres Alegres* (happy women), who are not registered and sell themselves for as little as five cents (11).

i want you women up north to know
how those dainty children's dresses you buy

at macy's, wannamaker's, gimbels, marshall fields,
are dyed in blood, are stitched in wasting flesh,
down in San Antonio, "where sunshine spends the winter."

I want you women up north to see
the obsequious smile, the salesladies trill
    "exquisite work, madame, exquisite pleats"
vanish into a bloated face, ordering more dresses,
    gouging the wages down,
dissolve into maria, ambrosa, catalina,
    stitching these dresses from dawn to night,
    in blood, in wasting flesh.

Catalina Rodriguez, 24,
    body shrivelled to a child's at twelve,
catalina rodriguez, last stages of consumption,
    works for three dollars a week from dawn to midnight.
A fog of pain thickens over her skull, the parching heat breaks over her
    body.
and the bright red blood embroiders the floor of her room.
    White rain stitching the night, the bourgeois poet would say,
        white gulls of hands, darting, veering,
    white lightning, threading the clouds,
this is the exquisite dance of her hands over the cloth,
and her cough, gay, quick, staccato, like skeleton's bones clattering,
is appropriate accompaniment for the esthetic dance of her fingers
and the tremulo, tremulo when the hands tremble with pain.
Three dollars a week,
two fifty-five,
seventy cents a week,
no wonder two thousands eight hundred ladies of joy
are spending the winter with the sun after he goes down. . . . (179–80)

Olsen works with Ibarro's letter to draw out its drama and intensify the
metaphoric power of the suffering it recounts. The title, "I Want You
Women Up North to Know," drawn from the letter, serves as a refrain line
that becomes a paradigm for North/South relations and for those who
benefit, often indifferently and sometimes in ignorance, from economic
exploitation. Olsen uses her own metaphors as well as Ibarro's, but her
poem remains an inventive extension of the original letter. Keeping true
to Ibarro's wish to have women up north understand the economic and

social relations that are hidden within the clothing they buy, Olsen adds a passage describing a department store where the children's dresses are sold. Notably, however, the poem's most explicit challenge—a challenge built into the original letter—is not to the businesspeople who hire the dressmakers or to the department store owners who sell them but to the consumers who buy them and thus fuel the entire set of transactions. Olsen is not alone in focusing on how ordinary people's actions help sustain economic exploitation—Kenneth Fearing, for example, often satirizes the way people's illusions reinforce the ideology of the market place—but attacks on industrialists were certainly more common during the period.

The primary change from Ibarro's text to Olsen's, as with most poems based on worker correspondence, is the generic shift itself, the move from prose to poetry. This is a shift Olsen embraces, but with uneasiness, as her effort, in one stanza, to emulate a bourgeois poet's lyrical evocation of Catalina Rodriquez's dying efforts at embroidery suggest: "White rain stitching the night, the bourgeois poet would say, / white gulls of hands, darting" (179). Yet with Olsen's poem a single witness's testimony about four women in one city becomes synecdochic in a double sense: these workers become representatives of their class, and their suffering becomes emblematic of a whole range of values the culture should either resist or espouse. The experience of working people thereby becomes a fitting ground for all the ideological investments the culture makes in literariness, particularly in poetry. Finally, to make poetry out of working-class experience, to return to working people their own narratives (or narratives about them) in poetic form, is explicitly to overturn much of the class prejudice inherent in the culture's hierarchical view of aesthetic value.

In all of this Olsen is effectively Ibarro's agent in the domain of literariness. The first person in the title of Olsen's poem is largely an extension of Ibarro's, even though Olsen amplifies what she feels we should know. Olsen thus draws out the structural implications of the underpaid work these women do and of the religious faith that helps keep them positioned as they are. Ibarro reports Ambrosa Espinoza's struggle to "pay rent for her shack, pay insurance, support the Catholic Church and feed herself." Olsen intensifies the ironies and adds an explicit antireligious commentary: "but the pennies to keep god incarnate, from ambrosa, / and the pennies to keep the priest in wine, from ambrosa, / ambrosa clothes god and priest with hand-made children's dresses" (180). Olsen also offers a more explicit revolutionary message. Espinoza's crippled brother, who lies "on a mattress of rags" and "dreams of another world," does not quite know that an alternative world "was brought to earth in 1917 in Russia, / by workers like him" (181). Except for a slight rearrangement of the words in the first line, however, the last stanza (with its revolutionary promise) is quoted directly from Ibarro's letter:

Women up north, I want you to know,
I tell you this can't last forever.

I swear it won't. (181)

Such motives animate much of the political poetry of the 1930s, which often focuses on economic hardship and revolutionary change, on general social conditions rather than private experience. Even when individual experience is recounted, it is often recounted because of its representative character, its simultaneous enabling and determination by current history. With individual poets each offering alternative versions of life in the depression and with poets hearing one another's work at group poetry readings and reading each other's work in books and magazines, it is not difficult to see how one is led not merely to read comparatively but to read chorally, to see these poems not as entries in a competition but as mutually responsive contributions to an emerging revolutionary consensus.

To read or write a 1930s political poem properly, then, is to be continually hailed by other voices. To give some sense of what that might be like, there follows a four-part poetry chorus assembled out of fragmentary quotations taken from poetry of the period. This collation of fragments gives particular emphasis to the years 1929–36, which had the strongest sense of a common revolutionary social mission, but the arrangement is conceptual not chronological. (After 1936 the rhetoric of revolution receded into the background as both the Communist International and the Communist Party U.S.A. [CPUSA] committed themselves to a broad united front to defeat fascism. In the summer of 1936 a new choral subject, the Spanish Civil War, began to occupy the international Left.)[3] The first two sections, "The City" and "The Farm," focus on descriptions of social conditions in the two major social environments of the depression. The third section, "Capital," gathers a few of the many passages of economic and social commentary and analysis that recur in 1930s poetry. The fourth and final section, "Revolution," evokes the figurative and political resolution that lies explicitly or implicitly behind much of the protest literature of the depression. Although the emphasis here is on a discursive formation rather than on individual achievement, the names of the authors are noted in parenthesis so that readers can have a sense of authorial participation in the continuing dialogue of the time:

I
THE CITY

This is the sixth winter.
This is the season of death
when lungs contract and the breath of homeless men
freezes on restaurant window-panes. (Edwin Rolfe)

See the set faces hungrier than rodents. In the Ford towns
They shrivel. Their fathers accept tear gas and blackjacks.
When they sleep, whimper. Bad sleep for us all.
Their mouths work, supposing food. (Genevieve Taggard)

We have grown used to nervous landscapes, chimney-broken horizons,
and the sun dying between tenements (Richard Wright)
The hungry digging the wild roots
From hillsides (Ruth Lechlitner), the parched young,
The old man rooting in waste-heaps, the family rotting
In the flat, before eviction (Stephen Vincent Benét)

This is the season when rents go up.
Men die, and their dying is casual, (Rolfe)
deep in the gangrened basements
Where Whitman's America
Aches, to be born. (Mike Gold)

Out there on the ruin of Kansas . . .
Downtown in the ruins called Denver (H. H. Lewis)
The crowds twisting over the maimed cement;
the unemployed with the bars of the L in their eyes (Ben Maddow)

the whimpering
stragglers at backdoors, the scratchy beggars
in the streets (Robert Gessner)
the ghosts in the burning city of our times (Benét)

Skeletons cast on a shore devoted to business (Ettore Rella)
Those heaps of plaster in the condemned house,
where the evicted slept last week;
the nailed doors. (Maddow)

The cardiac baby cries on the highest floor;
the relief potatoes boiled and blue
served on oilcloth. (Maddow)

You see the dead face peering from your shoes;
the eggs at Thompson's are the dead man's eyes. (Rolfe)
"Both rich and poor, my friends, must sacrifice," reechoes,
murmuring, through hospitals, death-cells. (Kenneth Fearing)

Maggots and darkness will attend the alibi (Fearing)

II
THE FARM

Outcries of unrest in a dream (Sol Funaroff)
pale children bowing in beetfields (Joseph Kalar)
And the men with bared feet in the grass:
their tired, heavy bodies hug the earth (Funaroff)

Tom's half-gone Ford
Stopped in the barn-yard middle. There the hens
Fluffed dust and slept beneath it. Desolation
Sat busy in the yard somewhere. The cows stamped on
Inside the barn with caking heavy udders (Taggard)

The wash-board cattle stagger and die of drought (Benét)
Drought walks in the furrows
And the young corn withers (Lechlitner)
Their farmer scrapes with his hoe the uniform heaven: drought
    (Maddow)

Last week from black pasturage the cattle stooped to
rasp the last mud (Maddow)
They sold the calf. That fall the bank took over (Taggard)

A headlong rain pours down all day to hide
the blackened stumps, the ulcerated hill, (Malcolm Cowley)
these stricken houses, dust-choked fields,
Starved beasts and starving men (Lechlitner)
And the giant dust-flower blooms above five states (Benét)

III
CAPITAL

The mills are down
The hundred stacks
are shorn of their drifting fume.

The idle tracks
rust . . .
Smeared red with the dust
of millions of tons of smelted ore
the furnaces loom—
towering, desolate tubes—
smokeless and stark in the sun . . . (John Beecher)

Flanking the freightyards: alleys, wooden shacks,
And hovels: a grim battalion
Of crouching rats covered down by the waters
Of fog that trickles down their slimy backs.
Near these: the blackened sheds
Of foundries, smelting furnaces,
And forges flanking the grey backs of the river (Stanley Burnshaw)

the earth smoked and baked;
stones in the field
marked the dead land:
coins taxing the earth. (Funaroff)

In these days of marking time,
While the whole tense land marks time (Burnshaw)
Where there is no life, no breath, no sound, no touch, no warmth,
no light but the lamp that shines on a trooper's drawn and
ready bayonet (Fearing)

Our age has Caesars though they wear silk hats (Joseph Freeman)
men, pig-snouted, puff
and puke at the stars (Herman Spector)
They burn the grain in the furnace while men go hungry.
They pile the cloth of the looms while men go ragged. (Benét)

Under the sign of the coin and the contract,
under the mask of the two-faced double-dealing dollar,
under the fetish of the document, stocks and bonds,
the parchment faces trade in securities. (Funaroff)
Men of paper, robbing by paper, with paper faces. (Benét)

The friend of caesar's friend murders the friend
who murders caesar. The juggler of knives
slits his own throat. Tight-rope walkers

find democracy in public urinals.
Black robed ministers stand with hatchet crosses;
the headsman hacks a worker's life to bone. (Funaroff)

Then an end, an end to this. Say enough . . . (Taggard)
The west is dying like a brood of aged birds
In the nests of their decay. (Norman MacLeod)

America today; its fields plowed under . . .
its wide avenues blistered by sun and poison gas (Rolfe)
And no lilacs bloom, Walt Whitman. (Gold)

There is a rust on the land (Benét)
an unseen hand
Weaving a filmy rust of spiderwebs
Over . . . turbines and grinding gears. (Kalar)

IV
REVOLUTION

We've eaten tin-can stew, tin-can java, tin-can soup
Inside the jungles of America!
We've slept in rain soaked gondolas, across ice-caked bars,
        On top of wind-beaten boxes. (Gessner)

    I'm not too starved to want food
not too homeless to want a home not too dumb
to answer questions come to think of it
        it'll take a hell
of a lot more than you've got to stop what's
going on deep inside us when it starts out
when it starts wheels going worlds growing
and any man can live on earth when we're through with it. (Kenneth
    Patchen)

The million men and a million boys,
Come out of hell (Horace Gregory)
From harvest fields rise up
Bone-aching and flesh-sore
Bondsmen (Lechlitner) and crawling back,
maybe they don't know what they're saying,
maybe they don't dare,

but they know what they mean:
Knock down the big boss . . .
hit him again, he cut my pay, Dempsey. (Gregory)

Brothers, Comrades, pool the last strength of men
In party, in mass, boil into form, and strike (Taggard)
let the workers storm from the factories,
the peasants from the farms;
sweep the earth clean of this nightmare. (Freeman)

If the dispossessed should rise,
Burning anger in their eyes . . .
Oh my brothers in the mire,
Clothe with lightning, shoe with fire . . . (Henry George Weiss)

I am black and I have seen black hands
Raised in fists of revolt, side by side with the white fists of white
    workers (Wright)
Fists tight-clenched around a crimson banner. (Rolfe)

And we think
Of barricades in some red dawn
On the East Side of New York City (MacLeod)
Split by a tendril of revolt
stone cedes to blossom everywhere (Muriel Rukeyser)
The blood's unvoiced rebellion brooding under
This sorrow, this despair. (Burnshaw)

We shall rise up, create our own new lands,
For the last frontiers are taken (Lechlitner)
Poets, pickets
Prepare for dawn (Rukeyser)

Red in the sky our torches write
Resurgence over death (Lechlitner)
Scarlet seas surge
exultant upon new shores (Funaroff)
into the red fields of sunrise (Funaroff)
to grind the streets into the single lens
of revolution, and converge their massing thunder
to the one pure bolt of proletarian red. (Maddow)

Listen, Mary, Mother of God, wrap your new born babe in

the red flag of Revolution (Langston Hughes).
Now, the red revolution comes. (Isidor Schneider)[4]

Since this compilation text was assembled in the 1990s, it was obviously not available to poets during the depression. Indeed, some of these
passages were not written until the middle and late 1930s, so this exact
metapoem could not have been assembled until then even if someone had
wanted to do so. In one sense, then, it represents a 1990s extension of the
dialogic poetics of the 1930s, evidence in part that these texts continue to
be available for rearticulation by contemporary readers, that we can enter this earlier conversation and keep it going sixty years later. Nonetheless, I would also argue that the poem exemplifies part of the implicit intertext that surrounded, animated, semanticized, and disseminated
revolutionary poetry throughout the decade. A full sense of how various
contemporary discourses informed, complicated, and enhanced individual poems would include not only other poems but also manifestos on
poetics, fiction, drama, journalism, editorials, essays, political speeches,
and sermons, as well as visual media. Putting all relevant discourses in
dialogue with one another would not, however, simply create one vast
intertext coextensive with all of 1930s culture, for poetry also had a degree
of autonomy and a series of distinctive social functions. Its own distinctive intertext was thus part of its social existence. The map of 1930s culture might be imaged as a series of overlapping intertexts in conversation
and debate with one another.

Of course poetry's revolutionary intertext was also in conflict with reactionary discourses, and it was in some contexts fissured from within by
competing visions of social change. But communists and Christian socialists alike also contributed to a broader revolutionary intertext whether they
chose to do so or not. The surrounding intertext thus provided a figurative analogue for the common ground of an alliance politics that the Left
could not really achieve in the early 1930s. Collectively, poetry from a
variety of socialist, communist, anarchist, and liberal democratic writers
offered a shared vision of human devastation, social and economic critique,
and revolutionary aspiration. The intertext to a notable degree dissolved
political differences while putting in their place an unstable but coalesc-
ing metonymics of representation.

In assembling this metapoem I deliberately mixed two techniques—
weaving fragments from multiple poems into coherent stanzas and giving
passages from other poems entire stanzas of their own. That is partly to
suggest that poems can both be dissolved in and make more individual

contributions to the intertext of their time. Neither pattern had absolute priority at the time; nor was such an intertext a fixed and stable entity. In its overall structure—a movement from descriptions of economic and social devastation to calls for revolutionary change—this metapoem imitates innumerable long and short poems throughout the period. It thus also bears out the way that 1930s poetry gave new political specification to the long progressive tradition it inherited, revived, and transformed. In one of the last Left historical anthologies of the decade, John Mulgan's *Poems of Freedom*, published in London in 1938, the editor calls its contents "a literature of protest and aspiration" (11). As this metapoem suggests, the conditions protested during the depression were no less specific than the mechanism of change toward which many poets aspired.

I have, however, deliberately constructed this metapoem as a fairly coherent intertext. Read aloud, without citing the author's names, it is easily assimilable to a single speaking voice; in an oral performance audiences would miss many of the places where individual poet's passages begin and end. They would also hear how one voice can be woven together out of many sources—an instance, if you will, of the *pleasures* of influence. This is consistent with my effort to enact the coeval, combinatory potential of these depression discourses. Of course an alternative (and far more discontinuous) 1930s poem could also be assembled. It might include polemical anticommunist passages and competing forms of idealization. A more complete study of 1930s intertextuality might thus credit several changing intertexts in competition with one another.

This is a good place to emphasize that I am not invoking some universalizing notion of intertextuality operating in all times and places. I would instead explicitly urge us to avoid partaking of that liberal elixir. Just what intertextuality means, what its grounds are, what kinds of reading and writing practices it inhibits and makes possible, what sorts of relations between texts it promotes, depends on the historical conditions at work in the period in question. There are other moments before, during, and after the modern period when other versions of the sort of revolutionary intertext I have assembled came into being and had cultural power. Such an argument could certainly be made for the renaissance in African-American writing in the 1920s. Like the revolutionary intertext of the 1930s, a Harlem Renaissance intertext would be grounded in a progressive movement for social change and in an awareness of intolerable material conditions. Both intertexts seek to empower the disadvantaged and the unemployed. At other times and in other contexts, however, upper-class and elite coterie intertexts have held sway in specific literary communities. That would make for a very different

story, one in which "intertextuality" would have quite different social meaning and quite different effects on subjectivity.

In the case of the poem I have assembled, one predictable response to
it would be to say that it shows how the monolithic core politics and nar-
rativity of 1930s poetry renders its surface variety irrelevant. It all reduces,
so the conservative argument would go, to a simple tale of blasted cities,
wasted farms, and unchecked exploitation—all these then cashed in with
revolutionary slogans. Indeed the presence of that recurrent core story was,
for many Communist Party functionaries, the only interest poetry had. Of
course there were many noncommunist Americans who found a call to
revolutionary change appealing during the depression and many journals
not under Communist Party control publishing radical poetry. Party publications themselves, moreover, often published poems on specific causes—such as the Scottsboro case or the effort to free Ernst Thaelmann from
a Nazi prison—that had no explicit revolutionary argument. But multiple
versions of the intertext assembled above were nonetheless influencing
how poems were written and read. As it happens, however, the semiotics
of political poetry does not operate as straightforwardly as the conservative attack would suggest. Such poetry has both its centripetal and its cen-
trifugal tendencies, and neither is precluded by its collaborative identity.
There is an irreducible, unstable mix of similarity and difference in each
of the metaphoric clusters above. Any image that enters into the compar-
ative interchanges these variations provoke is simultaneously drawn toward
a common identity and disseminated amongst multiple differences. The
presence of all these variations alongside the instances occurring in any
given poem inspires not only a sense of commonality but also the potential for endless displacement. The intertext enhances *both* these tendencies. It also reaches out to poems not part of its community of texts, se-
manticizing them against their will and co-opting them for a political
dialogue their authors might have preferred to avoid.

Even from this collation of fragments, it is possible to see that a variety of verbal styles and rhetorical strategies was in use in the revolutionary fervor of the 1930s. Looking for ways of capturing the suffering of the
depression and galvanizing readers, some poets aimed for a fairly neutral realism, while others tried to defamiliarize commonplace poverty
with more surreal and improbable images, such as Rolfe's "dead face
peering from your shoes." Some poets had no hesitation in provoking a
generalized pathos and sentiment, while others held themselves to precisely realized specific conditions. Some poets articulated a general critique of capitalism, while others mounted a specific attack on American

business. In all cases, however, this larger intertext of alternative images surrounded, supported, extended, and invaded any individual effort. A poet might thus write only about the farm or the city, but his or her work would inevitably be articulated to other depression settings. Similarly, a poem that focused on only one segment of the conceptual scheme I have mapped out would reverberate among the others as well. A poet who only wrote about misery on the farm would thus prompt revolutionary sentiments in readers regardless of whether they were voiced in the poem. A poem restricted to a critique of capitalism would inevitably remind readers of poems about how people were suffering and about the rising commitment to radical change. A poet like, say, Kenneth Fearing, who wrote numerous satires about modern business and commodified cultural life, was also contributing to the larger discursive formation evoked in the metapoem above.

Throughout this process, parallel images would echo and amplify one another, from the dust that seeps through all the dust-bowl poems to the dying cattle that haunt innumerable poems about depression farms to the unemployed and hungry who wander the streets of poems about American cities. Finally, to cite the most obvious case, a poet who found some inventive new invocation of the adjective *red* or made reference to the possibility of revolution would be explicitly understood as participating in the choral play of similarity and difference that ran through the poetry of the decade. Such images contribute to a rising tide of discourse that carries all revolutionary poems in its wake, making them coequal poems in a chorus of dissent. Richard Wright's sustaining vision of revolution "on some red day in a burst of fists on a new horizon" ("I Have Seen Black Hands 233) is also Louis Aragon's and Sylvia Townsend Warner's "Red Front" and Ben Maddow's "Red Decision," which may circle back to Wright's own call for change: "BREAD! / LAND! / FREEDOM! / I AM A RED SLOGAN." And Wright's "red day" is also MacLeod's "red dawn," Rolfe's "crimson banner," Taggard's "red banners" ("To My Daughter" 43), Funaroff's "red fields of sunrise," and Schneider's "red revolution," and these images in turn color every depression poem that describes a ruined present or yearns for a transformed future. Just as all these images gain a broader power of reference, then, so too do they partly give up their claim to a more controlled and narrow form of representation, for no such effort at representation can resist the chain of substitutions it invokes as soon as it is spoken. At the same time that one could argue every revolutionary poem holds a red banner aloft, one could equally well argue no thirties poem can decisively do so, for the banner slides into a slogan, which slips into a star, which substitutes for a flag. There is no *one thing* that all of these symbols could become because that one thing has no single, stable name. It is the nexus of radical change, the red site of signification. It reaches back into the history of progressive poetry to rearticulate older poems to this new synthesis. MacLeod's "red dawn" thus gathers Albert Young's 1915 "red dawn" into a contemporary configuration, and Ralph Chaplin's World War I antiwar poem, "The Red Feast," meets a countervailing semiotic force.[5] Indeed, even the element of whimsical or analytic distanciation in my diction is not wholly a 1990s phenomenon, for this site is also the wind flowing from "red steppes of peace and triumph" that Rafael Alberti heralds in his sardonically titled "A Spectre Is Haunting Europe" (15–16).

It is important to recognize that we are not just talking about image patterns in the poetry of the 1930s, about the kind of cultural patterns we can recognize retroactively whether or not writers at the time were aware of them. The broad categories above were very much part of contemporary public debate, and poets could not easily have avoided a sense of similarity and difference as they wrote. Moreover, there is repeated testimony to poets' and readers' sense of participating in a mass movement. The particular collective text assembled here is a retrospective one, but revolutionary writers and readers in the 1930s lived in a discursive environment much like the one I have assembled. I have worked for several years to recover the distinctive writing that individual 1930s poets did—partly to counter the reactionary claim that 1930s political poetry is all the same—but it may now be time to move in the opposite direction and recover the subsequently much-despised collective and choral features of the period. Indeed, some of the categorical revulsion that English professors have felt toward the poetry of the 1930s may reflect an unconscious awareness of these special literary conditions, about a time when no poem lived exclusively within its own boundaries and no poet's imagination seemed wholly private.

NOTES

1. For an important discussion of the cultural role of poems published in newspapers, see Furey.

2. I borrow the term *dialogic* from Mikhail Bakhtin, but my use of it is not narrowly Bakhtinian, at least insofar as Bakhtin deploys it most often to identify

polyphonic elements in individual works of fiction. Despite his tendency to see poetry as single-voiced, Bakhtin also invokes dialogism as a feature of all language, a necessary part of its social existence. There is thus, I would argue, some basis for taking the term in directions Bakhtin himself might not have anticipated. Here the term points to an additive or echolailic quality in a certain discursive formation—a formation to which many writers contributed—and to multiple effects and meanings embedded in individual words that are part of a social conversation taking place in poetry. In any case, it is the historical phenomenon, not its regulation by our vocabulary, that should have primacy here.

3. As I argue in *Repression and Recovery*, Popular Front poetry did not really replace the more aggressively revolutionary poetry of the Communist International's Third Period until the summer of 1936. Although the political period of the broad antifascist alliance of the Popular Front begins in 1935, the CPUSA continued, intermittently and inconsistently, to support some revolutionary Third Period poetry several months into 1936. See, for example, Malcolm Cowley's dramatically illustrated April 30, 1936, *Daily Worker* poem "A Poem for May Day," reproduced in my *Repression and Recovery*. By then, however, the Communist Party had withdrawn support for a number of radical publications and turned down some radical poetry projects, including Edwin Rolfe's *To My Contemporaries*.

"Poetry Chorus" is part of a book-length project on modern poetry. For other sections, see "Modern Poems We Have Wanted to Forget"; and "Lyric Politics: The Poetry of Edwin Rolfe." A companion essay—"Poetry Chorus: How Much For Spain?"—deals with Popular Front poetry.

4. The poems quoted are listed in the Works Cited under the authors' names; whenever possible, these sources were selected to maximize the reader's opportunity to obtain the poems and read other poems by that author from the same period, not to give information about their original date and place of publication, which in many cases was in 1930s books and journals that are now rare.

5. See the title poem in Albert Young's *The Red Dawn*. The cover adapts an image from IWW publications.

WORKS CITED

Alberti, Rafael. "A Spectre Is Haunting Europe." *A Spectre Is Haunting Europe: Poems of Revolutionary Spain*. By Alberti. New York: Critics Group, 1938. 15–16.

Aragon, Louis. *Red Front*. Trans. E. E. Cummings. Chapel Hill, N.C.: Contempo, 1932.

Bakhtin, M. M. *The Dialogic Imagination*. Ed. Michael Holquist. Austin: University of Texas Press, 1981.

Beecher, John, "Ensley, Alabama: 1932." *Collected Poems, 1924–1974*. By Beecher. New York: Macmillan, 1974. 18–19.

Benét, Stephen Vincent. "Litany for Dictatorships." *Burning City*. By Benét. New York: Farrar and Rinehart, 1936. 12–16.

———. "Ode to Walt Whitman." *Burning City* 26–41.

Burnshaw, Stanley. "I, Jim Rogers." *The Iron Land*. By Burnshaw. Philadelphia: Centaur Press, 1936. 99–102.

———. "Variations on a Baedecker." *The Iron Land* 81–83.

Chaplin, Ralph. "The Red Feast." *Bars and Shadows*. By Chaplin. 2d ed. New York: International Labor Defense, 1923. 54–55.

Cowley, Malcolm. "Mine No. 6." *Blue Juniata: Collected Poems*. By Cowley. New York: Viking, 1968. 9.

———. "A Poem for May Day." *Daily Worker*, April 30, 1936. Reproduced in Nelson, *Repression and Recovery* 220–21.

Fearing, Kenneth. "Denouement." *New and Selected Poems*. By Fearing. Bloomington: Indiana University Press, 1956. 31–53.

Freeman, Joseph. "Four Poems." Salzman and Zanderer 46–48.

———. "Six Poems." Salzman and Zanderer 40–44.

Funaroff, Sol. "Dusk of the Gods." *The Spider and the Clock*. By Funaroff. New York: International Publishers, 1938. 45–56.

———. "The Last Superstition." *The Spider and the Clock* 42–44.

———. "The Spider and the Clock." *The Spider and the Clock* 57–62.

———. "Unemployed: 2 A.M." *The Spider and the Clock* 15.

———. "What the Thunder Said: A Fire Sermon." *The Spider and the Clock* 25–32.

Furey, Hester L. "Raising the Specter: Poems and Songs of the American Radical Left." Ph.D. diss., University of Illinois, 1992.

Gessner, Robert. "Upsurge." *Upsurge*. By Gessner. New York: Farrar and Rinehart, 1933. 1–42.

Ghent, William J., ed. *Socialism and Verse: The New Appeal Socialist Classics*. No. 12. Girard, Kans.: New Appeal, 1916..

Gold, Michael. "Ode to Walt Whitman." Salzman and Zanderer 88–91.

Graham, Marcus. *An Anthology of Revolutionary Poetry*. New York: Active Press, 1929.

Gregory, Horace. "Dempsey, Dempsey." *Collected Poems*. By Gregory. New York: Holt, Rinehart, and Winston, 1964. 5–6.

Hughes, Langston. "Advertisement for the Waldorf-Astoria." Reproduced in Nelson, *Repression and Recovery* 212–13.

Ibarro, Felipe. "Where the Sun Spends the Winter." *New Masses*, Janaury 9, 1934, 1.

Kalar, Joseph. "Invocation to the Wind." Salzman and Zanderer 123–24.

———. "Papermill." Salzman and Zanderer 122.

Lechlitner, Ruth. "Clinical Prescription." *Tomorrow's Phoenix*. By Lechlitner. New York: Alcestis Press, 1937. 26–27.

——. "For Statisticians." *Tomorrow's Phoenix* 41–42.

——. "The Last Frontiers." *Tomorrow's Phoenix* 5–8.

——. "Nascent Root." *Tomorrow's Phoenix* 31–32.

——. "This Body Politic." *Tomorrow's Phoenix* 13–19.

Lewis, H. H. "Now What Good That Do?" Salzman and Zanderer 142–43.

MacLeod, Norman. "A Red Dawn in the East." Salzman and Zanderer 158.

Maddow, Ben. "Acts of God." Salzman and Zanderer 161–63.

——. "Images of Poverty." Salzman and Zanderer 163–65.

——. "Red Decision." *Symposium: A Critical Review*, October 1932, 443–53.

Mulgan, John, ed. *Poems of Freedom*. London: Victor Gollancz, 1938.

Nelson, Cary N. "Lyric Politics: The Poetry of Edwin Rolfe." Rolfe, *Collected Poems* 1–55.

——. "Modern Poems We Have Wanted to Forget." *Cultural Studies* 6 (May 1992): 170–97.

——. "Poetry Chorus: How Much For Spain?" *Disciplinarity and Dissent in Cultural Studies*. Ed. Cary Nelson and Dilip Gaonkar. New York: Routledge, forthcoming.

——. *Repression and Recovery: Modern American Poetry and the Politics of Cultural Memory, 1910–1945*. Madison: University of Wisconsin Press, 1989.

Olsen, Tillie. "I Want You Women Up North to Know." *Writing Red: An Anthology of Women Writers, 1930–1940*. Ed. Charlotte Nekola and Paula Rabinowitz. New York: Feminist Press, 1987. 179–81.

Patchen, Kenneth. "A Letter to a Policeman in Kansas City." *Collected Poems*. By Patchen. New York: New Directions, 1969.

Rella, Ettore. "Hieroglyphs." Salzman and Zanderer 213–15.

Rolfe, Edwin. *Collected Poems*. Ed. Cary Nelson and Jefferson Hendricks. Urbana: University of Illinois Press, 1993.

——. "Credo." *Collected Poems* 59.

——. "Season of Death." *Collected Poems* 95.

——. "These Men Are Revolution." *Collected Poems* 79–82.

——. *To My Contemporaries*. New York: Dynamo, 1936.

Rukeyser, Muriel. "City of Monuments." *Collected Poems*. By Rukeyser. New York: McGraw-Hill, 1978. 50–51.

Salzman, Jack, and Leo Zanderer, eds. *Social Poetry of the 1930s*. Philadelphia: Burt Franklin, 1978.

Schneider, Isidor. "Comrade—Mister." *Comrade: Mister*. By Schneider. New York: Equinox Cooperative Press, 1934. n.p.

Spector, Herman. "Outcast." *Bastard in the Ragged Suit*. By Spector; ed. Bud Johns and Judith Clancy. San Francisco: Synergistic Press, 1977. 57.

Spector, Herman, Joseph Kalar, Edwin Rolfe, and S. Funaroff. *We Gather Strength*. New York: Liberal Press, 1933.

Taggard, Genevieve. "Four Frescoes for the Future." *Calling Western Union*. By Taggard. New York: Harper, 1936. 64–65.

———. "A Middle-Aged, Middle-Class Woman at Midnight." *Calling Western Union* 13–15.
———. "O People Misshapen." *Calling Western Union* 28.
———. "To My Daughter, 1936." *Calling Western Union* 43.
———. "Up State—Depression Summer." *Calling Western Union* 50–53.
Trent, Lucia, and Ralph Cheyney, eds. *America Arraigned.* New York: Dean, 1928.
Warner, Sylvia Townsend. "Red Front." *Women's Writing in Exile.* Ed. Mary Lynn Broe and Angela Ingram. Chapel Hill: University of North Carolina Press, 1989. 363–66.
Weiss, Henry George. "If." *Lenin Lives.* By Weiss. Holt, Minn.: B. C. Haglund, 1935. 10.
Wright, Richard. "I Am a Red Slogan." *The World of Richard Wright.* By Michael Fabre. Jackson: University Press of Mississippi, 1985. 236.
———. "I Have Seen Black Hands." *The World of Richard Wright* 223–33.
———. "We of the Streets." *The World of Richard Wright* 247.
Young, Albert. "The Red Dawn." *The Red Dawn: A Book of Verse for Revolutionaries and Others.* By Young. London: Northern Division Herald League, 1915. 15–16.

3

LEFT OUT: THREE

ITALIAN-AMERICAN

WRITERS OF THE

1930S

In those hag-ridden and race conscious
   times
we wanted to be known as anti-fascists,
and thus get over our Italian names.
 —Felix Stefanile, "The Dance at
    Saint Gabriel's"

The project of creating a literary history of
the texts produced by American writers of
Italian descent is a recent development in
American cultural studies.[1] The many difficulties the historian faces in attempting to
place these contributions in any historical
context are compounded by the absence of
significant references to and legitimate analyses of these writers in the literary histories
that have been produced thus far. Although
there may be many reasons why contributions of this American subculture have never been adequately documented and examined in the context of American literary
history, this essay considers three possibilities
and applies them to three writers whose careers began in the 1930s and whose perspectives were shaped by the period.

   By 1940 three American writers of Italian
descent had established an important and
respectable presence in American literature.
John Fante, born in 1909, had already published half of his lifetime production of short
stories in such national magazines as the
American Mercury, the *Atlantic Monthly*,
Harper's Bazaar, and *Scribner's Magazine*.

He had also published two novels and a collection of his stories. Pietro di Donato, born in 1911, had published "Christ in Concrete," his first short story, in the March 1937 issue of *Esquire*; the story was reprinted in Edward O'Brien's *Best Short Stories of 1938* and expanded into a best-selling novel that was chosen over John Steinbeck's *Grapes of Wrath* as a main selection of the 1939 Book of the Month Club. Jerre Mangione, born in 1909, had numerous articles and book reviews to his credit and, more important, served as national coordinating editor of the Federal Writers' Project. In 1943 Mangione completed a book that Malcolm Cowley lauded as having "more lives than any other book of our time" (Cowley letter). The bulk of the subsequent writing of these three authors documented the 1930s and 1940s from an ethnic perspective.

Although most scholars are familiar with Nicola Sacco and Bartolomeo Vanzetti—two major figures and objects of Left writing of the period—most studies of the 1930s have not recognized Italian participation in American culture.[2] Only Warren French's *Social Novel at the End of an Era* (1966) includes a brief discussion of di Donato; however, while French acknowledges the "fresh and vigorous viewpoint" that di Donato's novel *Christ in Concrete* (1939) "brought to the American social scene," he portrays di Donato as an example of "the very irresponsibility that destroyed the age" (17). French includes di Donato, along with Richard Wright, in an epilogue subtitled "Beginners Luck."

The lack of formal experiment in their writing, which would have attracted the attention of the New Critics, and their attitudes toward Communist Party politics, which prevented their being taken up by left-wing critics, have combined to keep these writers out of the major studies of the period. More often than not, these writers, if considered at all, are not read in the context of their Italian-American heritage, and the ethnic-specific concerns they addressed in their work are not discussed. When their writing is recognized, they are usually (mis)read as members of the dominant white Anglo-Saxon culture. While this is a practice that might please those who wish to erase the stigma of an immigrant past and thus pass as Anglo-Saxons, it distorts (if it does not ignore or erase) the social and political problems encountered by Italian-Americans and overshadows the contributions they have made to American culture.

America's lack of exposure to the accomplishments of these writers and their impact on the development and evolution of Italian-American literature can be attributed to three claims I present, with the goal of helping us understand the absence of these three writers in historical accounts and critical writings of and about the 1930s. The first claim concerns the construction of historical categories used by scholars and critics to frame the study of this period; the second is based on the interpretative theoretical models that have been traditionally applied to works of this period; and the third concerns the religious orientation of these three writers. All three of these claims apply, in varying degrees, to each of the writers presented here. Although there may be other reasons as well, I offer these to explain why these three writers have been left out of every major literary and cultural history produced thus far.

The historical categories critics and scholars have constructed to characterize this era of American history have framed the way we see and study this important period in American history; unfortunately, until recently, most of the approaches have excluded from consideration those cultural products produced by members of such minority cultures as the Italian-Americans. One of the problems occurs when the definition of the period is limited to the writing published between the years 1930 and 1939. John Fante, Pietro di Donato, and Jerre Mangione all began their publishing careers in the 1930s and matured during the 1940s and 1950s. The constraints of periodization have contributed to their being left out, as evidenced by Warren French, who writes that "1939 and 1940 marked not only the end of an era in social and political history, but the end of a literary generation, especially in the creation of the social novel" (17). From this perspective, these writers could only be viewed as latecomers, stragglers in a cultural parade who pass the viewing stand long after the critics have left. In actuality those years mark the very birth of a generation of Italian-American writers, who as children of Italian immigrants, wrote stories and novels depicting their social environments. These are writers who would go on to produce what in retrospect can be labeled classics of Italian-American literature.

The traditional American Marxist criticism that is a characteristic, if not *the* dominant, critical approach to literature of the 1930s privileges class-conscious texts over those texts emphasizing ethnic, gender, or racial issues. As we know through the experience of Richard Wright, it was one thing to have one's writing accepted and quite another to have one's self accepted in social situations.[3] The Communist Party's attempts to establish a sense of a shared class identity among its writers, while important, was complicated by American racism and xenophobia. Although the desire to be supportive of a class struggle is important to such writers, their writing necessarily reflects other struggles created by racial and ethnic differences. By writing novels that did not follow important criteria established by such major Marxist literary critics of the period as Granville

Hicks, these writers could be easily ignored or overlooked by literary critics and historians.[4] By placing these writers in a culturally specific context (i.e., one that identifies and analyzes the Italian-American signifiers
in their writings), we can recover their works and acknowledge them as
vital contributions to the literature of the 1930s.

    None of these three writers identified strongly with what they perceived
as the ideology of Communist Party politics. John Fante, a loyal follower
of H. L. Mencken, stayed out of politics and described his attitude toward
party-line politics and Marxist aesthetics in a letter to his literary mentor:
"I haven't sucked out on Communism and I can't find much in Fascism.
As I near twenty-six, I find myself moving toward marriage and a return
to Catholicism. Augustine and Thomas More knew the answers a long
time ago. Aristotle would have spat in Mussolini's face and sneered at
Marx. The early fathers would have laughed themselves sick over the New
Deal" (Moreau 103). Fante's "return to Catholicism" and his choice not
to align himself with left-wing ideology would prove to hinder his consideration by cultural critics adhering to Marxist aesthetics. Fante never committed himself to any political cause. He registers his disappointment with
those who mix politics and literature in one of his many letters to Menck-
en in which he recounts his experience at the 1939 Western Writers' Conference in San Francisco: "My experience with writers is invariably disil-
lusioning. The more I meet them the less I think of the profession. There
is always the man's work—and then the man. That is excusable in hacks
and to be expected, but it seems to me the messiah on paper should not
step out of his role in real life. Mike Gold for example turns out to be a
platitude carrying a cross. He's so god-awful paternalistic, and yet so un-
mistakably adolescent" (Moreau 106).[5]

    In the recent resurrection of the late di Donato's contribution to the Third
American Writers' Congress, Art Casciato helps us understand why writers
like di Donato have been ignored by the established critics and scholars of
the period. As Casciato points out, di Donato, in his brief speech that Malcolm Cowley asked to be rewritten so it would conform to Cowley's expectations, refused to adopt "the prescribed literary posture of the day in which
the writer would efface his or her own class or ethnic identity in order to
speak in the sonorous voice of 'the people'" (70). As Casciato explains, di
Donato's style resisted the modern and "thus supposedly proper ways of
building his various structures." The result is that he is "less the bricklayer,
than a bricoleur who works not according to plans but with materials at
hand" (75–76). Di Donato was the only one of these three writers to join
the Communist Party, which he did at the age of sixteen on the night Sac-

co and Vanzetti were executed. The following excerpt from his contribution to the Third American Writers' Congress reflects di Donato's attitude
that Cowley found troublesome: "I am not interested in writing for class-
conscious people. I consider that a class-conscious person is something of a
genius—I would say that he is sane, whereas the person who is not class-
conscious is insane. . . . In writing *Christ in Concrete* I was trying to use this
idea of Christianity, to get an 'in' there, using the idea of Christ" (quoted in
Casciato 69). Needless to say, di Donato's use of "comrade-worker Christ"
(173) as a metaphor for the working-class man would prove to be quite problematic when viewed from a Marxist perspective.

Although sympathetic to the Communist Party in the United States,
Jerre Mangione never formally joined it because he recognized in it a
constraining dogmatism that reminded him of Catholicism. His memoirs
Mount Allegro (1943) and *An Ethnic at Large* (1978), along with *The Dream
and the Deal* (1972)—a study of the Federal Writers' Project—present a
very thorough account of the 1930s from an ethnic perspective.[6] His interest in writing and his encounters with American avant-garde artists of
the 1930s lead him to dismiss the "art-for-art's-sake" cult and to realize that
"no writer worth his salt could turn his back on social injustice" (*An Ethnic* 49). For a brief time he attended meetings of the New York John Reed
Club and taught literary criticism at the New School in New York. Though
uncomfortable with party-line politics, he became a dedicated antifascist
and contributed to the antifascist cause through news articles, book reviews, and social and political satire published in the *New Republic*, the
New Masses, the *Partisan Review*, and the *Daily Worker*. Many of these
he published under the pen names Mario Michele and Jay Gerlando. In
spite of his left-wing activity and his strong antifascist beliefs, Mangione's
work has never been adequately acknowledged in histories of this period.[7]

The writings of these authors were considered neither politically charged
nor stylistically innovative. When the traditional modernist/formalist standards of this period, established by proponents of the New Criticism, are
applied to their works, Fante, di Donato, and Mangione are, at best, relegated to minor-figure status. Much of their writing could be overlooked
because it lacked the experimentation that was typical of the modernist
movement.[8] All three writers wrote episodic bildungsromans in the natu-
ralist or realist tradition—obviously more influenced by Dreiser and Dos-
toyevsky than by Eliot and Joyce. Caught between the two dominant reading modes traditionally applied to texts of the period, their work falls
through the critical cracks into an oblivion that would only be detected
long after their publication. When cast in the spotlight of a culturally spe-

cific reading, however, their work can be read as the foundation upon which an Italian-American literature can be and is being created.[9]

My third claim is based on the issue of religion. The writing of Fante, di Donato, and Mangione is heavily imbued with an Italian Marianist Catholicism that is in many ways distinctly different from an American Catholicism institutionalized and controlled by Irish Catholics.[10] Discussion of their work thus requires the establishment of new interpretative frameworks that identify and include such contexts.[11] Such frameworks are only now being constructed. In a paper presented in a special session at the Modern Language Association's 1991 meeting, Thomas J. Ferraro proposed reexamining the period by focusing on the relationship between Mediterranean, Marianist Catholicism and American culture. Such an approach would make it impossible to ignore the writings of Italian-Americans, both proponents and opponents of American Catholicism, who documented what the Catholic church referred to as "The Italian Problem" (Malpezzi and Clements 108). Most of the works of these three writers present a variation of Catholicism that is often anti-institutional and is frequently referred to as "un-American." The Italian-Catholic background of all three writers, which strongly roots their works, is an area of American literary history that has yet to be adequately examined.

To illustrate these claims, I examine the content, style, and religious orientation of these three writers and offer readings that can be included in revised histories of the period. Space limitations in mind, the following is more of a historical orientation to, rather than a detailed analysis of, representative works of these three writers.

> We were all ideologists in the 30s; today there is suspicion of ideology. The current generation is more deprived than we were.
> —Jerre Mangione, in Thomas Lask's "Book Ends"

Unlike the few Italian immigrant writers who preceded them, whose work essentially argued for acceptance as human beings and pleas for recognition as Americans, the children of Italian immigrants used their writing both to document and to escape the conditions under which they were born and raised. Recovery and consideration of their works will aid us in re-creating a literary history that is sensitive to the process by which the children of immigrants create American identities. A common thread in the works of these three writers is the difference between the lives of their parents' generation and their own lives. Their parents' generation, characterized by hard work and the acceptance of injustices as destiny, would give way to the child's ability to fight injustice through writing. While all of the work of these three writers deals with the experiences and exploitation of the working class, none of them follows any of the expected and often prescribed formulas for creating proletarian literature. They all focus on what Richard Pells has called "a crisis of identity." But unlike writers who "spent an inordinate amount of time worrying about whether they had completely suppressed their bourgeois attitudes, whether they had truly been converted to the revolution, whether they were permanently immune to the temptations of the old world" (Pells 166), these Italian-American writers struggled with personal issues that complicated their sense of class identity. Analysis of their writings enables us to realize that when ethnicity intersects with class, it changes the dimension of one's perception of and identification with class struggle. Unlike the 1930s intellectuals V. F. Calverton and Michael Gold, whose name changes could be seen as attempts to avoid direct confrontation with their ethnic identity, di Donato, Fante, and Mangione chose to deal with their struggle to be perceived and accepted as Americans of Italian descent first. Because the 1930s is the period in which these writers begin their careers, the writing produced during these years is necessarily focused on personal development; this struggle is the essence of these writers' contributions to 1930s culture.

John Fante, the earliest of the three to publish, was aided by H. L. Mencken's desire to combat the Anglo-centric hegemony of the New England literary establishment. Among the books published in the 1930s, James T. Farrell recognized Fante's 1938 bildungsroman *Wait until Spring, Bandini* as one of the "few [novels] of genuine merit and value" ("End of a Literary Decade" 208).[12] Most of Fante's works concern the development of the social and aesthetic consciousness of a child of Italian immigrants. The subjects of much of his writing are the relationship between the individual and the individual's family and community and the subsequent development of a single protagonist's American identity that requires both an understanding and a rejection of the immigrant past parental figures represent. Fante's early writings focus on the development of an American identity through attempts to distance his characters from their Italian and working-class identities. Because of this, Fante's work reflects the more personal and thus ethnic aspects of his characters' experiences, rather than the political or class-based dimensions of his characters' lives.

Fante's four-book saga of Arturo Bandini, of which *Wait until Spring* is the first, tells the story of a young man who sets out for California to escape his family and its ethnicity. In the second novel, *Ask the Dust* (1939),

Bandini abandons his Italian-American home and makes his way to California. In the process he denies his ethnicity and calls attention to the ethnicity of others, such as Camilla, the Mexican waitress with whom he falls in love but continually calls a "greaser." Bandini believes the only way to become American is by identifying others as non-Americans.[13] After he does this, however, he identifies with their reactions and offers apologies with such explanations as "But I am poor, and my name ends with a soft vowel, and they hate me and my father, and my father's father, and they would have my blood and put me down, but they are old now, dying in the sun and in the hot dust of the road, and I am young and full of hope and love for my country and my times, and when I say Greaser to you it is not my heart that speaks, but the quivering of an old wound, and I am ashamed of the terrible thing I have done" (47). Such episodes provide insight into the process by which a child born of Italian immigrants struggles to fashion an American identity. Fante's characters do this by denying other immigrants and their children the same possibilities (i.e., to become an American one needs to identify the un-American and separate one's self from it). For Arturo Bandini, the development of this offensive behavior is a necessary defense, especially for one coming of age during the rise of Italian fascism.

During this period, Fante was at work on his first novel, *The Road to Los Angeles*, which had been contracted by Alfred Knopf but was not published until 1985, two years after Fante's death. In the novel, the protagonist, Arturo Bandini, uses references to European bourgeois intellectuals to set himself apart from the masses: "I said to Mona [the protagonist's sister], 'Bring me books by Nietzsche. Bring me the mighty Spengler. Bring me Auguste Comte and Immanuel Kant. Bring me books the rabble can't read'" (85). The key conflict in this novel, one that would separate Fante from the proletarian writers of this period, is a young writer's attempt to gain a sense of superiority over the working class by identifying with the literary models of bourgeois culture. Throughout the novel, Bandini comically regurgitates his readings as he rebels against his home environment. He uses his identity as a writer to separate himself from the working class, which reminds him of the past he is trying to escape. In *1933 Was a Bad Year* (1985) Fante depicts a young boy's desperate struggle to assimilate into American culture. The protagonist, Dominick Molise, attempts to separate himself from his poverty and ethnicity and rise above the masses through baseball. Fante juxtaposes the experiences of Molise's dream of "making America" through sports with the reality of the life of leisure led by the protagonist's wealthy best friend.

One impediment that continually keeps Fante's protagonists from identifying completely with mainstream American culture is their strong connection to Italian Catholicism. More than half the stories of his collection *Dago Red* (1940) deal with this subject. In 1933 the protagonist writes an essay on the mystical body of Christ (14) and believes the Virgin Mary has visited him in the night (37). Though Fante strays from this strong identification with Marianist Catholicism in *The Road to Los Angeles*, a novel in which Bandini constantly mocks his mother's and sister's Christianity in his attempt to separate himself from his background, he nevertheless does so through a character who is more comical than serious. Although Fante shares some of the concerns of those traditionally identified with the modernist movement, his ethnic and religious orientation combine to create philosophical obstacles that prevent critics and historians from including him in the Marxist and New Critical studies that have shaped the definition and thus our awareness of the modernist American literary tradition.[14]

While Fante was busy portraying characters who took to the road, traveling west and away from "Little Italy," Pietro di Donato was documenting the struggle of an Italian-American family facing the threat of disintegration posed by the American capitalist system. Di Donato, who died in January of 1992, left behind a considerable body of work dealing with the 1930s that deserves more attention than it has received. Born in Hoboken, New Jersey, in 1911 of Abruzzese parents, di Donato became a bricklayer, like his father, after his father's tragic death on Good Friday 1923. Unlike Fante, di Donato never dreamed of becoming a writer, but *Christ in Concrete*'s success placed him in a national spotlight that many critics believe blinded his literary vision for life. In a 1939 *Atlantic Monthly* review, E. B. Garside called him "a shining figure to add to the proletarian gallery of artists." Garside then went on to predict that di Donato "would never create a prose [sic] equal of Leopardi's *A Silvia*, nor will his latter-day rebellion rise to the supple power of *Pensieri*. But it must be understood that the Italian soul is essentially 'thin.' The Italian peasant and workman live themselves out fully as part of a family, or of an aggregate of some sort all committed to the same style" (7). Louis Adamic, more sensitive perhaps to di Donato's immigrant characters, saw that *Christ in Concrete* was unlike the staple fare of the laboring class that reflected "the economic treadmill on the tenuous cheesecloth fabric of an ideology" (5). In spite of this sensitivity, his review betrays a stereotypical notion of immigrant *italianita* (Italianness) when he characterizes the writing as "robust and full-blooded and passionate, now and then almost to the point of craziness; and also like Fante he has imagination and a healthy sense of the source of poetry in the Italian. . . . Sometimes one feels as though bricks and stones and trowelfuls of mortar have been thrown on the pages and from them have risen words" (5).

Italianita is vitally important to nearly everything di Donato has written. Through his work we can gain insight into the mysteries of Italian immigrant life and Italian Catholicism. Di Donato's style of writing is a strange synthesis of Theodore Dreiser's naturalism and James Joyce's stream of consciousness that rings with biblical echoes. His innovation can be found in his diction and word order, which re-create the rhythms and sonority of the Italian language. Whether he is describing a work site or a bedroom, di Donato's imagery vibrates with the earthy sensuality that early Italian immigrants brought to their American lives.

By directing his characters' rage at the employers who exploit immigrant laborers, di Donato argues for solidarity among American workers, and thus *Christ in Concrete* could be read in the tradition of the proletarian novels of James T. Farrell. Indeed, as Halford Luccock has noted, it was "written by a workman resembling more nearly the much heralded actual 'proletarian' author than any other [labor writer]" ((174). Unlike many writers of the proletarian literature of the period, di Donato continually inserts Catholicism as a force controlling the immigrants' reactions to the injustices of the capitalist system that exploits, maims, and kills the Italian immigrant. Di Donato's Catholicism has its roots in pre-Christian, matriarchal worship.[15] Annunziata, the mother in *Christ in Concrete*, controls her son's reaction to the work site "murders" of his father and godfather by calling on him to put his trust in Jesus, the son of Mary. By the end of the novel, Paul's faith is nearly destroyed, as evidenced by his crushing a crucifix his mother offered to him (296–97). The final image of the novel, however, suggests that the matriarchal powers still reign. The image we are left with is an inversion of the pietà, in which the son is holding a mother who is crooning a lullaby describing her son as a new Christ, one that her children should follow (303). Thus, while di Donato's novel depicts the injustices the immigrants face, it offers no revolutionary solution. The absence of such a solution, combined with the novel's Roman Catholic philosophical underpinnings, keeps *Christ in Concrete* out of the historical purview of proletarian literature and thus outside those literary histories devoted to such literature.

Jerre Mangione's contributions to American letters are fueled by a social conscience formed by the 1930s. While his literary works were not published during the 1930s, they were certainly written in response to

his experiences of this period. Unlike di Donato, Jerre Mangione wanted to be a writer since his college days during the late 1920s. As Mangione writes in *An Ethnic at Large,* "My true ambition, which I tried to
keep secret from my parents as long as possible, was to be a writer. It
seemed to me that I had no talent for anything else; that, moreover, it
offered the fastest avenue of escape to the world outside that of my relatives" (19). Mangione left that ethnocentric world of his family when
he entered Syracuse University, and during the 1930s he wrote extensively
about the effects of fascism on Italy and about those who fought fascism
in Europe. In fact, nearly all his fiction and much of his literary criticism is devoted to antifascist themes. One of his earliest book reviews is
of Ignazio Silone's *Fontamara.* Entitled "Happy Days in Fascist Italy," it
represents Mangione's earliest attempt to explain fascism to an American audience. "Fascism," Mangione wrote, "contrary to the impression
it tries to give to the world has made his [the peasant's] lot considerably
worse. It has borne down on him in many instances the naive faith the
ignorant peasant had in 'his government' and depriving him of his means
of livelihood" (37). Mangione uses this opportunity to present an alternative view of fascism, that of the illiterate Italian peasant who was
"tricked" into accepting the veiled offer of hope and progress extended
by Mussolini's black-shirt movement: "Silone's canvas takes in the whole
of Fontamara, the money-mad, tyrannical officials; the politician who
calls himself 'friend of the people' and then betrays them at every turn;
those peasants who, before they realized the true implications of Fascism
and implicit faith in God and 'their' government. . . . Fascism has wiped
Fontamara off the map, but Silone has put it on again in such a way that
no Fascist bullets can destroy its significance" (38).

   During this early stage of his writing career, Mangione, unlike di Donato and Fante, begins the task of interpreting Italian culture and life
under Mussolini. He reviewed translations of Pirandello's books *Better
Think Twice about It* and *The Outcast,* in the August 28, 1935, issue of the
New Republic. Entitled "Acrobat to Il Duce," the review points out Pirandello's influence on fascist literature:

> Long inclined to emphasize the cerebral and anti-realistic aspects of
> writing, Fascist literature needed only an impetus like Pirandello's to
> give it direction; that he has succeeded in giving it, is shown by the
> sheerly psychological and fantastic themes used and abused by mod-
> ern Italian writers in every branch of literature . . . it is hard to read
> very far in his two latest books without seeing Pirandello, the acro-

batic metaphysician, jostling aside the characters and stealing the stage for his own pet somersaults. (82–83)

During the same year, Mangione reviewed *Mr. Aristotle*, a translation of Ignazio Silone's collection of short stories. The review's title, "Pirandello Didn't Know Him," comes from the fact that when Mangione interviewed Pirandello during the playwright's visit to the United States, Pirandello said he had never heard of the author of *Fontamara*. This ignorance, wrote Mangione, "indicates that Italy has been more subtle than Germany in her suppression of intelligent books. Instead of making a bonfire of them, she has simply buried them, leaving no obituaries . . . [Silone] is an intellectual who can see clearly the plight and frustration of the peasant living under fascism" (23–24).

The predominance of Italy as a subject in Mangione's writing can be attributed to his travels there during Mussolini's regime. Mangione first visited Italy in 1936 and was an eyewitness to the methods of fascist control. He first documented this trip in articles he published during 1937 and 1938 in the *New Masses*, the *New Republic*, *Travel*, *Globe* magazine, and *Broun's Nutmeg*, and later they would become a significant portion of his first book, *Mount Allegro* (1943). His left-wing publications and his friendship with Carlo Tresca, an Italian anti-Fascist and anarchist who came to the United States in the early 1900s to aid the exploited Italian immigrant laborers, proved to haunt his first trip to Italy, during which his mail was censored and his movements monitored by fascist authorities. In 1936 Mangione traveled through Italy and Sicily fearing that at any time he could be arrested by fascist authorities and forced into military service. This trip is recounted in his classic memoir *Mount Allegro*.[16] In it he describes the effects of fascism on Italy and Sicily he observed in his encounters with Italians and his Sicilian relatives.

In 1937 Mangione left a New York publishing job to work for the New Deal. In the course of this period of politicization he came to understand the terrible threat that European fascism presented to the world. As he worked to understand it better, he befriended Carlo Tresca. His interactions with Tresca became the material upon which he would build his second novel, *Night Search* (1965). Based on the assassination of Tresca, *Night Search* dramatizes the experience of Michael Mallory, the illegitimate son of an antifascist labor organizer and newspaper publisher by the name of Paolo Polizzi, a character based on Carlo Tresca. Published in 1965, this novel follows Mallory as he searches for the murderer of his father. Mallory is an apolitical public relations writer inclined toward liberalism, who, through an investigation of his father's death, learns to take action and, in doing so, comes to an understanding of where he stands in relation to contemporary politics. Mallory very much resembles Stiano Argento, the Catholic protagonist in *The Ship and the Flame* (1948), Mangione's earlier and more strongly antifascist novel.

During this same period Mangione also read Sicilian writers, interviewed Luigi Pirandello, and convinced the publishing firm that employed him to accept the translation of Ignazio Silone's now classic antifascist novel *Bread and Wine*. Mangione explored in greater depth the effects of fascism on his relatives in his 1937 "Fontamara Revisited," in which he describes a visit to Realmonte, his ancestors' homeland in southern Italy. In *An Ethnic at Large*, based on his European experiences of the late 1930s, Mangione presents a more sophisticated overview of the effects of fascism. In *The Ship and the Flame* he creates an allegory for the sorry state of political affairs in Europe prior to America's entry into World War II. Aware of the dilemma of the liberal and the fate of the revolutionary in the world, Mangione created a microcosm of the larger world of his time, suggesting that the struggle against fascism could be won through heroic action that would not compromise one's Catholic beliefs.

Beyond the insights into Italian-American ethnicity we can gain by reading Italian-American representations of their struggles to "make America," to overcome prejudice and discrimination, and to negotiate an American identity without totally abandoning their *italianita*, closer readings of their writing reveal aspects of the mainstream writing of the 1930s. The radicalism of di Donato, the liberal pragmatism of Mangione, and the political apathy of Fante represent three different political positions available to writers at the time. In spite of their different political beliefs, their works are united by the social criticism of the larger American scene that comes from their positions at the banks of America's cultural mainstream. These three writers are but a few of the many unstudied Italian-American voices that can reward a revisionist history of the 1930s.[17]

A more thorough examination of the works these writers produced during and about the 1930s, would be, in most cases, a first critical and historical consideration. The next step, after analyzing their works as individuals and looking at the Italian-American aspects, is to compare their work with those created by other marginalized writers. Investigations of their contributions, especially when compared with the work that other marginalized writers (women, African-Americans, Mexican-Americans, and others), can provide us with new ways of seeing the past and subsequently with new ways of organizing the present, especially in terms of developing multicultural approaches to literary history and criticism.

NOTES

1. To date, there are only four book-length studies devoted to this phenomenon. See Boelhower; Green; Peragallo; and Tamburri, *To Hyphenate or Not to Hyphenate*.

2. Italian-American writers have been left out of such anthologies as Granville Hicks's *Proletarian Literature* (1935), John Herbert Nelson and Oscar Cargill's *Contemporary Trends: American Literature since 1900* (1949), Louis Filler's *Anxious Years* (1963), Harvey Swados's *American Writer and the Great Depression* (1966), and Jack Salzman's *Years of Protest* (1967). Not a word about these writers can be found in such major studies as Joseph Warren Beach's *American Fiction, 1920–1940* (1942), Alfred Kazin's *On Native Ground* (1942), Maxwell Geismar's *Writers in Crisis* (1947), Leo Gurko's *Angry Decade* (1947), Walter B. Rideout's *Radical Novel in the United States* (1956), Daniel Aaron's *Writers on the Left* (1961), Michael Millgate's *American Social Fiction* (1965), and Richard Pells's *Radical Visions and American Dreams* (1973). Even Marcus Klein's *Foreigners* (1981), a study that includes many noncanonical writers of the period, only briefly quotes Mangione and then only in reference to the WPA Writers' Project.

3. In his *American Hunger*, Wright goes to great lengths to explain that he left the Chicago branch of the Communist Party because he felt it was trying to dictate the writing of his *Native Son*. See also his "I Tried to Be a Communist," in which he discusses why he distanced himself from the Communist Party.

4. In spite of how these writers may have perceived the Communist Party's "line" on literature, recent criticism questions the idea of the hegemony of Communist Party thought and policy on literature in the 1930s. Most notable is Barbara Foley's *Radical Representations*, which posits, convincingly, that there was anything but a coherent party line on how literature should be produced and how it could function as a revolutionary vehicle.

5. Mencken, amused by the report, thought Fante's description of the conference should be worked into an article for the *American Mercury* or the *Saturday Review*, edited by the Italian-American Bernard De Voto. In a letter to Carey McWilliams, Fante presents a more detailed critique of the 1936 Western Writers' Conference (Cooney 136–40).

6. I examine these works in greater detail in "My House Is Not Your House."

7. For a more detailed look at Mangione's antifascist writings, see my "Fascism and Italian/American Writers."

8. Daniel Orsini identified this in di Donato's novel: "Thus, the true subject of the novel is not the history of a particular place or of a particular people but rather the author's own nonempirical ethnic awareness. As a result, when judged from a formalist, New Critical perspective, *Christ in Concrete* appears defective" (193).

9. For more on the development of approaches to Italian-American writers and the creation of Italian-American literature, see Tamburri's "In Recognition of the Italian/American Writers."

10. For more on Italian Catholicism in the United States, see Orsi; and "Folk Supernaturalism" in Malpezzi and Clements.

11. James T. Fisher's *Catholic Counterculture in America, 1933–1962,* is a good example of a study that examines the role American Catholicism played in the culture of the period; however, Fisher's study does not examine the many Catholic writers of Italian descent.

12. Farrell favorably reviewed Fante's *Wait until Spring, Bandini* in the January 1939 *Atlantic Monthly* ("Two Second Generation Americans").

13. Bandini's treatment of Mexicans in *Ask the Dust* is the same as his treatment of Filipinos in *The Road to Los Angeles.* Though this has been read as racism, readers must realize the irony created through such depictions.

14. Fante shares the modernist movement idea of America as a cultural wasteland: "I call my book *Ask the Dust* because the dust of the east and the middle west is in these streets, and it is a dust where nothing will grow, supporting a culture without roots and the empty fury of a lost hopeless people, frenzied to reach a peace that cannot ever belong to them" (Prologue to *Ask the Dust* 12).

15. Di Donato's devotion to the Catholic faith prompted him to write two religious biographies: *Immigrant Saint: The Life of Mother Cabrini* (1960) and *The Penitent* (1962), which tells the story of St. Maria Goretti through the point of view of the man who killed her. For a more thorough discussion of this element of his work, see my introduction to the 1993 reprint of *Christ in Concrete.*

16. This trip is also recounted in *An Ethnic at Large.* In the chapter, "Afraid in Fascist Italy," Mangione recalls his fear that he, like other Italian-American young men who had traveled to Italy, might be forced into the Italian military "as a reprisal for his [father's] having escaped army service by migrating to the States" (179).

17. In the early 1930s Luigi Fraina, who later changed his name to Lewis Corey, was one of the earliest to publish Marxist literary criticism. Frances Winwar is the only Italian-American writer besides di Donato to speak at a Writers' Congress. Winwar, who Anglicized Vinciguerra so that it would fit on the spine of her first book, spoke at the Second American Writers' Congress in 1937. Her paper, entitled "Literature under Fascism," described the effects of fascist repression on Italian literature of the 1930s and indirectly suggested that unless fascism were fought, similar consequences would face the writing of oth-

er countries. During the 1930s Winwar devoted her time to literary biographies, which could be read as allegories of the period. Louis Forgione and Garibaldi LaPolla are among other writers whose fiction has yet to be examined in the context of the 1930s. Michael De Capite's *No Bright Banner* (1944) is devoted to the protagonist Paul's coming of age during the 1930s. Angelo Pellegrini described his coming of age in the 1930s, which included a stint as a Communist Party member, in his memoir *American Dream* (1986). Recently Carl Marzani, who wrote a novel entitled *The Survivor* (1957) and a number of studies of American Cold War policy and Eurocommunism, has completed three volumes (out of a proposed five-volume series) of *The Education of a Reluctant Radical*, his memoirs reflecting a social conscience formed by the 1930s.

WORKS CITED

Adamic, Louis. "Muscular Novel of Immigrant Life." Review of *Christ in Concrete*, by Pietro di Donato. *Saturday Review*, August 26, 1939, 5.

Boelhower, William. *Immigrant Autobiography in the United States*. Verona, Italy: Essedue Edizioni, 1982.

Cooney, Seamus, ed. *John Fante: Selected Letters, 1932–1981*. Santa Rosa, Calif.: Black Sparrow, 1991.

Casciato, Art. "The Bricklayer as Bricoleur: Pietro di Donato and the Cultural Politics of the Popular Front." *Voices in Italian Americana* 2 (Fall 1991): 67–76.

Cowley, Malcolm. Letter to Jerre Mangione, April 29, 1981. Jerre Mangione Papers, Rush Rhees Library, Department of Rare Books and Special Collections, University of Rochester, Rochester, N.Y.

De Capite, Michael. *No Bright Banner*. New York: John Day, 1944.

di Donato, Pietro. *Christ in Concrete*. 1939. Indianapolis: Bobbs-Merrill, 1966.

Fante, John. *Ask the Dust*. 1939. Santa Barbara, Calif.: Black Sparrow, 1980.

———. *Dago Red*. New York: Viking Press, 1940.

———. *1933 Was a Bad Year*. Santa Barbara, Calif.: Black Sparrow, 1985.

———. Prologue. *Ask The Dust*. By Fante. Santa Rosa, Calif.: Black Sparrow, 1990.

———. *The Road to Los Angeles*. Santa Barbara, Calif.: Black Sparrow, 1985.

———. *Wait until Spring, Bandini*. 1938. Santa Barbara, Calif.: Black Sparrow, 1983.

Farrell, James T. "The End of a Literary Decade." *Literature at the Barricades: The American Writer in the 1930s*. Ed. Ralph Bogardus and Fred Hobson. University: University of Alabama Press, 1982. 204–10.

———. "Two Second Generation Americans." *Atlantic Monthly*, January 1939, in *The Atlantic* Bookshelf, an unpaginated section of bound volumes.

Ferraro, Thomas J. "Introducing the Italian/American *Risorgimento*." Paper presented at the Modern Language Association Convention, San Francisco, December 30, 1991.

Fisher, James T. *The Catholic Counterculture in America, 1933–1962.* Chapel Hill: University of North Carolina Press, 1989.

Foley, Barbara. *Radical Representations: Politics and Form in U.S. Proletarian Fiction, 1929–1941.* Durham, N.C.: Duke University, 1993.

Forgione, Louis. *The River Between.* New York: E. P. Dutton, 1928.

French, Warren. *The Social Novel at the End of an Era.* Carbondale: Southern Illinois University Press, 1966.

Gardaphè, Fred L. "Fascism and Italian/American Writers." *Romance Languages Annual.* Ed. Anthony J. Tamburri et al. West Lafayette, Ind.: Department of Foreign Languages and Literatures, Purdue University, 1993. 254–59.

———. Introduction. *Christ in Concrete.* By Pietro di Donato. New York: Signet, 1993. ix-xviii.

———. "My House Is Not Your House: Jerre Mangione and Italian/ American Autobiography." *Multi-Cultural Autobiography: American Lives.* Ed. James Robert Payne. Knoxville: University of Tennessee Press, 1992. 139–77.

Garside, E. B. Review of *Christ in Concrete,* by Pietro di Donato. *Atlantic Monthly,* July–December 1939, in *The Atlantic* Bookshelf, an unpaginated section of bound volumes.

Green, Rose Basile. *The Italian-American Novel.* Cranbury, N.J.: Associated University Press, 1974.

LaPolla, Garibaldi M. *The Fire in the Flesh.* New York: Vanguard Press, 1931.

———. *The Grand Gennaro.* New York: Vanguard Press, 1935.

Lask, Thomas. "Book Ends." *New York Times Book Review,* August 6, 1978, 35.

Luccock, Halford E. *American Mirror: Social, Ethical and Religious Aspects of American Literature, 1930–1940.* New York: Macmillan, 1940.

Malpezzi, Frances, and William M. Clements. *Italian-American Folklore.* Little Rock: August House, 1992.

Mangione, Jerre. "Acrobat to Il Duce." Review of *Better Think Twice about It* and *The Outcast,* by Luigi Pirandello. *New Republic,* August 28, 1935, 82–83.

———. *The Dream and the Deal: The Federal Writers' Project, 1935–1943.* 1972. Philadelphia: University of Pennsylvania Press, 1983.

———. *An Ethnic at Large: A Memoir of America in the Thirties and Forties.* 1978. Philadelphia: University of Pennsylvania Press, 1983.

———. (Pseud. Mario Michele). "Fontamara Revisited." *New Republic,* May 26, 1937, 69–71.

———.(Pseud. Mario Michele). "Francesco Becomes a Lion." *New Masses,* April 25, 1939, 10.

———. (Pseud. Mario Michele). "Francesco's an Aryan." *New Masses,* December 18, 1938, 17.

———. "Happy Days in Fascist Italy." Review of *Fontamara,* by Ignazio Silone. *New Masses,* October 2, 1934, 37–38.

———. *Mount Allegro.* 1943. New York: Harper and Row, 1989.

———. *Night Search.* New York: Crown, 1965.

———. (Pseud. Jay Gerlando). "Pirandello Didn't Know Him." Review of *Mr. Aristotle,* by Ignazio Silone. *New Masses,* November 12, 1935, 23–24.

———. *The Ship and the Flame.* New York: A. A. Wyn, 1948.

Marzani, Carl. *The Education of a Reluctant Radical: Growing Up American.* New York: Topical Books, 1993.

———. *Roman Childhood.* New York: Topical Books, 1992.

———. *Spain, Munich and Dying Empires.* New York: Topical Books, 1993.

———. *The Survivor.* New York: Cameron Associates, 1958.

Moreau, Michael, ed. *Fante/Mencken: A Personal Correspondence, 1930–1952.* Santa Rosa, Calif.: Black Sparrow, 1989.

Orsi, Robert Anthony. *The Madonna of 115th Street: Faith and Community in Italian Harlem, 1880–1950.* New Haven, Conn.: Yale University Press, 1985.

Orsini, Daniel. "Rehabilitating di Donato, a Phonocentric Novelist." *The Melting Pot and Beyond: Italian Americans in the Year 2000.* Ed. Jerome Krase and William Egelman. Proceedings of the Eighteenth Annual Conference of the American Italian Historical Association. Staten Island, N.Y.: AIHA, 1987. 191–205.

Pellegrini, Angelo. *American Dream.* San Francisco: North Point Press, 1986.

Pells, Richard H. *Radical Visions and American Dreams: Culture and Social Thought in the Depression Years.* 1973. Middletown, Conn.: Wesleyan University Press, 1984.

Peragallo, Olga. *Italian-American Authors and Their Contribution to American Literature.* New York: S. F. Vanni, 1949.

Stefanile, Felix. "The Dance at Saint Gabriels." *From the Margin: Writings in Italian Americana.* Ed. Anthony J. Tamburri, Paolo Giordano, and Fred L. Gardaphè. West Lafayette, Ind.: Purdue University Press, 1991. 158.

Tamburri, Anthony Julian. "In Recognition of the Italian/American Writers: Definitions and Categories." *Differentia* 6–7 (Spring/Autumn 1994): 9–32.

———. *To Hyphenate or Not to Hyphenate.* Montreal: Guernica, 1991.

Winwar, Frances. *Farewell the Banner.* New York: Doubleday, Doran, 1938.

———. "Literature under Fascism." *The Writer in a Changing World.* Ed. Henry Hart. New York: Equinox Cooperative Press, 1937. 81–91.

———. *Poor Splendid Wings.* Boston: Little, Brown, 1933.

———. *The Romantic Rebels.* Boston: Little, Brown, 1935.

Wright, Richard. *American Hunger.* New York: Harper and Row, 1977.

———. "I Tried to Be a Communist." *Atlantic Monthly,* August–September 1944, 61–70.

4

AFRICAN-AMERICAN

WRITING OF THE

1930S: A PROLOGUE

African-American literary production of the 1930s remains the perennially neglected stepchild in conventional accounts of African-American literary history. To the extent that a narrative of twentieth-century African-American literary history may be said to exist, the general tendency among literary critics has been to regard the 1930s as a transitional period—albeit one marked by continuing achievement of such established writers as Langston Hughes and Zora Neale Hurston and the powerful voice of Richard Wright toward the end of the decade. "The prevailing wisdom," Robert Bone notes, "postulates a Harlem Renaissance in the 1920s and a second literary flowering, associated with the Black Arts Movement of the 1960s. But our sense of the intervening years is at best vague and indistinct" (466). Indeed, the legend of the Harlem Renaissance is so deeply entrenched in most accounts of African-American literary history that it continues to overshadow other significant moments of literary production. "The term *Renaissance* in Afro-American cultural history," Hazel Carby points out, "has been most exclusively applied to the literary and artistic productions of intellectuals in the years between the end of World War I and the Depression" (163). Carby argues that "this particular moment has come to dominate Afro-American cultural history and overshadow earlier"—and I would add *later*—"attempts of the black intellectuals to

AFRICAN-AMERICAN WRITING   79

assert their collective presence" (54). The Harlem Renaissance is still widely viewed as the "happy hour of black literary and historical studies"—as
Clyde Taylor has so aptly put it (54)—and any attempt to construct a narrative about African-American writing during the 1930s must therefore
confront the problematics inherent in invoking the Harlem Renaissance
as *the* defining moment in twentieth-century African-American literary/
cultural production. When, in short, does the "Harlem Renaissance" end
and "the 1930s" begin? Robert Stepto has very adeptly charted how the
choice of terminology—in this instance such terms as *Harlem, Negro, New
Negro, Renaissance,* and *Movement*—both dictate and reveal the subtle
process of composing literary history ("Sterling A. Brown" 73–74) and how
the choice of language invariably reveals the ideological commitments of
the critic.[1] His analysis also highlights the necessity of disrupting the notion of the Harlem Renaissance as a "unique, intellectually cohesive and
homogeneous historical moment" (Carby 63) as a necessary first step toward retrieving the aesthetic and ideological antecedents of African-American writing during the 1930s.

African-American writing of the 1930s seems to have also suffered the
general fate of much of the literature of the period, relegated, as Carla
Cappetti has pointed out, to the second-rate status often accorded the literary works defined by the labels "naturalism" and "proletarian" (3). The
ideological and aesthetic baggage associated with these terms conveys yet
another implicit narrative: the predictable and dreary story about the tragic
encounter between the creative writer and political ideology. As Paul
Lauter has observed, this narrative insists that the art produced by politically committed writers "succeeded . . . only because its creators by accident or design moved outside this ideological orbit and thus from under
the stifling, humorless power of Communist Party functionaries" (332).
Repeated ad infinitum, this story thus emerges as a cautionary tale, designed to warn artists and intellectuals against the disastrous consequences on their work of the Left political enterprise in general and the intellectual tyranny of communism in particular. For African-American writers
of the 1930s, Lauter argues, this narrative has been cast in terms of the
supposed political seduction and subsequent redemption of Richard
Wright—the emblematic black writer of the period. In a broader sense,
this argument constitutes the basis of Harold Cruse's monumental but
flawed polemic *The Crisis of the Negro Intellectual,* a work that has been
central to shaping contemporary views about African-American artistic and
intellectual life during the 1930s. For Cruse, the historic encounter between African-American artists and intellectuals and the white Left—one

in which black thinkers functioned as apparently passive receptacles of Marxist orthodoxy—has had disastrous political and cultural consequences for the black community. This argument, too, will have to be contested as a step toward constructing a history of African-American writing during the 1930s. For the remainder of this essay I outline how a careful consideration of the cultural and political antecedents of African-American writing of the 1930s can lead to a richer understanding of this pivotal moment in African-American literary and cultural history.

RETRIEVING THE NEW NEGRO

When Richard Wright issued his manifesto "Blueprint for Negro Writing" in 1937, he signaled an apparently sharp departure from the literary practices and cultural practices of his predecessors, whom he described as "decorous ambassadors who go a-begging to white America. They entered the court of American Public Opinion dressed in the knee-pants of servility, curtsying to show that the Negro was not inferior, that he was human, and that he had a life comparable to that of other people. These were received as poodle dogs who have learned clever tricks" (37).

In spite of his critical assault on the aesthetic and ideological outlook of these writers, Wright, like those of the previous generation, participated in the general mood of the New Negro—a stance underscored by the epigram to his first collection of short stories, *Uncle Tom's Children:* "The post Civil War household word among Negroes—'He's an Uncle Tom!'— which denoted reluctant toleration of the cringing type who knew his place before white folk, has been supplanted by a new word from another generation which says—'Uncle Tom is dead!'"

Henry Louis Gates Jr. has demonstrated that the trope of the New Negro has served various generations of black intellectuals in search of a reconstructed presence in American public life (130), but the emergence of the term in the post–World War I era was foreshadowed by the debates within the African-American community about whether to support the United States's entry into the war (Vincent). New Negroes generally condemned the war effort, pointing out the hypocrisy of fighting abroad for rights denied at home, while many established black leaders endorsed it. Although it was difficult—and dangerous—to make this argument in a censored wartime press, New Negroes helped to create a contentious and defiant journalism (Kerlin)—one that coincided with the continuing transformation of the black community from a predominantly southern, rural population to an urban one; the return of black troops from fighting in Europe; and the tensions over employment, housing, and social relations, which finally exploded during the "Red Summer" of 1919, a year in which bloody race riots erupted in twenty-six cities across the country.

The mood of the New Negro was reflected in the name of many of the newspapers that flourished during this era—*Emancipator, Challenge, Advocate, Whip, Hornet,*—and its ethos was given its most radical expression in A. Philip Randolph and Chandler Owen's magazine, the *Messenger,* in which they published their 1919 "Thanksgiving Homily to Revolution":

> First, we are especially thankful for the Russian Revolution—the greatest achievement of the twentieth-century. . . .
> Fifth, we are especially thankful that radicalism has permeated America, giving rise to many of the greatest strikes in history. . . .
> Seventh, we are thankful for the New Crowd Negro, who has made his influence felt in every field—economic, political, social, educational and physical force. The New Negro has been in the front ranks of the strikes. He has taken his place in Socialist politics. He is an integral part of every great social movement. . . . On the field of physical force, the New Negro has been right on the job for the protection of his home, his life and his loved ones. The Washington, Chicago, Longview, Knoxville, Elaine and Omaha riots are bright spots in the New Negroes' attitude toward American lawlessness and anarchy. (quoted in Vincent 46)

If we see the "New Negro" as initially an expression of *political* insurgency, which will later find its cultural counterpart in the careful construction of the "Harlem Renaissance" by Alain Locke and others, it becomes possible not only to recover the radical content of the original usage of the term but also to recognize how sharply contested and coveted the term was among various strata of the black community: black leftists, nationalists, and the black bourgeoisie.

No account of the New Negro mood of the post–World War I era would be complete without recognizing the centrality of the Garvey movement to the period. Too often relegated to the margins of African-American political and cultural history, Garvey—and the particular vision of black nationalism and Pan-Africanism he advocated—must be seen as a central and competing vision in the fierce debates about race, class, and the future of the black community that engaged Marcus Garvey, W. E. B. Du Bois, the Friends of Negro Freedom, the National Association for the Advancement of Colored People (NAACP), the African Blood Brother-

hood, and other black intellectuals, nationalists, socialists, and communists during the 1920s. Garveyites played a central role in the cultural arena as well (Martin), primarily through the pages of the movement's newspaper, *Negro World*, but also through the efforts of such individuals as the
short-story writer Eric Walrond, whose collection of short fiction *Tropic
Death* won critical acclaim during the Harlem Renaissance; the scholar
William Ferris, whose 1915 historical study *The African Abroad* predicted
a worldwide cultural and political awakening of African peoples; and T.
Thomas Fortune, who founded the New York *Age* during the 1880s and
served as chief editor of *Negro World* during the mid-1920s.

When Garvey is reinserted into the picture of African-American life
during the 1920s, a more complex picture of the ideological currents swirling through the black community emerges—one that involves the voices
of W. E. B. Du Bois, A. Philip Randolph, Chandler Owen, Cyril Briggs,
Richard B. Moore, Hurbert Harrison, W. A. Domingo, Theophilus Lewis,
George Schuyler, and others—and it becomes clearer that Alain Locke's
construction of the "New Negro" was one of many competing for cultural and political authority during the 1920s. Harold Cruse is certainly right
when he argues that many of the unresolved artistic and political dilem-
mas that have plagued subsequent generations of African-American artists and intellectuals can be seen in sharp relief in the intellectual and
political ferment of the 1920s. When he argues, however, that the deepest
source of this "crisis" is the seduction of African-American intellectuals
by a "foreign cultural and political ideology" (51), his anticommunist bias
seriously skews his analysis.

AFRICAN-AMERICAN WRITERS AND THE LEFT

For Harold Cruse, "the Harlem Renaissance had too much to contend
with in the new Communist left wing and the new Garvey nationalism"
(53)—as if the Harlem Renaissance existed somehow independently of
those forces instead of being inextricably connected to them. "Unable to
arrive at any conclusions of their own as a *black intelligentsia*," Cruse
continues, "the leading literary lights of the 1920s substituted the Communist left wing philosophy of the 1930s, and thus were intellectually side-
tracked for the remainder of their productive years" (63). As one of the first
and foremost black writers to be associated with the Communist Party, both
nationally and internationally, during the 1920s, Claude McKay occupies
a central role in Cruse's narrative—and the larger narrative within which

it participates. The trajectory of his relationships with the white Left should therefore offer a particularly useful touchstone against which to test Cruse's thesis.

On November 20, 1922, Claude McKay joined Grigory Yevseyevich Zinoviev, the executive director of the Comintern, and other leaders of the Communist Party on the platform of the Bolshoi auditorium to address the Fourth Congress of the Third Communist International. Although McKay later denied in his autobiography that he had addressed the congress, implying that he would rather incur the disapproval of Zinoviev than sacrifice his integrity as a poet (A Long Way from Home 173), his remarks were summarized in International Press Correspondence the following day under the title "The Racial Question: The Racial Issue in the United States." McKay and Otto Huiswood, a member of the official American delegation, were the only African-Americans from the Western Hemisphere to attend the congress and the first in the brief history of the Third Communist International to address it. The sheer physical presence of McKay and Huiswood undoubtedly had an impact on the congress proceeding—notable for the first extended discussion in Moscow of the American Negro Question. The Negro Commission, chaired by Otto Huiswood, was established, and McKay was invited to address its members and participate in its proceedings. The commission subsequently produced a document, "Theses on the Negro Question," which represented the first real attempt on the part of the Comintern to formulate a position on the Negro Question (Foner and Allen 24–32). After the Fourth Congress concluded in December 1922, McKay remained in the Soviet Union, clearly enjoying his celebrity status. With the apparent complete confidence of the Party hierarchy, he met and corresponded with Trotsky, wrote poems and articles for the Soviet press, and met with and spoke before writers and other Soviet dignitaries. He was commissioned to write a book on African-Americans—which subsequently appeared as The Negroes in America (1923)—and was invited to gather materials for a book about the Russian Revolution for American readers, a task he apparently never completed. Although McKay's autobiography describes his experiences in the Soviet Union as one of the high points of his life, what appeared to be an intensified commitment to radical politics on his part turned out to be, in retrospect, the grand finale, the closing chapter of a distinct stage of his life and literary career. From 1923 to 1934, McKay lived and worked abroad—in Germany, France, Spain, and Morocco—returning to the United States at the height of the Great Depression. By then, McKay had become a relentless critic of the Communist Party in the

United States, particularly its activities in Harlem. Increasingly socially and culturally isolated, poverty-stricken, and plagued with illness, McKay gradually moved toward Catholicism as a source of spiritual refuge, converting four years before his death in 1948.

Although, on the surface, the outline of Claude McKay's career may suggest the familiar story of "seduction and betrayal," the reality, of course, is much more complex. At the very least, however, a careful examination of Claude McKay's activities during the early 1920s makes it very clear that African-American writers and intellectuals were, as Barbara Foley argues, "active contributors rather than passive respondents" to the emerging Marxist discourse about race and class during the 1920s (305).

McKay, it should be recalled, began his literary career not as an active participant in the Harlem Renaissance—which was orchestrated and publicized during the years of his extended absence from the United States— but as an associate of the radical and bohemian politics of Greenwich Village. The publication of his best-known poem, "If We Must Die," a direct response to the Red Summer of 1919, in the July 1919 issue of Max Eastman's *Liberator* not only gained McKay an entry into Greenwich Village's radical bohemia but also won him the admiration of the Garvey movement—whose newspaper trumpeted his fame in the black community—and brought him to the attention of the small but influential black cultural elite, particularly William Stanley Braithwaite, the literary critic for the *Boston Transcript*, and W. E. B. Du Bois, the editor of the NAACP's journal the *Crisis* (both of whom had previously rejected his poetry for publication). In short, "If We Must Die" brought McKay into contact with all of the major ideological formations swirling around African-American life in the post–World War I era—the white Left, the Garvey movement, the NAACP, and the New Negro mood. McKay therefore straddled the worlds of Greenwich Village and Harlem, negotiating among—and seeking to intervene in—the debates among white radicals, the Garvey movement, the NAACP, and the black literati who would become identified with the Harlem Renaissance.

McKay became closely connected with other prominent black radicals of the period through his close connection with Hurbert Harrison, a pioneering black socialist and one of the first and greatest of Harlem's soapbox orators, whom McKay had met when he first arrived in New York in 1914. Harrison had established two short-lived publications, the *Voice* and *New Negro*, and briefly edited Garvey's *Negro World* from 1920 to 1921. Through Harrison, McKay was drawn into a small but influential group of black radicals who emerged in Harlem toward the end of World War I, the group associated with Cyril Briggs, the editor of the magazine the *Crusader*, which organized itself as the semisecret African Blood Brotherhood in 1919.[2] Although much more needs to be learned about this fascinating organization, its outlook linked a sharply defined radical consciousness and commitment to national liberation movements with a radical critique of capitalism. McKay, in short, was linked to a coterie of black radicals that included Cyril Briggs, Richard B. Moore, Grace Campbell, Otto Huiswood, and others—many of whom became the first African-Americans to join the Communist Party. In spite of its small numbers, this cadre played a pivotal role in keeping the issues of race and racism at the forefront of the radical agenda and in interpreting the outlook of the Communist Party to the black community.

In Claude McKay's case, this work took the form of twenty-odd essays, reviews, and letters, which appeared in Sylvia Pankhurst's *Worker Dreadnought* during his sojourn in England in 1919 and 1920, the *Liberator* in 1921 and 1922, and the *Crisis* in 1923 and 1924 (Cooper, *The Passion* 45–47). From the beginning of his association with the white Left, McKay, like his allies in the African Blood Brotherhood, warned white radicals that the revolutionary movement in the United States and abroad would flounder unless the racial issue was honestly and directly addressed. When French troops, including several contingents of African-American soldiers, occupied Germany along the Rhine in 1920, the British Left, fearing that this action might topple the unstable Weimar government, sought to mobilize public opinion against the French action. The *Daily Herald*, Britain's leading socialist newspaper, crudely pandered to the racial fears of its readers by publishing a news report under the headline "Black Scourge in Europe: Sexual Horror Let Loose by France on Rhine." McKay's response, an open letter to George Lansbury, the prominent British socialist and Labour politician and editor of the *Daily Herald*, castigated the sexual mythology expressed in the article and challenged the racism of the British Left (Cooper, *The Passion* 54–57).

At the same time, McKay published several articles in Garvey's *Negro World*, sending back journalistic reports on the condition of London's black community. He also sought to reach the readers of the NAACP's *Crisis*, beginning in 1921 with an open letter to W. E. B. Du Bois, attacking him for "sneering" at the Russian Revolution and challenging the NAACP to take a more central role in organizing black and white workers under the revolutionary banner (Cooper, *Claude McKay* 141). During this period McKay seemed to subscribe to the broad goals of the African Blood Brotherhood: to keep the issues of race and racism in the forefront of the white radical agenda, to try to influence the Garvey movement and move its politics to the left, and to interpret the goals of the communist movement to the black community. Although McKay was sometimes critical of the racial attitudes of the white Left, there are few hints of his later disillusionment with communism in these essays. For this, perhaps, we need to turn to his brief experience as coeditor, with Mike Gold, of the *Liberator* in 1922.

McKay had met Max Eastman in 1919, beginning a friendship that would last throughout his life. After he returned to the United States from England in 1921, McKay resumed his association with the *Liberator* and joined its editorial staff. When Eastman resigned as editor in 1921, McKay and Gold were appointed coeditors. In his autobiography, McKay insists that this relationship was doomed from the beginning because of fundamental temperamental and ideological conflicts between the two men: "Michael Gold's idea of the *Liberator* was that it should become a popular proletarian magazine, printing doggerels from lumberjacks and stevedores and true revelations from chambermaids. I contended that while it was most excellent to get material out of the forgotten members of the working class, it should be good stuff that could compare with any other writing" (*A Long Way Home* 139). McKay also alludes to conflicts with the artist Robert Minor: "Robert Minor said he could not visualize me as a real Negro. He thought of a Negro as a rugged tree in the forest. Perhaps Minor had Negro playmates like that in Texas and could not imagine any other type" (*A Long Way Home* 103).[3] Writing from the vantage point of hindsight, McKay cast himself as an independent artist who resisted the role ascribed to him by American Marxist radicals and theorists—like Mike Gold—of proletarian culture. Nevertheless, as Wayne Cooper points out, McKay brought a distinct point of view to discussions of racial politics at the *Liberator*: "For McKay, the revolutionary's handling of the racial question was necessarily of decisive importance, while to other *Liberator* editors it was only one important point among many" (*Claude McKay* 20). These underlying tensions surfaced in Max Eastman's alarmed reaction when he discovered that McKay was hosting meetings with the African Blood Brotherhood and other Harlem radicals at the *Liberator* offices, and in the cool response of the other *Liberator* editors to McKay's proposal that the magazine devote at least 10 percent of its pages—roughly corresponding to the percentage of blacks in the U.S. population—to coverage of African-American life (Cooper, *The Passion* 20–21). The circumstances leading to McKay's final break with the *Liberator*, however, are more difficult to decipher.

Tyrone Tillery argues that the proverbial last straw occurred when

McKay, in his capacity as theater critic for the *Liberator,* was refused front-row seats reserved only for whites when he attended a production of Leonoid Andreyev's *He Who Gets Slapped* (55–57). Cooper sees McKay's growing disillusionment with the American Left in more gradual terms, pointing out that while he discovered a rare personal camaraderie in this community, he also discovered it lacked "the foresight he thought essential if radicals were to win the black masses to their cause" (*Claude McKay* 20). In June 1922 McKay resigned as coeditor of the *Liberator.* His last essay for the magazine, a review of T. S. Stribling's novel *Birthright,* can be read as a farewell address, his parting shot at critics—friendly and otherwise—who felt that his work should be "more broadly socialistic and less chauvinistically racial" (Cooper, *Claude McKay* 73): "Being a Negro, I think it is my proud birthright to put the case of the Negro proletarian, to the best of my ability, before the white members of the movement to which I belong. For the problem of the darker races is a rigid test of Radicalism. To some radicals it might seem more terrible to face than the barricades. But this radical question may be eventually the monkey wrench thrown into the machinery of the American revolutionary struggle" (quoted in Cooper, *Claude McKay* 73).

Yet neither McKay's growing disaffection with the white American Left nor his ideological disputes with Mike Gold and Robert Minor deterred him from traveling to the Soviet Union later that year to witness the results of the revolution with his own eyes. Nor, to judge by his two-part report published in the December 1923 and January 1924 issues of *Crisis,* was his enthusiasm for the Russian Revolution dampened by his experiences there. Moreover, there are no indications that McKay's intense involvement in radical politics had a deleterious effect on his art. On the contrary, he wrote his best poetry between the years 1919 and 1924 and produced a body of prophetic and provocative essays. It is difficult, then, to connect the drift of McKay's later life and literary career with a particular trauma deriving from his encounter with radical politics. Perhaps the clue to his drift can be more fruitfully found in the charge of "spiritual truancy" Alain Locke lodged against McKay in his 1937 review of McKay's autobiography in *New Challenge.*

Still, a careful scrutiny of Claude McKay's involvement with radical politics during this period helps to dislodge some of the assumptions that stand in the way of constructing a more complicated and detailed history of African-American writing in the 1920s and 1930s. This rearticulated narrative suggests there are important lines of continuity *and* disruption between the African-American literary production of the 1920s and its production in the

1930s. The writers of Richard Wright's generation did not emerge out of a cultural and historical vacuum but rather defined themselves against the backdrop of the aesthetic and ideological debates of the 1920s. African-American literary production of the 1930s signals in many respects a sharp departure from the aesthetic and ideological practices associated with the Harlem Renaissance, a "generational shift," as Houston Baker defined it: "an ideologically motivated moment overseen by young or newly emergent intellectuals dedicated to refuting the work of their intellectual predecessors and to establishing a new framework for intellectual inquiry" (67). Yet the writers of Richard Wright's generation were New Negroes, too, in the sense that—like their predecessors—they actively interrogated every ideology available to them in their attacks on the rigid restrictions of life in Jim Crow America: anarchism, socialism, communism, Pan-Africanism, trade unionism, revolutionary violence, and emigration.

As African-American writers drifted toward the Left during the 1930s, consistent with the general trend in the American literary community, they encountered in Marxist thought echoes of and reverberations from the debates of an earlier era. In the case of communism in particular, African-American writers—far from being dupes or innocent victims of Marxist orthodoxy—often embraced it, actively contested it, and helped shape its contours, finding within the analysis of the Left, as Barbara Foley notes, "a complexity and breadth—but also an ambiguity—that corresponded to their own problematic sense of the political position of U.S. Blacks" (305).

NOTES

1. See also Stepto's "Afro-American Literature."

2. See Hill; Solomon; and Turner and Turner. See also Cruse's discussion of the African Blood Brotherhood in *The Crisis of the Negro Intellectual* (45–47, 118–35).

3. A radical cartoonist, Robert Minor eventually abandoned his career as an artist to devote all his energies to the Communist Party. During the early 1920s he maintained a close working relationship with the African Blood Brotherhood. By the mid-1920s he had become a member of the Central Committee of the Communist Party in the United States, with primary responsibility for its work with the black community. He recruited Harry Haywood to the Communist Party in Chicago in 1925. In *Black Bolshevik* Haywood describes Minor's Southside Chicago apartment as a "virtual salon where black and white friends would meet to discuss the issues of the day" (139).

WORKS CITED

Baker, Houston A., Jr. *Blues, Ideology and Afro-American Literature.* Chicago: University of Chicago Press, 1984.

Bone, Robert. "Richard Wright and the Chicago Renaissance." *Callaloo* 9 (Summer 1986): 446–68.

Cappetti, Carla. *Writing Chicago: Modernism, Ethnography and the Novel.* New York: Columbia University Press, 1993.

Carby, Hazel. *Reconstruction Womanhood: The Emergence of the Afro-American Woman Novelist.* New York: Oxford University Press, 1987.

Cooper, Wayne. *Claude McKay: Rebel Sojourner in the Harlem Renaissance.* Baton Rouge: Louisiana State University Press, 1987.

———, ed. *The Passion of Claude McKay: Selected Prose and Poetry, 1912–1948.* New York: Schocken, 1973.

Cruse, Harold. *The Crisis of the Negro Intellectual.* 1967. New York: Quill, 1984.

Foley, Barbara. "Race and Class in Radical African-American Fiction of the Depression Years." *Nature, Society and Thought* 3 (1990): 305–24.

Foner, Philip S., and James S. Allen, eds. *American Communism and Black Americans: A Documentary History.* Philadelphia: Temple University Press, 1987.

Gates, Henry Louis, Jr. "The Trope of a New Negro and the Reconstruction of the Image of the Black." *Representations* 24 (Fall 1988): 129–55.

Haywood, Harry. *Black Bolshevik: Autobiography of an Afro-American Communist.* Chicago: Liberator Press, 1978.

Hill, Robert A., ed. *The Crusader.* New York: Garland, 1987.

Kerlin, Robert, ed. *The Voice of the Negro, 1919.* New York: Arno, 1968.

Lauter, Paul. "American Proletarianism." *Columbia History of the American Novel.* Ed. Emory Elliott. New York: Columbia University Press, 1991. 331–55.

Locke, Alain. "Spiritual Truancy." *New Challenge* 2 (Fall 1937): 81–85.

Martin, Tony. *Literary Garveyism: Garvey, Black Arts and the Harlem Renaissance.* Dover, Mass.: Majority Press, 1983.

McKay, Claude. *A Long Way Home.* 1937. New York: Arno, 1969.

———. *The Negroes in America.* Ed. Alan L. McLeod. Translated from Russian by Robert J. Winter. Port Washington, N.Y.: Kennikat Press, 1979.

———. "The Racial Question: The Racial Issue in the United States." *International Press Correspondence* 2 (November 21, 1922): 817. Reprinted in Cooper, *The Passion* 90–91.

Naison, Mark. *Communists in Harlem during the Depression.* New York: Grove Press, 1983.

Solomon, Mark. *Red and Black: Communism and Afro-Americans, 1929–1935.* New York: Garland, 1987.

Stepto, Robert. "Afro-American Literature." *Columbia Literary History of the United States.* Ed. Emory Elliot. New York: Columbia University Press, 1988. 785–99.

———. "Sterling A. Brown: Outsider in the Harlem Renaissance?" *The Harlem Renaissance: Revaluations.* Ed. Amritjit Singh, William S. Shiver, and Stanley Brodwin. New York: Garland, 1989. 73–81.

Taylor, Clyde. "Garvey's Ghost: Revamping the Twenties." *Black World* 25 (February 1976): 54–67.

Tillery, Tyrone. *Claude McKay: A Black Poet's Struggle for Identity.* Amherst: University of Massachusetts Press, 1992.

Turner, W. Burghardt, and Joyce Moore Turner. *Richard B. Moore, Caribbean Militant in Harlem: Collected Writings, 1920–1972.* Bloomington: Indiana University Press, 1988.

Vincent, Theodore, ed. *Voices of a Black Nation: Political Journalism in the Harlem Renaissance.* San Francisco: Ramparts Press, 1972.

Wright, Richard. "Blueprint for Negro Writing." *Richard Wright Reader.* Ed. Ellen Wright and Michel Fabre. New York: Harper and Row, 1978. 36–49.

———. *Uncle Tom's Children.* New York: Harper and Row, 1940.

5

THE PROLETARIAN

AS NEW NEGRO:

MIKE GOLD'S

HARLEM

RENAISSANCE

After a benefit for the Communist Party's *Daily Worker* held at the Savoy Ballroom in Harlem in 1937, Mike Gold used his long-running column in the newspaper to bestow two of the most flattering compliments he knew on the African-American social worker with whom he had jitterbugged: "she could dance like a dream, and she was a Communist!" ("Doing the Big Apple" 7). As the second compliment indicates, Gold had been moved to praise by more than an enthusiasm for his partner's intoxicating rhythm. Unlike other white tourists who trekked uptown to the Savoy in search of the raw African sensuality that Carl Van Vechten's *Parties* (1930) promised, he had come to the ballroom hoping to find ammunition with which to answer Sinclair Lewis's charge that Communists were as lifeless as their dreary proletarian literature.[1] In the heady atmosphere of a celebration that mixed Popular Front antifascism and music from a swing band that may have featured a young Dizzy Gillespie,[2] Gold had apparently decided that the dancefloor skill of the social worker and other African-American comrades was not really evidence of the innate kinetic capacities of black folk. Rather, it was evidence that rank-and-file Party members stopped being alienated from their own humanity the minute they left the workplace. His column praising the jitterbugging of his partner went on to brag that the "floor was crowded with our comrades. Communists do the Lindy Hop

too, Mr. Hill Billy Sinclair Lewis. Communists laugh, breathe, drink high-
balls, kid each other and even read your books. If you prick them, they
bleed" (7). Black Communists performing black dances to black music at
a ballroom that had been built a decade earlier to profit from the Black
Renaissance were emblems of the life of the Party.

To be sure, some present-day readers might charge this symbolic appropriation of black dancers with crimes as serious as ignoring the particu-
larity of an African-American cultural practice, subsuming race under
class, and judging the Other in terms of the self. In Gold's peculiar revision of Shylock's plea—If you prick us Communists, do we not bleed?—
African-American expression is cut from its specifically racial moorings and
meanings. Yet Gold's symbolism depends on much the same denial of the
association of blackness with subhumanity that Ralph Ellison praised in
his self-selected Anglo-American literary ancestors. From the American
Renaissance to Mark Twain, claims Ellison in "Twentieth-Century Fiction and the Black Mask of Humanity" (1953), the best of nineteenth-century Anglo-American writing conceived of the African-American as "a symbol of Man—the reversal of what he represents in most contemporary
thought" (49). Gold makes a bid to join Ellison's antiracist canon by recasting a stereotypic sign of black "animal spirits"—enthusiastic dance—
as a sign of the vibrant humanity of the interracial political party to which
he himself belongs. Through his recasting, he implicitly acknowledges that
his own humanity is threatened by racism and imagines this humanity
against the grain of the Enlightenment tradition in which it is often defined in opposition to a racialized Other.[3]

My flattering comparison of Gold to the figures Ellison reconstructs as
his nineteenth-century godfathers is not meant to suggest that Gold's radicalism somehow gave him the ability to leap outside of history and de-
tect every offense within the dominant racial discourse circa 1937. For
example, even as his *Daily Worker* column rejects some received ideas
about African-American dance, it distinguishes between authentic jazz and
Tin Pan Alley imitations by reiterating the familiar pseudobiological description of the genuine article as bred in black "bones" ("Doing the Big
Apple" 7). What I do mean to suggest is that Gold's radical engagement
with African-American expression is complicated and worth reconsidering, and not only because of the current academic faith that class and race
count as two fundamental and intersecting categories of literary production and reception. While Gold may not be typical, his case qualifies as a
strategic point through which to reapproach the exchanges between the
literatures of the Old Left and the New Negro. Thanks to his influential

novel-autobiography *Jews without Money* (1930), his ironic attachment to the modernist genre of the manifesto, and his long career as a faithful Stalinist and belligerent arbiter of working-class literary excellence, Gold, during his lifetime, became a synecdoche for the American proletarian literature that grew in the 1920s and flourished in the 1930s with the blessing of the Communist Party. His attitude toward African-American writing has thus been considered a master key by those few critics who have examined the relationship between proletarian literature and the New Negro (or Harlem) Renaissance, the African-American literary movement that was brewing only a subway ride away from Gold's Greenwich Village when he first directed young writers "towards proletarian art" in 1921 ("Towards Proletarian Art" 62).

The habit of envisioning Gold as proletarian literature incarnate marks Harold Cruse's *Crisis of the Negro Intellectual* (1967), to this day the most extensive treatment of Gold's contact with African-American writers and among the most frequently consulted studies of the relationship between blacks and whites, race and class, within the twentieth-century American cultural Left. Gold plays a leading role in the chapter "Harlem Background" that begins Cruse's epic genealogy of white radical manipulation and black radical capitulation, first as the tormentor of the Jamaica-born poet Claude McKay, then as the standard-bearer of the Jewish Communists who supposedly hoped to remake New Negro literature in their own image. As Cruse notes, Gold and McKay spent the first six months of 1922 sharing the position of executive editor at the New York socialist journal the *Liberator*, the successor to Max Eastman's *Masses* that took on the difficult task of synthesizing its precursor's diffuse and lyrical leftism with the more exacting and determinedly "scientific" Marxism that followed the Russian Revolution. The two editors occasionally disagreed over the direction of the publication, and McKay resigned in time to travel to the Soviet Union for the Fourth Congress of the Third Communist International that began in November 1922. In Cruse's eyes, McKay's departure reveals "that Gold was either envious or fearful of McKay" (49). "Without a doubt," Cruse asserts, "Michael Gold was not sympathetic to McKay's literary work or anything coming out of the Harlem Renaissance" (49).

This lack of sympathy is not just a foible to Cruse; in *The Crisis of the Negro Intellectual*, Gold stands for the prudery, imperial design, and Jewish will to power behind the Communist Party's congealing line on literature beginning in the early 1920s. Gold's criticism of what he considered Carl Van Vechten's legacy to African-American writers—"'Gin, jazz, and sex. . . . the gutter-life side of Harlem'"—is accordingly glossed as an "exam-

ple of Communist puritanical puerility," not a legitimate local intervention but a "critical bomb" directed at the heart of the Harlem Renaissance
(50). For Cruse, who defines the United States as "a nation dominated by
the social power of groups, classes, in-groups, and cliques—both ethnic
and religious" (7), Gold's and others' alleged efforts to discipline the New
Negro with a proletarian rod were intimately connected to the desire of
the Jewish Communist to master his or her black opposite number. The
attempt to draw African-American writers into the proletarian camp was
at bottom the attempt of "another minority. . . . [to] dictate cultural standards" to the black intellectuals just as "they were on the ascendant" (52).
"It should have been the [Langston] Hughes, the [James Weldon] Johnsons
and the McKays, who created the critical terms to be laid down on [the
New Negro]," Cruse protests, "*not* the Michael Golds" (51). Playing on
the "weak-kneed, nonpolitical, noncommittal naïveté of many of the Negro intellectuals" (53), these "Michael Golds" succeeded in speeding the
default of the Harlem Renaissance by persuading African-American writers to abandon indigenous artistic criteria for another ethnic/religious
group's criteria impersonating those of the entire U.S. working class. Gold/
proletarian literature/the Jewish Communist "expert" on black culture was
thus not merely guilty of opposing a movement that might have finally
liberated African-American writers from externally imposed standards but
also partially culpable for its early death. According to Cruse, the damage
done by this three-headed creature during the 1920s paved the way for the
thorough co-optation of African-American literature during the 1930s,
when such authors as Ellison, Hughes, and Richard Wright migrated toward the Communist Party and proletarianism in the wake of the stock
market crash and the new prominence accorded to what was then known
as "the Negro Question" after special Comintern resolutions were passed
on the subject in 1928 and 1930.

Any reopening of the question of Gold's relation to African-American
writing needs to start by reconsidering Cruse's portrait of the proletarian
artist as the enemy of black aesthetic decolonization. Clearly, Cruse's
findings against Gold are somewhat compromised by a suspicious fear and
respect for what he dubs "Jewish Nationalism" and are somewhat dated
by an imperative to discover white venality at the heart of interracial alliances that is rooted in the exigencies of the late-1960s turn to black nationalism. His monotone portrait of an absolute difference and an unfail-
ing hostility between Gold and McKay seems to indicate a need to repress
what can be called an anxiety of interracial influence, an unwanted awareness that the interlocking histories of the two writers might betray the

mutual construction and thus the racial impurity of proletarian and Harlem Renaissance writing. Nevertheless, neither the substance nor the influence of Cruse's charges can easily be dismissed. A work of passion and abundant scholarship, *The Crisis of the Negro Intellectual* continues to resonate with cultural critics, at its best offering an amply documented indictment that places painful historical weight behind the now ritual injunctions against "class reductionism" and "speaking for the Other." I will show here, however, that Cruse's treatment of Gold relies on a highly selective account of his interaction with McKay and the larger Harlem Renaissance while at the *Liberator* and neglects nearly all of his subsequent efforts to understand this interaction's significance for his own—and proletarian literature's—past, present, and future. More than the reputation of one well-known but hardly read radical author is at stake in setting the record straight. Recovering the complexity of Gold's attraction to and ambivalence toward McKay and the African-American literary movement that claimed him means beginning to challenge the prevailing assumption that proletarian and New Negro writing were always discrete, never reinforcing, even essentially antagonistic schools. Just as important, it also means beginning to question the tragic vision of the history of interracial cultural radicalism that helps feed the belief that both multiracial cultural histories and multiracial political coalitions—particularly those involving African-Americans and Jews—will inevitably succumb to a white need to dominate.

Although Cruse is justified in claiming that Gold and McKay sometimes argued during the six months in which they served as coexecutive editors of the *Liberator*—on one occasion the two were saved from a boxing match only by the pacifying effects of a bottle of red wine[4]—their disagreements never concerned McKay's race or status as the first poet laureate of the Harlem Renaissance. It is true that McKay himself reported to Max Eastman soon after resigning from the journal that one source of tension with Gold had been "the race matter" ("To Max Eastman: 3 April 1923" 82). What McKay meant by the term in this context, however, was not that his day-to-day relationship with his coeditor had been compromised by white racism. In McKay's opinion, the real race matter Gold needed to address was his lack of "a comprehensive grasp of the Negro's place in the class struggle." McKay informed Eastman that Gold had made "the race story in the June [1922] *Liberator* the basis of his attack on me" ("To Max Eastman: 3 April 1923" 82). Gold's criticism had probably centered on an article the two had published detailing a lynching in Texas and, more broadly, on McKay's proposal that since blacks composed a full 10 percent of the population and occupied a critical position within the class struggle in America, it was appropriate to devote around 10 percent of a socialist magazine to their struggles and achievements. Despite the weird echo of present-day debates over racial "quotas," Gold and others on the staff who opposed the proposal were not concerned about some lowering of standards. According to McKay's biographer Wayne F. Cooper, they instead feared the 10 percent solution "would jeopardize the magazine's appeal to white readers" (*Claude McKay* 162). Even in this, however, Gold and his colleagues showed themselves willing to indulge what they pictured as the lingering bigotry of their readership, uncharacteristically holding fast to the old Socialist Party dogma in the United States that since racial oppression was an exotic variety of class oppression, it would vanish with the triumph of the class that was to end classes.

By the time McKay's autobiography *A Long Way from Home* appeared in 1937, "the race matter" had been excised from his official memory of his disagreements with Gold. In this more public text, McKay identifies two main points of contention: what is characterized as Gold's abrasiveness and emotional intensity (Gold seems to have suffered a nervous breakdown in February 1921)[5] and his heightening conviction that publishing a proletarian magazine meant "printing doggerels from lumberjacks and stevedores and true revelations from chambermaids" (139). McKay recalls sharing Gold's privileged insight into proletarian literature, whose flowering the *Liberator* had begun to expect a year before the two began editing together. Unlike the many salon socialists affiliated with the journal, he as much as Gold had begun life as "an ordinary worker, without benefit of classic education" (139). McKay was quite literally a proletarian writer, a poet who earned a bare living waiting tables at a women's club and on the Pennsylvania Railroad, when his first work was published in the United States in 1917–18. Though he never admitted it outright, McKay seems to have relished the idea that his joint editorship with Gold was the sign of the dawning of what he calls the "proletarian *period* of literature, with labor coming into its heritage as the dominating social factor" (139), perhaps even a tiny foretaste of an interracial dictatorship of the proletariat. He was eager to point out that he parted company with Gold, however, whenever their special empathy for the "proletarian aspirant to literary writing" threatened to devolve into special pleading (139). "I knew that it was much easier to talk about real proletarians writing masterpieces," he reports, "than to find such masterpieces" (139).

Twenty-five years after he resigned from the *Liberator*, McKay was thus casting his feud with Gold as both a personality conflict and an early iconic exchange in a debate still raging over the relative importance of class origin and literary skill in evaluating proletarian writers. There may have been more behind the dropping of "the race matter" from this later account than a sometimes destitute writer's recognition that polemics over proletarian literature had become of increasing interest to American audiences between 1922 and 1937. By 1934 McKay appears to have been convinced that his hard-line antagonists at the *Liberator* had come to appreciate and appropriate his ideas on African-Americans and socialism. In a letter written to Eastman that year, McKay proudly contended that after his resignation from the journal, "the C.P. of America . . . carried on its own propaganda among Negroes from the very acute angle of my position" ("To Max Eastman: 19 Dec. 1934" 213). As I show later, McKay could have detected the influence of his position even in one of Gold's efforts to answer his own calls for proletarian fiction.

A look through the issues of the *Liberator* that McKay and Gold jointly produced suggests their clashes over the nature of proletarian literature and the place of African-Americans in the class struggle did not stop them from agreeing that a Marxist magazine was obliged to consider racism a threat to the entire proletariat. The first six monthly issues of the 1922 volume of the journal contain an increased number of items by or about blacks in the United States and the Caribbean, if not quite 10 percent of the total. The January issue alone, for example, features an essay answering the question "What Is Social Equality?" by Walter White of the National Association for the Advancement of Colored People; another comparing black and wage slavery by the frequent *Liberator* contributor Henry G. Alsberg; a book review by the West Indian radical orator Hubert Harrison, once editor of Marcus Garvey's *Negro World*; and a Whitmanesque poem by the now-obscure Daytie Randle titled "Lament" that opens with the declaration "I am a Negro Woman" and goes on to anticipate contemporary analyses of the "triple jeopardy" of race, class, and gender oppression. The February issue qualifies as an antilynching number. A two-page spread juxtaposes Onorio Ruotolo's nonstereotypic sketch of a seated, grieving black woman and two poems: E. Merril Root's "A Southern Holiday," a graphic arraignment of lynch law reminiscent of McKay's "The Lynching" (1920), and Ralph Chaplin's "Wesley Everest," an angry anti-elegy for a murdered activist that borrows the African-American conceit of the lynch victim as a crucified Christ. Taken as a whole, the spread invites both mourning and organizing, and associates sanctioned violence against African-Americans and socialists without completely collapsing one into the other.[6]

The *Liberator's* sharpened interest in black matters under the Gold-McKay partnership was not confined to its editorial policy. McKay's acquaintance Grace Campbell, one of the first blacks in the Socialist Party in the United States, was prevailed upon to recruit another black "first," the basketball referee Chris Husiwoud, as the star attraction for a fundraiser with "two black and white basketball games . . . [held] at the New Star Casino on the 10th of March" ("Something New"). A second interracial benefit held at Bryant Hall in May was a social and financial success until it was crashed by a squad of New York City police, who claimed that while the crowd broke no laws, it was guilty of breaking the color line.[7] However incompletely these events prefigured the color-blind society the magazine's staff trusted would be born from the death of capitalism, McKay in his autobiography fondly remembers the "large freedom and tolerance about the *Liberator* which made such a mixing possible" (149). Though he writes at a moment when Communist get-togethers in Harlem were not uncommon, he expresses the regret that no radical cultural institutions after the *Liberator* have so thoroughly blended "all shades of radicals . . . pink and black and red" (148). Considered more cynically, the journal's informal gatherings succeeded in providing black intellectuals, Red or otherwise, with some of the social capital they would invest throughout the 1920s to improve the material conditions in which black literature was produced and distributed. As Cooper suggests, the social orbit of the *Liberator* was among the first of the interracial scenes that increased black access to the white "publishers, editors, . . . theatrical producers and directors" who helped bankroll and market the Harlem Renaissance (*Claude McKay* 139).

McKay himself, of course, stood to profit from the *Liberator's* new enthusiasm for black intellectuals and their work. During the six months that he ran the publication with Gold, he not surprisingly became one of the journal's leading contributors, publishing nine poems, six essays, and one short story.[8] Both before and after his term as coexecutive editor, however, McKay was one of the *Liberator's* signature poets. From "If We Must Die," published by Max Eastman in 1919, to "The New Forces," published by Gold in late 1922, much of McKay's best-known poetry was initially printed in the *Liberator.*[9] The journal was the first home to more than one-third of the seventy-four poems collected in *Harlem Shadows* (1922), a text that is usually listed among the immediate causes of the Harlem Renaissance. Of the six poems by McKay included in Alain Locke's signal Harlem Renaissance anthology *The New Negro: An Interpretation* (1925), four were first published by Eastman, Gold, and company. It initially seems

strange that such a large part of McKay's seminal contribution to the poetry of the Renaissance—the rejection of dialect and the genteel in favor
of tightly controlled, epigrammatic expressions of black anger and racial
discord—was rehearsed in a Marxist journal with an almost completely
white staff. Yet the *Liberator* was among the very few American publications, black or white, that then welcomed carefully constructed Shakes-
pearian sonnets beseeching "the avenging angel to consume / The white
man's world of wonders utterly" ("Enslaved" 6). When it came to something like "The White House," depicting "passion [that] rends [the] vitals"
of McKay's speaker while walking past a shuttered building that may be
the home of the president (16), the *Liberator* was among the even fewer
publications that could be relied on not to demand moderation. Alain
Locke's *New Negro*, for example, featured the poem but prudently altered
its original *Liberator* title to "White Houses," a change that McKay protested had destroyed "the whole symbolical import of my poem" ("To Alain
Locke" 143). While McKay's work may have disturbed Eastman and Gold
in its implication that interracial working-class unity was something to be
built, not assumed, its tense and ironic expression of unrestrained black
rage within the measured pentameter of the archetypal English lyrical
form was readily accessible to the *Liberator* editors as poetry. McKay's
sonnets of black anger were similar to and partially informed by jailed
IWW poet Ralph Chaplin's ballads blasting ruling-class tyranny; the *Liberator* published both because they substantiated its vision of poetry that
might function as radical yet genuinely popular social commentary by
rearticulating traditional poetic forms with untraditional political content.[10]
    At least for the editors of the *Liberator* at the start of the 1920s—Gold
among them—the emerging categories of proletarian and Harlem Renaissance writing thus did not represent warring aesthetics inextricably bound
to opposing ethnic or religious interests. Gold's inaugural manifesto for
proletarian art published in the February 1921 *Liberator* in fact hints that
proletarian artists should take a cue from the New Negroes and humble
themselves before the earthy, so-called common people they had previously labored to transcend. "Towards Proletarian Art" substitutes the racially unspecific radical term "the masses" for the Harlem Renaissance
trope of "the black folk" to produce a command for reconnection with
"primitive" origins that could have been issued by a Bolshevik Alain Locke:
"The masses are still primitive and clean, and artists must turn to them
for strength again. The primitive sweetness, the primitive calm, the primitive ability to create simply and without fear or ambition, the primitive
satisfaction and self-sufficiency—they must be found again" (66). In the

style of Locke's invitations to "young Negro writers to dig deep into the racy peasant undersoil of the race life" ("Negro Youth Speaks" 51), Gold advises young proletarians to learn from the masses, who "are never far from the earth," and from the Russian practitioners of *Prolet-Kult*, who have realized that art "must grow from the soil of life" ("Towards Proletarian Art" 66, 69).

Gold's contact with McKay at the *Liberator* in the first half of 1922 seems to have only strengthened his perception that proletarian literature and the Harlem Renaissance were allied, not necessarily mutually exclusive projects. A May 1922 subscription offer that Gold must have written or approved, for example, testifies that he had no qualms about associating *Harlem Shadows* with the nascent proletarian movement. Dangled as a premium for new subscribers, McKay's shaping Harlem Renaissance text is touted as the work of the "foremost revolutionary poet of America" ("Subscribe to the *Liberator*: May 1922" 31). After McKay's departure, subscription bonuses in Gold's more self-consciously proletarian magazine replaced *Harlem Shadows* not with a collection of worker correspondence but with a translation of René Maran's *Batouala* (1922), the Goncourt Prize-winning novel that convinced many New Negroes the Black Renaissance was international in scope ("Subscribe to the *Liberator*: August 1922" 31). Nor did Gold's new regime consider it an offense against the working class to respect McKay's wishes and lend space in the September issue to the story "Carma" and the poem "Georgia Dusk" that would soon after appear in Jean Toomer's *Cane* (1923), the supergeneric text celebrated as the first fulfillment of the Harlem Renaissance's promise. If Gold was as unsympathetic "to McKay's literary work or anything else coming out of the Harlem Renaissance" as Cruse argues, he had an uncharacteristically subtle way of showing it while at the *Liberator*. Before, during, and after McKay's stint as his collaborator, Gold the editor acted as if he believed that proletarian and Harlem Renaissance writing were similar and sometimes even blended injections of the health of the oppressed into the tired body of bourgeois literature; despite his dubious apprehensions over disaffecting white readers, he, as well as McKay, helped to make the *Liberator* one of the small number of magazines in and around which the Renaissance took shape.

Whatever the toll of McKay's departure from the *Liberator*, Gold did not immediately attempt to erase the memory of their work together. His first book—the pre–Popular Front, patriotic hagiography *Life of John Brown* (1923)—is among other things a tacit commemoration of their joint edi-

torship that situates their collaboration within an old American tradition
of interracial revolutionary brotherhood. As James D. Bloom notes, Gold's
ostensible biography qualifies "at once [as] covert autobiography and a plan
for his own revolutionary career" (46). "Who knows but that sometime in
America the John Browns of today will not be worshipped in like manner?" asks Gold, leaving little doubt about his own qualifications as one
of "the outlaws of today, the unknown soldiers of freedom" who deserved
the abolitionist's mantle (*Life* 60). If Gold was due to be acknowledged as
an inheritor of the militant spirit of Brown, then it was only logical that
McKay was due to be recognized as a descendant of the five "dignified and
manly" African-Americans, carefully specified in Gold's list of Brown's
companions, who joined the raid on Harper's Ferry (48–49). Regarded in
the light of the historical imagination that Gold ascribes to a future socialist America, his turbulent friendship with McKay at the *Liberator* became a shadow of the more perfect love among Brown's interracial band
of brothers, the "young crusaders, thoughtful, sensitive, and brave," who
had similarly combined to provide ammunition for insurrection (46).

   This is not to claim that Gold would have failed to treat his biography
of Brown as a displaced confessional had he never met McKay. Bloom
points out that Brown was a constant presence on the "honor rolls . . . of
writers and freedom fighters with whom Gold sought to affiliate himself
and his agenda" (45). Bloom also observes that Gold always considered
the abolitionist crusade against slavery as a type of and stimulus for the
crusade against capitalism: in a 1953 biographical sketch, Gold claims that
"living echoes of the Civil War . . . helped to prepare [him] for socialist
ideas" ("The Writer in America" 183). Gold's very adult name was adopted from one of these living echoes, an old Civil War veteran who came
to mind as the Palmer Raids of 1919–20 forced him to choose a replace-
ment for his birth name of Itzok Granich. Neatly enough, the socialist
Liberator for which the renamed Gold went to work borrowed its name
from William Lloyd Garrison's flagship abolitionist newspaper. Despite all
the historical parallels, Gold's eagerness to define slavery as a horror "our
class has suffered" distanced him from the radical labor leaders of his
namesake's generation, whose rhetoric opposing "white slavery" in the
North often buttressed proslavery ideology ("A Secret Meeting" 96).[11]

   Gold's attachment to John Brown probably stemmed from a variety of
factors, but none more important than the Jewishness that his American-
ized pseudonym did not try too hard to hide. Affected by the black Christian comparisons between the historical enslavement and suffering of Jews
and African-Americans, Gold assumed that the fate of the two peoples was

linked and would be decided through a heroic struggle for socialism that required their pooled energies. Insofar as Brown was a national martyr, a precursor of the socialist militant, and an enemy of slavery to which Jews as well as blacks had been subjected, he afforded Gold with the same opportunity simultaneously to Americanize communism and to retain a secularized sense of Jewishness in its midst, as did the name he adopted from the Civil War veteran. The idea of the linked fate of Jews and African-Americans that helped attract Gold to Brown led him to the conclusion that it was self-destructive for Jews to adopt the course of other European immigrant groups and inch toward the status of full-fledged white Americans by learning to loathe blackness. He thus affirmed a bond between "Yiddish literature and music" and "Negro spirituals," like a good materialist avoiding speculation about the prodigious souls of the two peoples to note that their cultures were formed by the same "ghetto poverty" ("The Gun Is Loaded" 226). In a similar spirit, he christened one of the Jewish heroes of *Jews without Money* "Nigger," a risky attempt to affiliate black and Jewish resistance by subverting the worst of racist language from within. Poorest of the poor but "bravest of the brave, the chieftain of [the] brave tribe" of street-tough young Jews to which the narrator belongs (*Jews without Money* 43), Nigger is one of the text's few protorevolutionary models, a confirmation that defiance can be bred in the deprivation of the ghetto. As Bloom argues, "The figure of a Jewish 'white nigger' doctrinally advances communist internationalism, which holds racial and ethnic differences to be incidental" (61). It might even be claimed that Gold's character advances the notion that racial differences are slippery and easily overstepped. A more attractive relative of the racially indeterminate hero of Melville's *Confidence-Man* (1857),[12] Nigger with "his black hair and murky face" (42) transgresses the purportedly firm boundary between black and white that damages the prospects for African-American–Jewish identification. To reinforce this oblique point, Gold briefly wheels out a character who is Nigger's mirror image, not a Jewish black but a black Jew, a proudly pious, Hebrew-speaking Abyssinian, who does his best to convince the narrator's father and friends that it is they who may be "mere pretenders to the proud title of Jew" (175).

The idea that African-Americans and Jews were united not only by ghetto poverty but also by a need to rewrite impoverished representations makes an appearance in Gold's best-known post-*Liberator* statement concerned with the Harlem Renaissance, a "Notes of the Month" on "Negro Literature" printed in the *New Masses* in February 1930. Gold's main business here is denouncing Carl Van Vechten, quasi-official liaison between the

New Negro and young white intellectuals, as "the worst friend the Negro has ever had" and "a white literary bum who has created a brood of Negro literary bums" (3). Van Vechten's sin is the mortal one of corrupting the young: in Gold's judgment, "this night-club rounder and white literary sophisticate" had succeeded in infecting "young Negro literateurs" with his appetites for "gin, jazz, and sex" (3). Impressed by the great success of the novel *Nigger Heaven* (1926), Van Vechten's own controversial attempt to ironize the most hated racial epithet, many of these novices were "wasting their splendid talents on the gutter-life side of Harlem" (3). The result was an African-American fiction obsessed with low life and night life, a fiction that "slander[s] the majority of Negroes who must work so painfully in the mills, factories, and farms of America" by indulging the fantasy that black life is a cabaret (3). While Gold was capable of enjoying an evening at the Savoy Ballroom, he was certain that the place was not the proper metonymy for black America. Pretending otherwise for the sake of sales, he implies, helps uphold the gamut of ethnic and racial stereotypes, including those that defamed Jews without money, such as himself: "The Harlem cabaret no more represents the Negro mass than a pawnshop represents the Jew, or an opium den the struggling Chinese nation" (3). This critique likely derived its harshness not only from outrage at Van Vechten's poor example but also from an uncomfortable realization that the white Negro and his followers were like-minded practitioners of a realism that focused on populations outside the prevailing middle-class focus, writers to whom those who saw themselves as literary proletarians were related as much by similarity as by difference. In "Proletarian Realism," a manifesto published later in 1930 systematizing the views expressed in "Towards Proletarian Art," Gold takes time out to stipulate that "proletarian literature . . . portrays the life of the workers; not as do . . . the American jazzmaniacs, but with a clear revolutionary point; otherwise it is meaningless, merely a new *frisson*" (205–6).

As mentioned earlier, Cruse interprets Gold's criticism of Van Vechten's influence as (among other unpleasant things) a conclusive assault on the Harlem Renaissance as a whole and as an "example of Communist puritanical puerility." Cruse seems to have ground for this first contention—although Gold reserves his most energetic invective for Van Vechten and never explicitly refers to the Harlem Renaissance, his charges against the "brood of Negro literary bums" inspired by the white writer suggest that he worried over a misdirection of the African-American literary emergence. Yet a later comment argues that Gold probably had a single figure in mind as he reproached African-American writers for dulling their "splendid talents" to duplicate Van Vechten's success—namely, his old comrade McKay, who just two years earlier had become the first best-selling black novelist of the Harlem Renaissance with *Home to Harlem*, a text recommended by its publisher to "those who enjoyed *Nigger Heaven*" (quoted in John S. Wright 19). In the same 1953 sketch in which Gold testifies to the influence of "living echoes of the Civil War," he describes McKay's novel as "badly affected by the time and the influence of white writers like Carl Van Vechten" ("The Writer in America" 188). Using language nearly identical to that he used in 1930, but now naming the name that had then stood behind the abstraction of a "brood" of African-American writers, Gold summarizes the lesson that McKay had learned from Harlem's best-promoted white tour guide: "Negro authors could now reach a big audience among whites, but only if they forgot their people's wrongs and concentrated on gin, sex, and the cabaret" (188). The criticism of McKay is confined to the prose, however. The writer who, Gold reminds the reader, "served as co-editor of the *Liberator*" is also praised as "a fine lyrical poet," whose "poems of Negro liberation struggle are classics" (188).

The nuance of this late estimation suggests that while the Gold of 1930 detested *Nigger Heaven* and *Home to Harlem*, he may not have been convinced that their reign constituted the defining moment of a Renaissance he had come to know years earlier through McKay's poetry. Certainly nothing in Gold's 1930 note indicates he believed these novels would be the New Negro's last word. Near its conclusion, he expresses the belief "that Negro art and literature are only beginning. This cabaret obsession is but an infantile disease, a passing phase" (3). By 1936, in a piece echoing *The New Negro*'s call for a National Negro Theater, Gold had become confident that the Harlem Renaissance was about to recover its health. America's "first truly poetic theater" would be born in Harlem, he wagers, the "friendly soil" from which "the renaissance, as is well known, spread" ("At Last" 18). Though Gold holds that Harlem is "certainly no bed of roses, this region of shabby, overcrowded, tubercular tenements," there is no doubt in his mind that "its people have lost the chain-gang fears and have developed the intense pride and group consciousness in which a great theater is born" (18). Between 1930 and 1936, Van Vechten's presence on the "friendly soil" of Harlem had become less evident; *Home to Harlem* had become a bad but dim memory; and Gold's idea of the necessary ingredients of a working-class-friendly if not fully proletarian realism had absorbed the shift from the Communist Party's ultraleftist Third Period of 1928–30 to the more inclusive Popular Front. Portrayals of the lives of African-American workers without a "clear revolutionary point" could once more find a place under the big tent of literary radicalism.[13]

As for Cruse's reading of Gold's 1930 note on "Negro Literature" as an "example of Communist puritanical puerility," it is important to recognize that Gold's attack on the cabaret metonymy and the fascination with "gin, jazz, and sex" comes close to recapitulating the reviews of *Nigger Heaven* and *Home to Harlem* that the not-yet Communist W. E. B. Du Bois had written for the NAACP's *Crisis*. In his review of Van Vechten's novel, Du Bois, like Gold after him, undermines the assumption that "the black cabaret is Harlem" by presenting a capsule sociological profile (1216). "The overwhelming majority of black folk there never go to cabarets," he maintains. "The average colored man in Harlem is an everyday laborer, attending church, lodge and movie and as conservative and conventional as ordinary working folk everywhere" (1216). Describing his experience reading McKay's work, Du Bois divulges that "after the dirtier parts of its filth I feel distinctly like taking a bath." Again like Gold after him, he accuses McKay of pandering to those whites who dream of black life as a perpetual spree of "drunkenness, fighting, lascivious sexual promiscuity and utter absence of restraint" (quoted in Moses 121).

Whether or not Du Bois's reviews had actually been read by Gold, their strong similarity to the 1930 note argues that there was nothing peculiarly Communist or especially puerile about the fear that Van Vechten encouraged New Negroes to uphold the old racism. While charges of puritanism may put a finger on a squeamishness about representations of sexuality that Gold shared with the Victorian gentleman Du Bois, they do not explain the pair's assumption that post-Freudian notions of African-Americans as superior in their unabashed sensuality merely embroidered on past racial stereotypes. As Sterling Brown elaborated the idea, the new stock character of the urbanized, modernized yet still sensual black primitive was at bottom "a 'jazzed up' version" of the stereotype of the contented black slave, "with cabarets supplanting cabins, and Harlemized 'blues' instead of spirituals and slave reels" (quoted in Moses 119). Gold's 1930 note can be placed within a mainly African-American critical tradition warning of the dangers courted by a black Renaissance dependent on white patronage and white racial discourse. The very assumption that Van Vechten had fathered a "brood" of "young Negro literateurs," of course, indicates that Gold had not fully outgrown paternalistic notions of the white writer's generative burden. Nevertheless, he counsels against an African-American embrace of Van Vechten largely because he imagines its upshot as a determination to win a mass white audience, even if this entails refurbishing racial stereotypes that efface black labor in "mills, factories, and farms." The Communist Gold as much as the once-Socialist Du Bois believed that among their other harmful effects, such stereotypes blotted out the fact that the great majority of African-Americans were proletarians. White workers were prone imaginatively to consign their black counterparts to what Marx famously called the lumpenproletariat, the disaggregated mass of "vagabonds, discharged soldiers, discharged jailbirds . . . pickpockets, tricksters, gamblers, *maquereaus* [procurers], brothel keepers, porters, *literati* . . . [and] beggars" purportedly found at the base of reactionary movements (and at the top of McKay's *Home to Harlem* cast list) (*The Eighteenth Brumaire* 75). Until these workers recognized that proletarians came in black as well as white, African-Americans would be forced to prove their fitness to serve as union members and potential agents of revolution.

Gold's alertness to some of the pitfalls that confronted African-American writers who negotiated with the discursive and financial power of white patrons and audiences was the product not so much of extraordinary perceptual gifts as of difficult and contradictory work as an editor and author. He had been both something of an occasionally problematic white patron of the Renaissance while he and McKay had run the *Liberator* in 1922 and something of an aspiring "black" author wrestling with stereotypes while he had tried his own hand at proletarian literature in the late 1920s. *Jews without Money*, published the same month as his note on "Negro Literature," had been written against "lurid articles in a Sunday newspaper" and "Ku Klux moralizers" (35, 37)—in other words, against exoticizing and pathologizing accounts of a ghetto-dwelling "race apart," close to those with which Harlem writers were familiar. Like similar corrective work by these writers, Gold's book was criticized by some reviewers on the Left for excessive "nationalistic" passion and for insufficient attention to the growth of working-class consciousness; he had ignored the unionization of New York Jewish garment workers that had occurred during the period in which his text was set.[14] Even more instructive about the situation of black writers, however, was a play Gold had published three years earlier that Cruse is not alone in ignoring: *Hoboken Blues: Or, the Black Rip Van Winkle, a Modern Negro Fantasia on an Old American Theme.* One of the less principled reasons for Gold's assault on Van Vechten may have been that this overlooked three-act drama had undertaken the same racially transgressive project that *Nigger Heaven* had brought off so lucratively—to slip the bonds of whiteness and take part in, not merely comment on, the Harlem Renaissance.

Though *Hoboken Blues* was selected for Van Wyck Brooks's anthology *American Caravan* in 1927, it was not produced until a year later. Initially rejected by the Provincetown Players,[15] the piece found a home with the New Playwrights Theater, a short-lived company involving John Howard Lawson and John Dos Passos that Alexander Woolcott liked to dismiss as "the revolting playwrights" (quoted in Goldstein 26). Gold's play reflects the enthusiasm for the innovations of the postrevolutionary Soviet stage that most of the New Playwrights productions shared. During a 1925 pilgrimage to the Soviet Union, Gold had attended several plays directed by Vselvolod Meyerhold, the colleague of Eisenstein and Mayakovsky, who had vowed to bring the October Revolution into the theater. Meyerhold's promise to erase the gap between Soviet political and artistic development resulted in productions at his Actor's Theater in Moscow that featured agitprop, constructivist designs meant to "industrialize" theatrical space, and actors who would "present" rather than portray characters.[16]

Hoboken Blues faithfully and ambitiously attempts to bring the October Revolution into the American theater by fulfilling all of Meyerhold's program. Gold's agitprop subject matter is the revolutionary significance of the African-American attitude toward labor under industrial capitalism. His recommendations for stage sets specify that "it would be a calamity to treat the scenes in this play realistically. They must be done by an intelligent futurist" (*Hoboken Blues* 548). Directions on the composition of the cast indicate that Gold adapted Meyerhold's pre-Brechtian disruption of realistic, individualizing characterization to invert and parody the insistent artificiality and crude stereotyping of black characters in blackface minstrelsy. "No white men appear in this play," Gold insists, proliferating the ironies of his own racial masquerade. "Where white men are indicated, they are played by Negroes in white caricature masks" (549).[17] Suggestions for spirituals, blues, and jazz during and between the scenes are less indebted to Meyerhold, however, than to the postwar revival of African-American theater in both its "low" and "high" forms. Flournoy Miller and Aubrey Lyles's *Shuffle Along* (1921), featuring the songs of Eubie Blake and the voice of Florence Mills, was only the first of a string of black-produced and black-performed Broadway musical hits that showed no end as Gold wrote his own blues play. Ridgely Torrence's *Three Plays for the Negro Theater* (1917), a trilogy that Gold was not alone in considering the beginning of a dignified African-American drama, had, before *Hoboken Blues*, linked its three parts by means of a singing orchestra performing spirituals.[18] This wild mix of inspirations from Meyerhold to Torrence not only provides further evidence of the actually blurred margins between modernism and literary proletarianism but also suggests that Gold's hopes for a syncretic revolutionary–New Negro literature outlived his contact with McKay at the *Liberator*.

The plot and characters of *Hoboken Blues* owe their outline to the commonplace Harlem Renaissance theme of the rural migrant lost in the "Negro Metropolis," to the Washington Irving tale invoked in the subtitle *The Black Rip Van Winkle*, and to the central play of Torrence's trilogy, *The Rider of Dreams*. Act 1, set in an anachronistically black turn-of-the-century Harlem, introduces the protagonist, Sam Pickens. An analogue of both Rip and Torrence's impractical, guitar-playing Madison Sparrow, Sam prefers memories of his cabin down south to his apartment in New York and the banjo to unsatisfying wage labor. He is hounded by his wife, Sally, a less shrewish Dame Van Winkle, who convinces him that she will begin divorce proceedings if he breaks his word and fails to find work in Hoboken, like Ha(a)rlem, a locale with an appropriately Dutch association. Act 2 finds an obedient Sam seeking employment in New Jersey, even without a turnpike a far cry from the pastoral territory he had imagined. After a series of failed attempts to fulfill his wife's wishes, he takes a cue from Rip and mistakenly falls asleep for twenty-five years; in a pointed departure from Irving, the soporific is not alcohol but a white policeman's billy club. Sam dreams of his life in a factory town of the future, where three hours of sweat is all that is required, flowers bloom near plant gates, and his expert banjo playing cuts through prejudice and gets him elected president. His desire to work "cause [I] like to work," not for a "fat, nasty boss" (614), is fulfilled in this reverie of Hoboken as an industrialized Land of Cockaigne, Gold's fleshing out of Marx's atypical forecast of a socialist future in which one would "hunt in the morning, fish in the afternoon, rear cattle in the evening, criticize after dinner" (*The German Ideology* 160). Act 3 depicts Sam's inevitable awakening and return to the self-confident and fully industrialized Harlem of the 1920s. Here, jazzers, students, and followers of Marcus Garvey compete with greedy cabaret owners (friends of Van Vechten?) to define the New Negro. Sam's excited description of a "place for de poor men, black and white, where birds sing sweet, and every house is full of music, and dere's sunflowers round de factory door" is initially dismissed (626). The last word is his, however, along with the future, symbolized by the marriage of his daughter Emma Lou to Joe, a scholarly young neighbor who plans to inject the voice of "the black workers" into a Harlem Renaissance that has already guaranteed that "no one can laugh at the Negro thinkers and artists anymore" (610). Like Torrence's Sparrow, Sam closes the play reserving the right to dream; unlike him, he has convinced his community that dreaming is necessary and perhaps even politically useful.

As Marcus Klein suggests (240), *Hoboken Blues* may have made it into *The American Caravan* because its use of the story of Rip Van Winkle was in tune with the formula for new American writing then being proposed by the anthology's main editor. Brooks's recommendation that folk materials made the American past more usable was similarly followed by Hart Crane, who, in the same year that Gold completed *Hoboken Blues*, began sketching a modern Rip who forgets "the office hours" in "The Bridge" (58). Gold's borrowing is singular, however, in its attempt to tie both socialism and what appears to be a stereotype of black laziness to Irving's myth of national origin and archetype for the persistent American literature of masculine retreat. With Sam dreaming *of* revolution, rather than dreaming *through* revolution, *Hoboken Blues* proposes socialism as Rip's natural politics and a worthy goal for a second American War of Independence. With Sam shirking labor according to Rip's directions, the play also targets notions of black shiftlessness by linking a Harlem layabout to the heroes of that great American literary tradition honoring manly avoidance of compulsory labor and attendant domesticity. To summarize bluntly, *Hoboken Blues* appears to appropriate Irving's Rip Van Winkle to argue for a socialism American-style, made by white and black men united against women and industrial wage work. Thanks to this intertextual polemic, Gold's play seems a misogynous complement to his insistently gendered manifestos for proletarian literature. Sally, Gold's version of Dame Van Winkle, however, is distinguished from the original by surviving her husband's absence and accepting his love after his return. The variety of future freedom projected by *Hoboken Blues*, at least, involves a reconstitution of, not an escape from, male-female relationships.

More important, if only to my focus here, is another sticky question—that of the play's possible hostility to a variety of Harlem Renaissance efforts to reform black representation. *Hoboken Blues*'s dialogue often consists of the kind of distorted black dialect that James Weldon Johnson—inspired in part by McKay—identified as a primary enemy of Harlem Renaissance poetry as early as 1922. With characters assigned lines like "Is we or isn't we going to get any more testifications?" (559), African-American speech is transformed into what Johnson denounces as a "mere mutilation of English spelling and pronunciation" (41). This use of broad dialect is puzzling given Gold's later protests against the "vulgar" sounds the poet Archibald MacLeish had put in the mouth of a character subtly named "Comrade Levine" (quoted in Salzman and Wallenstein 238);

when it squarely hit home, he seemed to know that dialect could be an alienating and Othering force. Similarly, despite its intended parody of blackface minstrelsy, the play's comedy sometimes counts on the minstrel staple of travesty, by 1926 one of the main targets of serious African-American drama. To take only one example, Gold counts on the innate humorousness of a character called Achilles McGregor, "a short, fat jolly Negro in a big blue coat and driver's cap, with badge" (549). On the model of the blackface policemen and politicians who had wandered from the minstrel show to the more respectable American stage comedy by the 1920s, Achilles's classical name and nonclassical physique are intended to emphasize a comic disparity between the black man and his station. Ironically, however, *Hoboken Blues*'s most pronounced flirtation with racist representation derives from its faithfulness to the Harlem Renaissance strategy of celebrating blackness by inverting the hierarchy of terms within white-authored white-black oppositions. In a manner similar to the novels of McKay that Gold panned, the play's positive evaluation of its hero's refusal to work threatens to sanction the racial stereotype it recodes but does not displace—in this case, the stereotype of the indolent Sambo that Sam's name alone evokes and that Gold himself later sought to stamp out by exhibiting the hard facts of African-American labor.

Yet what is most interesting about *Hoboken Blues* is its campaign against interpreting Sam as just another version of Sambo. From the title onward, the play paints its hero as a relative of Irving's Rip and thus indicates that his distaste for work is not exclusively or necessarily a racial trait. More important, Gold repeatedly emphasizes that his hero rejects not work per se but the paid work available to the racially oppressed under American industrial capitalism. In Act 1, Sam himself suggests that he believes "in wuhk" (570) but that the positions offered in the North pervert the term. "When I wuz down south wid de fambly wuhkin' our little patch," he affirms, "I wuhked as hahd as anyboddy" (570). A pantomime preceding Act 2 reveals that self-hate is the main wage of the service jobs that are Sam's only alternative to the factories he abhors. He is shown kowtowing to detestable white-masked figures as a waiter in a restaurant, a shoeshine "boy," and the live target in a carnival booth labeled "Hit the Nigger and Get a Cigar," the last cast as a logical extension of the first two occupations (584–85). When he resists complete humiliation in each of the three positions, he is fired and beaten. Significantly, Sam's rejection of available paid work is throughout associated with enabling memories of sharecropping, creatively recast as unregimented preindustrial labor, and with enabling dreams of such labor's dialectical reinvention on a higher level under communism. His warm recollections of the "sunflowers at yo' own cabin door" (570) that could be meditated upon during workdays down home are transmuted during his twenty-five-year siesta into a utopian Marxist vision of sunflowers surrounding the entrance to a democratically managed factory.

Gold seems to have realized that a remarkably diverse white American working class achieved consciousness in part through "the idea that blackness could be made permanently to embody the preindustrialist past that [it] scorned and missed" (Roediger 97). As the historian David Roediger argues, the attractions of blackface—in its dramatic form something that *Hoboken Blues* both draws on and critiques—were "the result of the desire to project onto Blacks the *specific* behaviors that brought such conflicted emotions to whites during the formation of the first American working class" (97). With the coming of a work culture "that attacked holidays, spurned contact with nature, saved time, bridled sexuality, separated work from the rest of life and postponed gratification, profit-minded . . . Americans cast Blacks as their former selves" (Roediger 95). As a result, African-Americans were invested with the values censured and glamorized by the new industrial ethos. For all its flaws, *Hoboken Blues* attempts to rewrite the political meaning of blackface minstrelsy—and, by extension, the racist self-conception of its working-class audience—by embracing the identification of African-Americans with preindustrial values yet rejecting the moment of censure and the imprisonment of these values within a rigidly racialized and rapidly fading arcadian memory. The play's unambivalent defense of Sam's avoidance of work and its references to Irving's myth of national origin are meant to encourage the entire American working class to welcome what Du Bois had in 1924 described as the gift that black folk gave labor: "the idea of toil as a necessary evil ministering to the pleasure of life" (*The Gift* 79). Gold's projection of this contribution into American's socialist future as well as into its revolutionary past shows an eagerness to avoid mere nostalgia and to overturn the traditional racist assumption that Africa's people languish outside history, sealed within the archaic. *Hoboken Blues* represents African-Americans as neither relics nor historical exiles but as exponents of a historically rooted prospective vision that matches the stage sets Gold assigned to "an intelligent futurist." Even the most old-fashioned New Negro, the play suggests, is a symbol of and guide to the orthodox Marxist faith in history's teleological unwinding toward the liberation of work under communism.

Given Gold's usual paeans to muscular youths who break from labor "in the lumber camps, coal mines, and steel mills" only to scribble out rough proletarian verses ("Go Left" 188), how can we account for *Hoboken Blues*'s glorification of an African-American hero who declines to proletarianize himself? It is possible that Gold was impressed by the dissenting, epicurean Marxism of Paul Lafargue's *Right to Be Lazy*, a short, excited tract translated into English and published in New York in 1898. Taking cues from Charles Fourier and other socialists his father-in-law, Karl Marx, had rejected as insufficiently scientific, Lafargue prefigures Gold in affirming that the proletariat must recall the precapitalist past to prepare itself to enjoy the three-hour postcapitalist working day. The proletariat "must return to natural instincts," instructs Lafargue, "it must proclaim the Rights of Laziness, a thousand times more noble and more sacred than the anaemic Rights of Man concocted by the metaphysical lawyers of the bourgeois revolution. It must accustom itself to working but three hours a day, reserving the rest of the day for leisure and feasting" (quoted in Geoghegan 60). It is also possible to attribute *Hoboken Blues*'s peculiarity to Gold's desire to pay respect to his own receding bohemianism, cultivated on the fringes of the Provincetown Players and the old *Masses*. The play's salute to a nonworking member of the working class might then be interpreted as a reimagining of Gold's past, stemming from a desire to keep the peace between waning bohemian and emergent super-Communist selves. According to this reading, Sam is a slightly younger, "blacked-up" Gold as envisioned by the Gold of 1927, his taste for unalienated artistic labor elevated to a revolutionary virtue and his bohemianism understood as an embryonic communism.

What is more likely and less dependent on speculation about Gold's library or psychology is that *Hoboken Blues*'s hero emerged at least in part as a response to McKay's arguments. In his dream discovery of the indissoluble interests of African-Americans and the white working class, Sam reaffirms the interracial commitment of the 1922 *Liberator* that Gold shared with McKay when not worrying about the tolerance of white readers. In his embodiment of the idea that African-Americans are of special, disproportionate significance to the class struggle in America, Sam is also McKay's "very acute angle" on "the race question" dramatized. No wonder McKay could imply that Communists had begun to show him the sincerest form of flattery after his resignation from the *Liberator*. Beneath its sometimes inadequately critical internal critique of minstrelsy, Gold's play was an attempt by the long-expectant father of proletarian literature to advertise the kind of nonphilanthropic "revolutionary attitude towards Negroes" that McKay had called for in his parting article in the *Liberator* ("Birthright" 73). *Hoboken Blues* seems to qualify as Gold's belated acknowledgment of the validity of much of McKay's position in the *Liberator* debates over African-Americans and socialism.

Along with his other writings taking stock of McKay, Gold's play thus points out the error of assuming that white texts that take pleasure in speaking for and through the racial Other represent snippets of an uninterrupted white monologue. Recent studies of twentieth-century American literature that rely on theories of colonial discourse fail to account for the fact that, by the 1920s, an efflorescence of African-American writing thought to constitute a renaissance assured that loose talk about blackness would not go unanswered.[19] While they continued to enjoy unequaled access to cultural power, white Americans writing race in that decade began to be challenged by an agent that many European writers of imperialist fiction managed to avoid until the anticolonial movements after World War II: an Other within who not only had linguistic access to white writing but also had produced a sometimes widely popular literature that could contest white accounts of blackness and its meaning. In particular, Gold and other white American writers on the Left working within some of the nation's few integrated cultural institutions engaged in relatively free exchanges with black intellectuals on the subjects of race, representation, and the realism of pleas for interracial working-class unity. It should not be surprising, then, that *Life of John Brown*, *Hoboken Blues*, and other texts by Gold show the marks of a "dialogic race discourse" with McKay of the kind that has been found lacking in colonialist literature.[20]

In *The Hollow Men* (1941), a vindictive defense of the Hitler-Stalin Pact and the high-water mark of literary proletarianism during the Great Depression, Gold claimed that it was African-American writers of the 1930s, such as Richard Wright, Langston Hughes, and Sterling Brown, who, with the assistance of the "pioneers of proletarian literature," finally succeeded in "lifting to human dignity . . . the Negro people as portrayed in literature" (48). Gone is any intimation that Van Vechten and his followers did not represent the finest hour of the Harlem Renaissance that had promised to do this heavy lifting in the 1920s, let alone that proletarian literature and the Harlem Renaissance were confederate projects. Gold denounces Van Vechten for providing the ugly pattern of the black hero that the Renaissance followed and approvingly quotes Eugene Clay's portrait of New Negroes "'prid[ing] themselves on the fact that they could act, sing, paint and write as well as their white-skinned patrons'" (47). Nowhere is there an admission that the careers of two out of Gold's three exemplars—Hughes and Brown—straddle the 1920s and 1930s, the heyday of the Harlem Renaissance and proletarianism. The function of the comments on African-American writing in *The Hollow Men* is to construct a model of literary history in which the moment of the New Negro is confined to the 1920s and is linked to a corrupting white patronage and the moment of an uncringing black literature arrives with the 1930s and is linked to the inspiration of white proletarian forerunners. It is a model intended to introduce a series of stark conceptual divisions—between African-American literatures under the auspices of the Harlem Renaissance and proletarianism, between crippling and invigorating types of white influence on these literatures, and between the radical cultural politics of two decades, in which Gold had been arguing for and producing something that went by the name of proletarian literature.

A very different idea of the relationship between the Harlem Renaissance and proletarian literature was sometimes voiced during the period of the latter's greatest influence on African-American writers. In a 1937 address to the Communist-sponsored Second National Negro Conference, no less a midwife of the New Negro than Alain Locke emphasized "the considerable harmony . . . between the cultural racialism of the art philosophy of the 1920s and the class proletarian art creed of today's younger generation" ("Resume"). The New Negro had "aimed at folk realism which is involved in and is not so different from social realism or even proletarian expression," he noted. Locke cited "Langston Hughes and Sterling Brown, who belong to both generations," as clear proof that "in the expression of Negro folk life," the writing of the 1920s and 1930s has "a common denominator." The noblest task of the new generation of African-American writers was not to kill off their elders' Renaissance but to extend it, to "carry . . . motives of racial self-expression and folk interpretation out to sounder, fuller lengths." Locke's marching orders for a folk proletarianism were not issued in a void. Richard Wright admitted in his notoriously anti–New Negro "Blueprint for Negro Writing" (1937) that "the Negro has a folklore which embodies the memories and hopes of his struggle for freedom" and that any African-American writing worth its salt would have "continued and deepened this folk tradition" (56).

Nonetheless, mainstream, radical, and African-American literary histories have ignored Locke's contention that the literary movement he helped invent harmonized and linked with proletarian literature. If these histories agree with Gold on little else, they second his 1941 opinion that the Harlem Renaissance and proletarian literature are discontinuous; if related at all, related negatively. However much it is now common critical sense, this model of a complete break and opposition between the two bodies of writing had to be constructed after the facts of their fre-

THE PROLETARIAN AS NEW NEGRO   115

quent mingling and shared disrespect for the ideology of the literary decade, facts that might have supported a contrasting model. Gold was composing what he thought was proletarian literature in the 1920s; Zora Neale Hurston was making her best use of Harlem Renaissance topoi in the 1930s; and texts of writers as different as Gold, McKay, Hughes, Brown, and Arna Bontemps suggest that it was not too difficult to believe during either decade that one worked in both categories or some hybrid. The very language of Gold's disassociation of the Harlem Renaissance and proletarian literature in *The Hollow Men* reveals the arduousness of his task. In praising proletarianized African-American writers of the 1930s for "lifting to human dignity . . . the Negro people as portrayed in literature," he relies on the metaphor of black uplift that Locke, Du Bois, Johnson, and other old guard proponents of the Renaissance had overused until it became an object of parody by younger New Negroes. Even in his effort to construct opposition, Gold confesses the presence of the Renaissance Other in a black proletarianism he claims is indebted only to white proletarian pioneers.

As this essay has demonstrated, Gold's own extended engagement with McKay and the larger Harlem Renaissance supports much of Locke's commentary on the "considerable harmony" between that movement's "cultural racialism" and "the class proletarian art creed." None of this is to deny those episodes of blindness and paternalism in Gold to which Cruse draws attention, nor is it to wish away the significant differences between the Harlem Renaissance and proletarian literature, from the dissimilar racial identities of the majority of each school's writers to the dissimilar effects of figuring the people as either "the folk" or "the masses." It is to claim that the Harlem Renaissance lived and imagined by proletarian literature's leading symbol and theorist, not just in *The Hollow Men* but also twenty years earlier and ten years later, calls into question both triumphant narratives of the proletarian gift to black folk and what Henry Louis Gates Jr. has called "the usual remarks about 'cultural imperialism' [that] fail to acknowledge the specificity of cultural interactions" (191). What is needed in their place are a multiracial cultural history and cultural politics willing to recognize the moments of divergence and of interpenetration between the expressions of the New Negro and the Old Left. Even the Harlem Renaissance figure Cruse describes as Gold's nemesis might have approved of this concluding moral. Though he confessed he did not "expect the nice radicals" to see it, McKay considered his *Home to Harlem* "a real proletarian novel" (quoted in David Lewis 227).

NOTES

Thanks are due to the following people for commenting on earlier drafts of this essay: James D. Bloom, Wlad Godzich, Martin Hipsky, Andre Kaenel, Frank Lentricchia, Sherry Linkon, William Maxwell Sr., Bill Mullen, Alan Wald, Julia Walker, and Susan Willis.

1. For a taste of Lewis's unfavorable evaluation of Communists and their writing in 1937, see Sinclair Lewis 37.

2. The jazz historian Marshall Stearns reports that Dizzy Gillespie had just joined Teddy Hill's big band when it began working at the Savoy Ballroom in 1937 (233).

3. The ties between humanism and colonialism in the Enlightenment tradition are explored in Young.

4. McKay describes this fight-that-never-was and the healing bottle of "dago red" in A Long Way from Home 140–41.

5. For a brief treatment of Gold's 1921 breakdown, see Rideout 124.

6. This analogy between antiblack and antiradical violence can be compared with later efforts in the same vein considered in Nelson 119–22.

7. Wood offers a full account of the "police riot" that ended the 1922 Liberator party at Bryant Hall.

8. The useful checklist of McKay's writings that Cooper includes in The Passion of Claude McKay misses his review of Charlie Chaplin's My Trip Abroad.

9. Cruse mysteriously invokes a critique of McKay that Gold did not write to claim that "the Communists and Gold" disliked "If We Must Die" (49).

10. A suggestive discussion of how political poets in the first decades of the century manipulated and reinvested traditional poetic forms is contained in Nelson 22–24, 41–43.

11. The links between radical labor and proslavery views are discussed in Roediger 76.

12. For an analysis of the enigmatic racial identity of the Confidence Man in the Melville novel of the same name, see Karcher 186–257.

13. The mellowing of Gold's evaluation of the Harlem Renaissance between 1930 and 1936 was not unique on the cultural Left. Barbara Foley notes that for the length of the Third Period, "Communist cultural critics generally condemned the great majority of past and contemporary black writers for their neurotic subjectivism, their defeatism, and their snobbery (or conversely, their primitivism)" (186). Just as generally, these critics "more readily discovered progressive models in already existing [black] folk—and literary—culture" during the years of the Popular Front (188).

14. These left-wing critiques of Jews without Money are treated in Rideout 152.

15. Marcus Klein suggests that the Provincetown Players rejected Hoboken

Blues on "political grounds" (240), but he does not clearly describe these
grounds or provide supporting evidence for his claim.

16. Meyerhold's dramatic theory is explored in Hoover, especially 100–101.

17. To Gold's dismay, the New Playwrights wound up staging the play with
white actors in blackface, thus eviscerating much of its intended parody of minstrelsy (Goldstein 119).

18. For an account of the music used in Ridgely Torrence's *Three Plays for
the Negro Theater*, see Clum 101.

19. For an example of these studies, see Nielsen's otherwise stimulating and
original *Reading Race*.

20. Abdul JanMohamed argues that colonialist writing is marked by the absence of anything comparable to the dialogic class discourse of European literature (82).

WORKS CITED

Bloom, James D. *Left Letters: The Culture Wars of Mike Gold and Joseph Freeman.* New York: Columbia University Press, 1992.

Clum, John M. "Ridgely Torrence's Negro Plays: A Noble Beginning." *South
Atlantic Quarterly* 63 (1969): 96–108.

Cooper, Wayne F. *Claude McKay: Rebel Sojourner in the Harlem Renaissance.*
Baton Rouge: Louisiana State University Press, 1987.

——, ed. *The Passion of Claude McKay: Selected Prose and Poetry, 1912–1948.*
New York: Schocken, 1973.

Crane, Hart. "The Bridge." *The Complete Poems and Selected Letters and Prose
of Hart Crane.* Ed. Brom Weber. Garden City, N.Y.: Anchor-Doubleday,
1966. 43–117.

Cruse, Harold. *The Crisis of the Negro Intellectual.* New York: William Morrow, 1967.

Du Bois, W. E. B. *The Gift of Black Folk.* 1924. Millwood, N.Y.: Kraus-Thom-
son, 1975.

——. Review of *Nigger Heaven*, by Carl Van Vechten. *W. E. B. Du Bois: Writings.* New York: Library of America, 1986. 1216–18.

Ellison, Ralph. "Twentieth-Century Fiction and the Black Mask of Humanity."
Shadow and Act. By Ellison. New York: New American Library, 1966. 42–60.

Foley, Barbara. *Radical Representations: Politics and Form in U.S. Proletarian
Fiction, 1929–1941.* Durham, N.C.: Duke University Press, 1993.

Folsom, Michael, ed. *Mike Gold: A Literary Anthology.* New York: International Publishers, 1972.

Gates, Henry Louis, Jr. "Trading on the Margin: Notes on the Culture of Criticism." *Loose Canons: Notes on the Cultural Wars.* By Gates. New York: Oxford University Press, 1992. 173–93.

Geoghegan, Vincent. *Utopianism and Marxism.* New York: Methuen, 1987.

Gold, Michael. "At Last, a Negro Theater?" *New Masses,* March 10, 1936, 18.

——. "Doing the Big Apple for the *Daily Worker* Drive," *Daily Worker,* November 20, 1937, 7.

——. "Go Left, Young Writers!" 1928. Folsom 186–89.

——. "The Gun Is Loaded, Dreiser!" 1935. Folsom 223–30.

——. *Hoboken Blues: Or, the Black Rip Van Winkle, a Modern Negro Fantasia on an Old American Theme. The American Caravan: A Yearbook of American Literature.* Ed. Van Wyck Brooks et al. New York: Literary Guild of America, 1927. 548–626.

——. *The Hollow Men.* New York: International Publishers, 1941.

——. *Jews without Money.* New York: International Publishers, 1930.

——. *Life of John Brown.* 1923. New York: Roving Eye, 1960.

——. "Notes of the Month." *New Masses,* February 1930, 3.

——. "Proletarian Realism." 1930. Folsom 203–8.

——. "A Secret Meeting in the Pines." 1934. Sillen 95–96.

——. "Towards Proletarian Art." 1921. Folsom 62–70.

——. "The Writer in America." 1953. Sillen 181–88.

Goldstein, Malcom. *The Political Stage: American Drama and the Theater of the Great Depression.* New York: Oxford University Press, 1974.

Hoover, Marjorie L. *Meyerhold: The Art of Conscious Theater.* Amherst: University of Massachusetts Press, 1974.

JanMohamed, Abdul R. "The Economy of Manichean Allegory: The Function of Racial Difference in Colonialist Literature." *"Race," Writing and Difference.* Ed. Henry Louis Gates Jr. Chicago: University of Chicago Press, 1986. 78–106.

Johnson, James Weldon. Preface to the Original Edition. *The Book of American Negro Poetry.* Ed. Johnson. 1931. New York: Harcourt Brace Jovanovich, 1983. 9–48.

Karcher, Carolyn L. *Shadow over the Promised Land: Slavery, Race, and Violence in Melville's America.* Baton Rouge: Louisiana State University Press, 1980.

Klein, Marcus. *Foreigners:.The Making of American Literature, 1900–1940.* Chicago: University of Chicago Press, 1981.

Lewis, David Levering. *When Harlem Was in Vogue.* New York: Vintage, 1982.

Lewis, Sinclair. "Garland for Clowns." *Newsweek,* October 25, 1937, 37.

Locke, Alain. "Negro Youth Speaks." *The New Negro: An Interpretation.* Ed. Locke. 1925. New York: Atheneum, 1968. 47–53.

——. "Resume of Talk and Discussion." *Official Proceedings of the Second National Negro Congress.* October 15–17, 1937. Philadelphia: Metropolitan Opera House, 1937. n.p.

Marx, Karl. *The Eighteenth Brumaire of Louis Bonaparte.* 1963. New York: International Publishers, 1987.

——. *The German Ideology. The Marx-Engels Reader.* 2d ed. Ed. Robert C. Tucker. New York: W. W. Norton, 1978. 146–200.

McKay, Claude. "Birthright." Review of *Birthright*, by T. S. Stribling. Cooper, *The Passion* 73–76.
——. "Enslaved." *Liberator*, July 1921, 6.
——. *Harlem Shadows*. New York: Harcourt, Brace, 1922.
——. *A Long Way from Home*. 1937. New York: Arno, 1969.
——. Review of *My Trip Abroad*, by Charlie Chaplin. *Liberator*, May 1922, 28–29.
——. "To Alain Locke: 1 August 1926." Cooper, *The Passion* 143–44.
——. "To Max Eastman: 3 April 1923." Cooper, *The Passion* 82–87.
——. "To Max Eastman: 19 Dec. 1934." Cooper, *The Passion* 212–14.
——. "The White House." *Liberator*, May 1922, 16.
Moses, Wilson Jeremiah. *Black Messiahs and Uncle Toms: Social and Literary Manipulations of a Religious Myth*. University Park: Pennsylvania State University Press, 1982.
Nelson, Cary. *Repression and Recovery: Modern American Poetry and the Politics of Cultural Memory*. Madison: University of Wisconsin Press, 1989.
Nielsen, Aldon Lynn. *Reading Race: White American Poets and the Racial Discourse in the Twentieth Century*. Athens: University of Georgia Press, 1988.
Rideout, Walter B. *The Radical Novel in the United States, 1900–1954: Some Interrelations of Literature and Society*. 1956. New York: Columbia University Press, 1992.
Roediger, David R. *The Wages of Whiteness: Race and the Making of the American Working Class*. New York: Verso, 1991.
Salzman, Jack, and Berry Wallenstein, eds. *Years of Protest: A Collection of American Writings of the 1930s*. New York: Pegasus, 1967.
Sillen, Samuel, ed. *The Mike Gold Reader*. New York: International Publishers, 1954.
"Something New in the Field of Sports." *Liberator*, March 1922, n.p.
Stearns, Marshall W. *The Story of Jazz*. New York: Oxford University Press, 1956.
"Subscribe to the *Liberator:* August 1922." *Liberator*, August 1922, 31.
"Subscribe to the *Liberator:* May 1922." *Liberator*, May 1922, 31.
Wood, Charles W. "An Open Letter from Charles Wood." *Liberator*, June 1922, 11+.
Wright, John S. "A Scintillating Send-Off for Falling Stars: The Black Renaissance Reconsidered." *A Stronger Soul within a Finer Frame: Portraying African-Americans in the Black Renaissance*. Minneapolis: University Art Museum, University of Minnesota, 1990. 13–45.
Wright, Richard. "Blueprint for Negro Writing." *New Challenge* 2 (Fall 1937): 53–65.
Young, Robert. "Colonialism and Humanism." *"Race," Culture and Difference*. Ed. James Donald and Ali Rattansi. Newbury Park, Calif.: Sage Publications, 1992. 243–51.

SUZANNE SOWINSKA

6

WRITING ACROSS

THE COLOR LINE:

WHITE WOMEN

WRITERS AND THE

"NEGRO QUESTION"

IN THE GASTONIA

NOVELS

It was the first time that Marge had ever be-
held a colored person. True, she had seen
them around since early babyhood. But she
had never encountered one before—human
to human. Now, for an instant, Marge and
Martha looked at one another full in the
eyes. . . . For a moment, the distance which
lay between them was bridged and Marge
caught a glimpse across the miles.
—Myra Page, *Gathering Storm*

At the beginning of 1920, a seemingly minor
ideological shift in the political agenda of
the Communist Party in the United States
was made, after considerable pressure from
the Communist International, to address the
troubling problem of racial equality. The
success of the Soviet Revolution had in large
part been due to the support of ethnic minority groups, and the Soviet Party leaders
who dominated the International hoped to
translate this strategic formula directly to the
United States, where blacks represented the
largest and most oppressed minority group.
Soviet leaders began to invite prominent
black activists to visit the Soviet Union and
to witness firsthand the absence of racial
prejudice in Soviet society, at least in the
places where visitors went. The suggestion
that racism could dissolve under revolutionary conditions and the multiracial milieu at
Soviet schools, where African-Americans
mingled with Asians, Africans, and non-Eu-

ropean Soviet nationals, had a profound effect on blacks who went abroad and on those who read about Soviet developments in U.S. newspapers. A tiny group of African-Americans in Harlem was recruited by the Communist Party in the United States and was drawn into the difficult tasks of developing a new theoretical approach to what was known as the "Negro Question" and creating strategies to attract and increase black membership in the Party (Naison 3–126).

Once the Communist Party began to take up strategic discussions of the Negro Question and launched an enthusiastic campaign to include race as part of its radical agenda, other branches of the Left also began to move beyond their color blindness to define racial persecution as a matter of tremendous importance. While African-Americans themselves remained largely skeptical of the Communists until they launched their massive mobilization in defense of the Scottsboro boys nine years later, many white Communist Party leaders, organizers, and members were being carefully retrained and reoriented in their thinking about blacks. After continual agitation by black Communists and their white supporters within the Party, by the late 1920s to be a white revolutionary meant, at least theoretically, to embrace the principles of racial equality. For perhaps the first time in U.S. history, a systematic program by white radicals to unlearn racism was launched in the context of an organization committed to the struggle of the working class, the overthrow of U.S. capitalism, and the reorientation of American culture.[1]

To achieve its objective of expanding its influence in black America, the Communists realized they needed not only to increase black membership but also to educate its white membership that blacks, representing an important ally of the proletariat, had to be carefully cultivated for their support if the revolutionary movement was to succeed. A formal resolution of the Communist International, which dramatically changed the whole climate of the U.S. Party within which racial issues were considered, declared that "white comrades must be specially trained for work among the Negroes" and that "the Negro problem must be part and parcel of all and every campaign conducted by the Party." Additionally the resolution stated that Communists needed to work in the South and to "begin to organize the black agrarian population to struggle for control of the land and against . . . lynching, Jim Crowism, and segregation" ("Resolution of the Communist International" 110). A further resolution on the Negro Question, issued the following year by the Executive Committee of the Comintern, likewise affirmed that it was the duty of white workers to conduct a "relentless struggle against all manifestations of Negrophobia . . . to everywhere make a break in the wall of segregation and Jim Crowism which have been set up by the bourgeois slave market morality." These resolutions had an immediate impact on the Party and its activities, as its members began to work collectively to "stamp out all forms of antagonism, or even indifference among our white comrades toward the Negro work" and to attack "white chauvinism" within its ranks ("Resolution on the Negro Question" 156–58).

Although the potential for answers to the Negro Question to remain theoretical was strong, in reality the Communist Party and its followers on the Left tried hard to create an interracial political community that extended into the personal sphere. Given the cultural barriers separating black and white workers, the competition for jobs and housing, the stereotypes and myths that each race held of the other, and the differences in their experiences of class oppression, their task was at best awkward and at times overwhelming. Yet a utopian vision of racial equality combined with that of the eradication of class oppression fed the imaginations of many white radicals, who for the first time consciously attempted to undermine both their own assumptions about racial difference and the all-pervasive racism prevalent in white society. A developing proletarian aesthetic provided many radicals with the form and sometimes the formula for artistic representations of these issues, and the literary campaign that had been launched by radical writers on the Left and supported by the cultural wing of the Communist Party began to reflect these new priorities.

The Loray Mill Strike in Gastonia, North Carolina, in the spring and summer of 1929 was of great historical significance to the movement for industrial unionization and to the development of social realist writing during the depression era. While Gastonia erupted into violent conflict between pro-union southern textile mill workers and the reactionary forces at work in their communities, it also provided radical writers with an opportunity to witness and chronicle the revolutionary changes they hoped for in both society and literature. If, as Christina L. Baker remarks, "to go left was to go South, to Gastonia for rich material that fed the imaginations of novelists eager to employ art as a class weapon" ("Gastonia Strike" 256), Gastonia also stimulated visions of racial harmony and answers to the Negro Question for many of the white writers who wrote about the strike. Political equality for the Negro was a new militant tactic being stressed in the Communist-backed National Textile Workers' Union (the organization supporting the Gastonia strikers), and representations of cross-class and cross-race alliances moved to a more prominent place in radical discourse. Gastonia was one of the earliest opportunities the Party had to experiment with and enforce its new policies of eradicating "white chauvinism."[2]

Women writers were in the forefront of demonstrating that literary texts could be successfully used to combine important discussions of race with the class analysis that intellectual and political agendas in the 1930s had instituted as a virtual prerequisite to good writing.[3] They also brought a perspective on gender issues to their work and insisted that the emerging radical political program maintain some relevance to its female membership. Of the six novels about Gastonia, four were written by women: *Strike!* (1930) by Mary Heaton Vorse, *Call Home the Heart* (1932) by Fielding Burke, *Gathering Storm: A Story of the Black Belt* (1932) by Myra Page, and *To Make My Bread* (1932) by Grace Lumpkin.[4] Two additional novels about the Negro Question by these women writers act as semisequels to the Gastonia events: *A Stone Came Rolling* (1935) by Fielding Burke traces the further actions of one of her Gastonia characters, and *A Sign for Cain* (1935) by Grace Lumpkin outlines the continuation of the Communist Party's struggle for race equality in the South after Gastonia.

The four women novelists writing about Gastonia were in general agreement on the importance of representing the feminist aspects of the strike in their novels. Their texts contain realistic portrayals of strong, vibrant women mill workers and strike leaders bonding together across class lines, of heroic female protagonists, and of a strong sisterhood of women strikers refusing to give up their cause even when attacked, beaten, and bayoneted by police. As Sylvia Jenkins Cook has noted in her ground-breaking study of the Gastonia novels, these writers felt that women in general had been underrepresented as part of the revolutionary struggle, and they meant to demonstrate in their novels the degree to which women were responsible for changing history (*From Tobacco Road* 85–124). In addition to these concerns, the women Gastonia novelists, to varying degrees, hoped to bring their nascent consciousness of race relations to their largely white, middle-class, albeit radical, readership. For them, an emerging proletarian aesthetic would necessarily include answers to the Negro Question. As experts on that other testy question for radicals, the Woman Question, they felt they were particularly well placed to begin to bring an antiracist discourse to their novels and to their work in the movement.[5] Although the Gastonia novels say more about the hopes and visions of white radicals than about the historical realities of African-American workers, the positions that these women novelists take on the Negro Question provide a wide range of interesting and informative literary responses to white racism in the 1930s.

The first of the novels about Gastonia to appear in 1930, *Strike!* by Mary Heaton Vorse, is more concerned with addressing issues of gender and class oppression than in answering questions of racial equality. This is interesting in the light of the fact that Vorse based two of the main characters in her novel on women who were crucially involved in organizing black workers during the Gastonia strike. The novel's young female organizer, Irma, is modeled after Vera Buch, a close friend and confidante of Vorse during the period she was in Gastonia. Buch was sent to Gastonia by the national secretary of the Communist Party to "stiffen up" the strike leader and to "straighten him out," in particular about the issue of "white chauvinism" (Weisbord 173). Buch consistently tried to make contact with black workers, traveling to a waste mill in nearby Bessamer City to contact black women millhands and visiting Stumptown, a black hamlet where she was successful in getting a few blacks to sign union cards. She then enlisted the help of Ella May Wiggins, a well-liked troublemaker and much respected poor white union member.[6] Wiggins, who Vorse re-creates in *Strike!* as the character Mamie Lewes, organized among her black counterparts and helped Buch and the union establish connections in the African-American communities around Gastonia. Wiggins was murdered by an angry mob of townspeople intent on stopping the Gastonia strikers. In her recollections of the strike, Buch states, "I am certain it was as an organizer of the Negroes that Mrs. Wiggins was killed" (Weisbord 260).

In Vorse's fictional version of Gastonia, related in a sometimes sparse documentary-style narrative voice, racism is a pervasive part of the overall climate in her southern mill town, yet it consistently either remains in the background or is used as a counterpoint against which the relative terror of the white organizers is measured. Black characters are seen but not heard as they "shuffle off without thought of protest" (*Strike!* 279) during the Gastonia trials or are shyly heroic when they recover a white male union member after he has been "indescribably battered" by a mob and return him to a fellow worker's cabin (306). In addition to this absence of meaningful black characters, the presence of southern racism is internalized in the novel's white characters and manifested in their fear that their northern liberal viewpoints identify and associate them with the principal of racial equality and therefore make them the target of the town's vigilante mobs. Town toughs shout after the women organizers that they are "'nigger lovers,'" instilling in them a sense of "'imminent catastrophe,'" while the male strike leader becomes obsessed with the "lynch mob" that he fears is going to be sent after him (102, 311).

Unlike the rest of the women Gastonia writers, Vorse almost entirely

eliminates the race agenda of the union movement from her representations of the strike. On the one hand, she does not want to complicate issues; her goal is to depict "what one so rarely sees, a spontaneous uprising of the people" (7). To her this means representing the majority of the
workers (who in the case of Gastonia were white) regardless of ideological pressures to address the Negro Question. On the other hand, though
Vorse understands the importance of representing the underrepresented
in the case of the women involved in the strike, her notion of struggle is
based on what she sees as a common labor struggle, affecting its participants as collective members of the union without concern for their class,
race, or gender. Racism thus becomes anti-unionism; a hunt for "niggers"
becomes a hunt for "strike leaders" (103–4). While Vorse's narrator carefully records the special nature of women's oppression, the more complicated issues raised by the union's push for racial equality are ignored, and
Vorse chooses not to raise the Negro Question in her novel. Her concern
is with building a strong union. That the terms for unity within the structure of the union might be threatened by inequalities measured along race
lines is not a question she takes into consideration. More involved responses to the Negro Question, however, are very much a part of the agenda of
the other women writers of novels about Gastonia.

Two years after *Strike!* three more Gastonia novels by women authors
appeared, which address the question of racial equality and contain important representations of cross-class/cross-race alliances. In these novels,
the insistence that white organizers and intellectuals adjust their work to
include the integration of blacks into union activities and radical movements is an integral part of the aesthetic task of the authors. Each of these
novelists sees this task as part of her responsibility as a writer. In the Gastonia novels, most of the "Negro work" is, significantly, women's work.
While the union drive provides the impetus for contact between the white
and black workers, it is the women workers who are depicted as the first
to mingle with blacks on the picket lines. Additionally, the special hard-
ships suffered by women mill workers—the burden of large families abandoned by males, the double role of laborer and housewife, the struggle to
find adequate means of birth control, and the prevalence of sickness and
disease suffered by women regardless of their race—often provide the initial opportunity for communication between the black and white women
workers depicted in these novels.

Myra Page's novel *Gathering Storm*, for example, is organized around
a comparison between the struggles faced by two families of textile workers, one white and one black. The two families live "barely two hundred

yards" from one another, slightly separated by a field, yet Back Row, also known as "niggertown," represents the distance between two communities, an "invisible gulf" that "both sides took largely for granted" (50–51). Through a carefully constructed set of character doubles, Page matches the novel's white brother and sister protagonists, Marge and Tom Crenshaw, with their black counterparts, Martha and Fred Morgan. Both brothers leave the South for better jobs in the shipyards of New York, where, following similar narrative trajectories, they obtain a radical education and become union organizers. They also gradually become good friends and allies, learning to be "able to travel back and forth across the color line, studying and comparing the workers lives on each side" (75). For both characters, "the line" becomes "an indistinct, shadowy thing, robbed of its former reality and terror" (88).

Marge Crenshaw's parallel friendship with Martha Morgan, however, does not have a chance to develop before Martha is raped and brutally murdered by the arrogant son of one of the town's wealthy white families. Marge fondly remembers Martha and is "overcome by emotions she did not understand" when she hears the racist assumptions of other white millhands as they discuss the circumstances surrounding Martha's death (136). She is torn between the legacy of racism that is an essential part of her poor white upbringing and a sense of justice that recognizes its inhumanity, but she cannot decide which system of thinking represents the best path for her untrained mind to follow. Her dilemma is resolved when her brother, Tom, arrives for a visit and teaches her through his actions, and his "radical talk," to feel ashamed of her racist upbringing (147). Page demonstrates that while Marge's emotional response to Martha's murder prepares the way for her eventual transformation into an actively antiracist union organizer, she needs Tom's intellectual input to make the transition. Meanwhile, Tom's firsthand experiences with Fred, along with the ideological influences provided by his training as a radical in the North, bring about his conversion into an antiracist. In both cases, Page implies that a legacy of southern white bigotry can be unlearned only through a combination of internalized emotional change and external intellectual agitation. The shame that both Marge and Tom feel when they recognize the error of their earlier assumptions about racial difference is neutralized by action. Tom joins the Communist Party and returns to the South to help organize striking workers at Marge's mill. Similarly, Marge, "remembering her talks with Tom" about the need to see black workers as equals, learns to extend her friendship to other black women workers (168). Once educated by communism, the Crenshaws never waver in their commitment to integrate the union (297).

While Page's first attempt at novel writing realistically catalogs the potential horrors of southern bigotry, she does so at the cost of creating romanticized black characters, a utopian white proletariat, and somewhat idealized representations of bonds across race and class lines. If her white characters at first act with more than a little hesitation toward their black counterparts, they always quickly recover from their internalized notions of white superiority. Her black characters are saintlike; they patiently and even protectively wait for the whites to come to their senses about the Negro Question and hold no resentments for past injuries. By the end of the book, the white Communist organizers see themselves as engaged in a second civil war, a fight led by "white n' colored" Communists, a mass uprising "of ten million Negro peasants against their white masters" (327). As Page's injects her novel with Communist-inspired visions of a "Soviet America" that includes "a Negro Toilers' Socialist Republic" in the "Black Belt," her readers are left disappointed if not displeased with her utopian answers for more quotidian concerns (328).

On the one hand, Page wants to advance a "correct" representation of "good" black characters to a white liberal readership that she feels is accustomed to traditional stereotypes of black-white interaction. On the other hand, she wants to do justice to her sense of what communism is all about and how it can help workers organize and fight for social change. Given this second concern, she especially wants to push white radicals like Vorse, who, even when reminded to look, fail to see the importance of the race question and its connections to the proletarian cause. Even with these concerns prominently outlined on her agenda, however, Page remains an outsider to the very cause she tries to champion. Her response to the Negro Question is based in ideology rather than experience. She is a missionary hoping for converts rather than an observant participant hoping to learn from experiences gleaned from immersion in the task at hand. Her progressive characters suffer from the same malady; Page oversimplifies the terms of difference she establishes between her black and white characters in the beginning of the novel once their conversion to communism takes place. There is no real character development beyond the point of "joining up," as all difficulties between comrades are conflated once they become Communists. Instead of understanding the struggles of their black counterparts, the white characters, like Page herself, sink into a sentimentalization of blacks that subsumes the uniqueness of their fight for racial equality and their experiences of racial oppression. Although Page is astutely prescient in her depiction of cross-class/cross-race alliances, especially those among women, her narrative solutions to the problem of eliminating racism lack any concrete knowledge of black culture, black experience, or the long-term struggles by blacks themselves for social change.[7]

While Page's responses to the Negro Question cause her to invent white working-class characters who, once properly educated, instinctively overcome their race bias, Fielding Burke uses her first Gastonia novel to describe the perhaps more realistic dangers that accompany the forcing of radical solutions onto white mountain-bred workers previously unexposed to African-Americans or to the issue of racial equality. Although a relatively small portion of *Call Home the Heart* is devoted to an exploration of cross-class/cross-race alliances, these issues are central to the novel's climax. The overtly racist reaction of Burke's main character, Ishma, at the end of the novel contains a warning for northern idealists like Page. Burke's whites, even once they are "indoctrinated" by radicals with the "correct" mode of thinking about race, are slow to challenge or alter their assumptions about racial superiority. Burke wants to be sure that her readers recognize how difficult and often insurmountable the task of eradicating racism among southern white mountain folk can be. She also tries to represent ways in which her white characters can separate their personal feelings from their political convictions enough to be able to act in a politically responsible way. Burke allows that her white characters may never resolve their private, often conflicting, feelings and attitudes toward blacks. This does not prevent them in Burke's mind, however, from more progressive actions in the public realm.

Her heroine, Ishma, is similar to Page's Marge Crenshaw in certain respects. Both come from a strong matriarchal line of women kinfolk, whose families are forced to leave their mountain communities to find work and the promise of a better life in the mill towns. Both Page and Burke describe the awakenings of their female protagonists from a kind of murky, prelapsarian understanding of their place in the world as poor whites to a full-blown consciousness of themselves as participants in a class struggle. Unlike Page, however, Burke does not use the race issue as a central question; rather, it is one of many issues her heroine must grapple with as part of her radicalization. At least half the novel passes before Ishma gets up enough courage to leave the ignorance and harsh realities of her mountain life, including her impoverished but loving husband, for the uncertainties and potential advances offered by the mill town. Burke's central drama focuses more on Ishma's rejection of conventional womanly fulfillment in the form of romantic love, a rejection complicated by class and poverty, than on her rejection of racial stereotypes. But the principal of racial equality rears its head toward the end of the novel. Ishma's battle between heart and mind, between marriage and the promise of intellectual stimulation and world revolution that comes in the form of involvement with the cause of organized labor, also includes a fight to overcome her sense of racial superiority.

Burke somewhat bravely introduces the consequences and contradictions that come when attempts to promote an antiracist ideology are met with the emotional turmoil of institutionalized racism and the agonizing legacy of southern notions of white supremacy. Burke sees the recalcitrance with which poor whites meet the issue of racial equality as having its roots in the careful manipulation of poor whites by southern white capitalists. At the bottom of the economic scale, poor whites have essentially been duped into compliance with a system of white supremacy that, on the one hand, as an ideology of race relations offers them a sense of superiority over southern blacks while, on the other hand, as an ideology of class relations functions to keep them oppressed. Thus, once Ishma finally begins her education as a radical in the mill town, Derry Unthank, a country doctor turned Marxist who is also her intellectual mentor, explains:

> "Don't you know that if every white worker in the South were to join the union, the bosses could still chuckle and pat their paunches? They'd still have a big population of workers to draw from in the unorganized blacks."
>
> "They wouldn't make good workers."
>
> "Don't be a fool. In three years they could be trained to fill every white man's place in a Dixie mill. The only difference would be a little pigment under the skin, and that wouldn't affect the bosses' money." (352)

In Burke's view, ignorance has kept the poor white from seeing exactly how racism allows the capitalist to maintain control of the white workers as well as the blacks. The union encourages white workers like Ishma to embrace the notion of race equality logically even if they cannot accept it emotionally. This contradiction is one that Burke identifies as extremely problematic for her white heroine. Her novel resonates with the dangers of separating the emotions from the intellect, and Ishma's "knowing" about the evils of racism hardly affects her "feelings" on the subject.

Determined to defeat her prejudice against blacks for the sake of solidarity and to impress Unthank, who she feels taunts her with his intellectual superiority and knowledge of correct actions for radicals, Ishma gets her chance for heroic action in the novel when Butch Wells, a black union leader, is kidnapped by a lynch mob on a night when all the male union organizers are at a meeting in another town. In a tense and dramatic scene, Ishma rescues the bleeding Butch even though physical contact with Butch's unconscious body makes her "violently nauseated" (380). Yet Ishma also feels a sense of triumph "over that final error in her blood" (the one that causes her racism) and pride because she feels that Unthank "would know now that she too could act without prejudice." Ishma's jubilation at defeating what she sees almost as an inbred and therefore "natural" form of race prejudice veers toward the sanguine as she surveys the crowd gathered after the rescue and in unconsidered ecstasy decides she now loves "those black and bronze women with their big, tender eyes" (382).

Ishma's euphoria and complacent fantasy of race unity are short-lived, however, when Butch's "very fat and very black" wife arrives on the scene. Ishma experiences an "uncontrollable revulsion" when embraced by Butch's wife, an embrace that breaks all her newfound resolve to work for race equality. Burke purposefully overwrites the excesses of blackness in this scene to emphasize how, on an emotional level, Ishma's consciousness of race remains unchanged. Although intellectually able to cross the color line, Ishma reacts hysterically to physical contact with Butch's too-black wife; she "thrusts her off with a wild blow" and races back to the mountains in a state of "unutterable horror of herself" (385).

Ishma's radicalization has been fouled by her inability to take the final step across the color line. Her retreat from all she has learned about collectivity and social change is unavoidable because Unthank's lessons in the necessity of racial equality have failed to impart an understanding of otherness. Without a foundation for knowing or working with the blacks in her community, Ishma has no concrete knowledge of the realities and experiences of their lives. Like Page's Marge, Ishma is lectured to by male radicals about racism and dreams of putting their radical theories into practice. Yet without any contact with black working-class men and women, she finds herself unprepared for the severity of her own reactions when face-to-face with them for the first time. Burke represents Ishma, unlike Marge, as having no context for meeting blacks. They do not work in the mill with her, nor do they often appear in the union circles that Ishma frequents. Burke holds the union leaders responsible for this lack of contact and for a philosophical integration of black and white workers rather than a real one.

Burke is dismayed that the union's progressive race theories have not been put into practice within their own organization. Talk is cheap for the Communists and intellectuals, but the costs to the potential pool of working-class union members and future organizers is high. Burke's warning is clear: the danger is that "ideals, theories, the struggle of a world for breath" will be "thinned to nothing" (387). Strong union members will be driven out by the union's refusal to understand and combat the deep-seated race antagonism that mountain-bred workers like Ishma are taught from a very young age. Talk will not change a consciousness that attributes almost mythic qualities to the horrors of blackness. The union's policy of race equality is fruitless in the face of ignorance, fear, and habit. Burke's novel recognizes and challenges this absence of forethought on the part of Gastonia's Communist union leadership.

Unwilling to abandon her mountain-bred heroine to the degenerative effects of race antagonisms for long, Burke devotes the sequel to her first novel, *A Stone Came Rolling*, to Ishma's winning her battle between her primitive ideas about race and her intellectual training as an antiracist. Ishma conquers her irrational and emotional responses to African-Americans as part of a new identity she creates for herself as "a woman with vision and a conscience" (112). She begins to incorporate visits to "the Negro section" of the mill town into her regular routine, and she learns how to talk with black women directly about their experiences. She sees more clearly the connection between their condition and her own. Through the many conversations that Ishma now has with black women workers, Burke provides examples of the important differences between the Ishma of the earlier novel and this older and wiser character of the sequel.

Burke also uses the sequel to rewrite the lynch mob rescue scene of her first novel to provide a more "correct" depiction of a lynch mob intervention. The *New Masses* had condemned Burke's earlier representation of the rescue of Butch Wells for its unethical display of individualism. In *A Stone Came Rolling*, Burke, like Vorse, attempts to show solidarity among causes by linking whites' threat of violence against white organizers to the potential lynching of blacks by white mobs. One of her white male union members is thus beaten because he refuses to reveal where the black organizer Stomp Nelson is hiding. First the mob strips him of his clothing "'to see if he's black under his shirt,'" and then they hit him about the face and mouth so that he will bleed, thereby demonstrating to the mob that "'he's red sure enough'" (249). Burke's symbolic mixing of black and red strengthens the link between her black and white workers. The scene portrays a dramatic (and manly) act and provides necessary proof to the black union members that the white organizers will literally put their bodies on the line for the safety of black workers. It also conveniently positions the white radicals as suffering from the same level of oppression and subjected to the same abuses of power relations that their black counterparts are.

In the revised rescue scene, there is no individual responsible for Stomp's safety; it is the collective unity of the whole group of whites that sets him free. Women are returned to their proper place as part of, but not individually essential to, the collective goal. Ishma is part of the mob, but there is no heroic role for her to play. Burke symbolically describes her during the scene as dressed as a man, "standing aside in her husband Britt's overalls, and grasping Britt's arm" (294). Burke's revision downplays the feminist aspects of her character as a "strong woman" in favor of representations of Ishma as a "good organizer," whose main interest is participating in the collective solidarity of workers. Burke's revision of the lynch mob scene is less individualistic and leans toward group solutions, but her vision is still a romantic one. Only extraordinary events are symbols of antiracist actions. Her agenda regarding the Negro Question remains very much concerned with depicting the noble actions of her white radicals.

Although Burke opts for heroic solutions to show the commitment of white radicals to the cause of racial equality, she also offers more quotidian solutions for those who cannot completely heal the rift between the emotions and the intellect. Even though Burke's characters harbor racist attitudes, she insists they can still act in politically responsible ways. In the first novel, Ishma rescues Butch even though she is repulsed by him. In the second book, she returns to her progressive political work knowing that she has not completely resolved her feelings about the race issue. She struggles to overcome her racist feelings by beginning to make progressive political alliances with black women in her community. The gulf between her knowing the right thing to do about her black comrades and her feelings of racial superiority is almost as wide as it was in the first novel, but she does seem to have conquered her more primitive and emotional reactions to those of another race through rationality and reason. Her private thoughts remain tainted and confused, but her public actions more closely follow from her political beliefs. Notably, she accomplishes this unhappy harmony without being paralyzed by fear or guilt. She simply begins again, willing to let her somewhat tarnished record regarding race be rectified by time and her readjusted commitment to the cause of racial equality.

Grace Lumpkin's first novel, *To Make My Bread*, which won the Maxim Gorky prize for the best labor novel of 1932, describes two related social movements and their connection to her characters. The first is the migration of mountain-bred farmers to the mills, and the second is textile workers' emotional and intellectual awakening to the existence of class struggle. Almost as an aside, Lumpkin's characters take on the struggle for racial equality at the end of the novel after reactionary elements in the mill town try their hands at strikebreaking by circulating a racist handbill.

In *To Make My Bread*, the main audience for the question of racial equality is found in the women workers. They are represented as seeing the importance of the race issue most clearly and eventually taking action to begin bridging difference. Women workers, whose wages are considerably lower than their male counterparts and who traditionally represent the last hired, first fired category of workers at the textile mills, more quickly grasp the danger to their livelihood that the mill's potential threat of hiring black men and women as scabs will bring. Lumpkin's analysis of the problem is similar to Burke's: wealthy northern capitalists care little about who actually performs the labor in their mills as long as a profit can be made. A strong union, therefore, must incorporate all the workers at the mill, both white and black, both the weavers and those that perform the more menial tasks around the mill. As Lumpkin's white protagonist Bonnie McClure explains to her coworkers, if blacks aren't also recruited for the union cause, they will very likely be recruited by the mill owners for theirs. Alliances between white and black workers are necessary for the white workers because the alliance will help the white workers preserve their own place in the hierarchy of the mill system.

Lumpkin's first novel establishes an important concept that is not as clearly defined in the other novels about the Negro Question written by women. For Lumpkin, race alliances are based on mutual understanding and need. This is demonstrated in Bonnie's alliance with Mary Allen, a black woman who cleans at the mill. Their support of one another establishes an important cross-race alliance. Bonnie's position of friendship with and connection to the black community via Mary Allen is pivotal in opening up communications between the white union organizers and the black workers and in preventing the black workers from scabbing. Solidarity across racial lines is depicted as essential to the survival of both the black and white workers. Although the friendship between the two women is based in everyday experience, it has important progressive implications when put into a political context. By offering Bonnie her front porch as a speaking platform, Mary Allen also offers her black friends, coworkers, and neighbors the opportunity to have their ideas and viewpoints heard by the union. Later in the novel when Bonnie, like her historical counterpart Ella Mae Wiggins, is murdered, Lumpkin uses Mary Allen's prominent place-

ment at the very beginning of Bonnie's long funeral procession to demonstrate the commitment of white radicals to their black compatriots.
Everyday actions and occurrences, rather than large-scale symbolic acts
or heroic actions, form Lumpkin's view of how race alliances between
white and black workers might begin to grow. This theme appears even
more prominently in her second novel, which is primarily concerned with
depicting the interactions between black and white radicals in the "Black
Belt" after Gastonia.

A *Sign for Cain*, written in 1935, is unique among the novels about the
Negro Question in its representation of the evolution of a young, black
working-class girl into a Communist organizer. This transformation is a
central part of the novel's subplot. The main part of the narrative is similar
to Page's novel in that it compares the struggles of two Communist organizers, one black and one white, who attempt to agitate for the rights of workers in a small southern town. Lumpkin's progressive views on class and race
alliances are central to the text. While intentionally directing her ideological message to a mainly white audience, she manages to take more time and
considerably more care than any of the others in expressing the realities and
experiences of the black characters she has created. She neither sentimentalizes these characters nor worries about their potential negative influences on the whites in her novel and in this regard is perhaps the most "progressive" of the women who wrote novels about the Negro Question. She
gives her black female characters prominent roles in the novel, depicting
them as strong-willed, clearheaded, and intelligent in a way that anticipates
contemporary narrative representations of African-American women.

There are no large-scale union battles being fought in Lumpkin's second novel. The focus is on the everyday, basic, and often minor struggles
that radicals face when attempting to bring about social reform. The two
significant collective actions that the workers in A *Sign for Cain* participate in involve a small group of farmers and house servants approaching
a plantation owner for better rations and prompt payment of wages and a
few discussions of what to do about black washerwomen who are being
put out of business by a new white-owned laundry that has opened in town.
Lumpkin's attention to the quotidian allows her to concentrate on the
ordinary and everyday ways that race and class alliances occur. She also
hopes to show how deeply rooted, nonprogressive beliefs about race ingrained in both her black and white characters might be challenged and
eventually unlearned. Of all the novels written by women about the Negro Question, A *Sign For Cain* is the only one to attempt to portray the
lives and experiences of the black working class in realistic detail.

Lumpkin's use of Selah, a black, working-class, and female character, to represent a prototypical organic intellectual is unusual and notable, in the light of her sister writers' failings in this regard. Lumpkin, however, neither sentimentalizes nor promotes Selah as exceptional in any way. Selah's experiences and the possibilities for growth and change that open up for her over the course of the novel merely reflect the possibilities open to all of Lumpkin's workers, "men and women, black and white." Selah's character symbolizes the theme of political growth through knowledge, which is one of Lumpkin's concerns. Selah learns that both the bondage and futility of racism can be unlearned through education. Education for Selah takes two forms: learning to read and write and learning to channel the knowledge she gains from reading into collective action. According to Lumpkin, her attempts at self-education and her intuitive sense of injustice and willingness to act prepare her for her eventual education as a Communist. Selah's escape from the South at the end of the novel marks the beginning of a life of freedom for her, both concretely as it provides an end to her life of virtual slavery and metaphorically as it propels her toward New York, where she can educate herself in the ways of collective reform and action.

Throughout *A Sign for Cain*, the process of politicalization for Lumpkin's characters involves ordinary, daily exposure to and contemplation of the injustices that are close at hand. Lumpkin shows the basic and early steps that must be taken to build trust across race lines. When Denis, a black organizer, first meets with Lee Foster, a white farmer who has been identified as a potential ally, they carefully test each other's support:

Lee spoke gently, passing his hand along the neck of his horse. "Looks like there's going to be a war before long," he added in a soft careless voice.
"You think so?"
"Yes, it looks like it . . . a sort of war," he examined the horse's bridle . . . "between the rich and the poor."
"You think it would be all the poor?" Denis asked.
"Sure."
"Negroes, too?"
"Ain't they poor?" Lee Foster asked. (93)

Like many of Lumpkin's more race-conscious characters, Lee understands that given the imbalance of power implicit in race relations, he must make the first move toward Denis. He knows he cannot take it for granted that Denis will automatically trust him, even though they are both poor, and he understands it will take some time to establish a cross-race alliance.

Lee is willing to wait for their relationship to build slowly over time. When Denis later asks him to join the black sharecroppers in asking for the back wages and rations owed to them, Lee agrees to help. Lee's wife initiates perhaps an even more significant act in building trust between the white and black characters in the novel. She is open and friendly with Denis when she has no special reason to be; she invites him to "sit with" her and shares with him her domestic concerns. Her minor yet unpretentious acts of friendship help cement the bond between Denis and Lee (98).

Lumpkin is specific about the responsibilities of the white Communists to their black comrades and at the same time is realistic about the potential for change along race lines. This is seen most clearly in the novel as it functions as a bildungsroman for its principal white character, Bill Duncan. His belief at the beginning of the novel that "white tenant farmers and sharecroppers have the same interests as the nigra farmers" is a noble one, but by the end of the novel he understands clearly what the consequences of such actions are (16–17). He learns that although similarities in class background might bind workers together, blacks will inevitably pay the highest price and suffer the most for any transgressions.

As Duncan matures in his understanding of the consequences of crossing the color line, he becomes less idealistic and is able to act more responsibly on behalf of his black comrades. He organizes other whites to turn back a white mob determined to break into the jail where two black organizers are being held, and he subtly manipulates the town's racist judge into taking responsibility for further mob actions (280–84). Lumpkin hopes to emphasize that whites have a responsibility to fight against racism in their own communities. Although Duncan is a sympathetic listener and contributes to discussions among his black comrades, most of his political work takes place among his white peers. He neither fetishizes, internalizes, nor sentimentalizes the lives of his black compatriots. He sincerely sees in their struggle and advancement a link to the progress and advancement of the white working class. At the same time, however, he realizes that there are cultural barriers and historical differences that separate the realities and experiences of blacks and whites. He understands there are aspects of black community that remain outside of his reach and in which he has no place.

By the end of Lumpkin's novel it becomes clear that in her view revolutionary struggle for race equality also needs to move forward separately in white and black communities. Unlike the other women who wrote novels about the Negro Question, she often urges a cautious autonomy as well as unity between communities. Channels of communication must remain open between blacks and whites so that a sense of mutual trust is present. However, some of the most important antiracist work that her organizers do happens in relation to organizing within their own race. Thus Bill Duncan and Lee Foster break up a white lynch mob, and an entire black congregation walks out in "anger and protest" when a black preacher suggests that the jailed black organizers somehow got into "bad company" and were receiving a just punishment (281, 295). Whites learn to combat racism within their own ranks, and they do not necessarily need the help of blacks to do that. Blacks learn to promote independence from whites and resistance to forms of white ideology that has oppressed them. Both groups learn to form new terms for alliances based on mutual need and trust. At the end of Lumpkin's novel the "heroic" black and white men and women symbolically conjoined in the image of shadows on the wall whose race is indistinguishable leave the cabin where they have held a clandestine multiracial meeting to go out and organize in their individual communities. Through her symbolism, Lumpkin hopes to show the growing strength of a multiracial communist movement in the South. More than the other women who wrote novels about the Negro Question, Lumpkin carefully thought out her interpretation of the Party's mandate toward more progressive race relations ("Why I as a White Southern Woman Will Vote Communist" and "Southern Woman Bares Tricks"). She hopes to demonstrate through her novel how her characters are able to cross the color line long enough to make important and sometimes long-term alliances, while at the same time maintaining the integrity of differences represented by the intransigence of the line itself.

The novels about the Negro Question written by women offer a variety of viewpoints, opinions, and insights into how writers respond to and help create an aesthetic sensibility that demands that particular ideological constructions and political interpretations be foregrounded in a written text. As the question of race equality became an important concern for radicals of the 1930s, literary representations promised one avenue for presenting new arguments and defining the terms for the careful negotiations of race and class identities with which white radicals had begun to struggle. The women writing novels about the Negro Question share some similarities in their approach to the question of race equality. All, for example, believe and hope to demonstrate in their novels that coming to the question of race relations from an understanding of class relations is an important predisposition for challenging racism. Instead of sharing in a notion of a special women's culture, they posit the notion of a workers' culture. They hope to represent in their novels how class analysis makes it easier for them to identify with and form alliances across race lines. The strongest bonds in the novels occur between white and black working-class women, whose similarities in background, education, and experience and a shared connection to the local community provide both the basis and the need for cross-race alliances. Same-sex alliances across the race line occur most frequently because the "workers culture" they describe is primarily sex-segregated and sexist in nature, although Grace Lumpkin, in particular, judiciously includes cross-gender/cross-race alliances in A *Sign for Cain*.

The women writing novels about the Negro Question foreground gender concerns in their novels and consider them to be one of the principal methods for forming cross-race alliances. They always look, however, to similarities in class relations as the point of praxis. While their direct experience with gender oppression makes it relatively easy for them to form a critique of proletarian culture's intersections with women, the color line represents unknown and in some ways unexplorable terrain. They must develop new strategies for dealing with racial difference. These strategies often fail as they guess at what signifies for blacks in their novels or sentimentalize the lives of their black characters. Yet on other occasions the strategies they develop are more successful: they caution against a too-rapid mingling of race and class issues, or they ascertain that an unhappy separatism is the only route that black-white relations can follow. They also recognize that class struggle, the Woman Question, and the Negro Question cannot be divided into discreet categories and that the strongest cross-race alliances frequently are made in a context where men and women of differing classes do not perceive their situation as that of detached individuals but as embedded in relations with others.

For these writers of depression-era novels, there are specific actions and activities that constitute an antiracist discourse for whites. On a personal level, their characters must struggle with their emotional or learned responses to the blacks in their communities. They also believe a political program that includes the progressive understanding of race relations, like that offered by the Communists, can help individuals interrupt and reinterpret their responses to racial difference. Everyday actions and activities help build alliances between whites and blacks and foster a sense of interdependence. White characters who feel ashamed of or guilty about their former racist assumptions are encouraged to work out these feelings through action.

For the women writing novels about the Negro Question, the Communist Party and its unions provided a resource and avenue for such action.

On a political level, racist characters in their novels learn to separate their personal views about race and gender differences from their political actions. Whites also agitate for racial equality because it is in their interests to do so. The antiracist discourse for white organizers follows along these same lines. On a personal level, organizers need to expand their knowledge of the black community. They need to begin to feel a sense of responsibility for their black comrades. On a political level, white organizers need to learn to encourage discussions of race issues among other whites. They learn to make specific connections for the white workers that demonstrate the linkage of issues affecting both white and black workers. They teach white workers to combat racism in their own communities and to find ways of demonstrating their support of their black counterparts.

The final activity for promoting an antiracist discourse for the women writing novels about the Negro Question was the action of writing itself. Just as the Communist Party and its unions provided a resource and avenue for action, novel writing constituted a form of action. For these writers, progressive novel writing meant taking the Negro Question very seriously and incorporating its concerns into narrative representations. To represent the complexities of racial equality to other radicals in the form of a novel allowed for a continuous reminder of the responsibilities and commitment that white radicals made to all workers, regardless of their race. The women who wrote novels about the Negro Question provide some of the first examples of cross-class/cross-race alliances in American literature, and they expand our understanding of not only what commonalities link blacks and whites together but also how those connections can be strengthened. While the color line never quite becomes the "indistinct, shadowy thing" that Myra Page hopes for, it can be stepped across from both directions, with knowledge and information shared, in spite of its prescriptive separation.

Like no period before it, the depression era had a radicalizing effect on American women writers. In response to the widespread social and economic devastation of the era, many women writers turned to the genre of social realism as a tool for expressing their nascent concerns and began writing narratives filled with radical solutions and hope for progressive social change. Aligning themselves with movements of literary radicalism and assuming strong and unwavering voices of determination and commitment, they helped change the shape of American writing during the depression, imprinting their unique style on and adding important new priorities to representations of the era. Their agenda as radicals, as women, and as writers, however, diverged from that of their male counterparts.

The basis for this divergence necessitates further study and is one of the important areas of rediscovery and reevaluation in contemporary 1930s criticism.

Aware of the importance of gender difference as a basis for self-representation and as a potential bridge between class, race, and ethnic barriers, the women writing novels about the Negro Question developed and incorporated a radical political agenda within their writing both in response to and in defiance of the various literary, social, and political agendas of their male contemporaries. Representations of difference thus prominently figure in their writing and provide a new avenue of exploration for critical investigations of 1930s literary production. As these writers actively engage themselves in the project of expanding the radical agenda, they also affirm that discussions of difference and alliances between and among women of various race, class, gender, and ethnic positionalities were very much an important part of previous radical movements and constitute a significant history and tradition that has been lost to most contemporary readers of these texts. As these issues reappear in contemporary radical and feminist discourse, it is imperative to learn from the examples and mistakes of previous generations of women radicals committed to social change. The response these women writers made to the cultural moment of the depression and the radical agendas they advanced mark important and distinctive contributions to the literature of the 1930s.

NOTES

1. On the Negro Question and the relations between black and white Communists, see, for example, Cannon; Foley; Foner and Allen; Ford; Kelley; Meier and Rudwick; Naison; Record; Solomon; and Wolters. Foley, in particular, investigates the Communist Party's wavering between black nationalist analysis and class analysis during this period and the program that provides the historical backdrop for the troublesome interplay of race and class politics in novelistic treatments of these issues.

2. Many accounts, both historical and literary, describe the events that occurred in Gastonia in 1929. See, for example, Beal; Cochran; Cook, *From Tobacco Road*; Draper; Earle, Knudsen, and Shriver; Eller; Garrison, Introduction; Hodges; McCurry and Ashbaugh; Pope; Reilly; Rideout; Urgo; and Weisbord. For biographical information on the women Gastonia writers, see Baker, *Generous Spirit*; Cook, *From Tobacco Road*; Garrison, *Mary Heaton Vorse*; and Sowinska.

3. In relation to white women writers' exposure to literary texts written by African-American and other minority writers, Tillie Olsen recalled for Deborah Rosenfelt that "in the movement people were reading like mad. There was as in any movement a looking for your ancestors, your predecessors. . . . There was a burst of black writers. . . . I knew about W. E. B. DuBois before, but because the movement was so conscious of race, of color, we were reading all the black writers, books like Arna Bontemps' *Black Thunder*, Langston Hughes. We read Ting Ling, we read Lu Hsun, we read the literature of protest that was beginning to be written out of South Africa; we read B. Traven; writers from every country. The thirties was a rich, an international period. . . . And from whatever country or color this was considered to be part of our literature" (229).

4. The remaining two Gastonia novels are Sherwood Anderson's *Beyond Desire* and William Rollins Jr.'s *The Shadow Before*.

5. At least one 1930s reviewer of these novels argued that the constraints experienced by elite white women living in a gendered double standard created a sensitivity among them to the situation of black and white workers (Schachner).

6. Wiggins was known for her strike ballads—songs she wrote and sang daily on the picket lines. In Hall et al., *Like a Family*, which chronicles Wiggins music, she is described as having "lived in a black neighborhood outside the mill village," where she alone among local activists tried to persuade black workers to sign union cards (127).

7. For a historical account of the lives of African-American women workers during this period, see Jones.

WORKS CITED

Anderson, Sherwood. *Beyond Desire*. New York: Liveright, 1931.

Baker, Christina L. "Gastonia Strike." *Encyclopedia of the American Left*. Ed. Mari Jo Buhle, Paul Buhle, and Dan Georgakas. New York: Garland, 1990. 255–56.

——. *In a Generous Spirit: The First-Person Biography of Myra Page*. Urbana: University of Illinois Press, 1996.

Beal, Fred. *Proletarian Journey*. New York: Hillman-Curl, 1937.

Burke, Fielding [Olive Tilford Dargan]. *Call Home the Heart*. 1932. Old Westbury, N.Y.: Feminist Press, 1983.

——. *A Stone Came Rolling*. New York: Longmans, Green, 1935.

Cannon, James P. *The First Ten Years of American Communism: Report of a Participant*. New York: Pathfinder Press, 1962.

Cochran, Bert. *Labor and Communism: The Conflict That Shaped American Unions*. Princeton, N.J.: Princeton University Press, 1977.

Cook, Sylvia Jenkins. Critical Afterword. *Call Home the Heart*. By Fielding Burke. 1932. Old Westbury, N.Y.: Feminist Press, 1983. 447–62.

——. *From Tobacco Road to Route 66: The Southern Poor White in Fiction.* Chapel Hill: University of North Carolina Press, 1976.

Draper, Theodore. "Gastonia Revisited." *Social Research* (Spring 1971): 3–29.

Earle, John R., Dean D. Knudsen, and Donald W. Shriver Jr. *Spindles and Spires: A Restudy of Religion and Social Change in Gastonia.* Atlanta: John Knox Press, 1976.

Eller, Ron. *Miners, Millhands, and Mountaineers: Industrialization of the Appalachian South, 1880–1930.* Knoxville: University of Tennessee Press, 1982.

Foley, Barbara. *Radical Representations: Politics and Form in U.S. Proletarian Fiction, 1929–1941.* Durham, N.C.: Duke University Press, 1993.

Foner, Philip S., and James S. Allen, eds., *American Communism and Black Americans: A Documentary History, 1919–29.* Philadelphia: Temple University Press, 1987.

Ford, James W. *Communists and the Struggle for Negro Liberation.* New York: Communist Party, Harlem Section, 1936.

Garrison, Dee. Introduction. *Strike!* By Mary Heaton Vorse. 1932. Urbana: University of Illinois Press, 1991. vii–xxi.

——. *Mary Heaton Vorse: The Life of an American Insurgent.* Philadelphia: Temple University Press, 1989.

Hall, Jacquelyn Dowd, James Leloudis, Robert Korstad, Mary Murphy, Lu Ann Jones, and Christopher B. Daly. *Like a Family: The Making of a Southern Cotton Mill World.* Chapel Hill: University of North Carolina Press, 1987.

Hodges, James A. "Challenge to the New South: The Great Textile Strike in Elizabethton, Tennessee, 1929." *Tennessee Historical Quarterly* 23 (December 1964): 343–57.

Jones, Beverly W. "Race, Sex, and Class: Black Female Tobacco Workers in Durham, North Carolina, 1920–1940 and the Development of Female Consciousness." *The Great Depression and the New Deal: Women and Minorities during the Great Depression.* Ed. Melvyn Dubofsky and Stephen Burwood. New York: Garland, 1990. 251–61.

Kelley, Robin. *Hammer and Hoe: Alabama Communists during the Great Depression.* Chapel Hill: University of North Carolina Press, 1990.

Lumpkin, Grace. *A Sign for Cain.* New York: Lee Furman, 1935.

——. "Southern Woman Bares Tricks of Higher-Ups to Shunt Lynch Mob Blame." *Daily Worker*, November 27, 1933, 3.

——. *To Make My Bread.* New York: Macaulay, 1932.

——. "Why I as a White Southern Woman Will Vote Communist." *Daily Worker*, August 12, 1932, 4.

McCurry, Dan, and Carolyn Ashbaugh. "Gastonia, 1929: Strike at the Loray Mill." *Southern Exposure* 11 (Winter 1973–74): 185–203.

Meier, August, and Elliott Rudwick. "The Origins of Nonviolent Direct Action in Afro-American Protest: A Note on Historical Discontinuities." *Along the*

Color Line: Explorations in the Black Experience. By Meier and Rudwick. Urbana: University of Illinois Press, 1976.

Naison, Mark. *Communists in Harlem during the Depression*. New York: Grove Press, 1985.

Page, Myra [Dorothy]. *Gathering Storm: A Story of the Black Belt*. London: Martin Lawrence, 1932.

Pope, Liston. *Millhands and Preachers: A Study of Gastonia*. New Haven, Conn.: Yale University Press, 1942.

Record, Wilson. *The Negro and the Communist Party*. 1951. New York: Antheneum, 1971.

Reilly, John M. "Images of Gastonia: A Revolutionary Chapter in American Social Fiction." *Georgia Review* 28 (1972): 516.

"Resolution of the Communist International, October 26, 1928." *The Communist Position on the Negro Question*. New York: Workers Library Publishers, 1934.

"Resolution on the Negro Question in the United States." *Communist* 10 (February 1931): 157.

Rideout, Walter B.. *The Radical Novel in the United States, 1900–1954: Some Interpretations of Literature and Society*. Cambridge, Mass.: Harvard University Press, 1956.

Rollins, William, Jr. *The Shadow Before*. New York: Robert M. McBride, 1934.

Rosenfelt, Deborah S. "From the Thirties: Tillie Olsen and the Radical Tradition." *Feminist Criticism and Social Change*. Ed. Judith Newton and Deborah Rosenfelt. New York: Methuen, 1985. 216–48.

Schachner, E. A. "Revolutionary Literature in the United States Today." *Windsor Quarterly* 2 (Spring 1934): 27–64.

Solomon, Mark I. *Red and Black: Communism and Afro-Americans, 1929–1935*. New York: Garland, 1988.

Sowinska, Suzanne. Introduction. *To Make My Bread*. By Grace Lumpkin. 1932. Urbana: University of Illinois Press, 1995.

Urgo, Joseph R. "Proletarian Literature and Feminism: The Gastonia Novels and Feminist Protest." *Minnesota Review* 24 (Spring 1985): 64–84.

Vorse, Mary Heaton. *Strike!* 1930. Urbana: University of Illinois Press, 1991.

Weisbord, Vera Buch. *A Radical Life*. Bloomington: Indiana University Press, 1977.

Wolters, Raymond. *Negroes and the Great Depression: The Problem of Economic Recovery*. Westport, Conn.: Greenwood, 1970.

7

LITERATURE OF

RESISTANCE: THE

INTERSECTION OF

FEMINISM AND THE

COMMUNIST LEFT IN

MERIDEL LE SUEUR

AND TILLIE OLSEN

He confuses me about writing, for one thing.
—Josephine Herbst to Robert Wolf, on her
reluctance to get emotionally involved
with Michael Gold

This essay places two American working-class writers, Meridel Le Sueur (1900–) and Tillie Olsen (1912– or 1913–), in a contemporary critical context and addresses the complex intersection of feminism and the political Left as refracted in these writers' literary texts. Le Sueur's and Olsen's lives and literary texts span two generations of radical women, those affiliated with the Old Left and those who came of age with the New Left and the most recent women's movement. One of the salient features of the 1930s was the failure of any leftist organization to develop women's militance into a self-conscious feminism. Yet in more or less covert ways, Le Sueur's and Olsen's literature from the late 1920s and 1930s anticipates the concerns of feminists a generation later. We see in their texts a prescient if latent consciousness. During the 1930s Le Sueur's and Olsen's literature was considered "proletarian," the term generally reserved for working-class literature produced during the depression decade. This essay adopts Paul Lauter's definition of the broader term, "working-class literature," as texts by *and* about the working class that coincide with other literary categories, such as literature by women and people of color.[1]

Women's working-class literature provides a valuable historical record that is not as self-evident as many of its detractors—and its sympathizers—would have us believe. Cultural products refract rather than reflect history, suggesting the limits, in a given social formation, within which meanings are constructed and negotiated. But when 1930s leftist critics mined novels for their "revolutionary social content," their critical apparatus did not allow for the complicated mediation of social reality operating within the texts. Thus there is a need for a renewed historical and critical exploration of women's working-class literature.

Few scholars have examined American working-class literature since its flourishing in the 1930s. Since then, working-class literature has been generally considered crudely tendentious and aesthetically inferior to bourgeois literature. Impatient with this assumption, Lauter points out that the American literary canon has been defined by a privileged elite, primarily males of Anglo-Saxon or northern European origin. This essay implicitly supports the efforts of Lauter and others (people of color, women, radicals) to expand the canon and to examine the aesthetic and political bases on which it is constructed.

My approach, however, is also based on the premise that moments of textual conflict, often viewed as examples of "inferiority" or "weakness" in canonical, popular, or working-class literature, may be historically resonant, sometimes suggesting more about a given historical period than those moments that formalist critics might consider evidence of aesthetic excellence. Far from constituting a coherent reflection or central meaning, a piece of working-class literature, like any form of discourse, displays conflicting and contradictory meanings.

This is not to say that flaws exist in Le Sueur's and Olsen's literature that they should have recognized and corrected. Any writer is enmeshed in history and partially blind to the full range of events shaping that history. History precedes form, and tears in the textual fabric indicate the pressure that historical content brings to bear on form. That any text is "flawed" or incomplete, however, does not mean the critic should fill in the missing pieces; the critic's task is not to repair or complete the text but to identify the *principle* of its silences, "flaws," conflicted meanings (Eagleton 35).

In Le Sueur's and Olsen's 1930s literature, this principle lies partly in these writers' response to the sexism of the Communist Party U.S.A., an organization to which they were deeply committed. On the Communist Left, "proletarian" and "manly" were nearly synonymous; the worker-protagonist in proletarian literature "almost by definition was male; proletarian prose and criticism tended to flex their muscles with a particularly masculinist pride" (Rosenfelt 395). The androcentrism of Communist literary policy reflected that of the Communist Party as a whole. Party organizing during the early 1930s, for example, focused on the workplace, when only about 20 percent of women worked outside the home, and throughout the decade Party union activity centered on the mining, steel, maritime, and auto industries, in which few women were employed. The Party at least tacitly endorsed the traditional sexual division of labor, and domestic issues, when they counted at all, were not priorities.

However, the Party's work among women in the 1930s should be carefully evaluated as part of the struggle for women's liberation in the United States. Many women developed an awareness of their own potential, a sense of collectivity, and an understanding of America's social system through Party-related activities. Peggy Dennis, for fifty years an active Party member and the widow of the Party leader Eugene Dennis, reflects the views of Olsen and Le Sueur when she summarizes the contradictory experience of Party women: "Male Communists often responded to discussions of the 'woman question' with derision or condescension, but there were few other organizations in the country at the time in which women would even consider it their right to challenge such attitudes" (quoted in Isserman 141). That Party leadership was overwhelmingly male and that its bureaucracy functioned undemocratically "from the top down" is a matter of record, but the history of the rank and file, including its women, has yet to be thoroughly explored. Le Sueur's and Olsen's literary texts constitute an important part of that history.

Le Sueur and Olsen were at once loyal Party members and emerging feminists; their literature, straining toward and away from Party prescriptions, reveals conflicting impulses that I term "official" and "unofficial." Their texts address the physiological and sexual experiences that shape women's lives—sexual initiation, pregnancy, childbirth, miscarriage, sterilization, battery, rape—at a time when these topics seldom appeared in literature, including working-class literature. Olsen's emphasis on domestic labor in *Yonnondio*, a novel begun in 1932, implicitly questions orthodox Marxism's primacy-of-production theory and its concomitant privileging of the workplace and the industrial worker as the loci of struggle. During the 1930s the Party generally characterized psychological and emotional categories as unmaterialist, as unrelated to "real" politics, labeling introspective novels febrile, self-indulgent, and bourgeois. Despite this, Le Sueur and Olsen made familial relations, emotional deformation, and the developing consciousness of children the central subjects of their literature, overcoming the restraints of the very revolutionary organization that fostered them. Le Sueur's and Olsen's conscious and unconscious movement between official and unofficial categories was not limited, however, to the subjects and themes of their texts. Each writer also experimented with various literary forms.

Because Le Sueur and Olsen subvert not only bourgeois but also ortho-dox Marxist categories, "literature of resistance" in the context of this es-say means something directed not only against the dominant culture but also against restrictive elements within a leftist subculture. Le Sueur's and Olsen's texts foreshadowed, if only in a muted, provisional sense, questions about Marxism and Leninism that theorists, including feminists, have much more recently and more explicitly raised. They implied that "the personal is political" long before that phrase became a household slogan among younger feminists. By now old news, this slogan is nevertheless still timely.

One of my richest sources about the 1930s has been the writers them-selves, whom I extensively interviewed. But writing about living subjects, especially those with whom one feels political and personal solidarity, is a touchy, even painful, business. Attempting to be at once sensitive and critical, I resemble a character in Joanna Russ's *Female Man* who thinks of herself as standing in a puddle of water, holding two alternating elec-trical currents (138). The women's movement has made archetypes of Le Sueur and Olsen, who have become emblematic figures as much as his-torical ones, and yet I have more patience now than I once did with in-terviews that tend to be honorific rather than penetrating. I beg my sub-jects' forbearance while claiming that their rightful place is in history, not myth.

Conflicts between Le Sueur's "official" and "unofficial" views emerge in the tension between her theory and practice of literature. Le Sueur first publicly expressed her position on how radicals create a literature of re-sistance in "The Fetish of Being Outside" (1935). Written in the twilight of the Communist Party's proletarian period (or Third Period, 1928–35), this essay adopts the Party line that it is not only possible but requisite for enlightened middle-class writers wholly to leave their own class and to become ex officio members of the revolutionary working class. "The Fe-tish," which was a reply to Horace Gregory's defense of some middle-class writers' reluctance to join the Party, does not allow for oscillation between complicity and critique with regard to class sympathies. Le Sueur's lan-guage suggests rebirth, a baptismal cleansing of original sin, a Kierkegaard-ian leap of faith: "You cannot leave it by pieces or parts; it is a birth and you have to be born whole out of it." The "creative artist" must be "willing to go all the way, with full belief, into that darkness." With "a new and mature integrity" the writer does "not react equivocally" (23). The view expressed in "The Fetish" was popular among Party members and sympathizers. Sherwood Anderson, for example, thought it possible for intellectuals to join in a form of group suicide. In 1932 he declared, "If it be necessary, in order to bring about the end of a money civilization and set up something new, healthy and strong, we of the so-called artist class have to be submerged, let us be submerged" (10). And Joseph Freeman's autobiography, *An American Testament* (published in 1936 but "in progress" for nearly ten years), attempted to show that an intellectual committed to proletarian revolution could break irrevocably with the middle class.

Some of Le Sueur's "unofficial" literary texts, however, contradict the position articulated in "The Fetish of Being Outside." As a feminist within a male-dominated movement, she herself experienced, and expressed in her literature, the conflicting impulses for which "The Fetish of Being Outside" does not allow. In three short stories—"Our Fathers," "Annunciation," and "Corn Village"—Le Sueur frankly examines her own experience with the dual vision and divided loyalty that "The Fetish" proscribes. After providing some biographical information about Le Sueur, I will address these three texts.

Le Sueur was born on February 22, 1900, in Murray, Iowa, into a white, middle-class, and educated family. One of the most prominent women writers of the 1930s, she endured red-baiting, blacklisting, and twenty-five years of obscurity to become, in the 1970s, a regional folk heroine and nearly an archetypal figure within the women's movement.

Le Sueur has written extensively about her maternal grandmother, Antoinette Lucy, "one of the first settlers, gun in hand, of the Oklahoma territory" (*Ripening* 2), who had divorced her husband for "drinking up the farms her father left her" ("Ancient People" 22). Le Sueur's vivid memories of her grandmother, so full of the woman's courage and self-reliance, are nevertheless shadowed by a recognition of her emotional and sexual repression. Le Sueur has described Antoinette Lucy's "graceless intensity"; she was "earnest, rigid . . . spare as the puritan world" ("Ancient People" 31, 33). Lucy always dressed in black, considering bright colors sinful, and bathed in a loose-fitting shift. Her only emotional outlet was singing Protestant hymns, which she did with a telling fervor—through this hymn singing, Le Sueur has said, her grandmother made love to Jesus. But the hymn singing revealed other repressed feelings as well, Le Sueur believes: "Only through these songs did I know . . . her terrible loneliness, her wish to die, her deep silence. Sometimes I heard her cry in the night, but I could not humiliate her by going to comfort her. In the day there would be no sign" ("Ancient People" 34).

Le Sueur has said of her mother and grandmother that "their experience of this world centered around the male as beast, his drunkenness and chicanery, his oppressive violence" ("Ancient People" 23). Meridel was ten when her mother, Marian Wharton, left her first husband, William Wharton, a Church of Christ minister. Le Sueur describes him as "a charming womanizer, the village sex symbol . . . a raconteur, a vivant" (interview), as well as heavy-drinking, violent, and physically abusive.

As a single woman, Marian Wharton earned a living by lecturing on women's issues. While a lecturer, she was arrested for disseminating birth control information and for participating in the suffrage fight. Marian later headed the English Department at the People's College in Fort Scott, Kansas, where she met and married the socialist Arthur Le Sueur, president of the college (Eugene Debs was the chancellor). The school strove to attract working-class students and to teach from a working-class perspective. Marian and Arthur edited the college magazine, which bore the slogan "to remain ignorant is to remain a slave." Through her mother and her stepfather, both active socialists, Meridel was exposed as a girl to Populists, Wobblies, anarchists, union organizers, and members of the Socialist Party, the Non-Partisan League, and the Farmer-Labor Party; through her parents she met such luminaries as Debs, Emma Goldman, Alexander Berkman, John Reed, Mabel Dodge, Margaret Sanger, Theodore Dreiser, and Carl Sandburg. She joined the Communist Party in 1924.

On the basis of her long, admirable life as a radical, writer, and feminist, Le Sueur has become an emblematic figure, a "socialist tribal mother," as one admirer put it (Inman). Le Sueur both enjoys this status and finds it disturbing. "I haven't really revealed the brutality of . . . my own life," she has admitted. "And I think the women's movement has helped me to cover it up. . . . *Ms.* [Magazine] wanted to present me as [a] role model, [as a woman] who made it, who succeeded. . . . They don't tell the horrible violence of women's lives" (interview). When Le Sueur speaks candidly about her life, she reveals details that add rough edges to her public persona. But with a few exceptions, the popular feminist and leftist press has treated her as an ideal without contradictions, shortchanging not only Le Sueur but also students of women's history and the American Left.

Le Sueur is known for her reportage, especially "Women on the Breadlines" (1932) and "I Was Marching" (1934), which I categorize as "official" proletarian literature.[2] However, "Our Fathers" is one text in which an "unofficial" Le Sueur emerges. She has described "Our Fathers," which is somewhat autobiographical, as "one of the few [of my] stories that's not covered up. . . . It [is] really a naked cry" (interview). Through the fictional characters, she confronts her grandmother's, her mother's, and her own emotional deformation. Penelope, the story's adolescent protagonist, rebels as Le Sueur did against ascetic Protestantism. Penelope insists on knowing and feeling what her mother and grandmother have repressed, forgotten, denied.

"Our Fathers" takes place immediately before the funeral for Penelope's father, Tim, who had been active in the Unemployment Council and shot in a demonstration. Despite his irresponsibility toward his family, Tim had fostered his daughter's developing political consciousness. But Penelope is as disturbed by her grandmother's "triumphant" bitterness as she is by her father's death. The old woman sneers at a photograph of a man she left after twenty years of marriage: "'Samuel that no account. If I'd known what I do now about men it would a been different. Men . . . men . . . .' She was only glad to remember in order to deride him" (*Ripening* 120). Penelope wants desperately to know the stories of the forebears in the old photographs, to feel some connection to them, but the grandmother, revealing little, begins to quaver, "Jesus lover of my soul." She was "like a spouse of the Lord being betrayed by earth's little men" (122).

Tim's death has intensified Penelope's adolescent search for her identity. Studying the family photographs, she tries to comprehend her past and imagine her future by placing herself in a genealogy of immigrants, settlers, bitter women, rakes, and rebels. As a result "Our Fathers" has a searching, dreamy quality strikingly different from Le Sueur's "official" proletarian literature. The didacticism of "Women on the Breadlines" and "I Was Marching" is muted in "Our Fathers," except for Penelope's memory of Tim's identifying the class struggle and the proper side to support. Instead of providing slogans, solutions, and clear demarcations, "Our Fathers" permits questions, doubts, and fears to emerge and suggests that some aspects of life may remain mysterious to Penelope, despite her craving to know.

The threat is not simply the "wheat, lumber, and coal kings" about which Tim had sermonized: Penelope senses that she will not escape the "bitter drouth" so affecting her mother, grandmother, and the stern women in the photographs, and she fears that eventually she, too, will taste the "brew" and "never be cured of it" (*Ripening* 114, 177). "Our Fathers" acknowledges some of the complexity of the emotional/sexual legacy Le Sueur and other women of her generation inherited.

One can wish that Le Sueur had further explored the marks left on her by the towering presence of an absent father and by a grandmother who could not cry unless "her bad eye" ran water, "as if weeping alone, unknown to her" (*Ripening* 115). Le Sueur explains that she became a writer to speak for the "oppressed, mute, forgotten, or lost," specifically identifying her grandmother: "My grandmother was mute. She had no words for her terrible life" (interview). While we get a valuable glimpse of unemployed women during the depression in Le Sueur's reportage, we do not come to know these women as we come to know Penelope and her forbidding grandmother. Le Sueur's reportage is perhaps limited by her class. She does not penetrate the consciousness of the characters in "Women on the Breadlines" or "I Was Marching" but does so acutely in "Our Fathers," whose characters were based on people she knew only too well.

"Annunciation" departs even more than "Our Fathers" from typical proletarian literature. The title alludes to the angel Gabriel's announcement to Mary that she will give birth to the Son of God (Luke 1:26–38), and Le Sueur originally wrote the story in 1928 to her first, unborn child. Set in the depression, this narrative prose poem represents a pregnant woman's dreamlike state of mind, imposing a theme of fertility and regeneration upon a secondary theme of contrasting deprivation.

Because pregnancy, labor, the moment of birth, and the nurturing of a newborn are among life's most profound experiences, it is striking that they appear so rarely in literature. One explanation for this silence is supplied by Hortense Calisher, who, in referring specifically to labor and delivery, also describes the experiences surrounding them: "Childbed is not a place or an event; it is merely what women do" (quoted in Olsen, *Silences* 230). "Annunciation" suggests the powerful, inexplicable bond between mother and unborn child, a bond at once common and singular in women's experience and yet almost entirely excluded from proletarian as well as canonical literature. And the story's lush, sensual, evocative language is hardly the stuff of "official" proletarian literature: "I look at myself in the mirror. . . . My hips are full and tight. . . . I am a pomegranate hanging from an invisible tree with the juice and movement of seed within my hard skin. I dress slowly. I hate the smell of clothes. I want to leave them off and just hang in the sun ripening . . . ripening" ("Annunciation" 86). Images move in circles—the magnolia tree, pear tree, and landlady appearing, disappearing, and reappearing—as opposed to the linear progression Le Sueur associates with masculine form. Here we see one of Le Sueur's deliberate subversions: she intends this style as the "antithesis of what she sees as the male style of linear movement toward a 'target,' or a conclusion to be 'appropriated'" (*Ripening* 251).

"I've never heard anything about how a woman feels who is going to have a child," observes the narrator of "Annunciation" (86). When Le Sueur wrote the story, pregnancy was considered unacceptable as a literary subject, as much by the *New Masses* as by the magazines that gave that reason for rejecting her manuscript (*Scribner's Magazine* and the *Atlantic Monthly*). Although the story has been frequently reprinted, it was originally published only in a small private edition (Platen Press, 1935). A favorite Le Sueurian anecdote recalls her retort to the editor at Scribner's who, as he rejected the story, suggested that she write more like Ernest Hemingway: But "fishin', fightin', and fuckin'," she quipped, "are not the sum of my experience" (interview). "Annunciation" similarly defies protocol.

Like "Annunciation," "Corn Village" (*Scribner's Magazine*, 1931) has little in common with orthodox proletarian realism or reportage. In writing about Midwest farmers, Le Sueur was not writing about workers considered by the Party during the Third Period to be the key to revolution; the Party gave priority in this period to organizing efforts among workers in basic industry because of its assumed importance to the economy. In "Corn Village" Le Sueur has consciously or unconsciously almost wholly discarded the Party discourse. "Official optimism" and its corollary, what I term "official certainty" ("we know that not pessimism, but revolutionary elan will sweep this mess out of the world forever") are noticeably absent from the text (Gold 5). Like Penelope's grandmother, corn villagers have no love song other than "Jesus, Lover of My Soul." Their bodies are awkward, "held taut for some unknown fray with the devil or the world or the flesh" (15). Sexual and emotional repression are the human equivalent of the barren, frozen landscape, which is colorless and lifeless—all whites, grays, "emptiness and ghostliness." In Corn Village, it is "as if some malignant power were in the air" (10, 11). Mystery, uncertainty, and fear prevail.

"Corn Village" also departs formally from Le Sueur's consciously proletarian literature. In her reportage and her novel *The Girl*, for example, Le Sueur resisted lyricizing experience, partly as a response to the problem of poeticizing oppression. She also felt her writing should take a revolutionary form presumably divorced from bourgeois forms. Some 1930s Marxists considered unembellished prose an act of good faith, a break from bourgeois writing, and regarded stylistic experimentation suspiciously. "Corn Village," however, subverts the Party aesthetic. Like "Annunciation," it is less a short story than an evocative prose poem, a vortex of incident, image, and symbol. Moreover, the didacticism evident in her "official" literature is noticeably absent from the text, while it acknowledges the complexity of "the people," who were often romanticized in Party—and in Le Sueur's own—discourse.

"Corn Village" is not constrained by the limited understanding of ideology that characterizes much of proletarian realism and reportage. For example, in Le Sueur's "I Was Marching," ideology is seen as merely a superstructure produced by an economic base, a false consciousness obscuring society's "real" structures. In contrast, ideology pervades "Corn Village," prefiguring the more current understanding of ideology as the way in which we actively but unconsciously perform our roles within the social totality. The story supports Antonio Gramsci's notion of dominance and subordination as a "whole lived social process," saturating even the most private areas of our lives and consciousness. If we accept Wendell Berry's definition of regionalism as "local life aware of itself" (975), "Corn Village" qualifies as an extraordinary piece of regionalist writing precisely *because* Le Sueur adopts the double consciousness and the oscillation between complicity and critique that "The Fetish of Being Outside" condemns as neither possible nor desirable for the radical writer. Le Sueur resides at once within the corn village culture and outside it, negotiating difference and sameness with divided loyalty and consciousness.

This text seems as authentic as it does, I suspect, largely because it examines Le Sueur's own experience. She chronicled the lives of other oppressed people, sometimes at the expense of exploring her own oppression as a middle-class woman and a member of the male-dominated Communist Party. "I don't know how to write about women. I feel like I have to learn to write the final book about myself as a woman," Le Sueur has said, even though she has been writing about women for over seventy-five years, ever since she first recorded bits of conversation while hiding under the quilting frame as a ten-year-old (interview). Yet we sense that in "Corn Village" Le Sueur's untold story begins to emerge.

Le Sueur's motives for adopting the working class as her literary milieu were overdetermined: surely a strong sense of justice and collective responsibility sparked her concern; she also disliked the strains of ennui, nihilism, and self-absorption in twentieth-century American literature; and she was influenced by the Party's focus during the Third Period on the proletariat as the key to overturning capitalism and by its contradictory attitudes toward women. As a whole, Le Sueur's treatment of the working class contributes to American literature and social history a valuable record of people whose lives have rarely been chronicled. Yet in such pieces as "Our Fathers," "Annunciation," and "Corn Village," an unofficial Meridel Le

Sueur appears, moving toward the oracular voice she sought but did not achieve in her "official" proletarian literature.

We can understand why demarcations seemed clear in the midst of the sharpening class struggle that accompanied the economic crisis in the 1930s. However, we have moved beyond the 1930s Marxist assumptions about working-class literature that place a resistance culture in binary opposition to bourgeois culture. Working-class literature is, at best, a sub-species of bourgeois literature, just as any culture of resistance remains, for the historical moment, a subspecies of bourgeois culture. Leftist criticism must try to account for the conscious and unconscious movement of working-class literature between marginality and inclusion, and it must view working-class literature relationally, gauging which of its forms oppose, which strategically adopt, and which unconsciously borrow the forms of "high" and mass culture. As we have seen, some of Le Sueur's own texts subvert the reductive opposition she established in "The Fetish of Being Outside" and support a more contemporary view of how we might usefully approach elements of a resistance culture. In "Our Fathers," "Annunciation," and "Corn Village," we see that discourse lives, as Mikhail Bakhtin suggests, on the boundary between its own and an alien context and that one culture "can define itself only by becoming imbricated in another" (Klancher, *Making* 103).

This complex intersection of feminism and the Old Left is also refracted in illuminating ways in Tillie Olsen's literary texts. Olsen's career includes two periods: all of her 1930s publications appeared in 1934, when she was only twenty-one; her "second period" dates from 1953, when the youngest of her four children entered school. Olsen's writing from the 1930s, like Le Sueur's, is marked by a tension between official and unofficial views of proletarian literature.

Olsen's writing from her two "periods" also represents two distinct types of oppositional form. Whereas the content of her 1930s literature is culturally and politically agitational, the discursive model has been borrowed, unmodified, from dominant modes of representation, taking the processes of signification for granted. These texts foreground the "message" rather than the production of meaning. Openly tendentious, Olsen's published 1930s writing is marked by an uncontested authorial voice and a completion and closure of meaning. In what Bakhtin terms monological discourse, these texts directly address the reader, anticipating responses and deflecting objections; meanings are seen as delivered, unchanged, from source to recipient. In the tradition of muckraking, social journalism, and reportage, Olsen's writing during this period, like Le Sueur's "Women on the Breadlines" and "I Was Marching," was intended to spark political resistance. At the same time, however, its didacticism, like that of Le Sueur's more tendentious writing, actually limits involvement by undercutting the reader's role as an active producer of meaning. As we will see, Olsen's *Silences* (1978), on the other hand, challenges the ideological character of the signification process itself. The production of meaning, as much as the message, becomes a site for dissent.

Olsen's birth was not recorded, although she has determined that she was born either near Mead or in Omaha, Nebraska, in either 1912 or 1913. Her parents, Samuel and Ida Lerner, were Jewish working-class immigrants who had participated in the abortive 1905 Russian Revolution. Although the family was poor, the Lerners' active socialism added a rich dimension to Tillie's childhood. She became politically active in her mid-teens as a writer of skits and musicals for the Young People's Socialist League. In 1931, at eighteen, she joined the Young Communist League, the youth organization of the Communist Party.

Olsen did not share the problem of the enlightened middle-class writer who, like Meridel Le Sueur, contemplated in the 1930s how best to identify with the working class. Hers was a different dilemma: whereas our social system defines Olsen's intellectual and professional aspirations as middle class, her personal and emotional identification remained, profoundly, with the class of her birth. Olsen appreciated the power of class origin, which Le Sueur unintentionally trivialized in "The Fetish of Being Outside." Both intellectual pursuits and the struggles of working people to improve their lives were crucially important to Olsen, and how to live in both worlds remained her insoluble riddle.

Like Meridel Le Sueur, Olsen recognizes the debt she owes the Communist Left for nurturing her writing. The Party provided publishing outlets for beginning writers and established the John Reed clubs specifically to encourage unknown young writers and artists. Although Olsen was occasionally obliged during her years as an activist to write short pieces "on demand" for political events, her 1934 publications were not consciously written to accommodate the Party literary credo. Olsen was well aware that proletarian realism was "the standard that was set . . . by the leading columnists and polemicists" of the *New Masses*, which she read "faithfully—sometimes lovingly, sometimes angrily," but she insists that the Party literary line "did not touch" her (interviews).[3] Nevertheless, Olsen's published writing in 1934 is consistent with the tenets of proletarian realism, which the Communist Party promoted from 1930 to 1935. Her literature shows "the *real conflicts* of men and women who work for a living"; includes details of the workplace; and portrays the "horror and drabness in the Worker's life" while emphasizing that "not pessimism, but revolutionary elan will sweep this mess out of the world forever."[4]

That hopes were high among leftists in 1934 is evident from the notes about contributors when Olsen's short story "The Iron Throat" appeared in *Partisan Review*: "Tillie Lerner is at work on a novel of mining life. She is a 21-year-old Nebraska girl at present living in Stockton, California. Last year she took a leave of absence from the Young Communist League to produce a future citizen of Soviet America" (2). As Olsen began her writing career, workers started pouring into the available unions. Section 7A of the New Deal's National Industrial Recovery Act (1933) guaranteed workers the right to organize and bargain collectively, and many workers felt that "the tide of history had finally turned" (even though the NRA was skirted far more often than it was enforced by the establishment of "company" unions and was declared unconstitutional in 1935 [Green 143]). Three major strikes of 1934, the year in which all of Olsen's publications from the 1930s appeared, demonstrated the great potential for working-class militancy. In February, nine hundred National Guardsmen failed to break a massive picket of ten thousand workers from the community surrounding the Toledo Auto-Lite plant. The San Francisco maritime strike, which involved Olsen directly, began in May. And in July the Minneapolis teamsters strike, chronicled in Le Sueur's "I Was Marching," closed down the trucking industry and tied up the entire city.

As one might expect, then, Olsen's 1930s publications are more polemical, more akin to orthodox proletarian literature than is her later writing. The two poems she published during the 1930s—"I Want You Women Up North To Know" and "There Is a Lesson"—are representative. In these poems Olsen consciously resists lyricizing experience. She works in the muckraking and reportage tradition, wanting her readers "to see and feel the facts"—to *"experience"*—oppression's iron heel (Hicks et al. 211). The source of the discomfort that these poems cause for readers is, however, ambiguous. While the texts succeed in forcing us to confront oppressive working conditions in the United States and the rise of fascism in Europe, they are also unsettling because their exhortatory language preempts our emotional and moral responses. Marked by closure, the poems resist a reader's collaboration in constructing meaning. This earlier writing is marked by a didacticism, an "us/them" opposition, and an "official certainty" absent from the later period. Olsen's 1934 publications respond soberly to grave historical conditions and buoyantly to a working class that

was on the move. These texts deal less with the complexity of consciousness and more with the economic causes of oppression than do her more
recent works.

As Deborah Rosenfelt points out, however, this tension between discursive models is already apparent in *Yonnondio*, which Olsen began in 1932
at age nineteen (389–99). The novel, which provides a bridge formally and
politically between Olsen's 1934 literature and her more recent writing,
was her most important literary effort during the 1930s. Olsen completed
the first four chapters, or almost half, of the novel before regretfully abandoning it after the birth of her second child in 1937. In 1972–73, Olsen
completed *Yonnondio* "in arduous partnership" with "that long ago young
writer." The first four chapters, in final or near-final form, presented only
minor problems. The succeeding pages, which became four more chapters, were increasingly difficult to reconstruct. "But it is all the old manu-
scripts—no rewriting, no new writing," Olsen explains in a note appended to the novel. She felt that she "didn't have any right" to revise what "that
long ago young writer" had intended for print (interview). *Yonnondio*, then,
is a cultural product more of the 1930s, when it was written, than of the
1970s, when it was published. Varying tendencies coexist uneasily in the
text (some elements adhere to the tenets of proletarian realism, while other
elements subvert them), indicating Olsen's increasing ambivalence about
the Party aesthetic, as Rosenfelt suggests. But this tension also hints at
fundamental problems within the 1930s Communist Party and Marxism
itself.

Yonnondio confronts one of the differences within the working class that
the 1930s Communist Party minimized—the divisive effects of sexism. At
a time when Avram Landy, representing Party leadership, denied "any
conceivable antagonism" between working-class women and men, the
novel implicitly emphasizes the way in which the sexual division of labor
militates against working-class unity (Shaffer 86). While Jim Holbrook
descends into "the iron throat" of a Wyoming coal mine, Anna Holbrook,
lacking the barest essentials, struggles to care for their growing family. A
psychic division of labor accompanies the material one. Anna frets that her
children will go uneducated and does not dismiss a friend's wish that their
daughters enter convents rather than live in poverty and bear more children "to get their heads blowed off in the mine." Jim, on the other hand,
wonders "what other earthly use can a woman have" except childbearing.
As a man, he must never reveal his fear of the mine, and when Anna push-
es him to consider its dangers, he tells her, "Quit you woman's blabbin"
(10). The novel depicts Jim and Anna taunting one another and his aban-

doning the family for days at a time. Jim "struck Anna too often to remember" and, at one point, raped her while their young daughter, Mazie, listened in terror (15).

Since tensions between Anna and Jim ease considerably during their one brief period of relative prosperity, *Yonnondio* implies that gender-based antagonisms are related in a simple cause-and-effect way to economic oppression. According to the prevailing view of 1930s Party members, a socialist revolution would sweep away sexual oppression in its wake (one *Daily Worker* headline proclaimed about the Soviet Union, "All [Sex] Inequality Abolished by the October Revolution"), and Party women tended to defer their hopes for a feminist future.[5] Nevertheless, whatever Olsen's intention at the time, *Yonnondio* provides evidence that the social construction of gender is an entrenched, unconsciously reproduced phenomenon that will not overturn itself simply by "tailing" a transformation in economic relations.

The novel includes four didactic intrusions by an omniscient narrator, separated typographically from the text, which contain several conventions of proletarian literature. One such passage appears after an explosion occurs at the mine. While miners' families wait anxiously for survivors to emerge and for bodies to be dug out, the editorial voice, like a Greek chorus, interjects, "And could you not make a cameo of this and pin it onto your aesthetic hearts? So sharp it is, so clear, so classic. The shattered dusk, the mountain of culm, the tipple; clean lines, bare beauty—and carved against them, dwarfed by the vastness of night and the towering tipple, these black figures with bowed heads, waiting, waiting. Surely it is classical enough for you—the Greek marble of the women, the simple, flowing lines of sorrow, carved so rigid and eternal" (30). This interjection attacks formalism, which elevates aesthetic concerns over sociopolitical ones. The standard call to revolution, in the form of an imaginary letter threatening the mining company, occurs later in this passage: "*Dear Company. . . . Please issue a statement; quick, or they start to batter through with the fists of strike, with the pickax of revolution*" (31). Three of the novel's four interpolations echo this battle cry, and a reference to Marx, common in proletarian novels, functions as a refrain in the fourth insertion ("nothing to sell but his labor power" [77–78]). Olsen views her art as pedagogical; "I was writing the reason why we have to have a revolution," she has said about *Yonnondio*. She did not trust the novel, if stripped of these didactic passages, fully to affect her readers, to make them "feel the impact," and to indicate the causes and remedies for the Holbrooks' misery, which they themselves perceive and articulate only in a limited way (interview). Olsen may also have been unconsciously adhering to one of the principles of proletarian realism, which as defined by Edwin Seaver in the *New Masses*, demanded that the writer "take a conscious part in leading the reader through the maze of history toward Socialism and the classless society" (23–24).

These four passages interrupt *Yonnondio*'s narrative much as Bertolt Brecht's *Verfremdung* disrupts his plays (although, since Brecht's literary work had not yet been translated into English and circulated in the United States, it is unlikely that Olsen knew that she was employing a Brechtian device). Such intrusions counter traditional realism, in which the present social order appears as natural, static, and immutable rather than contradictory, discontinuous, and, potentially, the object of revolutionary change. The interpolations also announce the gulf between art and reality, which realism effaces but Brecht's epic theater foregrounds. Conventional realism assumes the reader to be a passive recipient of representation, whereas Brecht and Olsen attempted to jolt the audience/reader into an active spectatorship that may lead to questioning the status quo.

However, Olsen's Brechtian intrusions support as well as undermine the classical ideologies of representation. Although the interpolations are politically and culturally oppositional, they draw upon a culturally dominant form—the dualistic rhetorical model of a message conveyed, unchanged, from an authoritative source to a compliant recipient. They announce themselves as the official "reading" of the novel, attempting to impose a closure of meaning on the reader. These editorial passages, then, like Olsen's 1934 publications, at once attempt to activate and to constrain the reader.[6]

The editorial voice of the indented passages is joined by those of three other narrators—Mazie, Anna, and Jim. Together these four constitute a collective protagonist, which Rachel Blau DuPlessis defines as a way of structuring a text so that neither an individual nor a heterosexual couple dominates the novel (163). One of the progressive effects of the collective protagonist is a merging of the public and private spheres that a patriarchal and capitalist system would have us keep separate. The use of a collective protagonist also implies that problems bourgeois culture would have us view "as individually based are, in fact, social in cause and in cure" (179–80). Since form is profoundly dependent on historical change, the best working-class literature can do is prefigure postindividual forms in some diminished, provisional sense, and *Yonnondio*'s four narrators represent an attempt to move beyond an individual point of view toward more collective forms—in narrative structures suggesting possibilities for social change.

The presence of a feminist voice in the novel also pluralizes the text. Writing over thirty years before the existence of the women's movement that would welcome *Yonnondio*'s publication in 1974, Olsen countered Communist Party literary prescriptions by focusing on domestic labor and the point of *re*production. Her unsentimental presentation of institutionalized motherhood has forced on the American literary canon a subject hitherto forbidden except in idealized form.

What Jim derisively calls "woman's blabbin'," in a variety of forms, is central to the novel. Mazie, with her special sensitivity to language, lists the words she knows, tells her brother stories, recites poetry. Moreover, she vocally opposes the sexual division of labor, even though neither of her parents does: "Why is it always me that has to help? How come Will gets to play?" (142). In the penultimate, packing-house scene, it is a woman "who [has] a need to put things into words," who chants the workers' plight in kitchen imagery (144). And when Mis' Kryckski takes care of the children after Anna's miscarriage, she sings them "not lullabies, but songs of her own country in which her fierce anger flashed" (90). The novel concludes with baby Bess announcing and celebrating her emerging identity by banging a fruit jar lid.

As any other text of working-class literature, *Yonnondio* remains subsumed by bourgeois form and content. However, it subverts elements not only of bourgeois culture but also of the 1930s Communist Party and orthodox Marxism. While *Yonnondio*'s critique of capitalism is foregrounded and full-blown, its prescient questioning of some tendencies of Party politics and orthodox Marxism—such as productivism and its concomitant privileging of the industrial worker; the separation of public and private spheres; the subordination of gender-related issues to those of class; and the teleological notion that revolutionary struggles will achieve an ideal, static "state"—is only half realized. In *Yonnondio* Olsen strains away from her early 1930s "official" proletarian literature, her evolving lyrical style lending itself readily to the novel's two major themes—working-class familial relations and the complexity, susceptibility, and potential of human consciousness. Despite the Party's minimizing consciousness as a site for ideological struggle, *Yonnondio* suggests that "one of the major powers of the muted is to think against the current" (DuPlessis 196). "Reader, it was not to have ended here," Olsen laments in the note appended to the unfinished novel. On the contrary, in *Yonnondio* Olsen has written "beyond the ending."[7]

While Olsen's "message" continues to be oppositional in her more recent writing, the rhetorical model is more dialogic than that of her 1930s publications, challenging the signification process itself. Culturally main-stream modes of representation lend themselves to forms of domination that can be countered by alternative modes of representation, such as those prefigured in *Silences* (1978), a nonfiction book that catalogues impediments to a writer's productivity. By now a classic of American feminism, *Silences* employs the strategy of a pluralized text, suggesting one form that a literature of resistance might take.

When the authorial voice is granted exceptional status, writers appear to need no complement, as Bakhtin has noted; the natural state of being appears to be solitary, independent of others. *Silences*, however, subverts unicentered discourse and the concept of textual ownership, affirming the reader not as an object but as another subject, a reciprocal "thou." Whereas dominant discursive practices take for granted that the act of reading will be a *subjection to* a fixed meaning, *Silences* offers an alternative way of conceiving the writer's and reader's roles: it foregrounds the process by which it constructs meaning, disrupting and activating its reader-subjects while subverting authorial control. *Silences* implicitly acknowledges that in the act of reading, reader-subjects engage in an active, complex, and creative process not unlike that of writing. An anticonjurer, Olsen refuses to lull her readers with the illusion of mimetic representation. The reader is no longer simply a consumer, a passive receiver of a representation. In the tradition of Brecht's theater and Jean-Luc Godard's cinematic montage, *Silences* turns readers into collaborators.

The first half of the book consists of three essays by Olsen; the second half is a montage, including excerpts from writers' diaries and letters spliced together with Olsen's headings and commentary. Crossing gender, race, and class boundaries, Olsen quotes male and female, white and black, known and unknown writers. Through frequent citations, *Silences* undercuts the conventional rhetorical model of speaker/message/listener by adding not only a third voice but dozens of voices. Both writer and reader must address themselves not simply to each other but also to the extra, complicating party or parties. This third (or fourth, fifth, etc.) speaker in the language act changes the discourse from a dualistic exchange to a complex social one (Klancher, "Dialogue" 4).

Olsen unmasks the fact of work and production, one of the keys to historical thinking and a "carefully concealed" secret of a commodity culture, which by definition effaces the signs of work on its products (Jameson 407). *Silences* demystifies book-as-final-product by recalling its own often precarious progression from silence to speech (two of the three essays evolved from unwritten talks) to writing. More important, *Silences* unmasks the hidden labor that often supports literary production, exposing the class and patriarchal character of the structures in which literature is produced. Olsen foregrounds domestic labor—especially child care, which may be the most "naturalized," invisible labor of all, the secret *most* carefully concealed.

In Olsen's oeuvre we see a shift from one form of cultural resistance to another. This was not a deliberate, conscious shift. "I never *thought* in terms of form," Olsen insists, her voice resonating. "I thought in terms of *content*. When people ask me about form, I'm still that way. . . . I don't *think* in terms of form" (interview). Form is not, however, the initial mold from which a writer starts but the final articulation of content (Jameson 328–29). *Silences'* democratic content realizes itself in its multivocal form, resisting the present social order at the level of narrative. Olsen may not be conscious of a relationship between her own antiauthoritarian impulses and the way she constructs a text; and when she has "completed" a work, she may not be aware of all of its implications, especially its formal ones. A writer's intention, after all, does not circumscribe the range of meanings evoked by a text. That Olsen may not be fully aware of her own achievement does not lessen it, however. The form of Olsen's later texts suggests, as Virginia Woolf's "Leaning Tower" proclaims, "Literature is no one's private ground; literature is common ground. . . . Let us trespass freely and fearlessly and find our own way for ourselves" (125).

Le Sueur and Olsen asserted their difference within the forced unity and closure of not only the dominant culture but also an androcentric Communist Party, providing a wedge into problems that have historically plagued the Left. In so doing, they prefigured a younger generation of feminists. Politically and culturally, Le Sueur's and Olsen's texts represent what Raymond Williams describes as a "*pre-emergence*, active and pressing but not yet fully articulated, rather than the evident emergence which could be more confidently named" (126).

Their texts resist, for example, orthodox Marxism's reduction of the social terrain's heterogeneity to centers and margins, such as males in the industrial workplace and women in the domestic sphere. At a time when the "proper" subjects and settings of working-class literature were workers waging strikes in the factory, *Yonnondio*, for example, focused largely on working-class familial relations and ended with an image of a baby realizing her power by gleefully banging a fruit jar lid.

Against the transcendent Party, Le Sueur and Olsen asserted the importance of their own concrete experience. They implicitly questioned Marxism's primacy-of-production theory, which defines production as *the* distinctively human activity. This theory encodes activities carried out in the home, to which women have historically been disproportionately consigned, as less valuable than men's activities outside it. When Michael Gold challenged proletarian writers to "write with the courage of [their] own experience," addressing himself to machinists, sailors, ditch-diggers, and hoboes, he thought he was speaking broadly, inclusively (5). Ironically, it is as if both Le Sueur and Olsen took Gold at his word: their texts subvert the Party's productivism and sexism, legitimating the point of *repro*duction, work that Olsen terms "the maintenance of life" (*Silences* 217).

One critical element of this "maintenance of life" may be the crucible of the women's movement: responsibility for children. This issue has not been a priority for the movement because during the 1960s and 1970s many feminists forewent or delayed childbearing. With the 1980s baby boom, however, even the women the movement has most helped to advance, its educated professionals, have with a sense of déjà vu felt that old shock of sudden recognition, that familiar "click": equal professional opportunity collapses around the issue of who will take care of the kids. Olsen's and Le Sueur's literature illuminates the cracks in an idealized, good-housekeeping Comrade/Wife, a creature not unrelated to today's mythic Superwoman, who, politically mainstream or Left, can presumably "do it all." That more women than men have valued Le Sueur's and Olsen's iconoclasm reminds us that textual meaning, rather than being absolute, is a consequence of a reader-subject's being in a particular situation in the world.

The Communist Party U.S.A. was not a monolith; democratic centralism notwithstanding, the views and daily experience of rank-and-file women often differed from those of male Party bureaucrats, as Tillie Olsen and Meridel Le Sueur insist. And yet, despite valuable documentaries made during the 1970s and 1980s, such as *Union Maids, With Babies and Banners, The Life and Times of Rosie the Riveter,* and *Seeing Red,* the history of rank-and-file Party women remains largely unrecorded. Le Sueur's and Olsen's literature, and that of other radical and working-class women writers, constitutes an important part of that record. This literature suggests that a counterhegemony created by connecting many different forms of struggle—including those not primarily "public" and "economic" as well as those within "the fibres of the self and in the hard practical substance of effective and continuing relationships"—would lead to a more profound and compelling sense of revolutionary activity (Williams 212).

NOTES

This essay, with minor editorial changes, was originally published in *Left Politics and the Literary Profession*, ed. M. Bella Mirabella and Lennard J. Davis, © 1990 by Columbia University Press, and is reprinted with the permission of the publisher.

1. Lauter designated as members of the working class those who sell their labor for wages, have relatively little control over the nature or products of their work, and are not professionals or managers. He includes not only factory workers but also slaves, farm laborers, and some of those who work in the home.

2. In my dissertation, from which this essay derived, I made a distinction between what I termed Le Sueur's "official" and "unofficial" writing. Although the Communist Party U.S.A. promoted reportage in the early 1930s, I no longer see "official" and "unofficial" as distinct categories and do not employ them in my book *Better Red: The Writing and Resistance of Tillie Olsen and Meridel Le Sueur*. However, the book maintains this essay's argument that while Le Sueur's reportage resisted the dominant culture, other Le Sueur texts—such as *The Girl* and the three short stories considered here—subvert not only the dominant culture but elements of a patriarchal leftist subculture as well.

3. Interviews conducted by Constance Coiner, July 11–12, 1986, and by Deborah Rosenfelt, December 20, 1980. With Rosenfelt's permission, I have identified subsequent quotations from these two interviews parenthetically in the text, without distinguishing between them. I wish to thank Deborah Rosenfelt for generously allowing me to use her taped interview of Tillie Olsen to supplement my own. Rosenfelt's essay (see Works Cited), the touchstone for Olsen criticism, provides a wealth of biographical information about the writer. I am indebted to Le Sueur and Olsen for their permission to quote from taped interviews and for their legacy of courageous resistance.

4. These are some of the elements of proletarian (or socialist) realism outlined by Mike Gold in "Notes of the Month." Exemplar of a new proletarian tradition in American literature, Gold was from 1926 to 1932 one of the editors of the *New Masses*, a Communist Party journal. During the early 1930s Gold was "perhaps the best known Communist writer and critic" (Gilbert 119), and at the 1935 American Writers' Congress, he was hailed as "the best loved American revolutionary writer" (Rideout 168). Gold's classic proletarian novel *Jews without Money*, which has been translated into sixteen languages, went through eleven printings in the first year of its publication (1930) and six more by 1938.

5. This proclamation appeared September 2, 1935, as a secondary headline in an article credited only to "Irene" and titled "Legend of the 'Weaker Sex' Effectively Smashed by the Position of Women in the Soviet Union."

6. My analysis of these four editorial interpolations is significantly different in my book *Better Red*, which has a far more extensive discussion of them.

7. I have borrowed this phrase and concept from DuPlessis's *Writing beyond the Ending*, which defines "writing beyond the ending" as "the invention of strategies that sever the narrative from formerly conventional structures of fiction and consciousness about women" (x). However, I believe that "strain away from" is often more accurate than "sever."

WORKS CITED

Anderson, Sherwood. "A Writer's Note." *New Masses*, August 1932, 10.

Berry, Wendell. "The Regional Motive." *Southern Review* 6 (Fall 1970): 972–77.

Coiner, Constance. *Better Red: The Writing and Resistance of Tillie Olsen and Meridel Le Sueur*. New York: Oxford University Press, 1995.

DuPlessis, Rachel Blau. *Writing beyond the Ending: Narrative Strategies of Twentieth-Century Women Writers*. Bloomington: Indiana University Press, 1985.

Eagleton, Terry. *Marxism and Literary Criticism*. Berkeley: University of California Press, 1976.

Gilbert, James Burkhart. *Writers and Partisans: A History of Literary Radicalism in America*. New York: John Wiley and Sons, 1968.

Gold, Michael. "Notes of the Month." *New Masses*, September 1930, 3–5.

Green, James R. *The World of the Worker: Labor in Twentieth-Century America*. New York: Hill and Wang, 1980.

Hicks, Granville, Michael Gold, Isidor Schneider, Joseph North, Paul Peters, and Alan Calmer, eds. *Proletarian Literature in the United States*. New York: International Publishers, 1935.

Inman, Will. "Meridel Le Sueur." *We Sing Our Struggle: A Tribute to Us All for Meridel Le Sueur*. Ed. Mary McAnally. Tulsa, Okla.: Cardinal Press, 1982. n.p.

Isserman, Maurice. *Which Side Were You On? The American Communist Party during the Second World War*. Midddletown: Wesleyan University Press, 1982.

Jameson, Fredric. *Marxism and Form*. Princeton, N.J.: Princeton University Press, 1971.

Klancher, Jon. "Dialogue from Rhetoric to Literature: Bakhtin's Social Text." Paper presented at the College Composition and Communication Convention in New Orleans, 1986.

———. *The Making of English Reading Audiences, 1790–1832*. Madison: Wisconsin University Press, 1986.

Lauter, Paul. "Working-Class Women's Literature: An Introduction to Study." *Radical Teacher* 15 (December 1979): 16–26.

Le Sueur, Meridel. "The Ancient People and the Newly Come." *Growing Up in Minnesota: Ten Writers Remember Their Childhoods*. Ed. Chester C. Anderson. Minneapolis: University of Minnesota Press, 1976.

——. "Annunciation." *Salute to Spring*. By Le Sueur. New York: International Publishers, 1977. 75–89.

——. "Corn Village." *Salute to Spring*. By Le Sueur. 1940. New York: International Publishers, 1977. 9–25.

——. "The Fetish of Being Outside." *New Masses*, February 26, 1935, 23.

——. Interview conducted by Constance Coiner, March 26, 1985.

——. *Ripening: Selected Works*. Ed. Elaine Hedges. Old Westbury, N.Y.: Feminist Press, 1982.

Olsen, Tillie [Lerner]. Interviews conducted by Constance Coiner, July 11–12, 1986; and by Deborah Rosenfelt, December 20, 1980.

——. "The Iron Throat." *Partisan Review*, April–May 1934, 2–9.

——. "I Want You Women Up North to Know." *Partisan*, March 1934, 4.

——. *Silences*. New York: Dell, 1978.

——. "There Is a Lesson." *Daily Worker*, March 5, 1934, 7.

——. *Yonnondio: From the Thirties*. New York: Dell, 1974.

Rideout, Walter. *The Radical Novel in the United States, 1900–1954*. New York: Hill and Wang, 1956.

Rosenfelt, Deborah. "From the Thirties: Tillie Olsen and the Radical Tradition." *Feminist Studies* 7 (Fall 1981): 371–406.

Russ, Joanna. *The Female Man*. New York: Bantam, 1973.

Seaver, Edwin. "Socialist Realism." *New Masses*, October 22, 1935, 23–24.

Shaffer, Robert. "Women and the Communist Party, USA, 1930–1940." *Socialist Review* 9 (May–June 1979): 73–118.

Williams, Raymond. *Marxism and Literature*. Oxford: Oxford University Press, 1977.

Woolf, Virginia. "The Leaning Tower." *The Moment and Other Essays*. By Woolf. London: Hogarth, 1952. 105–25.

JESSICA KIMBALL PRINTZ

8

TRACING THE
FAULT LINES OF
THE RADICAL
FEMALE SUBJECT:
GRACE LUMPKIN'S
THE WEDDING

Although Grace Lumpkin was one of the most prominent female activists affiliated with the radical movement during the early 1930s, none of the reviewers of her third novel, *The Wedding* (1939), considered it part of the genre of revolutionary fiction. Lumpkin's first novel, *To Make My Bread* (1932), won the Gorky Prize for the best labor novel of the year. Her second novel, *A Sign for Cain* (1935), achieved modest critical success as a spirited, if stylistically flawed, piece of "communistic propaganda" (Daniels 10). *The Wedding*, however, only elicited a litany of patronizing—albeit positive— diminutives from reviewers, who embraced it as a quaint Austenesque comedy of manners, "the soberest little novel that ever carried its tongue in its cheek" (Wallace 7).[1] The few reviews of the novel that even mention the author's previous work do so only to assert the novel's complete dissociation from her former thematic and ideological concerns. One reviewer hails Lumpkin for "turning from propaganda to people" (Pruette 10), while another calls the novel a "slight simple story as far from the subject of her first book as a picket line is from a pulpit" ("Bride's Strike" 7). The paltry secondary references to this work follow suit in labeling the novel as a delightful "retreat from the acerbity of social propaganda to social comedy" (Mellard 353).[2] Despite the praise this apparent "retreat" seems to have garnered, the novel's virtual neglect by scholars

of radical fiction and southern fiction alike suggests that such an evaluation of the novel helped relegate it to an obscurity that even its recent
(1976) reprinting in the Southern Illinois University Press's Lost American
Fiction Series has not been able to dispel.

This essay reclaims *The Wedding* as a significant text for 1930s criticism,
not as a charming period piece but as a profoundly disturbing example of
women's "dystopian radical fiction." Like the more familiar representatives
of the genre, Tess Slesinger's *The Unpossessed* (1934) and Josephine Herbst's *Rope of Gold* (1939), Lumpkin's novel explores the themes of middle-
class decay and revolutionary aspirations, fleshing out a dystopian world
through the evolving subjectivities of middle-class female characters.
Nevertheless, *The Wedding* takes the idea of dystopia one step further by
eradicating the possibility of a gender-, race-, and class-conscious bourgeois
female subjectivity. In Slesinger's and Herbst's novels, already radicalized
middle-class female characters struggle to make sense of the peculiar combination of sexual oppression and class privilege that defines their social
position and affects their revolutionary capacity.[3] Through the parallel
stories of a reluctant bride, Jennie Middleton, and her younger sister,
Susan, however, Lumpkin bifurcates what would be the ideal narrative of
the development of a radical female middle-class subject into two separate narratives: a protofeminist one,[4] crippled by its myopia about class and
race relations, and a potentially revolutionary one, rendered ineffective by
a lack of gender awareness. This essay demonstrates that it is precisely the
absence of a radical female intellectual character in *The Wedding* that
marks the novel as part of the subgenre of women's dystopian radical
fiction. Through the traces of this absent character found in Jennie's and
Susan's unconnected, fragmented, and ultimately impotent lines of development, Lumpkin poignantly and self-consciously questions the radical
potential of the middle-class female subject.

"STRANDED IN A MIDDLE PLACE": THE ARRESTED DEVELOPMENT OF JENNIE MIDDLETON'S FEMINISM

Given the proverbial nature of the novel's central plot device, a bride's
sudden case of "cold feet," it is not surprising that most of the "official"
readers of *The Wedding* have mistaken it for another southern comedy of
manners. Except for brief excursions into memory, the entire action of the
novel takes place in the twenty-four hours before the wedding. Jennie
Middleton, the eldest daughter of a pedigreed yet postbellum-impover-

ished southern family, is engaged to Dr. Shelley Gregg, a self-made man of humble origins. For the sleepy town of Lexington, Georgia, the wedding is the event of the season, but it does not come off without a hitch. The evening before the ceremony, Jennie and Dr. Gregg have a disagreement about the furnishings for their new home that escalates into a shouting match. The next morning Jennie announces she will not go through with the wedding; her refusal sends shock waves throughout the wedding party. Hoping to cajole and reason her out of her stubbornness, Dr. Gregg's best man, Dr. Greve, escorts Jennie and Susan on a visit to Old Rosin, a former servant of the Middletons now dying of tuberculosis in the penitentiary. After the visit, Dr. Greve takes Jennie back to the hotel where her fiancé is staying and ultimately engineers a reconciliation. Meanwhile the father of the bride, Mr. Middleton, quarrels with Dr. Grant, the new "Yankee" minister of the church, about the use of Confederate memorabilia in the ceremony and agonizes over his finances. Outraged at the news of his daughter's imprudent excursion with the best man, Middleton arrives at the hotel just in time to witness the reconciliation. Jennie returns home to regroup the harried bridesmaids and rehearse the last-minute changes in the ceremony. Like most novels typed as "romantic comedies," the novel concludes with the wedding ceremony.

Even if one ignores the subplot involving the development of Susan Middleton's radical consciousness, a reading of the novel as a slight or frivolous comedy cannot do justice to its intricate portrait of Jennie's peculiar predicament as a postbellum "southern lady," her complex awareness of the gendered dimension of her situation, or her equally complex shortcomings. In refusing to marry her fiancé, Jennie enacts her own private rebellion and asserts a subjectivity apart from and resistant to the dominant perceptions of southern womanhood. Nevertheless, Jennie's desire to be an object of male desire and contestation profoundly compromises this claim and ultimately makes her resistance impossible to sustain. Forever trapped in the insular world of her sometimes protofeminist, sometimes self-defeating narrative of personal desire, Jennie remains unreflective about the privileges that her own class and race afford her. She remains oblivious to marriage as the instrument of a political state or economic order rather than just an instrument of sexual oppression. Lumpkin's sympathetic portrayal of her heroine's limitations suggests that without incorporating a more inclusive historical perspective, narratives of female desire and the feminist impulses they engender and rely on are destined to self-destruct.

In exposing the contradictions that accumulate around Jennie as a post-

bellum "southern lady," *The Wedding* draws on the traditional concerns
of the southern women's domestic novel, even as it lends itself to interpretation by feminist theories of female desire and subjectivity. In tracing
the development of this domestic genre from the sentimental tomes of
Augusta Jane Evans to Margaret Mitchell's best-seller, Anne Goodwyn
Jones suggests that the southern woman in female-authored fiction and
in real life often "found herself at the center of the paradoxes that informed
her own southern culture, yet she had experience and a point of view that
diverged in some ways sharply from those of her southern white father,
husband, brother, and son. . . . She was torn, too, between her love for the
men and boys central in her life, her pride at what she symbolized for
them, and her perhaps buried anger at the repressiveness implicit in their
reverence and the fear implicit in their habit of commanding her" (24).
As a young "lady" in the South of 1909, pledged to be married to a "self-
made" man in a church presided over by a northern minister, Jennie finds
herself at a cultural nexus. Her wedding functions as a transaction between
men who represent the competing discourses of the "old" and the "new"
and the oppositional sectional allegiances in the ever-present history of the
Civil War.[5] Yet even as her wedding serves as the contested ground for
masculine discourses of power, Jennie also feels trapped in her own peculiar version of the old/new binary and sectional cleavages. Unlike the
men's identities, which appear in a stable, metonymic relationship with
the "sides" men take up in various debates, Jennie's identity seems perpetually created "in the fissure of a radical split" set up by these binaries.[6]
Like the narratives of desire Jones discusses, Jennie's narrative is fractured.
It mirrors the division she experiences between the "old" and the "new,"
between southern allegiances and visions of northern independence.

On the one hand, Jennie wants to see herself as the Confederate veterans have envisioned her: as "the fairest ornament of the South" (41), "the
daughter of the Veterans," and "a symbol of their past" (292). By embracing her status as an object of male veneration and as an emblem of a romanticized version of southern history, Jennie embodies the "old" in a way
all too familiar to contemporary theorists of female subjectivity under
"patriarchal" systems. According to the French feminist Luce Irigaray, such
systems treat women as, and encourage them to desire to be, objects of
male discourse and exchange rather than subjects. In accepting and fulfilling her assigned role as the magnolia blossom of the Confederacy, Jennie, like the women in Irigaray's market model of patriarchy, "assure[s] the
possibility of the use and circulation of the symbolic" by her own "non-
access to the symbolic" (Irigaray 189). So, too, Jennie's intrafamilial rela-

tionships confirm the toll the system can take on women's relationships with each other. As daddy's little girl, Jennie aspires to be her father's ally in domestic disputes, confirming his opinions of her mother's shortcomings and lending herself to his expectations of a listening, complicit female sensibility. She thinks of their "special relationship" (78) as a "little conspiracy" that makes her "feel that she and her father were in some way superior to the mother" (67). Jennie thus participates in what Irigaray sees as patriarchy's devaluation and impoverishment of women's bonds with one another: "For uprooted from their 'nature,' [women] no longer relate to each other except in terms of what they represent in men's desire and according to the 'forms' that this imposes on them. Among themselves, they are separated by his speculations" and required to "maintain" themselves as "object[s] of desire" (188).

On the other hand, Jennie's experiences as a "new" woman of the South, a young woman who pursues an education and obtains a modicum of financial and emotional independence, give her a desire to live beyond the confines of the South and its traditional strictures on womanhood. Jennie "leave[s] home to earn her own living" (19) and becomes a "brilliant student" (21) at a New York acting school. She then returns to the South with a stable teaching job in "dramatic expression" (21) and a newfound awareness of the narrowness of the position that southern society allows her; in effect, she becomes a kind of protofeminist "female intellectual." Although Jennie is certainly not a "radicalized" intellectual, the link between her bifurcated narrative of desire and her ambivalence toward motherhood confirms Paula Rabinowitz's assessment of the radical female intellectual's relationship with that institution: "The trope of maternity, which reembodied the working-class woman within narrative and within history, cannot contain the female intellectual and thus fractures her narrative" (139). So Jennie tells her father, "'You want me to be like mother, sacrificing myself like her. You are old and think in an old-fashioned way. You don't understand. I don't want to be timid and just a mother. Of course I want to be a mother, but not that only . . . I want to be a person'" (80, ellipses in original). In part, Jennie's private rebellion originates in the inadequacies of that traditional role for women, its inability to encompass or express the range of Jennie's desires and subjectivity— her personhood. The indeterminacy of this term, along with the presence of a literal lacuna in the text itself (formed by the ellipses), foreshadow the problematic nature of female desire and the evanescence of its feminist impulses in subsequent pages.

Although Jennie verbalizes her refusal to marry Dr. Gregg as a refusal "'to be a slave . . . to a man who is coarse'" (80, ellipses in original), her private analysis of her situation as a bride-to-be shows that the essential quarrel runs much deeper than mere personal antagonism or frivolous disputes about furniture. It is a quarrel with the system itself and the sexist constructions of female identity and desire that it produces and enforces. Jennie's refusal to marry Dr. Gregg thus gives her a site of resistance, a vantage point from which to view her own present and pending oppression, and allows for the possibility of a female subjectivity in excess of the forms that southern society imposes on her. In her imagined "dungeon" of self-awareness (143), Jennie realizes that the bargain-reconciliation Dr. Greve suggests—that she accept Dr. Gregg as he is because he agrees to take her as she is—is no bargain at all because the man necessarily does all the taking: "It was stupid for anyone to say this. Because she was giving up her individual life and so her energies must be used for her husband. And she must push him on to do more because he would be her ambition also. He must carry out her life in the world as well as his own. He must because she was giving up her individual life for him" (202). Just as the women in Irigaray's market model are required to "yield" to men "their natural and social value as a locus of imprints, marks, and mirage of his activity" (Irigaray 177), Jennie will be required to submerge her ambitions, her desires, her very self in the doctor's "activity." The repetitive structure and diction of this passage underscores its theme of loss, the loss of independence and "life" that marriage represents for women, and the lack of choice it predicates for Jennie in the future. However, the initial line allows the reader and Jennie to break away from the passage's compulsory language of "musts"; it offers a kind of respite from the circularity of the passage that follows and signifies Jennie's (temporary) ability to distance herself from that depressing future she is pressured to "choose."

Still, the way Jennie exposes the whole framework of sexist assumptions that define this future as a viable or even desirable choice for women leaves her in an impossible situation. Ironically, her protofeminist refusal to choose the life that marriage has mapped out for her threatens to deprive her of any "life" at all. As inspiring and self-affirming as her site of resistance may be, it ends up confirming Jennie's place in a no-win situation, in a no-man's-land of desire: "The sound of [her father's] feet going down the hall and the stairs seemed to represent the steps of her old life going away leaving her alone stranded in a middle place where she had neither the old nor the new, but some indeterminate position which was empty of all joy and hope. And it was intolerable to her to be in this neutral position" (83). Whereas earlier in the novel Jennie's complication of the old/new binary seems to offer her a subjectivity beyond the roles made available to her in society, here the binary assumes an overwhelmingly repressive force over Jennie's interpretation of her situation. Why is it that Jennie is compelled by the "intolerable circumstances" of her life into a "private rebellion,"[7] only to deem such a rebellion itself "intolerable"? Given the gendered dynamics of power in Jennie's subsequent capitulation, her resistance may be impossible to sustain precisely because of what Catharine MacKinnon calls the essentially self-compromising and complicitous nature of female desire:[8] "sexual desire in women, at least in this culture, is socially constructed as that by which we come to want our own self-annihilation; that is, our subordination is eroticized in and as female — in fact, we get off on it, to a degree. This is our stake in the system that is not in our interest, our stake in the system that is killing us" (110). One can certainly debate the totalizing tendency of MacKinnon's argument.[9] Her effort to define women's "stake" in a system geared to their own oppression, however, proves valuable to understanding Jennie's final acquiescence.[10] In Lumpkin's novel, Jennie's "desire for self-annihilation" translates into a desire to maintain an illusion of power by subscribing to the roles of emotional creature and object of desire that men have given her. Because Jennie is unable to link her private torment to a greater understanding of oppression as a collective affair, her protofeminist impulses end up only making her feel completely isolated from others and alienated from any possibility of happiness. Crippled by a profound lack of awareness of her own position and the positions of others in a system of racial and economic injustice as well as sexism, Jennie ends up colluding with the systemic practices that oppress her just to obtain some modicum of "self." Her subjectivity thus becomes a site of hegemony as she exercises her "choice" to work within that system, to exist in its rules and share its blind spots, and to narrate the female subjectivity and desires that it cripples and confines. Jennie's need to feel power *within* such a system therefore tips the balance in favor of her acceptance of the wedding and destroys her feminist aspirations and any chance of her radicalization.

Within this sexist value system, the men of the novel perpetually attempt to define sexual difference as a dichotomy between reason and emotion. In the quarrel that precipitates Jennie's rebellion, Dr. Gregg thinks of the house that he has already furnished for his bride as a reasonable and practical gift and views Jennie's anger as the temper tantrum of "a child [that] would never grow up in her emotions" (46). Similarly, Mr. Middleton dismisses any chance of a rational discussion with his wife and daughter through a simple assertion of female histrionics: "'I won't have hysterical women about'" (64). When he goes to coerce Jennie into her marriage, Middleton reminds himself to behave as a cold, rational (male) thinker because "'women are more at home in emotion. They know instinctively what to do in that sphere while I am lost . . . lost. Emotion is a tyrant if not controlled by reason'" (76, ellipses in original). Despite the fact that the male characters often lament the affective control women have over them, emotional strength is virtually the only pretense of power that their value system affords and prizes in women; consequently, Jennie and other women in the novel cannot resist making the most of this "power." Their desires therefore often become synonymous with those that men construe as their "innate" qualities and desires. Jennie's perceptive analysis of her situation during her rebellion clearly reveals she is more than a bundle of nerves and raw feelings. Nevertheless, Jennie subsequently thinks she can find her own lifeline of desire only by becoming the emotional creature that men want; her desires are described as a dependency, an addiction to the feelings she inspires in men: "It was emotion which gave her greatest pleasure. She wanted emotion, and if she could not have it in love, she wanted it in anger. Emotion made her feel she was living, and she could not live without it" (266).

Jennie's proclivity for passionate performance not only complements her talent as a teacher of dramatic expression but also goes hand in hand with an intense desire to be an object of contestation and adoration. Ironically, her impending marriage, an event that will take her out of circulation in the courtship game, inspires her to make the most out of her current status as an object of exchange. She transforms the ambiguity of her own status as a commodity, as a woman already "spoken for" but temporarily "on the outs" with her possessor, into an opportunity to flirt with another man and to inspire her father's and her fiancé's jealous anger. During her falling out with Dr. Gregg, Jennie turns on the charm for his confidante and best man, Dr. Greve; such behavior assures her that she is not in a "neutral position" in relation to desire but occupies the prestigious place of an object prized for the male competition it inspires. Borrowing MacKinnon's terminology, one might say Jennie thrives on being the recipient of "the gaze that constructs women as objects of male pleasure" and "gets off on" being an object of male desire (110). Her flirtatious behavior assumes the status of an imperative; it becomes an essential means to the elusive agency she craves so desperately. Thus, on the subject of Dr. Greve as a potential admirer, Jennie thinks, "She must do something to restore her lost dignity, her lost importance. She could not go on until she had impressed her very self on him" (205).

The illusory feeling of power Jennie obtains by playing the role that the social order has provided for her shows itself most forcefully in the confrontation scene (262–68) between "her" three men: Dr. Greve, Dr. Gregg, and Mr. Middleton. In a series of exchanges that seems to illustrate the gendered dimensions of René Girard's "triangulated desire,"[11] Jennie symbolically becomes the object of male "homosocial" conflict even as she is literally passed from one man's arms to another's.[12] As the reconciled bride, Jennie revels in Dr. Greve's "crestfallen" deportment[13] even as she migrates from her seat on the couch beside him to the "large arm[s]" of Dr. Gregg (263). When she sees the "two men star[ing] at each other" with "hard and cold" eyes and feels the erotic tension her presence initiates, Jennie believes "without saying it to herself, that she was in control of the situation, that they would do what she said, and be what she said, and this feeling gave her a peculiar joy" (263). When her father subsequently arrives on the scene, Jennie again takes pleasure from the "cock fighting" that ensues on her behalf as an innocent pawn of masculine machinations. By calling her "'Daughter'" again and again, her father temporarily reclaims her as his own private property even as he voices his resentment of the interlopers present, the men who have also had a hand in her commodification:

> Robert looked over Jennie's head to the two men who were standing silently across the room. All his anger was suddenly directed toward these two men. He looked at his future son-in-law and wondered how he could ever have thought of trusting his daughter to him. And the thought came to him . . . that this strange man . . . was to take possession of his daughter, this young innocent girl whose head pressed against him. And that other stranger, the little Doctor, had imposed on his daughter. He had taken Jennie away from her home on the day of her wedding and exposed her to scandal and gossip. (266)

Whereas earlier in the novel Middleton unconsciously characterizes his daughter as a possession to be unloaded because of the risks associated with it,[14] here he thinks of Jennie as a precious investment, one that requires protection to ensure its marketability to the appropriate, trustworthy buyer. In both instances, Jennie seems largely deprived of agency, but at this point her own self-compromising desire enables her to obtain a parasitic pleasure from witnessing inter-male conflict, "taking their misery and making it into her joy" (267). Her identity functions as the space where men's relationships take place, but Jennie no longer seems to resent this full-scale appropriation; rather, she becomes good at being the goods "on the market" and takes pride in the privilege of self-abnegation and the paradoxical semblance of control it brings.

Thus, while in her rebellion Jennie says that she refuses to "'sacrifice'" herself "'so that everyone else can be happy'" (79), as the radiant bride Jennie learns to relocate her desires within the system and is duly "reward-ed" for her martyrdom: "all of them looked on her with admiration and confidence. She had regained their confidence and they would do what-ever she wished and what she wished was for the good of them all. She *was good* once more and happy and joyful once more" (278, emphasis added). Communal acceptance necessitates her conformity to the male-authored system's standard of "good." By taking on the social role that has been fashioned for her, Jennie allows her desires and expectations, her identity, to be remade in "man's image."

Although the conclusion of Jennie's narrative on marital "bliss" has been used to type the novel as a romantic comedy, the careful delineation of Jennie's predicament earlier in the novel and the toll this resolution takes on Jennie's already crippled subjectivity makes the "happiness" of this final moment profoundly questionable. From the limited perspective of Jennie's insular world, the only alternative to an assertive yet isolated protofemi-nist subjectivity seems to be a complete retreat into and identification with a patriarchal value system. Given the attention the novel has devoted to the debilitating effects of such a system on the lives and development of its characters, it comes as no surprise that this "delightful comedy of man-ners" actually ends with a gruesome description of those characters about to participate in the system's most cherished institution: "'They are like a couple of aristocrats marching to the guillotine'" (302).

"A WEIGHT ON HER HEART": SUSAN AND THE BIRTH OF A RADICAL CONSCIOUSNESS

If *The Wedding* only concerned itself with exploring the tragic limitations set on the desires and dreams of a "southern belle" in a world of middle-class decay, the novel might simply be placed into the genre of southern women's protofeminist fiction. The novel's intricate portrait of female development in a deteriorating social order is certainly reminiscent of Ellen Glasgow's *Sheltered Life* (1932), while its critique of "southern lady-hood" makes it a polite precursor to the caustically ironic wit of Flannery O'Connor on the same subject in *A Good Man Is Hard to Find* (1953). Katherine Anne Porter's Miranda figure in the *Pale Horse, Pale Rider* (1939) collection and Eudora Welty's Virgie Rainey in *The Golden Apples* (1949) have protofeminist impulses and feelings of estrangement similar to those of Jennie Middleton.[15] Nevertheless, the perpetual presence of Susan Middleton's narrative allows the novel to move into the thematic arena more typical of the genre of revolutionary fiction: the birth of a radical consciousness. In a sequence that parallels her older sister's crisis of "cold feet," Susan enacts her own rebellion by asserting solidarity with an African-American servant wrongfully accused of stealing and by exposing the willful deceit of his privileged white male accuser. Nevertheless, Susan's rebellion is doomed to be at best only temporary and ineffectual by the very circumstance that allows her radical perspective to flourish: her relative detachment from the strictures of the adult social order and of southern womanhood, as well as from the narratives of desire, female subjectivity, and feminist impulses that they evoke or cripple.

In many ways, Susan's potential for developing a social conscience seems directly related to her status as a child, a being poised at the margins of her culture. Unlike her older sister, Susan has not yet been completely socialized either as an adult or as a woman in the southern social order. Because she is a child, Susan has mobility and a mental openness that allow her unique access to the otherwise hidden lives of the working class. In frequenting the workrooms, barnyard, and kitchen areas of the Middleton manor house, Susan becomes steeped in the history behind the scenes: the stories and temperaments of Louisa and Ed, the African-Americans whose thankless industry keeps the house running, and those of Old Rosin, the white woman who repairs mattresses. Susan initially gravitates toward these figures with a child's gut-level appreciation of storytelling and the kindness they show her. For example, although "Susan could not have told anyone exactly what Louisa was or about her appearance," she knows at a deeper, emotional level "that from Louisa's mouth came good stories and laughing and wisdom, and from her eyes which saw clearly when Susan did anything the wrong way, there came also a feeling of friendliness" (102–3). Similarly, she obtains a simple "comforting feeling" from watching Rosin finish a mattress and hearing her say, "'Now it's done. Now you will sleep well and have good dreams'" (211).

Susan's childlike curiosity and attention to detail allow her to see these characters' histories of suffering in things or events that remain invisible to the privileged adults of Susan's world. Whereas Mrs. Middleton's tired feet arouse the concern of Jennie and the bridesmaids during the rehearsal (275), only Susan notices the feet that are swollen and tender every day from hard work, the feet of a woman "on her feet" all day long: Louisa's feet, shod in "old felt slippers that had belonged to one of Susan's brothers" (102). When Dr. Greve escorts Jennie and Susan to visit Old Rosin in prison, Jennie tells Dr. Greve about her family's discovery of Rosin's tuberculosis and the official story of the murder Rosin committed; however, Susan and her young brother, Bobby, are the ones who know "more than any of the others about Rosin's life, because Rosin had talked to them while she sewed on the mattresses" (209). Jennie's version of Rosin's story narrates the public events of Rosin's life; she recounts Rosin's publicized infectious state and her prosecution for killing a man while in a drunken state. Only the children know about the painful personal experiences that preceded these events. Rosin tells the children of her grueling childhood as a mill girl, a child so isolated by her long workdays that "she might have met her own brother and sister on the street and would not have recognized them" and so eager to escape the drudgery that she derives "special pleasure" from thinking of the cotton in the carding room as a "cloud" passing by (211).

Nevertheless, at this point in the novel Susan's powers of observation only allow her to see and feel the evidence of suffering around her; they do not give her an understanding of that suffering within a broader social context. Similarly, when she encounters a socialist novel, Susan's heightened emotional response remains largely uninformed by the novel's practical implications for interpreting her own history. Bobby brings the book home from the local secondhand store and shares it with his sister. The novel predicts a secular apocalypse in which a charismatic worker and his followers destroy a nightmarish industrial capitalist social order: "The story said that many years in the future all people in the country except a few would be made into miserable slaves. They were the victims of machines and of the few rich men who owned the machines. . . . And then a powerful workman, the son of a blacksmith, came up from the South and roused all the poor ones who were in slavery. And when he and his followers had killed all the rich people, the blacksmith leader had his followers build a great pyramid on a public square . . . of the dead bodies of the rich" (246). Instead of interpreting this fictional account of the future as a key to the origins of the past and present suffering she has witnessed, Susan reads it as another biblical allegory, one full of the mystery of divine wrath and forbidden pleasure, of oppressive sin and the cleansing power of retribution. Even the vision of a "terrible pyramid built of the dead bodies of the rich" only results in an outpouring of morbid curiosity and emotion in the children, sending "shivers of excitement and dread" down their spines and inspiring them to make a blood-pact to prevent such a future (246). The oath that the children make after reading the book, "'We do solemnly swear we will not let the poor people suffer and we will not let the rich people make them suffer'" (247), may sound like a classic declaration of a radical awareness; however, in this context it is nothing but a series of ominous words to chant in the elaborate rituals of child's play.

Although Susan's exposure to the socialist novel and her sympathetic observations of the working-class men and women in her life are necessary precursors to a radicalized subjectivity, *The Wedding* does not present Susan's radicalization as a gradual process of discovery from emotional moments to a highly intellectualized rebellion. Rather, in a structural move that underscores the psychological tension occurring throughout the novel, Lumpkin telescopes the development of Susan's radical consciousness into a brief and incredibly complex account of the process of memory and mental associations. This account is stimulated by a recent event Susan finds "impossible not to remember" (243): the theft of the silver wedding bowl, her involvement in it, and its outcome. Susan is persuaded by her wealthy, spoiled cousin, Saint John Middleton, to act out an episode of familial history that has been mythologized as an emblem of southern rebellion: hiding the family silver from the "Yankees." After taking the bowl from the table of wedding presents in the hall and wrapping it up in a coat, Saint John orders Ed, the African-American servant, to play the role of "the faithful slave" and bury the bundle without knowing its contents (108). Ed becomes an unwitting participant in the theft and in the rehearsal of a glorified history of racism. Intrigued by her cousin's air of importance and secrecy, Susan watches as Ed buries the "treasure" and Saint John acts as overseer. When the adults finally notice the absence of the bowl, Saint John publicly accuses Ed of the theft, and Susan remains self-consciously silent. Her complicity helps engineer Ed's fate as a wanted man.

Ironically, Susan's initial failure to defend Ed triggers a painful recognition of the historical context of her privileged subject position and the disturbing connection between her own past (of noninvolvement) and those narratives of suffering she has seen, heard, and read but never quite understood. After placing her own insidious silence in the context of the socialist novel and an earlier memory of her own passive observation of white children hurling rocks and racial taunts at black children, Susan suddenly realizes that "because she loved Ed and Louisa, and because of what had just happened to Ed, all this came back and became a weight on her heart" (248). Susan's radical consciousness is thus a consciousness

of "the burden of southern history" on an intellectual and emotional level.[16] In this dramatic and traumatic awakening of her radical self, Susan
confronts the legacy of hatred and neglect she has been given and her own
perpetuation of the plight of working-class men and women in a racist and
highly stratified social order. At the same time, she reaffirms those feelings of solidarity and affection that run counter to the ideological lessons
of her childhood, those lessons about the "difference between herself and
Ed and Louisa and that in order to be loyal to her own people she must
preserve this difference" (245).

Armed with the confidence this awareness brings her, Susan stages a
rebellion against "her own people" by violently exposing Saint John as a
liar and defending the character of the man he maligned.[17] In speaking
out about Ed's innocence and her own participation in the theft, Susan
attempts to counteract the devastating effects of her own guilty silence and
the silence imposed on Ed by a racist society. She tries to retell the past,
to construct a narrative of history that begins to acknowledge the perspectives of those men and women oppressed by the literal and systemic "lies"
of the Saint Johns of this world.

Susan convinces her father of Ed's innocence and Saint John's culpa-
bility, but her rebellion and the radical consciousness she achieves are
never capable of orchestrating any real change in the dominant attitudes
and structures of oppression present in the little, local world of the novel.
Ed remains banished, Old Rosin remains imprisoned, and Louisa and
Annie May are sequestered at the wedding in "the gallery which was reserved for colored people. It was the old slave gallery" (289). Like Jennie,
Susan retreats from her rebellion, but she retreats into the language and
images of religious allegory to make sense of the terrible injustice that has
been committed and allowed to stand: "She saw Ed running with fire trying to overtake him, a fire in a cloud, like the fire that came down over
the ark of the Israelites in the Bible" (282). Still, the inefficacy of this one
little girl's rebellion comes as no surprise. As a child, Susan retains but a
minute, powerless, and marginal position in a system engineered by adults.
As a little girl who plays dress-up, Susan understands the physical sensa-
tion of "petticoats weigh[ing] her down" but not the burden of southern
womanhood that awaits her and cripples the dreams and desires of her
older sister (140). Although Susan bristles at Saint John's accusation that
she has used language improper for a little girl,[18] as a child she cannot have
any sophisticated sense of herself as a gendered subject, an understanding that might enable her to achieve an awareness of the future that awaits
her or a feminist sympathy for the predicament of the women around her.

Accordingly, as the symbolic separate halves of a bifurcated radical middle-class female subject, Susan and Jennie inspire narratives that forever talk past one another, leaving the economic, sexual, and racial structures of domination intact.

THE WEDDING AS "MIDDLE PLACE"

Although most literary disciplines engage in the recovery of lost texts and the articulation of generic categories, 1930s criticism identifies itself with such projects more than the other disciplines do. In part, this focus reflects the relative newness of the field, but it is also encouraged by the texts themselves; their obvious, and often self-proclaimed, differences from other types of literature in terms of political and social concerns have shaped our appreciation of them, even as such seeming separateness helped hasten them to obscurity. From Walter Rideout's *Radical Novel in the United States, 1900–1954* (1956) to Paula Rabinowitz's *Labor and Desire: Women's Revolutionary Fiction in Depression America* (1991), 1930s criticism has been devoted to recovering, reevaluating the cultural significance, and defining the generic parameters of this body of texts that has been quietly dismissed from most literary histories of twentieth-century America because of its size, inaccessibility, and lack of conformity to typical aesthetic standards. Because of the overtly political nature and goal of the texts it studies, 1930s criticism has also been committed to exploring the complex relationship between authors' literary endeavors and their radical activities.

The Wedding is precisely the kind of text that should be targeted for recovery by this kind of criticism because it complicates the generic categories established for the radical novel. Lumpkin's deployment of radical themes in one of the most unlikely subject matters, a middle-class southern wedding, expands current concepts of dystopian radical fiction. The novel's unlikely subject matter, however, is itself significant; it underscores a generic hybridity that may help us better recognize affinities between "radical" novels and other currents in twentieth-century American fiction. In tracing Jennie's ambivalent assumption of the pedestal of southern ladyhood and the development of Susan's radical consciousness, Lumpkin draws on a variety of literary traditions in addition to that of the radical novel: the southern domestic novel, bourgeois feminist literature, and women's protofeminist fiction of the South. As a text that functions as a generic crossroads and has gone unnoticed by scholars of all those traditions, *The Wedding* silently seconds Rabinowitz's call for "reconsiderations" of "notions of the feminine (literary) tradition in much feminist historiography" (5). Recognizing the transgeneric concerns that animate women's contribution to the radical novel would enable 1930s criticism to attract the larger audience that its texts certainly deserve.

The novel marks another crossroads of sorts, one that provides insight into the relationship between a radical author's political orientation and her literary work. Although I have argued for this novel's inclusion in the subgenre of women's dystopian radical fiction precisely because of the absence of a unified radical female intellectual, the liminal position of *The Wedding* in Lumpkin's own literary and political career suggests that the "fault lines" the novel traces are not simply those of a generic radical female subject; they are those of Lumpkin herself, a radical intellectual woman embroiled in a very personal crisis of commitment. The novel is located chronologically between Lumpkin's overtly radical novels and 1941, the year of her religious conversion and formal renunciation of communism. Whereas Lumpkin's early 1930s novels, *To Make My Bread* (1932) and *A Sign for Cain* (1935), display the radicalization of the working class and the participation of (male) intellectuals in a heroic light, *The Wedding* (1939) shifts the thematic focus to the problem of middle-class female subjectivity.[19] In bifurcating the ideal radical female subject into a narrative of protofeminism and a race- and class-conscious narrative that remain disconnected and ineffective, Lumpkin registers her growing pessimism about the possibilities of solidarity and radical social change. She reveals her uneasiness about the precarious position of the female intellectual within the movement and as a character in a "radical" novel. Actively including this "slight simple story of a southern wedding" in the literary history of the radical novel thus may lead 1930s criticism to a more nuanced understanding of gender, genre, and the "real-life" predicament of the radical female subject.

NOTES

1. Of the seven original reviews of the novel (Armfield; "Bride's Strike"; Ferguson; "Grace Lumpkin's Tale of Interrupted Romance"; Pruette; Salomon; and Wallace), five characterize it as a comedy of manners (Armfield; "Bride's Strike"; Pruette; Salomon; and Wallace). Only three try to relate it to Lumpkin's previous work (Armfield; "Bride's Strike"; and Pruette).

2. These consist of Gilkes's afterword to the 1976 reprint of the novel and Mellard's essay.

3. For the concept of dystopian radical fiction and this description of Slesinger's and Herbst's novels, I am indebted to Rabinowitz. For a more detailed discussion of the position of the radical female intellectual, see Rabinowitz 132–72.

4. I have chosen to refer to Jennie's awareness of sexual oppression as a "protofeminist" because it lacks an understanding of oppression on a broader collective scale that one would expect of a "feminist" perspective. Jennie is acutely aware of her own experience of sexual oppression, but she never translates this personal experience or the glimmering of feminist reflections it inspires into an appreciation of the "predicament" of other women, not even other women in a similar social position. Born in isolation, her feminist impulses remain stunted and ultimately ineffectual.

5. The reenactment of Civil War history in which the men and Jennie participate throughout the novel does not ever lead to a deeper understanding of the costly "past" of their social positions—the price they and their value system have exacted on others to keep their privileged position intact. Theirs is a romanticized version of war waged for God and country, not a history that recognizes racism and class privilege.

6. I borrow this phrase from Jacques Lacan, who uses it to describe the essentially problematic nature of sexual identities in a world where "sexual desire can only exist by virtue of its alienation . . . [and] any satisfaction that might subsequently be attained will always contain this loss within it" (quoted in Mitchell 5). Although Lacan's "split" places a slightly different emphasis on the eroticization of lack, the phrase's connection to a dilemma of desire seemed particularly appropriate in describing Jennie's situation.

7. Sylvia Jenkins Cook uses these terms to describe the typical narrative of the working-class woman in women's revolutionary fiction in the 1930s. She refers to the story of a "poor white heroine who was driven by the intolerable circumstances of her life into various forms of private rebellion. . . . these rebellions ended invariably in defeat or compromise, not merely because women were isolated from any sympathetic group who might give moral sanction to their rebellion but because they themselves felt finally compelled to admit their duties lay with home and family" (99). Although Jennie and these characters would certainly define their "intolerable circumstances" differently, the terms themselves still seem appropriate for describing the predicament of this confused and isolated middle-class woman.

8. Because MacKinnon believes that "sexuality *is the social* process that creates, organizes, expresses and directs desire" (107, emphasis added), distinguishing between female desire and women's sexual desire at this point would be virtually meaningless.

9. Ellen Willis does an admirable job of laying the groundwork of this de-

bate and its potential relevance to a novel centering on one woman's "refusal" to accept the role society has given her. In the discussion session transcript following MacKinnon's essay in the Nelson and Grossberg anthology, Willis suggests that MacKinnon's theorized model of the sex/gender system is like "another version of Marcuse's closed system in which capitalism is so pervasive in its ability to manipulate that any resistance is turned around and made part of the system; at best one has the opportunity for refusal. Yet even refusal would seem to contradict the closed system, since refusal implies the power to define one's own situation, to feel enough pain so as to invent the concept of feminism" (117).

10. Mrs. Middleton's description of marriage aptly conveys its overwhelming impact on female identity through the register of the familiar old/new binary: "And she remembered how it had seemed that marriage was like dying and waking up into a new life. It was painful to die in the old life, but there was the new ahead" (63).

11. In an early theory of male homosocial relations, René Girard coins this term to describe the eroticized relationships that occur between men because of their mutual interest in a woman. For details, see his *Deceit, Desire and the Novel*.

12. The word *homosocial* is borrowed from Eve Sedgwick's landmark study *Between Men: English Literature and Male Homosocial Desire*. Sedgwick uses the term to describe "social bonds between persons of the same sex," noting that the peculiar "pattern" of male homosocial bonds cannot be "understood outside of its relation to women and the gender system as a whole" (1).

13. This description actually belongs to a larger collection of avian metaphors Lumpkin uses to denote virility in male homosocial relations. Earlier in the novel, Lumpkin uses the peculiar trope of cock fighting to describe Mr. Middleton's confrontation with Rev. Grant over the marriage ceremony (173). Just as roosters fight to resolve territorial questions of dominance, Middleton and Grant's altercations stem from a certain angst about virility; each man feels his potency and masculine authority challenged on the "turf" he considers his own: the wedding ceremony. One of the most crucial events in a woman's life in southern society, one that irrevocably determines her position in the social order, ends up being reinscribed as a battlefield for male egos in which only the "felt" strictures of genteel society prevent men from vulgar displays of power. Hence, when Pamela deconstructs her cousin Jennie's expectations of "'chivalry from the man she is to marry'" (145), her use of another rooster analogy appropriately serves as a reminder that neither marriage nor chivalry has much to do with respect for women or their desires.

14. Even before he encounters Dr. Gregg, Robert Middleton feels that "the responsibility for her weighed heavily on him so that without realizing he did so, Mr. Middleton looked forward to the time when he might transfer his responsibility for Jennie to a husband" (21).

15. Of course, this type of female character is certainly not the exclusive province of either southern women's fiction or the dystopian radical novel. Marie Rogers and Ishma Waycaster, the working-class heroines of, respectively, Agnes Smedley's *Daughter of Earth* (1929) and Fielding Burke's *Call Home the Heart* (1932), certainly share Jennie's hesitations about marriage and the narrow compass of self it inscribes for women; they are also torn between desire for independence and a craving for a kind of emotional power or security.

16. I borrow this phrase from the title of C. Van Woodward's influential study of the history and culture of the South.

17. After telling her own narrative of the events, Susan demands that Saint John "tell the truth" as well; when he refuses, she slaps him.

18. To deflect attention from his own bad behavior, Saint John accuses Susan of calling him a "bad name" (250).

19. Although *A Sign for Cain* also addresses this problem through the character of Caroline Gault, Lumpkin portrays her in a very unsympathetic light, and her narrative does not really take precedence over the heroicization of the activist Bill Duncan and the radicalization of the working class in the novel.

WORKS CITED

Armfield, Eugene. "Cross Section of a Southern Town." Review of *The Wedding*, by Grace Lumpkin. *Saturday Review of Literature*, February 25, 1939, 7.

"Bride's Strike." Review of *The Wedding*, by Grace Lumpkin. *Time*, February 27, 1939, 79.

Cook, Sylvia Jenkins. *From Tobacco Road to Route 66: The Southern Poor White in Fiction*. Chapel Hill: University of North Carolina Press, 1976.

Daniels, Jonathan. "Old Devil Cotton." Review of *A Sign for Cain*, by Grace Lumpkin. *Saturday Review of Literature*, November 9, 1935, 10.

Ferguson, Otis. Review of *The Wedding*, by Grace Lumpkin. *New Republic*, April 5, 1939, 259.

Gilkes, Lillian Barnard. Afterword. *The Wedding*. By Grace Lumpkin. 1939. Carbondale: Southern Illinois University Press, 1976. 309–19.

Girard, René. *Deceit, Desire, and the Novel*. Baltimore: Johns Hopkins University Press, 1984.

"Grace Lumpkin's Tale of Interrupted Romance." Review of *The Wedding*, by Grace Lumpkin. *Springfield Republican*, April 9, 1939, 7e.

Irigaray, Luce. "Women on the Market." *This Sex Which Is Not One*. By Irigaray; trans. Catherine Porter. Ithaca, N.Y.: Cornell University Press, 1985. 170–91.

Jones, Anne Goodwyn. *Tomorrow Is Another Day: The Woman Writer in the South, 1859–1936*. Baton Rouge: Louisiana State University Press, 1981.

Lumpkin, Grace. *A Sign for Cain*. New York: Lee Furman, 1935.

———. *To Make My Bread*. New York: Macauley, 1932.

———. *The Wedding*. 1939. Carbondale: Southern Illinois University Press, 1976.

MacKinnon, Catharine. "Desire and Power: A Feminist Perspective." Nelson and Grossberg 105–16.

Mellard, James. "The Fiction of Social Commitment." *The History of Southern Literature*. Ed. Louis D. Rubin Jr. Baton Rouge: Louisiana State University Press, 1985. 351–55.

Mitchell, Juliet. "Introduction to Lacan." *Feminine Sexuality: Jacques Lacan and the École Freudienne*. Ed. Juliet Mitchell and Jacqueline Rose. New York: W. W. Norton, 1982. 1–26.

Nelson, Cary, and Lawrence Grossberg, eds. *Marxism and the Interpretation of Culture*. Urbana: University of Illinois Press, 1988.

Pruette, Lorine. Review of *The Wedding*, by Grace Lumpkin. *New York Herald Tribune Lively Arts and Book Review*, March 5, 1939, 10.

Rabinowitz, Paula. *Labor and Desire: Women's Revolutionary Fiction in Depression America*. Chapel Hill: University of North Carolina Press, 1991.

Rideout, Walter B. *The Radical Novel in the United States, 1900–1954: Some Interrelations of Literature and Society*. Cambridge, Mass.: Harvard University Press, 1956.

Salomon, Louis. "South Carolina Town." Review of *The Wedding*, by Grace Lumpkin. *Nation*, March 11, 1939, 301.

Sedgwick, Eve. *Between Men: English Literature and Male Homosocial Desire*. New York: Columbia University Press, 1985.

Wallace, Margaret. "Twenty-four Hours." Review of *The Wedding*, by Grace Lumpkin. *New York Times Book Review*, February 26, 1939, 6–7.

Willis, Ellen. "Discussion of MacKinnon's 'Desire and Power: A Feminist Perspective.'" Nelson and Grossberg 117–21.

Woodward, C. Van. *The Burden of Southern History*. Rev. ed. Baton Rouge: Louisiana State University Press, 1968.

9

MARGARET

BOURKE-WHITE'S

RED COAT; OR,

SLUMMING IN

THE 1930S

A popular Irving Berlin song from 1930 invited its financially strapped middle- and working-class listeners to "go slumming on Park Avenue." Written in the midst of the worst year of the Great Depression, when unemployment soared to between 25 percent and 33 percent, the song sarcastically played on the downward class mobility caused by the 1929 crash. The turning of the class tables was also a common theme in Hollywood, where spunky golddiggers displayed their goods ("We're in the Money") to entice wealthy bankers and lawyers who visited the seedy nightclubs in which they performed before the men retreated to the safety of their men's clubs. During the 1920s wealthy whites had traveled uptown to take in the atmosphere of jazz and high living offered in Harlem's famous night spots. Michael Gold describes how the poor Jewish kids hurled missiles of garbage and paving stones at the carriages of wealthy up-towners touring the Lower East Side during the years before World War I. The class boundaries superintending America's cities were rigid, yet popular culture encouraged their permeability; after the stock market crashed, popular culture unleashed a new pastime—working stiffs gleefully surveyed the lives of the tragically rich, whose means left them incapable of adapting to tight times.

If we take Irving Berlin at his word, we can begin to understand class as both a social practice and a representation (precisely the way that Joan Wallach Scott and Teresa de Lauretis argue gender operates in culture).[1] In his famous sentence describing the peasants and small landowners of postrevolutionary France, Marx asserted, "They cannot represent themselves, they must be represented " (*Eighteenth Brumaire* 124). His double sense of representation is a political practice; someone must speak for, stand in for, perform as the inchoate and unformed group—not yet a class because it cannot represent itself, yet surely a class because it can be represented to and for itself and others. If representation is crucial to class formation and expression, then class, like gender, is performative—divined in the exchanges among representatives of and for classes. These exchanges were themselves the subject of intense representation and theorizing during the 1930s—a decade when class, racial, and gender divisions were both more pronounced and more thoroughly contested than they are today.

To analyze how class represents, I want to explore the politics and meaning of boundary crossing—of slumming, so to speak. These crossings occur tellingly at moments of *visual* encounters between those whose lives were privileged to observe, regulate, and detail the behaviors of others—journalists, novelists, photographers, and social workers—and their subjects, usually, in the depression decade, the poor. As vehicles of regulation, exposé, and reification, photography and fiction became central mechanisms of class representation. This essay looks at the complicated relations of cross-class looking encoded in the lives, novels, and images of working-class and middle-class women during the 1930s. It seeks out the tensions at the borders of class and racial boundaries when women cross them. Fiction and reportage by radical women—both middle class and working class—describe one horn of the dilemma I am tracing. Margaret Bourke-White, among the highest paid women of the 1930s, whose photographs helped propel *Life* magazine's spectacular success, embodies another. When a middle-class woman looks across her class privilege at another woman, what does she see? And because she herself is also an object under investigation, how is she seen in turn? Can a working-class woman see herself? And because she is already under surveillance, might she refuse to look at others?[2]

Middle-class inspection of the poor begins long before the 1920s slumming, and its purpose was more likely the regulation of working people's desires than the expression of middle-class pleasures. Nancy Armstrong has detailed the way in which the rise of the domestic woman figured in eighteenth-century British novels placed middle-class women in a position to regulate their own lives and the lives of their children. According to both

Denise Riley and Linda Gordon, the consolidation of feminism and social reform movements in nineteenth-century Britain and America ensured
that middle-class women would also regulate and superintend the lives of
poorer females who failed to live out proper standards of housekeeping
and femininity. Oversight brought into view all deviations so that they
could be ameliorated. Being able to see into the dark spaces of poverty had
accompanied the invention of the mercury flash in the 1890s; Jacob Riis
could not only enter the tenements of the Lower East Side and inspect
but also record "how the other half lives." The projects of state and capitalist regulation, reportage and fiction, documentary photography and
feminism are curiously interwoven; each mode oversees itself, its object,
and its others. But in the 1930s a radical critique of capitalism turned the
lens through which middle-class women looked over (and after) their
poorer sisters.[3]

In 1928 Virginia Woolf powerfully etched the intimate links between
feminism and writing. She produced a new understanding of British literary history by acknowledging the history of women's oppression and their
achievements as writers. Her formula—to be a writer, a woman needed
"five hundred pounds a year and a room of one's own" (A Room 113)—
signaled that literature was the province of the middle-class that could
afford time and space to meditate, study, and write: "the poor poet has not
in these days, nor has had for two hundred years, a dog's chance" (107).
In her perambulations traced in the lecture/essay, the narrator periodically
finds herself alone in a room looking out her window at the absurd, but
everyday, bustle below.

This image of the writer separated from the streets as surveyor and overseer of the lives of her subjects links the project of literary production to
that of bourgeois domestic maintenance. There, too, as Nancy Armstrong
has demonstrated, the middle-class woman learned to display her skill by
self-inspection and projection onto the objects surrounding her. She assumed authority as the supervisor of her domestic surroundings, her qualities of perception indicating her intrinsic value. Like the early bourgeois
"domestic woman" Armstrong analyzes, Woolf's writer is set apart in her
own room because of class differences. Rebecca Harding Davis had portrayed this in her 1861 novella Life in the Iron Mills, which begins as another unnamed middle-class female narrator stands at her window watching the mill workers trudge along the path before her as they return from
work. Like Davis before her, Woolf notes that it is unlikely we will find
many working-class artists—male or female. Nevertheless, in the pages of
contemporaneous socialist journals, writers were calling for a new "pro-

letarian" poetics to replace that of a defeated high modernism. Woolf herself wrote an introductory essay for a book of working-class women's tales collected by the Co-operative Working Women's Guild a few years later, entitled *Life as We Have Known It*.

The idea that literary production was the result of observations of life — rather than from what one has known of it—simply reinforced the sense that writing and looking were privileges of the middle class. Michael Gold's novel *Jews without Money*, an enactment of his calls for proletarian art— writing that would dramatize the lives of those in the tenements—brought the narrator downstairs. Smashing the pane of glass separating writer from the street below, he insisted that stories and their telling were the activities of the poor and working class.

Usually the poor represented an absence in literary discourse, the *non-dit*, to use Pierre Macherey's term, of the words and works of both high realism and high modernism. But Gold's call for proletarian literature opened up a new arena for middle-class writers as well. Still, their desire to know and transmit (if not transform) the lives of poor and working-class subjects maintained the conventional boundaries separating art from life, seeing from knowing. The form of reportage was, in some measure, an attempt to refigure these relations; yet, when these boundaries were violated, they confounded generic (and gender) conventions. For example, when the journalist Martha Gellhorn traveled throughout the United States to record *The Trouble I've Seen* (1936) and found "Ruby," the eponymous girl of the first part of the book, she was at a loss to account for Ruby's behavior. No convenient story emerged to trace either the defiant pride (as well as outlandish clothes) prostitution offered Ruby or her shame at her mother's ineffectual morality that restricted them to poverty. But Gellhorn was also uneasy with the social worker who saves Ruby from her unfit mother and lodges her safely among a middle-class family. It is not clear just what the "trouble" is here—poverty, childhood prostitution, improper mothering, or straight-laced social workers—or what the "I" who has seen it has learned or intends to do about it. As a reporter, Gellhorn is troubled by what she has seen, but she maintains her "traditional" distance.[4] Is she slumming, even if her travels across class boundaries never yield a thrill?

Writings by and about radical women intellectuals, whose metaphoric annihilation as actors in the historical movement of the proletariat was doubled because of both class *and* gender differences, stressed that they were always "foreigners" among the American people and within the American Left.[5] "Ruby" presented a typical feature of much radical women's writings of the 1930s: the inevitable scene in which the white middle-class social worker—proper representative of the state—enters the home of the working-class mother to supervise her failed attempts at homemaking. The occasion for the state's interest in the home of the poor was usually the arrest of a wayward daughter for prostitution. The blame for her transgressive sexuality—the money that did not always see its way back to the home but was used selfishly to buy pretty things for the young girl—was securely lodged in the inept mother. As the social worker surveys the filthy apartment cluttered with laundry, rancid food, and howling babies, she registers the distance between her classed understanding of proper femininity and maternity and offers a view on the slovenly housekeeping of the poor. Despite being beaten down, the mothers fight back, if only to comment on the impossibility of living up to the standards of bourgeois housekeeping on a few dollars a week from relief.[6] Their anguish—the pain registered on the face of Dorothea Lange's "Migrant Mother" or the blank stare of a sharecropper's wife caught by Margaret Bourke-White—was a shameful admission that the middle-class culture had failed to make over the face of America in its image.

Even when the heroine of a feminist proletarian novel like Fielding Burke's *Call Home the Heart* was an "organic intellectual" like Ishma, the mountain-woman-turned-mill-worker-and-union-activist, rather than a well-to-do newspaper woman, the motives of the female intellectual were suspicious. In the penultimate scene of the novel, Ishma single-handedly saves the black union organizer Butch Wells from being lynched by her former husband and his friends. Shaming them with the threat that she will kill herself and leave them with the reputation of having attempted to rape her, Ishma uses her whiteness and femininity to save a fellow worker. Burke restages the highly charged gender, racial, class, and sexual dynamics of lynching and rape through a subversion of stereotypes. Inverting the historical myth that the rape of a white woman by a black man causes his lynching at the hands of white men, Ishma, a working-class white woman, stops Butch's lynching by charging the white men with rape. Later, at Butch's home, she is confronted with her own racism, marring the heroism of her act, when his wife Gaffie grabs Ishma in an embrace and kisses her:

Her lips were heavy, and her teeth so large that one needed the sure avouch of eyes to believe in them. It was impossible to associate her with woe, though tears were racing down her cheeks. As her fat body moved she shook off an odor that an unwashed collie would have disowned.

> "Bressed angel, bressed angel ob de Lawd," she kept repeating, and
> with a great sweep enveloped Ishma, her fat arms encircling the white
> neck, her thick lips mumbling at the quivering white throat. . . . The
> fleshy embrace, the murky little room, the smoking ashes, the warm
> stench, the too eager faces shining greasily at the top of big, black
> bodies, filled Ishma with uncontrollable revulsion. (383)

The heavy hint of interracial lesbianism so disturbs Ishma that she rein-
states racial stereotypes of black womanhood—as an animal, a mammy, a
sexual predator. Disgraced in the eyes of the community, especially Derry Unthank, a white doctor and Party member who has overseen Ishma's
political education, she flees back to the mountains and her first husband.

As the protagonist of the novel, Ishma holds center stage in the drama
unfolding around her during the mill workers' strike. Her sexuality, limited by lack of contraception to a series of heterosexual "marriages," sparks
her political commitments. Her pursuit of sexual freedom *and* economic
equality set her apart from the proper white middle-class women of the
mill town and the less assertive women of her class. She is exceptional,
but she can never fully become a radical because of her racism. Here, the
white female (organic) intellectual again is separated from other women,
whose bodily excess—too much money, too many children, too much
flesh, whatever—threatens her political identity.

In both cases, the authors, themselves middle-class women, could not
overcome through their prose the racial or class differences dividing wom-
en. The ideal of fraternity, often figured in the image of the maternal
collective engulfing disparate workers in its embrace, escaped their wom-
en characters, as if class and racial divisions—marked by tasteless clothing and expressive sexuality, on one hand, a well-cut suit and heroic behavior, on the other—were more extreme among women.[7] Writing
produced by working-class authors during the 1930s also dramatized class
and racial divisions through the awkward instances produced when one's
body is on display, but they challenged the stance of either passive observation or flight from confrontation. Women's radical fiction in the 1930s
reversed a classic image from Dickens's novels through *Stella Dallas*: the
poor waif (or elderly mother) looking in at the opulent dining rooms of
the wealthy. It often placed poor and working women inside and subject
to the view of those passing by.

For instance, in Ramona Lowe's painful story "The Woman in the Window," a wry revision of Fannie Hurst's 1933 melodramatic novel *Imitation
of Life*, Mrs. Jackson answers an advertisement for a cook, only to discover

she must dress the part of Aunt Jemima and fry chicken in the window of Mammy's restaurant. Her children, shamed by the taunts of white children who see her, challenge her to quit her demeaning job, but she explains that her job is cooking and it puts food on their table and shoes on their feet and that "*when a body say nigger. You turn roun' 'n' give'm such a thrashin' they woan never forget.*" Her self-possession in spite of her public humiliation, her demands that her employers address her as Mrs. Jackson and raise her pay, her insistence to her children that some work is dignified and some not "but it all got t' be done" inverts Woolf's use of the window (83). Here the window is for display, not for observation. It provides a glimpse of the object at work, not a view for the writing subject. Mrs. Jackson may be the spectacle, but she is also the theorist of her position. She is an object who speaks back by simply asserting the need that drives her to claim her objectification: "She leaned against the table and looked out, and the world looked in curiously at the embodiment of a fiction it had created" (82). This woman in the window challenges Woolf's observer to cross through the glass, like Alice, and enter another world, to think of a set of relations other than observer/observed, subject/object, inside/outside. But that project is terribly difficult, as Mrs. Jackson is forced to realize when her daughter comforts her: "'Mama, I thought you looked pretty in the winda'" (83). The awkward and often tragic attempts to cross class divides highlight social exclusions among women. These divisions—distinguishing those who belong from those who do not—are central to social privileges learned and experienced in childhood.[8]

However, in her epic 1934 story "I Was Marching," Meridel Le Sueur traced the clumsy awakening of a middle-class woman to the experiences of working-class solidarity. Written in part to assuage the condemnation she had suffered at the hands of the *New Masses* editor Whittaker Chambers for her earlier piece of reportage, "Women on the Breadlines," the first-person narrator is wary: a woman, a middle-class woman, a middle-class woman writer, who watches herself as much as she watches others and for whom language, the representation of an event, is more profound than its experience. "For two days," she writes, "I heard of the strike. I went by their headquarters, I walked by on the opposite side of the street and saw the dark old building that had been a garage and lean, dark young faces leaning from the upstairs windows. I had to go down there often. I looked in . . . I stayed close to the door, watching. I was afraid they would put me out. After all, I could remain a spectator. A man wearing a polo hat kept going around with a large camera taking pictures" (159–60). This introduction establishes the narrator as an outsider, the middle-class onlooker

who, as Georg Lukács theorized in *History and Class Consciousness*, per-
ceives social relations as a "passive observer," much as one might view a
theatrical performance (100). But Le Sueur's narrator is drawn into the
union hall, where the masses of bodies worked together and suffered in
unison, and after days on the picket lines and pouring coffee, she finds
herself an insider. "I was marching," she declares finally,

> with a million hands, movements, faces, and my own movement was
> repeating again and again, making a new movement from these many
> gestures, the walking, falling back, the open-mouthed crying, the
> nostrils stretched apart, the raised hand, the blow falling, and the
> outstretched hand drawing me in. I felt my legs straighten, I felt my
> feet join in that strange shuffle of thousands of feet, and my own
> breath with the gigantic breath. As if an electric charge had been
> passed through me, my hair stood on end, I was marching. (171)

Where the narrator began her tale by emphasizing sight, her looking in
and looking on, the concluding ecstatic push of humanity incorporates
feet, hands, nostrils, mouths, and hair but refuses to name the eyes.

By erasing the presence of the eye, Le Sueur clearly wants to ease the
separation that vision, the observation of working-class others, produces.
Her final cry, "I was marching," despite its individualism, subsumes her
body into the masses, the "we" that has begun its funeral march. In a ges-
ture repeated endlessly in women's proletarian fiction, the collective en-
gulfs its characters and re-forms them into an earth-shuddering force. Still,
the narrator reasserts her presence here, I believe, because it is so important to Le Sueur that she indicate that the relationship between middle-
class woman and worker could be other than one of merely onlooker. She
needs to return to her embodied presence to alert us to the fact that she
does not merely see but also moves. She is not slumming; she has crossed
the threshold.

As in Lowe's story, the workers are inside, their heads glimpsed on the
street below, where "artists, writers, professionals, even businessmen and
women" watch with "longing" and "fear" the dark and solemn faces within
(160). Those on the street (and notice how women are joined with the
representative types of the middle class) remain unnoticed and uncom-
prehending. Despite gathering before the union hall, they appear as cut
off from the history as Woolf's or Davis's narrator. They need to enter the
space behind the workers' doors and windows to enter history. And they
need to do so with their marching feet, not their watching eyes. It was by
passing through the door that Le Sueur's narrator could overcome her

distance from the working class—a distance, she noted in "The Fetish of Being Outside," that was fundamental to bourgeois, particularly romantic, notions about artists and writers—and transform fiction from a tool of (self-) exploration into a space where boundaries between self and other blurred. Only then might she "change worlds," as Anna Louise Strong emphatically proclaimed.

If looking at the bodies of working-class women marks a separation between professionals and the poor, then surely photographers, particularly female photographers, presented the most troubling figure of reform during the 1930s. The depression spawned the careers of some of America's most prominent women photographers: Dorothea Lange and Marion Post Wolcott, who both worked for the Farm Security Administration (FSA); Berenice Abbott, who worked for the Works Progress Administration; and Margaret Bourke-White, who was the only *Life* photographer with photo credits. These women negotiated precarious positions for themselves as artists, documentarians, and commercial photographers by using the signs of middle-class femininity—their supervising eyes—to track the impact of the depression and the New Deal on the lives and landscapes of America's poor.

Paradoxically, the depression provided middle-class women opportunities to move out of their previously restricted roles. They could travel the world as journalists, social workers, photographers, organizers, and teachers. In their desire to make this opportunity meaningful, to "change worlds," they found their poorer sisters a moving target for their work. Certainly these women made their mark on the backs of the poor women who filled their accounts and peopled their photographs, but without the middle-class incursion into the private lives of the poor, their stories and faces would barely be heard or seen at all. Moreover, the mobility open to middle-class women meant that poor and working women could get a close look at their more comfortable sisters. As Muriel Rukeyser noted in a poem, what they saw—"more of a corpse than a woman"—was not always desirable. This doubled and contradictory interaction is mirrored in the curious status of the 1930s period in American literary and cultural history.

Nancy Armstrong argues that the modern bourgeois individual is most fully embodied in the woman because she is the repository of feelings, not information, and is the center of desire rather than wealth. But what are the consequences of recognizing the female worker whose body transverses the spaces of the domestic and the economic? If we agree that the engendering of knowledge is an aspect of bourgeois society, we might fruitfully describe one project of the radicals writing novels or taking pictures during the 1930s as discovering a working-class form of knowledge. But proletarian theorists described class divisions through gender differences: the effeminate bourgeoisie was bound to be replaced by the virile working class. Knowledge was still deeply gendered, and this formula left out women as agents of history. A working-class woman could have no place, no knowledge, because in this configuration she is insufficiently gendered and inappropriately classed. Not fully feminine because she works, she is also not a worker because she does women's work. Her body is the sight of the dual labor of productivity and reproduction and so appears outside the divisions constituting knowledge. Understanding the reconfiguration of gender, class, and knowledge might provide one means of revisioning the 1930s.

What fiction and photography from the 1930s establish are the contradictory relations among the state, capitalism, family, art, and sexuality in the bodies positioned in and among those institutions. Thirties literary and photographic works by committed intellectuals—both male and female—attempted to refashion the domestic narratives of nineteenth-century realism by foregrounding the objects of labor—workers' bodies, spaces, and tools. This reconstruction of the bourgeois relations embodied in the fiction of domesticity deforms conventions separating words, pictures, classes, and genders by making connections between political action and aesthetic representation, interpellating (male, workers') history in (female, bourgeois) fiction.[9]

For example, the final volume of Josephine Herbst's trilogy *Rope of Gold*, which brings the story of the Trexler family into the 1930s, cleverly refashions one plot of nineteenth-century domestic fiction—the family saga—through the interpolation of documentary intertexts. Herbst uses excerpts from some of her own reportage, blurring the line between fact and fiction. The novel further blurs the gender and class divisions separating intellectual and manual labor, the home and the workplace. The domestic place is brought into the workplace as the Flint auto workers set up house during the sit-down strike; political strategizing in Realengo 18, the Cuban sugar soviet, goes on over dinner and cards. Victoria Chance, the radical journalist, writes herself out of the narrative as she rides a bus north to participate in a strike; Steve Carson, the militant striker, begins to write his narrative on the shop floor.

Documentary reportage and photography embraced these confusions, bringing the observing, (usually) bourgeois individual writer or photogra-

pher into the participating (usually) proletariat to show the horrors of capitalism at home or fascism abroad. However, the presumptions of political efficacy lodged in the documentary project are based in the same ideal of depth modeled by bourgeois forms of knowledge: the psychological
reading of the image. The documentary desire to "expose" the crimes of
bourgeois culture constructs an other class known not through the penetration of the subject but through the display of objects. Paradoxically, that
objectified class then assumes the function of the psychological subject;
its surface masks another layer of meaning to be penetrated. In this sense,
the Left's use of the documentary image to reveal classed relations of power
is an attempt to let the objects speak—in much the same way that Marx
allowed the commodities a voice in *Capital* to speak of their lack of value—and thus challenges the construction of bourgeois subjectivity. Yet this
challenge to the workings of subjective realism through the object falters
at the precise moment the image is read by the audience. To whom do
the objects speak, those bourgeois subjects slumming among them?

In the appendix to *Let Us Now Praise Famous Men*, James Agee includes
a New York *Post* clipping about Margaret Bourke-White. Quoted in its
entirety, it stands as the only place where middle-class women enter the
text. May Cameron's breezy article describes Bourke-White's presence as
flamboyant and flashy; her entrance signaled by the "reddest coat in the
world" (454). After the thousands of words Agee has used to detail the
meager wardrobe hanging on the nails of the tenant farmers' bedroom
walls and his meditation on the impossibility of fulfilling desire when space
is so cramped and the body so exhausted by daily chores, this flagrant display of wealth and female sexual allure is intended to stun the reader and
to discredit the most popular and widely known female photographer of
the decade. Bourke-White's career as a Luce photographer, for *Fortune* and
for *Life*, parallels Agee's own history of employment for the Time/Life
empire, except she was among the highest paid women in America, while
he eked out a meager salary there. It is perhaps his uneasiness about this
fact that gives his citation an extra bite. The column stands unremarked—
it needs no comment—save a footnote indicating its source as a "liberal
newspaper" (454). But why do we feel Bourke-White to be so brazen in
her red coat? Clearly, it has something to do with the coat juxtaposed with
the threadbare denim and calico of the tenant farmers who were photo-
graphed for the book *You Have Seen Their Faces*, produced with her second husband, Erskine Caldwell.

Bourke-White's signature style, "the caterpillar view," which she
achieved by, as she said, "literally crawl[ing] between the legs of my com-

petitors and pop[ping] my head and camera up for part of a second" (*Portrait* 147), was unseemly. It displayed her arrogance toward her subject as she purposely imaged black preachers and white tenant farmers from unflatteringly low angles. Caldwell recalled, "She was in charge of everything, manipulating people and telling them where to sit and where to look and what not" (quoted in Goldberg 168). Moreover, these images are captioned with quotations gleaned from the conversations Caldwell had as Bourke-White shot: "The legends under the pictures are intended to express the authors' own conceptions of the sentiments of the individuals portrayed; they do not pretend to reproduce the actual sentiments of these persons" (*Faces* frontispiece). Agee himself had ventured into the minds of tenant farmers, inventing soliloquies for them, but the layout of *You Have Seen Their Faces* juxtaposed captions and image. Walker Evans's photos in *Let Us Now Praise Famous Men* stand as testaments on their own.

Even more than FSA photographers, Bourke-White made her living as a voyeur, as a middle-class tourist among the neediest people, sending dispatches back to the comfortable living rooms of *Life* magazine's readers. Her first assignment for *Life*, which coincided with its inaugural issue for which she provided the cover story, traced the new boomtowns of the West growing up around the multimillion dollar water projects of the Columbia River Basin. Her pictures from the town of New Deal, Montana, disarmed her editors, who had expected the architectural shots characteristic of Bourke-White's earlier career. What they received—"everything from fancy ladies to babies on the bar," she wired the New York office—"surprised" her editors (*Portrait* 142). They expected "construction pictures as only Bourke-White can take them. What the Editors got was a human document of American frontier life, which to them, at least, was a revelation" (Editors 3).

Bourke-White's revelation about New Deal was not only that there were women living amid trailers and cement block cabins but also that these fancy women might be mothers carting children along with them. This slice of life, the basic theme of all *Life* magazine articles, opened the lives of the poor and working-class to widespread public scrutiny and confirmed an image of the poor as derelict rather than either defeated or defiant, as FSA photographers or literary radicals might portray them.[10] Bourke-White's invasion of the homes of the impoverished meant she was a

foreigner who acted like one. I remember one occasion when we went into a cabin to photograph a Negro woman who lived there. She had thick, glossy hair, and I decided to take her picture as she combed it.

She had a bureau made of a wooden box with a curtain tacked to it and lots of homemade things. I rearranged everything. After we left, Erskine spoke to me about it. How neat her bureau had been. How she must have valued all her little possessions and how she had them tidily arranged *her* way, which was not my way. This was a new point of view to me. I felt I had done violence. (*Portrait* 126–27)

We wonder at Bourke-White's naïveté and her arrogance.

Touching and rearranging objects had been something that Agee and Evans agonized over as they perused the shacks of the three tenant families that became the subject of *Let Us Now Praise Famous Men*. Bourke-White's breezy entrance into a poor black woman's private space clearly marked off class and racial positions: one the photographer from the North, the other the sharecropper of the South. Letting *"you,"* her middle-class audience, "see *their* faces" preserved the distance between her and her audience and the photographic objects contained in the book.[11] Despite recounting this incident, Bourke-White seems to have learned nothing. We still know nothing of the woman—not her name, her town, her occupation: she is a Negro woman with thick, glossy hair. The "violence" that Bourke-White performed is akin to slumming. Still, something instructive is going on in this encounter about disjunctures between women and the attempts to overcome them. Their failures need recognition; they are crucial to revisioning the 1930s as a lived moment in our histories.

Looking across classes, like all transgressive looking, makes public the spectacle of private desire. Because the poor live outside the realm of bourgeois privacy, their lives are open to the inspection and regulation or amelioration of both the state and its radical opponents. The New Deal projects to document the effects of the depression and the benefits of government intervention helped erase the divide between public and private. The photographs to come out of the New Deal (including those of New Deal) melded the two spheres by bringing "their" faces to "you." However, no matter how "surprised" the editors of *Life* magazine were at Bourke-White's photographs of New Deal, Montana, the folks there end up revealing a familiar story, the story of *Life*.

The abuse Agee poured on Bourke-White was picked up by the critic William Stott, who condemns Bourke-White's photographs as "maudlin" and "sensationalistic," with their fake quotations for captions and their excessive craft (222–23). His most telling condemnation comes because *You Have Seen Their Faces* was so successful; it netted Bourke-White a great deal of money. This "double outrage: propaganda for one thing and profit-making out of both propaganda and the plight of the tenant farmers . . . was morally shocking to Agee and me," says Walker Evans. "Particularly so since it was publicly received as the *nice* thing to do, the *right* thing to do. Whereas we thought it was an evil and immoral thing to do. Not only to cheapen them, but to profit by them, to exploit them—who had already been so exploited. Not only that but to exploit them without even *knowing* that was what you were doing" (quoted in Stott 222–23). Evans calls Agee's attack "vicious" but justified and goes on to repeat it for another generation.

Their "vicious" critiques of Bourke-White were fully justified, but there is more to it. To my mind it has to do with the gendered terms by which 1930s Left intellectuals described themselves and their work. In an effort to divorce themselves from the doubly feminized realms of popular and bourgeois culture, radical male intellectuals were fervently committed to a "virile" poetics that would give voice to the new worker. For instance, Hugo Gellert's illustrated edition of Marx's *Capital*, published in 1934, presents the picture of a masculine proletariat—man, woman, and child— bulging with muscles and ready to walk triumphantly into the future once the shackles of wage slavery are overthrown.[12] Bourke-White's image of a peasantry defeated pandered to middle-class sympathy for this vanishing breed—the tenant farmer. Yet it also resisted the vision of the powerful masculine worker who fired the imagination of the male intellectuals. Perhaps this was part of her crime.[13]

In *Sensational Designs*, Jane Tompkins discusses the vilification Harriet Beecher Stowe received for writing (and making money from) *Uncle Tom's Cabin*. Contemporary criticism, fearing the feminization of American culture, railed against the dangerous sentiment oozing from Stowe's book. The cultural work of middle-class women is rendered suspect by aligning its popularity with femininity, thus marking off the serious work of men as unsentimental, unpopular, and artful. Women's political interventions, if they rely on popular sentiments, and the gender divisions privileging certain kinds of cultural practices over others ensure that their cultural work will be unrecognized. *You Have Seen Their Faces* is a direct heir to *Uncle Tom's Cabin*, complete with equating blacks, the poor, and women with suffering.[14] Margaret Bourke-White's "superior red coat," made for her by Dietrich's designer Howard Greer and presumably paid for with profits from her book (which she worked on by taking a leave without pay from her *Life* job), makes Agee and Evans's project all the more morally superior. Evans eschewed sentimentality in the pictures; he claimed to have "brought photographic style back around to the plain relentless snapshot" (Evans 136), fighting, according to Stott, "against the gigantism and bathos of Margaret Bourke-White, against the lurid excitements of *Life*" (267–68). Agee catalogued simple objects in his prose; he remarked obsessively on their roles as "spy and counter-spy." And Evans and Agee never made a dime off their book. Thus *Let Us Now Praise Men* is a "classic," and we are left feeling embarrassed by Bourke-White's efforts.

Bourke-White's retroactively acknowledged "violence" was represented in countless incidents recorded in radical women's writing of the 1930s. Their dilemma about giving voice to working-class women was foregrounded when the "foreigners," representatives of the state or public realm—writers, organizers, social workers, photographers—encountered poor women walking picket lines, hustling drinks, fixing stews, or retreating to silence. Recognizing the uneasy differences between women was crucial to women's revisioning class relations in 1930s America. For some, this led to radical action, to an attempt to cross the threshold separating women, through identification, even glorification; for others, it remained a kind of socially responsive slumming, moving through the lives of the poor, not for pleasure or thrills but out of a sense of largesse, which left both working-class and middle-class women fixed in their conditions, though perhaps offering each a glimpse of the restraints limiting their lives and the possibilities of changing them.

The working-class female body was a vivid text in 1930s America. From Mae West strutting her stuff before Cary Grant or W. C. Fields, to Ruby Keeler dancing her heart out on top of a taxi, to Ginger Rogers hawking her goods in Pig Latin, Hollywood presented "working girls" whose bodies were traded as show girls or as prostitutes to keep off the dole. Their energy and voluptuousness contrasted with the image of the hollowed out, empty men on the breadlines. These Hollywood dream girls were a far cry from the Migrant Mother's gaunt cheekbones and sad eyes, from the tough, grim faces of the women in New Deal, Montana, who were just barely getting by and hanging on. Yet these contrasting images, coupled with the vital "revolutionary girl" celebrated in poetry by Maxwell Bodenheim and sketched in cartoon by Hugo Gellert—the women who "sure [we]re scrappers" as they fought police and scabs on picket (Dahl 252)— all indicate the varied space that a working woman could occupy in 1930s American culture. There was a gap between what a working-class woman could look like and by extension accomplish and what her middle-class sister could only imitate, imagine, or observe.

Looking at the bodies of working-class females was certainly not a new activity in the 1930s. When Henry Mayhew walked the streets of London in the 1840s and found "the little watercress girl . . . [who] although only eight of age had already lost all childish ways, was indeed, in thoughts and manner, a woman," her curiousness was her failure to express proper femininity (151). But the 1930s in America opened up a particular kind of visualization of the working-class female body, one which was founded on a transaction between middle-class women's opportunities to write, to photograph, to organize, and to reform and which faltered on the very inequities that made poorer women their objects of narrative, image, and action, for rarely could either escape their lots.

The 1930s provided an opening for middle-class women to enter the public sphere, often through the inspection of the private lives of women poorer, darker, and less powerful than they. As ethnographic imperialists, as tourists amid the other half, they sometimes had suspect motives, and their projects were often corrupted. Lacking a place within dominant or radical cultures, these women looked to the objects traditionally left to their care—poor women—for inspiration, knowledge, guidance, and use. Yet even in their most arrogant and sentimental appropriations, the silences and invisible objects of capitalist and patriarchal oppression could be heard, their faces could be seen. Without Fielding Burke's attempt to unpack southern racism and its corrosive effects on working-class solidarity, without Meridel Le Sueur's push through the doorway of the union hall, even without Margaret Bourke-White's invasion of the homes and churches of black and white tenants, working-class and poor women's determination, struggles, and failures might have remained unremarked or unremarkable. In this transaction, we find an earlier incarnation of the "politics of disparity" and "entrustment" theorized by contemporary Italian feminists—a politics that acknowledges women's class and generational differences as "an exchange between these two moments of female humanity, between the woman who wants and the woman who knows" (Milan 123). A politics based on a recognition of a "regime of exchange" that insists "women owe women."[15]

The stories and images we do have are not simply transparent views of social reality. The working-class woman resists theorizing in the usual terms, but that does not mean we must assume she is any less of a theorist. To do so is surely to reproduce the terms and marginalize or romanticize the working class and women. Failed resistance is not the same as no resistance.[16] Still, we too need to be aware of our position as we revision the 1930s. Are we a new generation of committed female intellectuals overseeing and regulating the stories and pictures of that other time? What is it we expect to know about them? How is our gaze shaping the

1930s into something other than what those years were for the women who lived through them? What do we want from the archives when we go slumming in the 1930s? These open-ended questions draw attention to our complicity in the representations of class, racial, and gender differences operating in our work, even when our work is committed to exposing and eradicating the inequities caused by those differences. An earlier generation of women was moved to represent those who "must be represented." Their attempts often resembled slumming, especially when they sported a "superior red coat" as they worked; still, they left an array of images that speaks to us across time about deprivation and struggle—and the importance of women's urge to step out of bounds.

NOTES

Another version of this essay appears as a chapter in *They Must Be Represented: The Politics of Documentary* by Paula Rabinowitz, © Verso, London, 1994, and is published with permission of the publisher.

1. Scott maintains that "gender is a constitutive element of social relationships based on perceived differences between the sexes, and gender is a primary way of signifying relationships of power" (42). De Lauretis asserts, "The construction of gender is both the product and the process of its representation" (5). Judith Butler challenges these perspectives by suggesting that although they see gender as a signifying practice, they still rely on foundationalist assumptions about subjectivity. "Gender," she says, "proves to be performative—that is, constituting the identity it is purported to be. In this sense, gender is always a doing, though not a doing by a subject who might be said to preexist the deed" (25).

2. For a discussion of a contemporary encounter between working-class female poets and a middle-class female critic, see Maria Damon's "Tell Them about Us," in which she introduces poetry by three young women living in South Boston during the 1970s busing crisis. Here is how one of the D Street writers describes their situation: "We're watching ourselves watching you watching us, we look at ourselves *through* you" (253).

3. Elsewhere I have theorized about the implications of cross-gender and cross-class looking. In "Voyeurism and Class Consciousness," I look in detail at *Let Us Now Praise Famous Men* for clues about the history of specular relations. These I take to be founded on a classed sexuality that empowers bourgeois men to regard poor women as embodiments of sex/knowledge. For an indepth history of the politics of documentary rhetoric, see my *They Must Be Represented*.

4. This is Gramsci's term for the intellectuals whose function is to maintain order and hegemony for the ruling class, in contradistinction to "organic intellectuals" who rise from within the subaltern classes to forge revolutionary movements. By maintaining an objective pose, Gellhorn's journalism shied away from the radicalism of reportage that impelled activism from observation.

5. Margaret Bourke-White described herself as a foreigner, as did the journalist and Smith College graduate Lauren Gifillan, whose book-length account of her life among striking coal miners, *I Went to Pit College*, outlined the limits of middle-class women's ability to enter the lives of the working-class. See my discussion of the work in *Labor and Desire*.

6. This scene can be found in Caroline Slade's *Triumph of Willie Pond* (147–57) and Ruth McKenney's *Industrial Valley* (36–39) as well as Martha Gellhorn's *Trouble I've Seen*; variations can be found in Marita Bonner's "The Whipping," a story of how a young black mother is jailed for murdering her son after relief fails to help her feed him, and Meridel Le Sueur's "Sequel to Love," which reveals how the state invades the reproductive bodies of women. Slade was a prominent New York social worker, whose novels often criticized the welfare institutions for which she worked. *Triumph of Willie Pond* damns the logic of Aid to Dependent Children that says an unemployed father is more valuable to a family dead than alive. McKenney's account of Akron, Ohio, during the depression contrasts ineffectual social services with militant Unemployed Councils and industrial unions.

7. For a moving tale of the politics of refusal and envy animating one working-class woman (and as such defying the cultural criticism defining working-class identity), see Steedman.

8. Two books from the mid-1980s, Carolyn Steedman's *Landscape for a Good Woman* and Sandra Cisneros's *House on Mango Street*, begin their explorations of 1950s girlhood lived without resources with an image remarkably similar to those I have been tracking in 1930s texts. Steedman's tale of working-class women's differences in postwar London turns on the disdain expressed by an official, a representative of the state, whose comments tacitly confirm Steedman's (and her mother's and sister's) illegitimacy, while Cisneros begins her novel with the story of a nun quizzing Esperanza, her young narrator, about where she lives. Neither the health visitor nor the nun inhabits the seat of power; they are representatives sent to supervise the lives of those outside the view of power yet subject to it. They remain guardians of the street and the home, of decency, patrolling the lives of these young girls, reminding them of the things they lack, of their terrible needs that can barely be spoken much less met. Both stories condemn the female representative's insensitivity; blind to the hurt produced by her distance from the lives of those she visits and instructs, she offers no hope of ever learning about them—or herself.

9. In effect, this is Susan Rubin Suleiman's point in her marvelous study of French *roman-à-thèse*, *Authoritarian Fictions*.

10. Follwing Agree and Evans, Terry Smith claims Bourke-White's "scoop" of the FSA projects in both *You Have Seen Their Faces* and the *Life* spread is evidence of her complicity with "Corporate State modernity" (346).

11. Notice how the title of the book, *You Have Seen Their Faces*, foregrounds the difference between "you" and them by emphasizing voyeurism—seeing. Contrast this with the D Street writers exhortation to Damon to "tell" "them" about "us." The girls demand action from Damon as they claim their subjectivity: "us" writers over and against "them," academic critics.

12. These images from the Left resemble those detailed by Barbara Melosh in *Engendering Culture* emanating from New Deal liberals.

13. I should note that I wrote this essay during the "Nannygate" disclosures involving Zöe Baird and Kimba Wood and the parallels were inescapable. When a woman makes a lot of money, it is scandalous. Glaring class differences among women ignite tremendous public fury, even when Baird struggled to play down her class privilege. She spoke at her confirmation hearings about her plight in terms of gender (she was acting as a mother) and ethnicity (as a Jew, she was concerned about how babysitters would respond to her household), but she failed to register the plight of her exploited employees.

14. Stott quotes a review of *You Have Seen Their Faces* by Norman Cousins that dares to assert that Bourke-White's photographs will do as much to ameliorate the plight of tenant farmers as Stowe's novel did to arouse antislavery sentiments (220).

15. See *Sexual Difference* by the Milan Women's Bookstore Collective for a detailed history of the genealogy of women's freedom in the "entrustment" of one woman to another. Their theory is radically anti-Enlightenment, rejecting a rights-based analysis of liberation. However, its focus on disparity and the retrieval of the symbolic mother leaves it open to the critiques that the translator Teresa De Lauretis launches in her introductory essay to the collection.

16. I am indebted to Asha Varadharajan's useful distinction between failed resistance and no resistance that she offered in conversation with me.

WORKS CITED

Agee, James, and Walker Evans. *Let Us Now Praise Famous Men.* 1941. Boston: Houghton Mifflin, 1980.

Armstrong, Nancy. *Desire and Domestic Fiction: A Political History of the Novel.* New York: Oxford University Press, 1987.

Bodeneim, Maxwell. "To A Revolutionary Girl." *New Masses*, April 3, 1934, 16.

Bonner, Marita. "The Whipping." Nekola and Rabinowitz 70–78.

Bourke-White, Margaret. *Portrait of Myself.* New York: Simon and Schuster, 1963.

Bourke-White, Margaret, and Erskine Caldwell. *You Have Seen Their Faces.* 1937. New York: Arno, 1975.

Burke, Fielding. *Call Home the Heart.* 1932. Old Westbury, N.Y.: Feminist Press, 1983.

Butler, Judith. *Gender Trouble: Feminism and the Subversion of Identity.* New York: Routledge, 1990.

Cisneros, Sandra. *The House on Mango Street.* Houston: Arte Public Press, 1984.

Dahl, Vivian. "'Them Women Sure Are Scrappers.'" Nekola and Rabinowitz 252–54.

Damon, Maria. "'Tell Them about Us.'" *Cultural Critique* 14 (Winter 1989–90): 231–57.

De Lauretis, Teresa. *Technologies of Gender: Essays on Theory, Film, Fiction.* Bloomington: Indiana University Press, 1988.

Editors. "Introduction to the First Issue of *Life.*" *Life,* November 23, 1936, 3.

Evans, Walker. *Walker Evans at Work.* New York: Harper and Row, 1982.

Gellert, Hugo. *Karl Marx's "Capital" in Lithographs.* New York: Ray Long and Richard R. Smith, 1934.

Gellhorn, Martha. *The Trouble I've Seen.* New York: William Morrow, 1936.

Gilfillan, Lauren. *I Went to Pit College.* New York: Literary Guild, 1934.

Gold, Michael. *Jews without Money.* 1930. New York: Carroll and Graf, 1984.

Goldberg, Vicki. *Margaret Bourke-White: A Biography.* Reading, Mass.: Addison-Wesley, 1987.

Gordon, Linda. "Family Violence, Feminism and Social Control." *Women, the State and Welfare.* Ed. Linda Gordon. Madison: University of Wisconsin Press, 1990. 178–98.

Gramsci, Antonio. "The Intellectuals." *Selections from the Prison Notebooks of Antonio Gramsci.* Trans. Quintin Hoare and Geoffrey Nowell Smith. New York: International Publishers, 1971. 3–23.

Herbst, Josephine. *Rope of Gold.* New York: Harcourt, Brace, 1939.

Le Sueur, Meridel. "The Fetish of Being Outside." Nekola and Rabinowitz 299–303.

———. "I Was Marching." *Salute to Spring.* By Le Sueur. New York: International Publishers, 1940. 157–59.

———. "Sequel to Love." Nekola and Rabinowitz 36–38.

Lowe, Romona. "The Woman in the Window." Nekola and Rabinowitz 79–83.

Lukács, Georg. *History and Class Consciousness.* Trans. Rodney Livingstone. Cambridge, Mass.: MIT Press, 1971.

Macherey, Pierre. *A Theory of Literary Production.* Trans. Geoffrey Wall. London: Routledge and Kegan Paul, 1978.

Marx, Karl. *Capital.* Vol. 1. Trans. Samuel Moore and Edward Aveling. New York: International Publishers, 1967.

———. *The Eighteenth Brumaire of Louis Bonaparte.* New York: International Publishers, 1963.

Mayhew, Henry. *London Labor and London Poor.* Vol. 1. London: George Woodfall, 1851.

McKenney, Ruth. *Industrial Valley*. New York: Harcourt, Brace, 1939.

Melosh, Barbara. *Engendering Culture: Manhood and Womanhood in New Deal Public Art and Theater*. Washington, D.C.: Smithsonian Institute Press, 1991.

Milan Women's Bookstore Collective. *Sexual Difference: A Theory of Social-Symbolic Practice*. Trans. Teresa De Lauretis and Patricia Cicogna. Bloomington: Indiana University Press, 1990.

Nekola, Charlotte, and Paula Rabinowitz, eds. *Writing Red: An Anthology of American Women Writers, 1930–1940*. New York: Feminist Press, 1987.

Rabinowitz, Paula. *Labor and Desire: Women's Revolutionary Fiction in Depression America*. Chapel Hill: University of North Carolina Press, 1991.

———. *They Must Be Represented: The Politics of Documentary*. London: Verso, 1994.

———. "Voyeurism and Class Consciousness: James Agee and Walker Evans, *Let Us Now Praise Men*." *Cultural Critique* 21 (Winter 1992): 143–70.

Riley, Denise. *"Am I That Name?": The Category of "Women" in History*. Minneapolis: University of Minnesota Press, 1988.

Rukeyser, Muriel. "More of a Corpse Than a Woman." Nekola and Rabinowitz 142.

Scott, Joan Wallach. *Gender and the Politics of History*. New York: Columbia University Press, 1988.

Slade, Caroline. *The Triumph of Willie Pond*. New York: Vanguard Press, 1940.

Smith, Terry. *Making the Modern: Industry, Art, and Design in America*. Chicago: University of Chicago Press, 1993.

Steedman, Carolyn Kay. *Landscape for a Good Woman: A Story of Two Lives*. New Brunswick, N.J.: Rutgers University Press, 1986.

Stott, William. *Documentary Expression and Thirties America*. 1973. Chicago: University of Chicago Press, 1986.

Strong, Anna Louise. *I Change Worlds: The Remaking of an American*. 1935. Seattle: Seal Press, 1979.

Suleiman, Susan Rubin. *Authoritarian Fictions: The Ideological Novel as Genre*. New York: Columbia University Press, 1983.

Tompkins, Jane. *Sensational Designs: The Cultural Work of Fiction, 1780–1860*. New York: Oxford University Press, 1985.

Woolf, Virginia. "Introductory Letter." *Life as We Have Known It*. By Co-operative Working Women; ed. Margaret Llewelyn Davies. 1931. New York: W. W. Norton, 1975. xv–xxxix.

———. *A Room of One's Own*. New York: Harcourt, Brace, 1929.

10

POLITICS MEET

POPULAR

ENTERTAINMENT

IN THE WORKERS'

THEATER OF

THE 1930S

When Warren Susman characterized the 1930s as the "age of Mickey Mouse" rather than the "age of Franklin D. Roosevelt," he paved the way for new approaches to the study of American cultural history (197). He and his successors looked beyond the established literary canon, recognized political and philosophical writings, and elite artistic production, and they focused instead on advertisements, how-to manuals, movies, and popular songs to understand "the culture" of an age more broadly defined. For the 1930s, this alternate view has resulted in the depiction of a collective American psyche torn between feelings of fear, shame, and anxiety, on one hand, and faith, confidence, and desire for the solace of security, on the other.

The split personality that such scholars as Lawrence Levine, David Peeler, and, more recently, Mark Fearnow have posited as characteristic of the 1930s presents a compelling interpretation of this period. What must be remembered, however, is that other voices outside mainstream American culture existed alongside those highlighted by these scholars and maintained an animated dialogue with them. Despite transformations wrought by commercial entertainment and mass media, regionally and ethnically distinct cultural practices and beliefs, for instance, persisted through the 1930s.[1] Moreover, where intellectuals and academics developed a new understanding of culture and sought to define American culture, others sought to redefine this culture based on particular concepts of the American past or visions of the American future. On the Right, twelve southern intellectuals looked to a (mythical) agrarian past as a model for undoing the destruction that industrialism had wrought on American society.[2] On the Left, labor and radical movements envisioned a society that distributed its wealth more equitably and accorded more dignity to its working people. In working toward this latter vision, the labor movement developed an alternative culture around unions and political parties. The strikes and organizing drives of the 1930s took place amid a cultural life that included music, theater, sports, and classes in parliamentary procedure, among others.

This labor culture consciously distinguished itself from what it saw as a mainstream culture permeated with the destructive values of capitalism and bourgeois hypocrisy. Yet it did not reject American culture wholesale. On the contrary, as this essay shows, labor and the Left maintained a stance toward American culture that was profoundly ambivalent. Organized labor and left-wing movements presented themselves as outsiders that taunted institutions and dared them to be more responsive to the needs of working people, while, at the same time, they asserted the need to change the culture with which they identified themselves.

This ambivalence vis-à-vis American culture is most evident in the workers' theater of the 1930s. Unlike other elements of the labor culture of the period, the theater conveyed specific messages about labor through both its content and its form. As a platform for labor, workers' theater expressed the goals and visions of contemporary organizing campaigns and sought to develop among working people loyalty to the labor movement and to their individual union. Through collective action and unions, working women and men, according to the plays of the workers' theater movement, could achieve what American society had long denied them: justice and dignity in the workplace and in their communities. The language that workers' theater used to convey its lessons about the power of an effective labor movement was that of American popular entertainment.

Labor-oriented theater carefully wove together union politics and mainstream entertainment, expressing the former in the idioms and imagery of vaudeville, radio, Tin-Pan Alley, and the melodramatic morality play. One could certainly dismiss the presence of these genres in workers' theater as reflecting nothing more than the American culture within which the creators of workers' theater existed; in creating their own plays, theater-oriented working people and politically oriented theater people could be expected to use the language and forms with which they were most familiar. Nevertheless, other models of political theater were available, and some political theater artists did attempt to further German and Soviet theatrical experiments in the United States. The existence of alternative models for expressing political ideas on the stage thus suggests that the workers' theater movement made a clear choice in its use of the tunes and themes of popular theater. The choice of popular culture as primary idiom and the specific popular culture images and references in workers' theater therefore provide important clues for understanding how the labor movement sought to position itself vis-à-vis mainstream American culture and, ultimately, how unions in the 1930s identified themselves as agents of change in American society.

Workers' theater combined education and entertainment, teaching participants as well as audience members about the importance of solidarity and collective action and associating the labor movement with good times. In this process, labor plays used the styles of melodrama, comedy, movies, radio, and popular fiction that had already proven themselves entertaining to working people. They also borrowed from the variety show and the musical revue, with a liberal dose of popular songs, many rewritten with topical lyrics.

The theater artists and labor educators involved in workers' theater were very much aware of the political theater that had developed in the Soviet Union and Germany, and many drew their inspiration from that source.[3] The first pieces that the Workers' Laboratory Theater performed in the 1930s, for instance, were translations of pieces produced by a German-language theater group in New York City, the Proletbuehne. The director of this group, John Bonn, had been active in political theater in Germany before coming to the United States in the mid-1920s. The Proletbuehne productions that the Workers' Lab translated and performed, *Tempo, Tempo* and *The Belt*, reflected German and Soviet political theater's use of actors' voices and bodies to dramatize the conditions of workers in modern industrial society.

Members of the Workers' Lab labored to perfect this style of performance and admired the work of European groups.[4] Nevertheless, after a couple of years, the Workers' Lab abandoned such styles for what one of its key members called "native forms of entertainment" (Saxe 5). Indeed, after 1933, experiments with this particular style of European political theater were relatively few. Moreover, the notorious failure of one of the most ambitious of these experiments, the Theater Union's production of Bertolt Brecht's *Mother*, suggests crucial differences between European and American workers' theater and illuminates the cultural stance of workers' theater in this country.

The Theater Union was an organization made up of theater artists and political activists who mounted professional productions of plays oriented to working people and their middle-class allies. Different participants in the production of *Mother* have offered their own explanations for the show's dismal failure—with audiences and critics alike. The Theater Union argued that the production's genre was unintelligible to the American public, and Brecht accused the Theater Union of bastardizing his concept of Epic Theater, which was to revolutionize theater by appealing to audiences' reason rather than their emotions (Wolfson; Ellstein; Brecht 81–84; Davis, telephone conversation). The accusations that flew, however, all missed a central point about the direction that workers' theater was taking in the United States: it was concerned far less with introducing audiences to new genres of performance than with introducing them to unionism or reinforcing their knowledge of unionism. Where Brecht sought to reshape theater as well as class politics, the Theater Union, the Workers' Laboratory Theater, and the scores of other groups producing theater for audiences of workers around the nation accepted the major premises and conventions of popular performance and even used them to communicate their lessons about working-class power and politics.

The failure of this expensive experiment signaled the Theater Union and other workers' theater companies that they should remain close to the known and tested in popular entertainment and draw on the strengths and virtues of established genres rather than attempt to educate audiences in a new theatrical language. For the Theater Union, whose plays were performed by groups across the country with varying degrees of professionalism and skill, the genre of choice—from which *Mother* proved to be the only exception—proved to be melodrama. This particular theatrical genre drew its popularity with audiences from the use of shared symbols of good and evil and from its efforts to move spectators to share the pain and therefore the determination of characters on the stage.

By the 1930s, melodrama already had a long history in the United States as a vehicle for moral and political crusades. Where in the mid-nineteenth century, stage versions of *Uncle Tom's Cabin* called audiences to the fight against slavery, in the 1930s, the strike plays of the Theater Union, complete with clearly identifiable good guys (workers and their allies) and bad guys (bosses, sheriffs, and bankers), rallied spectators to the struggle for higher wages and better working conditions (Hyman, "Culture" 279–81; Rahill 247–54; Toll, *Show* 151–55).

The strike melodrama clearly demarcated working people's territory and, like other forms of workers' theater, defined class conflict to include life outside as well as inside the workplace. These plays take place where working people spend their lives and share joys and sorrows with one another: in the mining camp, in their homes, and in the coffee shops where they gather before and after work. In the case of John Howard Lawson's *Marching Song*, the action takes place entirely in an abandoned factory building that is now home to an evicted family and unemployed transients. It also serves as the working-class community's village green and union organizers' meeting hall. The appearances of the banker and the owner of the property constitute a clear intrusion into the lives and physical space of working people, and the owner's plans to tear down the building threatens the daily life of the community.[5] When the members of this community join together to organize and support a strike at the local automobile plant, it is not only because their jobs are at risk at the factory but also because the ties of kinship, romance, and neighborhood are about to be destroyed. In an ending characteristic of melodramas, the last scenes lead to a "public recognition of where evil and virtue reside," and virtue resides, quite literally, among working people, identified not only by their jobs but by their bonds to one another as well (Brooks 32).[6]

Despite the popularity of the strike plays among working-class audiences, however, much of workers' theater consisted of semi-improvised mobile productions, which were easy to develop, stage, and transport from park to union hall to rally. For this, the variety show and musical revue proved to be the most easily adaptable. Once it abandoned German-influenced productions, the Workers' Lab, for example, produced programs composed of a selection of songs, skits, and puppet shows (Elion 2, 17; Buchwald 19–20; Williams 138; Friedman 71–77). A bill of fare that included several different numbers was far better suited than the melodrama to the diverse settings in which the Workers' Lab performed, which included union meetings, picket lines, subway stations, and public parks (Robinson; Bruskin; Williams 79–83). In contrast, the full-length play required a hall, a stage, and a whole evening.

Producers of workers' theater were sharply conscious of borrowing from mainstream culture: when Brookwood Labor College began sending out troupes to perform in mining towns, mill villages, and urban workers' communities in the early 1930s, it called its productions the Labor Chautauqua. While the diverse content of each bill justified the label of "variety show," the name "chautauqua" alerted audiences to the educational content of the show.

The Brookwood Labor College chautauqua program was usually made up of a series of "acts" alternating with songs. One 1934 chautauqua opened with three songs from the songbook that was sold to audience members, an introduction to the school and the troupe, a short play about relief programs titled *Saving the Country*, more songs, a mass recitation, songs, a ventriloquist, a performance by an a cappella quartet, another play, more songs, a third play, and a closing song. Chautauqua programs also included puppet shows and other variety acts, and the performers made changes in response to specific requests or feedback on their programs, just like other traveling shows.[7] On the whole, however, they stuck to this format of ten to twelve fast-moving numbers for an evening's entertainment.

The "chautauqua movement," which dates back to the early twentieth century, was a largely middle-class reformist effort to educate and uplift the public. The decision to call Brookwood's traveling show chautauqua reflects the ambivalence toward mainstream culture that workers' theater seems to have cultivated. While the name might have prepared audiences for staid bourgeois productions, the show subverted such expectations—and the meaning of chautauqua—by its anticapitalist, prounion content. The choice of the name chautauqua announced Brookwood's intention of making chautauqua-like programs more responsive to the needs and interests of labor and working people. Like other Americans, the Labor Chautauqua proclaimed, working women and men were entitled to education. That education was to meet their own class interests, however, just as conventional chautauquas addressed the interests of middle-class audiences.

As Brookwood's Labor Chautauqua suggests, labor-oriented theater continually prodded mainstream culture, remonstrating it for not taking working-class Americans into account in developing educational and recreational programs and pressing it to do so. The tone of the debate established by Brookwood's traveling performances was quite tame, however, compared with the work of others in the workers' theater movement. Where Brookwood accepted the chautauqua largely on its own terms of providing educational entertainment and entertaining education, workers' theater frequently went much further in its critique of mainstream entertainment and subjected popular culture to merciless parody. Ironically, at the same time it expressed its most stinging indictment of popular amusements, workers' theater placed itself squarely within an established tradition of popular entertainment. Parody and self-parody lay at the heart of popular performance genres in the late nineteenth and early twentieth centuries: nineteenth-century burlesque played upon and inverted gender conventions of theater as well as society; vaudeville skits simultaneously mocked and sympathized with the immigrants that appeared in stereotypes in its shows; and Tin-Pan Alley songs outdid each other in wittiness while also drawing attention to their own preciousness (Allen 26–30, 81–108; Snyder 110–12; Furia 6–8, 153–55).

In this context, workers' theater could easily maintain its love-hate relationship with popular entertainment. On one hand, the workers' theater movement could level a biting critique at American popular entertainment, blaming it for a variety of ills, the greatest of which was distraction of working people from their own interests (Hyman, "Culture" 268–76). On the other hand, leaders of the workers' theater movement could call for the use of well-known genres in developing shows for working-class audiences.

The Workers' Laboratory Theater (WLT) production *World Fair* epitomizes the dialectical relationship between politics and popular entertainment that characterizes workers' theater. This elaborate mobile production was developed in the summer of 1933, the year of the Chicago World Fair. It transformed this most American of entertainment media into a stinging critique of New Deal politicians while simultaneously skewering such fairs and circuses for preying on the public's gullibility.[8] At the same time, it clearly based its own appeal on the appeal of circuses and tent shows.

The Workers' Lab inaugurated its own "World's Fair" at a picnic for the Communist Party's *Daily Worker* in Pleasant Bay Park on July 30. As the picnickers entered the park, they were greeted by the boom of a big brass band. Following the direction of the noise, they saw a large tent, a clown, "a freakishly dressed person in a college cap, and general barkers, all ballyhooing for the show inside, 'Only ten cents, the Greatest Show on Earth.'" Once inside, spectators were treated to a "Rogues' Gallery" of New Dealers; the "House of Culture" against a backdrop depicting Rockefeller Center; the "House of Morgan," featuring "the speculators, bulls, bears and jackasses buying, selling and shouting"; and finally, the "House of Agriculture," featuring "The Song of the Landowners and the Bankers" (to the tune of "Old MacDonald Had a Farm"). Powerful leaders in business and politics were, the show intimated, no different from the cheap entertainers audience members encountered at fairs and amusement parks.

As a piece of political entertainment, the WLT's *World Fair* operated at three different levels. First, the form itself announced to its audiences that they would find the same kind of amusement they would find at the World's Fair. Second, the genre provided the troupe with images that would convey the WLT's views of various political leaders. Finally, and most important, in presenting its own "World Fair," the WLT attacked the Chicago exposition for obscuring the important issues of the day. Where the fair in Chicago was billed as celebrating "A Century of Progress," the WLT's announced a "Capitalist Century of Progress."

World Fair contrasts sharply with Brookwood's Labor Chautauqua. The Labor Chautauqua's critique of its mainstream counterpart remained largely implicit and did not challenge its premises. *World Fair*, in contrast, took direct and explicit aim at the World Fair itself, making its critique of that institution central to its own raison d'être: the Workers' Lab devised its production as a direct response to the injustices it saw embodied in the Chicago exposition.

In the context of the overall outlook of workers' theater, however, *World Fair* functioned in ways similar to Brookwood's Labor Chautauqua. By taking on this form of entertainment with such an elaborate production, the WLT indicated visually and aurally that it knew American culture from the inside; members of the troupe could undertake such a knowledgeable critique because they themselves were Americans. At the same time, however, they indicated that current institutions of politics and entertainment were not meeting their needs or the needs of workers and the poor. Even more pointedly than the Labor Chautauqua, the *World Fair* demanded redress not only in the political and economic realm but in the realm of amusement as well.

By its very existence, workers' theater posited the need for entertainment oriented to working-class Americans. Indeed, workers' theater construed its mission as twofold: to build a strong and effective labor movement and to provide for working people's leisure. These two goals would reinforce each other, as entertainment oriented to the needs of working people would support their demands for justice and dignity and a militant labor movement would create and support a demand for class-conscious entertainment.

In working to provide explicitly political amusements, however, workers' theater constantly ran the risk of upsetting the delicate balance that it needed to maintain between its outsider's critique and its insider's techniques. The show *Pins and Needles*, produced by the International Ladies' Garment Workers Union (ILGWU), represents the apogee of the adaptation of the variety show and theatrical parody to the politics of labor-oriented theater, but it also represents the pitfalls of working too closely within accepted modes of popular entertainment.

Workers' theater's efforts to use entertainment idioms with which audiences were familiar opened up the possibility of being caught in the conventions of those genres, unable to differentiate itself from the culture that it was critiquing and thus unable to make its critique heard. In *Pins and Needles*, we see most clearly how workers' theater could lampoon the upper class and ridicule the state in clever parodies of popular genres without causing the least discomfort to the targets of its barbs.

Pins and Needles was the labor movement's most elaborate venture into theater production. Initially produced on Broadway, the revue toured the United States several times and was one of the most successful Broadway shows of its day. *Pins and Needles* also inspired numerous productions in local unions and remains a landmark in the history of union-sponsored cultural activities (Goldman, "When Social Significance Came"; Smith).

Pins and Needles elaborated on both the work of earlier workers' theater troupes and the mainstream revue format, which, like WLT productions and the Labor Chautauqua, combined parodies of popular shows and current events with song-and-dance numbers (Toll, *Entertainment* 305; Cohen-Stratyner xvii-xx). This musical revue highlighted the lives and loves of garment workers, using contemporary popular culture to comment on current social and political developments. "Mussolini Handicap" mocked the Italian dictator's domestic policies by comparing them to games of chance. In a reference to the popular Irish sweepstakes of the 1930s, the number introduces the winners of "the greatest contest of its kind in the history of the world—the All-Italy Maternity Sweepstakes": "Winner of the Sardinian Marathon Endurance . . . In sixteen years, nineteen bouncing bambinoes!"

The revue also took aim at U.S. government policies, reminding audiences of the political opposition hampering Franklin Roosevelt's New Deal programs. "FTP Plowed Under" exemplifies the multiple layers of reference characteristic of not only 1930s political theater but also the popular entertainment it parodied. The skit took its name from the Federal Theater Project production "Triple-A Plowed Under," a critique of the Supreme Court decision ruling the Agricultural Adjustment Act unconstitutional. "FTP Plowed Under" ridiculed the Federal Theater Project bureaucrats who censured the Project's plays and, by its title, suggested that they were rendering the FTP as meaningless as the Supreme Court had rendered Roosevelt's program for agricultural reform. Another number, "We'd Rather Be Right," borrowed its title from the Rodgers and Hart revue *I'd Rather Be Right* and its music from the dance tunes of the 1920s and 1930s. The piece features three 100 percent Americans discussing ways to carry out their campaign to "Make America Bigoted and Better." Their theme song begins with the verses "If you find you can't reply to your / Opponents, why don't [you] try to / Call them Un-American."

The revue to which this skit referred, *I'd Rather Be Right*, belongs to a musical genre that was a mainstay of the musical theater and vaudeville in the early twentieth century. Writing for the current season rather than for posterity, songwriters filled their works with references to politics, fashion, inventions, and the latest fads. The songs were liberally sprinkled with allusions to sports figures, clothes, social and political scandals, and newspaper headlines (Cohen-Stratyner xvii-xviii).

This medium thus proved most compatible with a form of entertainment that had an explicit political message to convey about working people and their unions. Audiences were drawn into the production by their recognition of the style and then called to task for uncritically accepting the genre as well as the conditions it ignored. Producers of such shows demonstrated that they too could compete in the arena of popular entertainment and could meet their audiences' needs and desires for engaging amusements while working for their dignity in the workplace.

Satire and social commentary were so deeply ingrained in popular entertainment, however, that, in incorporating them into its productions, labor-oriented theater ran the risk of encountering audiences that were inured to the combination of entertainment and political critique. While political theater has frequently been accused of sacrificing audiences' amusement to their indoctrination or propaganda (such criticism of the workers' theater in the 1930s was as common as it is of Oliver Stone's movies in the 1980s and 1990s), *Pins and Needles*, which tailored its portrayal of garment workers' trials and tribulations to the tastes of Broadway audiences, ended up losing much of its political bite in its efforts to entertain. Indeed, as the journalist Heywood Broun commented in his review of *Pins and Needles*, "while stout ladies in ermine must realize that they are being kidded, few if any have rushed screaming into the night" (249–50).

In *Pins and Needles*, then, politics ended up bowing to entertainment. The revue certainly sparred with contemporary culture: "I'm tired of moon songs / Of stars and of June songs," sang the garment workers in the show's opening number, "Sing Me a Song of Social Significance" (*Pins and Needles* Program). Nonetheless, in ceding as much ground to popular amusement as it did, *Pins and Needles* effectively lost its ability to challenge American culture and the society in which it functioned, belying the difficulties inherent in workers' theater wanting to identify itself as simultaneously inside and outside of mainstream American culture.

To a large extent, the nonthreatening nature of *Pins and Needles* reflects the ILGWU's own centrist position. It was no doubt the union's moderate politics as well as the show's mild critique that attracted such a broad audience and the request for a command performance at the White House (Goldman, "Pins and Needles"). Indeed, David Dubinsky, the union's president, used *Pins and Needles* as a public relations tactic aimed at currying favor with a broad spectrum of political, labor, and industrial leaders. I would argue here that, in an inversion of an inversion, the close relationship between workers' theater and popular entertainment that had developed during the 1930s allowed workers' theater to be used almost against itself. Where the workers' theater movement used popular genres to indicate its Americanness while challenging American institutions and politics, *Pins and Needles* used the cover of workers' theater to stress its identity with the labor movement while rejecting the movement's militance and asserting its own willingness and ability to work within established structures. The ILGWU, which through most of the 1930s remained at odds with older American Federation of Labor unions and with the more militant unions forming the Congress of Industrial Organizations, thus used culture as a strategy for redefining the politics of labor to coincide with its own social-democratic political agenda (Dubinsky and Raskin 219–38; Stolberg 173–201).

If *Pins and Needles* reveals the risks workers' theater ran in aligning itself with the tradition of parody in American popular performance, the productions of Local 65, United Wholesale and Warehouse Workers Union, illuminate the potential of other genres for presenting and preserving a militant edge while donning the comfortable garb of popular entertainment. Local 65 had one of the most extensive theater programs in the labor movement (Hyman, "Culture" 76–83). Its preferred genre was the musical comedy, which could provide clear models for working-class action that satire frequently did not, in either *Pins and Needles* or Workers' Lab vaudeville.

The musical comedy, first developed in the 1880s and perfected in the first three decades of this century by George M. Cohan and Jerome Kern, "told a story about average people and used vernacular music and dance to do it," unlike older musical shows, which derived their entertainment value from elaborate production numbers or mockery of different social groups (Toll, *Show* 183–97). When the musical moved onto the silver screen in the late 1920s and the 1930s, it was once again distinguished by extravagant productions—most notably in the movies of Busby Berkeley—but here still, the characters were often young working women whose livelihood depended on the success of their show (Toll, *Entertainment* 137–41; Sklar 178; Bergman 62–65).

Local 65's *Wholesale Mikado* and *Sing While You Fight* could not offer lavish production numbers, but through songs they did tell stories of earnest young people whose financial security depended on their ability to secure a union contract. In *Curly*, the shy, pushed-around office clerk is accompanied in his transformation to militant unionist by a chorus of workers promising that "anything your heart desires will come to you" when you join the union. Like Hollywood, Local 65 offered escape from grim reality and visions of hope for those with little in their pockets. For 65ers, however, this came not from making a hit show or marrying a millionaire but from joining the union: "Join up Local 65, your dreams will come true," promised one of the songs from *Curly*. And while the Gold-diggers of 1933 sang "We're in the Money," leaving audiences to imagine its provenance, for 65ers, riches came from union membership: "The skies will be sunny, / We'll make more money / In the drive of '65."[9]

The benefits of unionism were not exclusively monetary, however. Curly finds a whole new set of friends, and in *Sing While You Fight*, the two main characters find meaningful recreational activities and, ultimately, love. Jean and Bill, who meet at the union hall, are each involved in different union activities—Jean in the union's newspaper, Bill on athletic teams—but they meet again at a Saturday night social, where Bill sings "I Met My Love at the Social Hall." In joining the union, working people could thus find gratifying leisure activities and, in the process, romantic bliss.

Sing While You Fight makes explicit some of the strategic assumptions of workers' theater and the labor movement of the 1930s as well as the reality of working-class identity in those years. The labor movement was a movement of young people, who had grown up with commercial entertainment and its promises of sensual gratification and amusement.[10] They did not check these aspirations at the door when they entered campaigns for union contracts. The women and men who produced workers' theater were members of that same generation. They worked to shape a labor movement that provided space where young working people like themselves could find fulfillment of their personal, emotional needs as well as gratification of their material needs for adequate wages and safe working conditions.

The idiom that workers' theater adopted in creating this space, which recognized both "bread and roses" as central to working people's lives, also took up the question of the relationship between the labor movement and, on one hand, the young activists, and, on the other, the broader society in which they lived. Unlike the songs of Woody Guthrie, the Almanac Singers, and the People's Song movement in the 1940s and 1950s, which identified militance with a romanticized, rural "folk" America, workers' theater clearly situated a militant labor movement and its constituencies within modern commercial culture.[11] The result was a redefinition of labor militance as "all-American." By the same stroke, "all-Americanness," as embodied in Bill and Jean of *Sing While You Fight*, was redefined to include labor militance.

In subsequent decades, however, these redefinitions were rejected by labor leaders, who found no better response to their opponents demanding greater militance within the labor movement than to "call them un-American." Where the labor movement of the 1930s identified itself with various traditions of amusement and entertainment in American culture, organized labor in the postwar years more closely fit in with American traditions of bigotry and xenophobia. By the 1950s, the labor movement's ambivalence toward American culture during the 1930s had given way to a shameless acceptance of the saccharine pieties of Cold War America, and from this new position, organized labor abdicated the responsibility of working for change in American society and culture that had invigorated the labor movement in the 1930s.

NOTES

Another version of this material appears in *The Drama of Labor: Worker's Theater and the American Labor Movement* by Colette Hyman, © by Temple University Press, 1996, and is published with the permission of the publisher.

1. Major works on ethnic cultures in the 1920s and 1930s include Moore; Morawska; Buhle; and Cohen.

2. For a complete text of this critique of this industrial society, see Twelve Southerners.

3. On workers' theater in Europe in the same period, see Deak; Bradby and McCormick; Stourac and McCreery; and Mally.

4. Writings of the members of the Workers' Laboratory Theater appeared frequently in the magazine *Workers' Theater*, which they founded in 1931. Among the articles the magazine published on European workers' theater are Reines; "How the 'Workers' Theater' Works in Germany"; Vaughn; and Boyarsky. On the magazine itself as documentation of political theater in the United States in the 1930s, see Liss.

5. On spatial dimension of melodrama, see Brooks.

6. The significance of community in workers' theater is explored in Hyman, "Women, Workers and Community."

7. Materials on the Brookwood Labor Chautauqua are available in the Brookwood Labor College Papers, Box 96, Folder 24; and in the Josephine Colby Papers, Box 1. See also "Sacrifice Vacations to Chautauqua Trip."

8. The script to this production was published as "*World Fair.*" All further references to this production are from this article. The Chicago World Fair was a popular target of the Left, as is evident by the publication, just a few weeks earlier, of "The Chicago Fair," a lengthy article in the *New Masses* denouncing the "rot beneath the glitter" and the "ballyhoo" of the fair.

9. References to Local 65 lyrics are drawn from the *District 65 Songbook*. I would like to thank Sol Molovsky for providing me with a copy of the full script of *Curly*.

10. On youth culture in the 1920s and 1930s, see Lynd and Lynd, *Middletown* and *Middletown in Transition*.

11. In recent years, the folk music movement of the 1930s and its heirs have been the targets of curiously venomous attacks characterizing them as naive and misguided at best, retrograde and even dangerous at worst. See, in particular, the debate aroused by Lemisch, "Letters"; Lemisch, "I Dreamed" and "The Politics of Left Culture"; and Davis, "Music from the Left." For a vivid but flawed discussion of the People's Song movement, see Lieberman.

WORKS CITED

Allen, Robert C. *Horrible Prettiness: Burlesque and American Culture*. Chapel Hill: University of North Carolina Press, 1991.

The Belt: An Agit-Prop Play by the Prolet-Buehne. Trans. B. Stern, Workers' Laboratory Theater, New York. *Workers' Theater*, March 1932, 6–8.

Bergman, Andrew. *We're in the Money: Depression America and Its Films*. New York: New York University Press, 1971.

Boyarsky, Y. "Fifteen Years of Soviet Theater." *Workers' Theater*, March 1933, 7–8.

Bradby, David, and John McCormick. *People's Theater*. London: Rowman and Littlefield, 1978.

Brecht, Bertolt. "Criticism of the New York Production of *Die Mutter*." *Brecht on Theater*. Ed. and trans. John Willett. New York: Hill and Wang, 1964. 81–84.

Brooks, Peter. *The Melodramatic Imagination: Balzac, Henry James, Melodrama and the Mode of Excess*. New Haven, Conn.: Yale University Press, 1976.

Brookwood Labor College Papers. Archives of Labor and Urban Affairs, Wayne State University, Detroit, Mich..

Broun, Heywood. "Pins and Needles." *Out of the Sweatshop: The Struggle for Industrial Democracy*. Ed. Leon Stein. New York: Quadrangle/New York Times Books, 1977. 249–50.

Bruskin, Perry. Interview with author, November 26, 1985.

Buchwald, Nathaniel. "A Theater Advancing." *New Theater*, January 1934, 19–20.

Buhle, Paul. "Jews and American Communism: The Cultural Question." *Radical History Review* 23 (December 1980): 9–36.

"The Chicago Fair." *New Masses*, June 1933, 20–21.

Cohen, Lizabeth. *Making a New Deal: Industrial Workers in Chicago, 1919–1939.* New York: Cambridge University Press, 1990.

Cohen-Stratyner, Barbara, ed. *Popular Music, 1900–1919: An Annotated Guide to Popular Songs.* Detroit: Gale Research, 1988.

Colby, Josephine. Papers, Tamiment Library, New York University.

Davis, R. G. "Music from the Left." *Rethinking Marxism* 1 (Spring 1988): 7–25.

———. Telephone conversation with author, March 8, 1989.

Deak, Frantisek. "Blue Blouse." *Drama Review* 17 (March 1973): 35–46.

District 65 Songbook: Songs Reprinted from District 65 1941 and 1952 Songbooks. District 65 Papers, Wagner Labor Archives, Tamiment Library, New York University.

Dubinsky, David, and A. H. Raskin. *David Dubinsky: A Life in Labor.* New York: Simon and Schuster, 1977.

Elion, Harry. "Two Workers' Theater Spartakiades." *Workers' Theater*, May–June 1933, 2, 17.

Ellstein, Sylvia Regan. Interview with author, November 15, 1985.

Fearnow, Mark. "A Grotesque Spectacle: American Theater of the Great Depression as Cultural History." Ph.D. diss., Indiana University, 1990.

Friedman, Jean. "From the Workers' Laboratory Theater to the Theater of Action: The History of an Agit-Prop Theater." M.A. thesis, University of California, Los Angeles, 1968.

Furia, Philip. *The Poets of Tin Pan Alley: A History of America's Great Lyricists.* New York: Oxford University Press, 1990.

Goldman, Harry M. "Pins and Needles: The White House Command Performance." *Educational Theater Journal* 30 (March 1978): 90–101.

———. "When Social Significance Came to Broadway: 'Pins and Needles' in Production." *Theater Quarterly* 7 (Winter 1977–78): 25–43.

"How the 'Workers' Theater' Works in Germany." *Workers' Theater*, May 1931, 6.

Hyman, Colette A. "Culture as Strategy: Workers' Theater and the American Labor Movement in the 1930s." Ph.D. diss., University of Minnesota, 1990.

———. "Women, Workers and Community: Working-Class Visions and Workers' Theater in the 1930s." *Canadian Review of American Studies* 23 (Fall 1992): 31–34.

Lawson, John Howard. *Marching Song.* New York: Drama Book Services, 1937.

Lemisch, Jesse. "I Dreamed I Saw MTV Last Night." *Nation*, October 18, 1986, front cover and 374–76.

———. Letters. *Nation*, December 13, 1986, 658, 672, 674.

———. "The Politics of Left Culture." *Nation*, December 20, 1986, 700–704.

Levine, Lawrence W. "American Culture and the Great Depression." *Yale Review* 74 (Winter 1985): 196–223.

Lieberman, Robbie. *My Song Is My Weapon: People's Songs, American Communism, and the Politics of Culture, 1930–1950*. Urbana: University of Illinois Press, 1989.

Liss, Felicia N. Frank. "The Magazine *Workers' Theater, New Theater, New Theater and Film*." Ph.D. diss., City University of New York, 1976.

Lynd, Robert S., and Helen Merrell Lynd. *Middletown: A Study in American Culture*. 1929. New York: Harcourt Brace, 1956.

———. *Middletown in Transition: A Study in Cultural Conflicts*. New York: Harcourt Brace, 1937.

Mally, Lynn. *Culture of the Future: The Proletkult Movement in Revolutionary Russia*. Berkeley: University of California Press, 1990.

Moore, Deborah Dash. *At Home in America: Second Generation New York Jews*. New York: Columbia University Press, 1981.

Morawska, Ewa. *For Bread with Butter: The Life-Worlds of the East Central European Immigrants in Johnstown, Pennsylvania, 1890–1940*. New York: Cambridge University Press, 1985.

Peeler, David. *Hope among Us Yet: Social Criticism and Social Solace in Depression America*. Athens: University of Georgia Press, 1987.

Pins and Needles. International Ladies' Garment Workers' Union Papers, Martin P. Catherwood Library, New York State School for Industrial and Labor Relations, Cornell University, Ithaca, N.Y.

Pins and Needles Program [1938]. Harris Collection, Brown University, Providence, R.I.

Rahill, Frank. *The World of Melodrama*. University Park: Pennsylvania State University Press, 1967.

Reines, B. "The Experience of the International Workers' Theater." *Workers' Theater*, December 1931, 1–4.

Robinson, Earl. Interview with author, December 11, 1985.

"Sacrifice Vacations to Chautauqua Trip." *Brookwood Review*, December 1933, 1.

Saxe, Al. "Take Theater to the Workers." *New Theater*, July 1934, 5.

Sklar, Robert. *Movie-Made America: A Cultural History of American Movies*. New York: Random House, 1979.

Smith, Gary L. "The ILGWU's and Labor Stage: A Propagandistic Venture." Ph.D. diss., Kent State University, 1975.

Snyder, Robert W. *The Voice of the City: Vaudeville and Popular Culture in New York*. New York: Oxford University Press, 1989.

Stolberg, Benjamin. *Tailor's Progress: The Story of a Famous Union and the Men Who Made It*. Garden City, N.Y.: Doubleday, 1944.

Stourac, Richard, and Kathleen McCreery. *Theater as a Weapon: Workers' Theater in the Soviet Union, Germany, and Britain, 1917–1934.* London: Routledge and Kegan Paul, 1986.

Susman, Warren I. "Culture and Commitment." *Culture as History: The Transformation of American Society in the 20th Century.* By Susman. New York: Pantheon Books, 1984. Originally appeared as Introduction to Warren Susman, ed., *Culture and Commitment, 1929–1945.* New York: Pantheon Books, 1973.

Tempo, Tempo: An Agit-Prop Play by the Prolet-Buehne, N.Y. Trans. B. Stern, Workers' Laboratory Theater, New York. *Workers' Theater,* January 1932, 18–21.

Toll, Robert C. *The Entertainment Machine: American Show Business in the Twentieth Century.* New York: Oxford University Press, 1982.

———. *On with the Show: The First Century of Show Business in America.* New York: Oxford University Press, 1979.

Twelve Southerners. *I'll Take My Stand: The South and the Agrarian Tradition.* 1930. New York: Harper and Row, 1962.

Vaughn, Mary. "From the Report of the TRAM Theatres." *Workers' Theater,* Fall 1932, 13.

Williams, Jay. *Stage Left.* New York: Charles Scribner's Sons, 1974.

Wolfson, Victor. Interview with author, October 30, 1987.

"World Fair." *Workers' Theater,* September–October 1933, 14–18.

11

DEPRESSION

CULTURE: THE

DREAM OF

MOBILITY

Cultural history is often seen as soft history, our effort to make sense of what otherwise falls through the cracks: sensibility, moral feelings, dreams, relationships, all hard to objectify. My theme here is at once concrete—the books, the films of an era—and quite intangible, the look, the mood, the feel of the historical moment. Most of us think we *know* what the 1930s were about. Like the 1960s, the 1930s belong not only to history but to myth and legend. To this day the period remains our byword for economic crisis, a permanent warning of what could yet happen again. The 1929 crash was on everyone's mind when stocks plummeted in the fall of 1987; it remained an unspoken fear during the long, intractable recession that began in 1989 and lasted through the early 1990s, leaving many without jobs and with diminished hopes. In recent years we have witnessed the contraction of not only American industry but also the old sense of unlimited possibility: the career open to talents, the promise of American life. My concern here is not with jobs but with the state of mind that goes with lower economic horizons. My subject is the role of culture in reflecting and influencing how people feel about their lives.

The mood of the Great Depression was defined not only by hard times and a coming world crisis but also by all the attempts to cheer people up—or else to sober them up into facing what was happening. Though

poor economically, the decade was rich in both popular fantasy and tren-
chant social criticism. This is the fundamental split in depression culture:
on one hand, the effort to grapple with unprecedented economic disaster, to explain and understand it; on the other hand, the need to get away,
to create art and entertainment to distract people from their trouble, which
became another way of coming to terms with it. Keeping our eyes on both
sides of this cultural divide, we can see how closely linked they are.

Thanks to the intersection of new technology and certain deep human
needs, the 1930s proved to be a turning point in American popular culture.
Radio came of age, binding audiences together as they shared amusements
as well as anxieties. Photography, photojournalism, and newsreels provided the visual images that even those great radio voices—H. V. Kaltenborn
from Spain, Edward R. Murrow from London, Orson Welles from Mars—
could not convey. This was also the era that saw the consolidation of the
Hollywood studio system and the classical style of American sound films.
The great movie genres of the 1930s—the gangster movie, the horror film,
the screwball comedy, the dance musical, the road movie, the social-con-
sciousness drama, the animated cartoon—have since shown amazing vitality. They still influence the way our movies are made, while the old films
themselves remain objects of nostalgia or affectionate imitation.

Woody Allen's clever movie *The Purple Rose of Cairo*, a pastiche of
depression-era clichés, lovingly portrays the Janus-faced culture of the era.
Mia Farrow is a waitress in a jerkwater town who lives out her fantasies
by going to the movies, while Danny Aiello plays her unemployed husband, a blue-collar lout who belongs to the drab and boring life she is trying to forget. Jeff Daniels plays a character who literally steps off the screen
to add a little magic and romance to her pinched world.

If you look at the movie within the movie, the film she keeps going back
to see, you get Woody Allen's version of the fantasy itself. We get incoher-
ent glimpses of some wealthy, frivolous idlers making silly banter on movie-
sets designed to look like cavernous living rooms, glitzy nightclubs, or
"Egyptian" tombs. Such cheesy but exotic settings parody the famous
depression-era idea of the careless rich living a life of pure swank and style.
But the movie also shows us the other side of the story: the small town so
idle and empty it looks like a picture postcard; the husband out of work,
supported by a waiflike wife as he hangs out with the boys; the movie theater as the scene of communal daydreaming, where ordinary people feed
on escapist images of wealth, adventure, and romance.

Woody Allen is a master at manipulating movie clichés, simplifying
them, satirizing them, infusing them (as Chaplin did) with his own kind

of little-man pathos. Dennis Potter did the same thing for the English common man, depression-style, in his wildly original series *Pennies from Heaven*. There Bob Hoskins played a sheet-music salesman with a bossy, repressed wife and a shy, dreamy love for the music and lyrics that light up his gray, constricted world. They are his romantic outlet as he lipsynchs his feelings to the incongruous sound of the old recordings. He looks longingly to America as the place the best songs come from but also as the fantasy land where those songs come true.

Psychological studies of the Great Depression have shown how economic problems were complicated by emotional problems, since hard times, no matter how impersonal their origin, undercut their victims' feelings of confidence, self-worth, even their sense of reality. The psychological pain was exacerbated by the American ethic of self-help and individualism, remnants of a frontier mentality—the same dream of success, dignity, and opportunity that had inspired immigrants, freed slaves, and natives alike. This made people feel responsible when their lives ran downhill. *Purple Rose* and even *Pennies from Heaven* are stories about fighting off depression, in every sense of the word.

It has been forcefully argued that more people during the 1930s, especially the poor, lived vicariously by turning on the radio than by going to the movies. (The movie audience actually peaked in 1946, shortly before the coming of television.) Woody Allen complemented his picture of the depression in *Purple Rose* with his more autobiographical treatment of a noisy Jewish family in Brooklyn in *Radio Days*, a tribute to the role radio had played in melding a larger community out of an ethnic stew. The nightly fifteen-minute dose of the tribulations of Amos 'n' Andy, which was often piped into theaters—otherwise few would have gone to the movies—propelled traditional dialect humor onto a national stage. New York's mayor, the inimitable Fiorello La Guardia, read the comic strips over the radio on Sunday mornings. Franklin Roosevelt's fireside chats gave people a feeling of intimate connection with their more activist government; radio, by intervening pervasively in people's lives, thus became the electronic equivalent of the New Deal.

"Amos 'n' Andy" was an ongoing epic of daily life, setting the practical man against the quixotic dreamer whose schemes, especially money-making schemes, were always going awry. Behind the laugh lines it was a program about ordinary people trying to get by. This was typical of depression-era "escapism": obliquely reflecting deeply felt concerns yet also containing and neutralizing them, spinning out problems to show they could somehow be worked out. This was not so different from the way

Roosevelt himself, despite his patrician tones, put a warm human spin on the news of the world. He spoke with authority but also simply and directly, as if to each listener individually. By showing he cared, he fostered real hope after the deepening despair of the Hoover years. While forwarding the new federal role, he reassuringly affirmed traditional values.

But the myth of the 1930s was far more than the sum of its movie images and radio sounds. A battalion of gifted photographers helped create an indelible iconography that we still associate with hard times. Everyone recalls the urban images of apple-sellers and their pushcarts, the southern chain gangs, and haggard but dignified sharecroppers. Epic scenes from the Dust Bowl are part of our permanent shorthand for rural poverty and natural desolation. Much that we know about the human spirit in adversity can still be found in Dorothea Lange's "Migrant Mother," the great 1936 photograph of a woman whose brow is furrowed like tractored-out land, the look on her face more pensive and distant than pained or troubled. Two children, with their backs to the camera, have nuzzled into her shoulders, and the bony fingers at her chin seemed to extend from some armature sculpted to support the weight of her head. Like other Lange photographs of migrants, she is all angles, a zigzag of intersecting lines. Anxious but reserved and self-contained, she speaks to our humanity without soliciting our sympathy. Yet she has a look of entrapment, of someone with her back to the wall.

As we look back at it today, the depression is a study in contrasts. At one extreme, the "look" of the 1930s is in the flowing art deco lines of the new Chrysler Building, the Radio City Music Hall, the sets of Astaire-Rogers musicals such as *Top Hat, Swing Time,* and *Shall We Dance.* At the other end is the work done by such photographers as Lange, Walker Evans, Arthur Rothstein, and Ben Shahn for Roy Stryker's photography unit of the Farm Security Administration, conceived as a way of bringing home the unthinkable pain of rural poverty to urban Americans. If the FSA photographs give us the naturalistic art of the depression at its most humane, the Astaire-Rogers musicals convey an elegant, sophisticated world in which the depression is barely a distant rumor. Yet both are equally characteristic of the period.

In his fine book *Documentary Expression and Thirties America* William Stott described how the government, business leaders, and even economists suppressed or sweetened the unpleasant facts during the early years of the depression. Until *Fortune* published an article in September 1932 called "No One Has Starved," establishment newspapers, magazines, and radio programs downplayed or ignored the depression and portrayed the country, as Hoover himself did, in business-as-usual terms.

This virtual blackout gave impetus to the documentary movement, to radical journalism, and to a few independent films, such as King Vidor's utopian pastoral fable *Our Daily Bread* (1934), which shows the old American individualism giving way to the sense of community on a Russian-style collective farm. A few years later, an upbeat *Life* magazine, founded in 1936 as the vehicle for a new photojournalism, complained that "depressions are hard to see because they consist of things not happening, of business not being done" (Stott 67–68). Needless to say, *Life* published none of the stomach-churning pictures of rural misery taken by its star photographer, Margaret Bourke-White, in 1936 and 1937. They appeared instead in a book she wrote with Erskine Caldwell, *You Have Seen Their Faces*, whose accusing title reminds us that a great deal of suffering, poverty, and unemployment was invisible, except to those who cared to look at it.

Trying to grasp the essential spirit of the 1930s would seem to be a hopeless task. How can one era have produced both Woody Guthrie and Rudy Vallee, both the Rockettes high-stepping at the Radio City Music Hall and the Okies on their desperate trek to the pastures of plenty in California? To readers of the journalist Eugene Lyons's 1941 bestseller, it was the "Red Decade." Revisionist historians, including Warren Susman and Loren Baritz, countered by drawing attention to the conservative heartland of the middle class, with its deep economic fears yet also its interest in sports, mystery novels, self-improvement, and mass entertainment. Some historians, such as Daniel Aaron, James B. Gilbert, and Richard Pells, focused on the intellectual history of the 1930s, analyzing the radicalism of the era in terms that reach back to prewar socialism and progressivism. Other writers in the popular tradition of *Only Yesterday* and *Middletown* concentrate on the social history of everyday life. Still others, such as Arthur Schlesinger Jr., center on the administrative and political history of the New Deal and the dramatic figure of Roosevelt himself, whose dominating presence became a force of mythic proportions. Most recently, younger students of the 1930, including Paula Rabinowitz, Deborah Rosenfelt, Constance Coiner, and Nora Roberts, have reemphasized the radical Left, especially the unsung role of such women as Josephine Herbst, Tillie Olsen, and Meridel Le Sueur in bringing gender concerns, family histories, and deep personal emotions into the committed fiction and journalism of the era. Less convincingly, a few scholars have excavated and set out to defend virtually all the proletarian writing of the 1930s, in part because they feel it has been unjustly neglected but more because they identify with its political program.

When I was in college in the late 1950s, the 1930s appeared to us in the hazy distance as a golden age when writers, artists, and intellectuals developed strong political commitments and enlisted literature on the side of the poor and the destitute. We were able to mythologize the 1930s because we never read most of what was written then. (Most of it was long out of print.) We hated the blandness and repressive limits of the political culture of the 1950s and looked back wistfully at the excited ideological climate of the 1930s, about which we knew next to nothing.

Years later, when I finally looked into some of the ideological debates of the 1930s, whose radical intensity I had admired from afar, I was horrified by the mean-spirited brutality of many sectarian polemics, more concerned with doctrinal purity than with advancing any real social change. For all their dialectical ingenuity, they were deaf to the free play of ideas, and they breathed an atmosphere of personal aggression and fundamentalist dogma.

Yet this was also a period when writers as well as photographers keenly pursued an interest in the backwaters of American life: the travail of the immigrant, the slum, the ghetto, the failures of the American dream, and above all the persistence of poverty and inequality amid plenty—a subject with few parallels in earlier American literature.

One attempt to grapple directly with social reality was the proletarian novel, a middle-class experiment in creating militant, revolutionary fiction about the working class. Many of these novels centered on industrial conflict. At least six of them dealt with the same strike in the cotton mills of Gastonia, North Carolina, in 1929. These writers reshaped journalistic material into ideological fables. In this they were encouraged by the Communist Party, which in the early 1930s saw literature as a weapon, a way of fostering class consciousness. Debates on proletarian writing were commonplace in left-wing journals all through the early 1930s, with some critics discounting books that merely portrayed working-class life without stressing its revolutionary potential.

The standard view of these novels used to be that of Malcolm Cowley, who drew a composite sketch of their plots as follows:

> A young man comes down from the hills to work in a cotton mill (or a veneer factory or a Harlan County mine). Like all his fellow workers except one, he is innocent of ideas about labor unions or the class struggle. The exception is always an older man, tough but humorous, who keeps quoting passages from *The Communist Manifesto*. Always

the workers are heartlessly oppressed, always they go out on strike, always they form a union with the older man as leader, and always the strike is broken by force of arms. The older man dies for the cause, like John the Baptist, but the young hero takes over his faith and mission. (250–51)

Described in this reductive and amusing way, the novels seem even more absurdly formulaic than they actually were. Partly inspired by Soviet experiments in proletarian art, these books have never fared very well with readers or critics. By 1939 the editor of *Partisan Review*, Philip Rahv, once a theorist of proletarian writing, could dismiss the whole episode as "the literature of a party disguised as the literature of a class" (299–300). Yet proletarian writing was part of a much broader tradition of fiction and poetry in the 1930s and 1940s. Many key works of depression journalism and social documentation resemble proletarian fiction, which also overlaps with mainstream social novels such as James T. Farrell's *Studs Lonigan* and John Dos Passos's *U.S.A.* that have few working-class characters and depend on no simple conversion fable. There are also strong similarities between proletarian fiction and the 1930s road novel, as well as the hard-boiled crime fiction of writers such as James M. Cain and W. R. Burnett and their ubiquitous Hollywood progeny. Stylistically, they all came out of Ernest Hemingway's sleeve.

Malcolm Cowley reduced proletarian fiction to a simple formula by limiting his selection to works built on that formula. If most of the strike novels seem thin and ideological today, there remains a more enduring kind of "proletarian" novel than Cowley's. I mean fiction dealing with what Edward Dahlberg called the "bottom dogs" of society, the *Ironweed*-style characters at the very base of the social ladder. Reading Dahlberg's novel *Bottom Dogs* not long before his death, D. H. Lawrence took note of the "mass of failure" that underlay America's "huge success" (267). He was horrified and fascinated by what he took to be the latest wave of American primitivism, a brutal reduction of the human animal to "a *willed* minimum" (271). "The next step," he prophesied, "is legal insanity, or just crime" (267, 271, 272). Besides Dahlberg, this raw, grim vein of writing includes such books as Edward Anderson's *Hungry Men* and Tom Kromer's Kafkaesque *Waiting for Nothing*, both republished and well received in the mid-1980s.

Nelson Algren was one of the best of these writers. Walter Rideout described his first novel, *Somebody in Boots*, as "fascinatingly hideous" (185). It foreshadowed the work of later hard-boiled pulp writers, such as Jim

Thompson. But Algren was anything but to the manner born. Partly Jewish, partly Scandinavian in origin, his real name was Nelson Algren Abraham, and he had been to college and to journalism school. For him, as for many others, becoming a writer meant taking to the road to see how the other half lived: riding boxcars, cadging meals, stopping in hobo jungles and Salvation Army soup kitchens, and learning which town threw drifters in jail for vagrancy. Men and even children went on the road simply because there were no jobs or because their families were disintegrating around them.

In later interviews Algren estimated that there were a million people out on the road in the early 1930s. Falling into their world made him a writer. "The experience on the road gave me something to write about," he told H. E. F. Donohue. "You do see what it's like, what a man in shock who is dying looks like. He knows he's going to die, and he's shocked by the idea that he's dying. Or you're waiting for a boxcar and it seems to be going a little too fast and some kid makes a try for it and then you get the smell of blood and you go over and you see it sliced off his arm. . . . And all the tens of thousands of Americans literally milling around at that time trying to survive" (Donohue 53).

The road, says Algren, not only gave young writers something to write about but also conditioned their attitudes toward the larger society: "Everything I'd been told was wrong. That I could see with my own eyes. I'd been told, I'd been assured that it was a strive and succeed world. What you did: you got yourself an education and a degree and then you went to work for a family newspaper and then you married a nice girl and raised children and this was what America was. But this was not what America was. America was not socialized and I resented very deeply that I'd been lied to" (Donohue 54). Algren in his tough-guy manner may have romanticized his life on the road, like Jack London several decades earlier, but since it was based on experience, not formula, it became a truer form of discovery than the contrived conversions we find in the strike novels.

Empathetic writers, burdened by middle-class guilt, were invariably radicalized by what they saw on the road, by their exposure to so many marginal and miserable people, the detritus of the American dream. While few women took to the road as Algren did, they often had similar experiences in breadlines, on picket lines, or among the homeless. They got involved in the labor wars, witnessing factory lockouts and seeing goons beating up strikers to prevent unions from organizing. Writers, both men and women, moved back and forth between journalism and fiction or poetry. John Steinbeck's *Grapes of Wrath* emerged directly out of the wrenching articles he wrote for the *Nation* and the San Francisco *News* on the conditions of migrant labor. Often the writers became Communists, or worked with the Communists, not because they were strongly political but simply because the Communists, especially at the local level, seemed the most committed to changing society and helping those at the bottom.

Writing in the 1930s was thus in many ways an experiment in downward mobility. Only a few of the "proletarian" authors—Jack Conroy and Tillie Olsen, for instance—actually came from the working class. Others felt ashamed of their own background and upbringing. Still others (such as Algren) may have been seeking adventure and risk, in the style of Hemingway—then writing about it, also in Hemingway's style. (A number of writers followed Hemingway to Spain after 1936.) Though many middle-class or ethnic authors and filmmakers grew up in circumstances that were but one step above poverty, their education alone vaulted them into the ranks of the privileged. Many, however, sloughed off the comforts of the middle class, for a time at least, to explore a way of life that seemed more emblematic of depression-era America.[1]

There was no doubt a comic side to this quest for the lower depths that so many were desperate to leave behind. I'm sure more writers nurtured their radicalism in the Hollywood hills than in riding the rails. As the depression ended, Preston Sturges brilliantly satirized Hollywood's social conscience in *Sullivan's Travels* (1942)—by sending a frivolous director of inane comedies (a character named Sullivan, played by Joel McCrea) out on the road looking for the poor, with an entourage of studio retainers following close behind. Instead of another edition of *Ants in Your Pants*, his usual kind of movie, Sullivan wants to make a serious epic of social concern called *O Brother, Where Art Thou?* though his thoughtful butler warns him that only "the morbid rich" have an interest in poverty, which is really a plague to be shunned at all cost.

At first the director's cushioned life and his absurd play-acting prevent him from making even superficial contact with the poor. (A limousine ferries him to where he can hop a freight train.) But then, in a series of circumstances that could happen only in a movie, he loses his memory and his identity, is given up for dead, gets railroaded by the judicial system somewhere in the South, and is propelled without appeal into a world of "real" suffering—that is, the chain-gang world of such movies as *I Am a Fugitive*, with a chorus of black prisoners singing "Go Down, Moses." Sturges shifts from satirizing social-problem movies (and the shallow Hollywood types who make them) to reenacting them in a setting of dreamlike intensity. He traps his well-meaning director in just the kind of movie he wanted to make, a stylized world of arbitrary punishment and grim endurance. After merely slumming in social misery, he is swallowed up by it, with no lifeline to his familiar world.

But the movie does not end here. Along with his fellow prisoners, Sullivan finds some momentary relief watching cartoons about Mickey Mouse and Pluto. *This* is what depression audiences really needed, says Sturges: escape, lighthearted enjoyment. The point is pungently philistine and a trifle complacent: Sturges the comedy-director is telling us that laughter, not lower-depths sociology, is the universal solvent. The entertainer, not the revolutionary, has the common touch. Comedy eases the burden of the wretched of the earth and unites the privileged artist for a brief moment with his suffering brother, that 1930s myth, the common man. Yet *Sullivan's Travels*, though self-congratulatory, pays handsome tribute to the genre it satirizes and re-creates, the lower-depths movie. Even for a comic artist, as Chaplin showed, the way down, into life's pratfalls and social embarrassments, was the way out.

The kinds of protest movies Sturges had in mind stretch from the Warner Brothers problem movies of the early 1930s, such as *I Am a Fugitive from a Chain Gang* and *Wild Boys of the Road*, to the grand summation of the decade's social consciousness, John Ford's remarkably faithful 1940 adaptation of *The Grapes of Wrath*. Significantly, all three of these films are road movies, not about observers doing research on the poor but about ordinary people uprooted from a stable life and forced to wander in search of something better, only to find more hellish conditions among other displaced, unwanted, or viciously mistreated people. The social disintegration, violence, and human isolation in these films are akin to the atmosphere in the gritty gangster films from which they emerged, often made at the same studio, Warner Brothers.

Like some of the gangster films, *I Am a Fugitive* traces the roots of social turmoil back to the Great War, which had exposed the men who fought in it to violence and carnage but also to a wider world than the one they came from. Based on a controversial magazine serial that was turned into a novel, *I Am a Fugitive* shows us how James Allen (played by Paul Muni) returns from the war to confront a different world and a family that cannot understand what he has been through or how he has changed. This is exactly what happens in Hemingway's great story "Soldier's Home." Just as Hemingway's returning soldier, having seen what he's seen, can no longer summon up the will or purpose to do *anything*, James Allen finds his old factory job too confining. After so much army regimentation, he recoils at the rigid industrial routine. He does not want to be a "soldier of peace," a soldier of anything. He wants to be creative, an engineer who can work with his hands and build projections of his own dreams. Instead he is chained to a desk job he can do with his eyes closed. "I've changed . . . been through hell," he tries to explain.

So he leaves his steady job, crisscrosses the country, gradually becoming a hobo as he is unable to find work. He tries to pawn his war medals, but the pawnshop already has a case full. The time frame is vague, but we are still in the early 1920s, a relatively prosperous period. We soon understand that the film is projecting the social crisis of the depression onto the earlier decade, thinking about the 1920s in 1930s terms: scarcity of work, a mobility born of ambition but soon fueled by desperation, the disruption of social bonds and promises embodied in the discarded medals, which speak to us of discarded values, dreams, and ideals.

Soon, caught up in another hobo's stickup attempt, James Allen is railroaded by a crude legal system into ten years on a chain gang. But what made the movie famous was something more visceral and concrete: the concentration-camp atmosphere of the prison barracks, the casual brutality of the overseers and the chain gang itself, the wasting away of a desperately ill prisoner who is still forced to work, the torture of the sweatbox and the inedible food, and the excruciating feat of the escape, from the removal of James Allen's leg-irons with blows from a sledgehammer to his flight through the swamps as he is pursued by vicious armed guards with snarling dogs. These scenes have the sensory and social impact of the early Soviet films. Their memorable imagery would reappear in later films from *Sullivan's Travels* to *Cool Hand Luke* and *Down by Law*, set in the Louisiana bayous. *I Am a Fugitive*, like Upton Sinclair's *The Jungle* and Steinbeck's *Grapes of Wrath*, was one of those works that actually made a difference in the real world, provoking violent controversy and leading to reform of the grotesque system of "justice" it vividly exposed. But the really radical twist in the movie has not been fully understood.

After escaping north and reversing his two names, James Allen manages to invert his position in society as well. He gets the job in construction he has always wanted—a job that his work on the chain gang had obscenely parodied—and between 1924 and 1929, in Chicago, under his new identity, he builds himself up into one of the upstanding citizens of the community. Blackmailed and eventually betrayed by a woman he is forced to marry, he returns voluntarily to the South, by agreement, to serve out a symbolic ninety-day sentence. But the unnamed state—actually Georgia—goes back on its word, subjects him to even more brutality than before, then refuses to release him at the promised time.

His only way out is another escape. Now, at top speed, all he did must
be done again. But the frenzied, desperate, utterly disillusioned creature
who flees this time is not the cocky, confident person who made it out
before. During the escape he loses the old man who embodies the only
bit of humanity he has ever encountered on the chain gang: the cynical
realist who was stunned that he had returned but also the symbol of his
own dwindling humanity and resilience.

Careening along in a truckload of dynamite, James Allen has gone from
being an unfairly victimized citizen, still resourceful and full of hope, to
an explosive desperado hell-bent on freedom or self-destruction. Now there
is no question of his putting his life together again, not just because of the
depression but because of his own depression. His self-assurance has crum-
bled with his trust. The man who was stupid enough to walk back into the
chain gang now sees through everything: "The state's promise didn't mean
anything. . . . Their crimes are worse than mine." The bedrock faith in the
system, which brought him through the war, which survived impoverishment, injustice, and physical torture, has now disintegrated, leaving him
a haunted and a haunting man.

The last lines of the movie are a famous exception to the Hollywood
cult of the happy ending. James Allen appears in the shadows, a shadow
himself, for a furtive goodbye to his second wife. "How do you live?" she
asks him. A hollow, frightened voice hisses, "I steal." His crazed eyes tell
us that his second escape, for all its reckless bravado, did not really work.
He is a wreck of a man, unable to function except as the criminal and
fugitive he was falsely accused of being. Quite literally, society has made
him what he is: a man who, in his half-demented, half-realistic fears, sees
through society, sees the lie of its official values. The unusual title of the
film, like the last line of dialogue, places this man in an ongoing, open-
ended, unresolved present: I *am* a fugitive, I still am. He points a finger
at us, for he is the homeless, shadowy outcast who haunts our world, whom
we would all prefer to forget. The movie ends, but his flight continues. It
would be a long time before another American film would end on such a
hopeless, accusing note.

I haven't room here to discuss in detail the other side of 1930s culture, the
supposedly escapist side. In contrast to proletarian novels, radical documentaries, and films like *I Am a Fugitive*, the popular arts in the 1930s were
legendary for their lightheartedness and frivolity. Sometimes the fun was
anarchic in a way that bordered on savagery. From the first half of the
decade, think of the zaniness of the Marx brothers and their scenarist, S. J.

Perelman; the black humor fiction of Perelman's brother-in-law, Nathanael West; and the snidely insinuating comedy of W. C. Fields and Mae West. At other times this popular culture was buoyant and sophisticated, as in the witty lyrics and clever patter songs of Cole Porter, Rogers and Hart, and the Gershwins and the screwball humor of the Thin Man series, *It Happened One Night*, and the many breakneck romantic comedies that followed. The same period that produced the histrionic Paul Muni, who clumped through *Scarface* like a childish, menacing oaf, also gave us as one of its icons, the lean, lightfooted, whimsical figure of Fred Astaire, who embodied the grace and filigree of the era as definitively as Muni conveyed its heavy, brooding seriousness.

The conventional picture we get from *The Purple Rose of Cairo* or even *Sullivan's Travels* of people going to the movies or listening to the radio to escape their troubles—to daydream and fantasize—is thus seriously inadequate. The relation of the arts to the social mood was far more complex. A period's forms of escape, if they can be called escape, are as significant and revealing as its social criticism. Under the guise of mere entertainment, "Amos 'n' Andy" transposed people's daily problems, especially money problems, into a different key and made them seem more manageable—interminable, perhaps, but manageable. The mass audience could identify even with black people in a period when *everyone* felt beset and beleaguered.

Immensely popular historical romances like *Gone with the Wind* and *Anthony Adverse* transported readers into different eras, such as the post–Civil War period in the ravaged South, which in its mixture of feelings of defeat, futility, and plangent hope had striking resonance for many in the depression era. The anarchic comedies of the early 1930s, with their legendary speed, wit, sexiness, and irreverence, showed how our moral limits and social conventions had been undermined by the depression. Finally, it is no accident that so many screwball comedies, stage musicals, and Astaire-Rogers films are set in the world of the very rich, for that world had not only the money but also the mobility that was denied to so many during the depression.

This is the ultimate irony: in a world where so many took to the road, so few had any real mobility. James Allen on his flight from the chain gang, a flight to nowhere; the men and boys hopping freights and pitching camp outside towns that did not want them; the Joad family on its biblical trek through town and desert, Hooverville and sanitary camp: this is not travel but desperation, a way of standing still or running in place. As Nicholas Lemann showed in *The Promised Land*, even the great black migration from

the South slowed down; there were so few jobs to be found. Migrant workers like the Joads were grasping at survival, not reaching for freedom. This
is one reason photography became such a central mode of expression in the
1930s. The migrant pictures, with their sharp angles and their clashing lines,
are all about going nowhere; the people are pinned like social specimens,
frozen into postures that allow little movement, no escape.

The fantasy culture of the 1930s, on the other hand, is all about movement, not the desperate simulation of movement we find in the road stories but movement that suggests genuine freedom. This was why, with
Busby Berkeley, with Fred Astaire, and with George Balanchine and
Martha Graham, choreography became as important as photography for
this decade. The look of the great 1930s musicals is everything that Lange's
"Migrant Mother" or "Woman of the High Plains," so angular and static,
are not. It is all circle and swirl, all movement and flow. Think of it: the
rose-petal effect in Berkeley's big numbers, the sweepingly elegant curva-
ture of the art deco sets, the brilliance of movement of Astaire and Rogers, locked together in breathtaking dips and turns, he in top hot, white
tie, and tails, she in elaborate gowns that create rococo line drawings in
space.

We tend to forget the considerable dramatic tension generated in these
films. The musical numbers are always embedded in a story line that con-
trives every possible conflict, hesitation, and misunderstanding to keep
Astaire and Rogers apart. Like the couples in screwball comedies, they are
treated as an incongruous pair, always at cross purposes. Apparently, no
one informed them in advance of how perfect they were together or let
them in on the critical cliché—"He gives her class and she gives him sex."
Their talk is the banter of two ill-matched people, unable to agree on
anything *except* when they dance. "Let Yourself Go," says one signature
number; "Never Gonna Dance," says another. Dancing is not simply what
they *do*, it is what their films are about.

And when they do dance, an astonishing metamorphosis takes place.
Feelings they could never articulate are suddenly acted out in movement.
Like all genuine couples, together they are something they could never
have been separately, not simply romantic, not simply a dream of swank
and elegance inherited from the nightclub era of the 1920s, but a dream
of motion that appealed to people whose lives were pinched, anxious,
graceless, and static.

With the coming of sound films, the 1930s also became the great age of
dialogue comedy, the spoken equivalent of Astaire's dancing and Cole
Porter's songs. The great couples in 1930s comedies—William Powell and

Myrna Loy, Katherine Hepburn and Cary Grant, Cary Grant and Irene Dunne, Carole Lombard and *any* of her partners—were wonderful talkers rather than ideal lovers. In the age of the strict production code, which descended like a velvet curtain in 1934, the zest and effervescence of sharp repartee and the look that accompanied this thrust and parry were the only effective ways of being sexual (rather than merely sentimental). The crackle and speed of the dialogue, the frantic, farcical pace of the action, represented yet another form of freedom and mobility.

The screwball comedies were usually set in a comic-opera world of wealth and ease, but also a world hemmed in by stuffy conventions and rigid family proscriptions. The bubbly, unpredictable women played by Lombard or Hepburn in such films as *My Man Godfrey* or *Bringing Up Baby* represented the lure of sexual or social irresponsibility. Think of the sheer lunacy of Hepburn and Grant singing "I can't give you anything but love" to a leopard on someone's roof. The zany freedom of their behavior is made possible by money but also by energy, spirit, insouciance, and independence, qualities with which their hard-pressed audience was quick to identify. The huge dinosaur skeleton that collapses at the end of *Bringing Up Baby* represents the dry bones of the past, rigid, sexless, and sterile, while Hepburn's daffy effervescence and mobility suggest an unstoppable life-force daringly oriented toward the unknown, toward the future.

This suggests that the real dream of the expressive culture of the 1930s was not money and success, not even elegance and sophistication, but mobility, with its thrust toward the future. Certainly the crucial aspect of 1930s architecture and design is its dedication to the ideal of motion, its famous streamlining, the loops and curves of its deco modernism, which pretended to be clean and functional but were actually so decorative and stylized. At first the completion of such large projects as Rockefeller Center, the Chrysler Building, and the Empire State Building was an act of blind faith carried forward during the worst years of the depression. But after 1933, when few large buildings were built, a new and more genuinely hopeful note enabled this architectural style to be applied to the world of consumer goods, furniture styles, and industrial design.

Streamlining was a way of putting speed and motion into consumer goods by associating them with the dynamic energy of the machine, at just the moment when consumer demand was low and so many in the work force and the industrial plants were idle. As Eva Weber writes in *Art Deco in America*, "The style's main function was to attract new customers by means of its persuasive allusions to modernism, high style, efficiency, and speed" (145). From the Century of Progress exhibition in Chicago in 1933 to the great New York World's Fair of 1939–40, with its famous GM Futurama, this decade of near-stagnation, in which the world was also spiraling down toward totalitarianism and war, devoted itself to imagining a sleek, streamlined consumer culture, which would not come into being until after 1945.

The age of industrial decline was also the golden age of industrial design. The man who took the motor off the top of the refrigerator made a fortune, for sales skyrocketed, even in the depressed 1930s. The GM Futurama rightly predicted the automotive America of 1960, crisscrossed by ribbons of new highways. The loops and curves of art deco eventually became the cloverleafs of the interstate highway system, superseding the right-angle grid of downtown traffic patterns. Out of the stagnation of the present, the 1930s had invented the future. Again Americans would take to the road, but not as drifters or fugitives. In the postwar years, with the growth of suburbia, Americans at last achieved the mobility that had been denied to them during hard times.

Thus what began seemingly as a world of fantasy, a denial of the depression, was in fact a response to it, an effective antidote to it. Perhaps the most far-reaching legacy of the depression was the consumer culture, the automotive culture, the suburbanized one-family house culture that followed the war. But this brought new problems in its wake: decaying central cities, traffic jams, and a polluted environment. America discovered that prosperity too had its price. Even before the huge migrations to the Sunbelt and California, social critics of the 1950s (such as William H. Whyte) suggested that America was becoming a much more rootless society. After the privations of the depression and war came the stupefaction of affluence, the boredom and anomie of suburbia.

In the end, the dream of mobility turned into a terrible disappointment for some who succeeded and others who were left behind, and the depression era, like the wartime, would come nostalgically to seem more authentic, more genuine—a time when life seemed more real and Americans lived much closer to the bone.

NOTE

1. Murray Kempton neatly avoids precise class origins by paying tribute to the "plebeian" writers, such as James T. Farrell, who came from the lower middle class but carried the freight of early poverty through their whole writing

lives. He cites an epigraph that Farrell borrowed from Chekhov: "What writers belonging to the upper class have received from nature for nothing, plebeians acquire at the cost of their youth" (128).

WORKS CITED

Cowley, Malcolm. *The Dream of the Golden Mountains*. New York: Viking, 1980.

Donohue, H. E. F., *Conversations with Nelson Algren*. 1964. New York: Berkley, 1965.

Kempton, Murray. *Part of Our Time: Some Monuments and Ruins of the Thirties*. New York: Simon and Schuster, 1955.

Lawrence, D. H. *Phoenix*. London: William Heinemann, 1936.

Rahv, Philip. *Essays on Literature and Politics, 1932–1972*. Ed. Arabel J. Porter and Andrew J. Dvosin. Boston: Houghton Mifflin, 1978.

Rideout, Walter B. *The Radical Novel in the United States, 1900–1954: Some Interrelations of Literature and Society*. 1956. New York: Columbia University Press, 1992.

Stott, William. *Documentary Expression and Thirties America*. New York: Oxford University Press, 1973.

Weber, Eva. *Art Deco in America*. New York: Exeter Books, 1985.

12

POPULAR CULTURE

AND CRISIS:

KING KONG MEETS

EDMUND WILSON

Even as it inscribes one powerfully imagined moment of discontinuity in our sense of national history, the "depression" obscures the continuities of a whole other, more persistent, and less mythic national narrative. "The negro was born in depression," Clifford Burke explains to Studs Terkel in *Hard Times*. "It didn't mean too much to him. The Great American Depression, as you call it. It only became official when it hit the white man" (82). Some white men and women in the early 1930s might have shared Burke's irony, especially the thousands of American miners, farmers, and industrial workers adversely affected by the massive economic and social reorganization of American capitalism that fueled New Era prosperity. To accept Burke's challenge, however, is to accept the challenge of understanding how the economic crisis of the early 1930s came to be defined as a crisis for and within "official," or dominant, centers of social and cultural power.

As Antonio Gramsci reminds us, this passage from economic to national crisis is neither so simple nor so direct as we might imagine. "It may be ruled out," Gramsci wrote in *The Prison Notebooks*, "that immediate economic crises of themselves produce fundamental historical events; they can simply create a terrain more favourable to the dissemination of certain modes of thought, and certain ways of posing and resolving questions involving the entire subsequent development of national life" (184). For Gramsci, the politics of crisis are played out on the terrain of culture, that place where "the great masses become detached from their traditional ideologies" (276). Consequently, to understand how the economic crisis of the depression was recognized, interpreted, and imagined as a crisis of and within dominant ideologies, I turn to a series of representative cultural moments in the early 1930s. Each of these moments, which range from the popular fiction of the *Saturday Evening Post* to Edmund Wilson's revision of modernist intellectual identity and authority to the Hollywood spectacle of *King Kong*, represents the depression crisis as an eruption of class difference, an explosion of repressed social conflict that threatens to overwhelm dominant ideological narratives of collective identity and unity.

Tracing these figures of crisis within American culture, high and low, we can also trace out a new structure of feeling as it emerges within the increasing gaps between ideology and affect; in high and low texts of the early 1930s, affective investments in the outsider, the subaltern, and the other begin to contradict and compete with the authority of "official" ideological boundaries and oppositions. Writing in 1931, both Edmund Wilson and John Dewey identified this rupture of affect and ideology as "the collapse of a romance." Wilson described "the distinct psychological change" of the depression as a general recognition that "the romance of the legend of the poor boy [that] was the romance of democracy, of the career open to the talents" served only to conceal "the monstrosities of capitalism" ("Appeal" 236). Explaining a similar "breakdown of that particular romance known as business" (294), Dewey cited a crisis in which "the normal insecurity [of market society] has got out of hand to the extent that it cannot be concealed from general recognition" (293). For both social critics, the myths and legends of New Era prosperity remained, but the emotional investment that turned these ideological narratives into collective "romances" was fast ebbing. More often than not in the cultural texts of the early 1930s, this breakdown is narrativized as a failure to contain and to manage agents of class difference who both provoke and, ultimately, subvert "official" boundaries between inside and outside, self and other, and order and anarchy.

Located within this generalized cultural scene of difference and disruption, familiar texts are constellated in new ways. We can see, for instance, how Edmund Wilson's 1931 critical masterpiece, *Axel's Castle*; William Faulkner's only bestseller, *Sanctuary* (1931); and the movie *King Kong* (1933) share a similar set of narrative preoccupations and perform their cultural work *for* different audiences but *within* a common ideological problematic. Adopting this kind of synchronic perspective on 1930s culture, historians of the decade stand to gain a more complicated, less secure, but more productive map of the period and its struggles over and within culture. From this perspective, for example, critics and historians attracted to the decade's radical culture and politics might begin to see that the preoccupation with class and class conflict was not confined during the 1930s to a "Stalinized," avant-garde, "proletarian literature." Instead, representations of class recur in displaced form all across the spectrum of popular and elite, dominant and oppositional cultures. Situated in this broader context, representations of class might better be viewed as contested, discursive terrain around and through which a variety of texts negotiated their ideological and cultural business. This essay charts the conditions out of which class and class identity surfaced as central terms in the struggle over different versions of "national life."

By the end of the 1920s, mass advertising in the United States had perfected a highly sophisticated poetics of consumer desire. Weaving images and text together, advertising in the 1920s gradually eschewed direct, syllogistic, or "reason-why" ad copy in favor of elaborately scripted scenarios that promoted commodities as the natural, all-purpose solution to the crisis of everyday life. As the organic intellectuals of mass-consumption capitalism, American ad men quickly seized on the "therapeutic" value of the commodity; in modern advertising, the once simple "product" now became an intricate commodity-text, a phantasmic object whose true value was to be found in a shifting cultural economy of meanings and pleasures. As T. J. Jackson Lears notes, within this new configuration of culture and commodity, "face power, for example, could be sold to both flappers and anti-flappers — depending on whether the [ad] copy appealed to restless sexual energy or self-conscious sophistication" (383). Modern advertising invited its readers not just to purchase refrigerators, hair tonic, or color-coordinated bath sets but also to enjoy the values and pleasures of a world and self able to be transformed by the power of the commodity and the act of consumption.

For readers of the glossy, ad-packed pages of the *Saturday Evening Post* in October 1931, the advertisement featuring a hearty proletarian male and his proud declaration of solidarity on the magazine's back pages (see figure 12–1) must have appeared as a shocking intrusion into the usual parade of commodities and their "magical solutions." The ad announces the arrival of the working class into the popular arena of cultural representation, a moment of arrival that would be extended across the decade in forms as

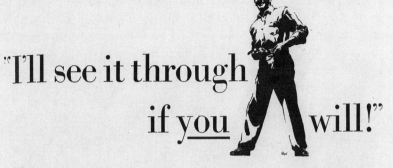

"I'll see it through if y<u>ou</u> will!"

"THEY tell me there's five or six million of us—out of jobs.

"I know that's not your fault, any more than it is mine.

"But that doesn't change the fact that some of us right now are in a pretty tough spot—with families to worry about—and a workless winter ahead.

"Understand, we're not begging. We'd rather have a job than anything else you can give us.

"We're not scared, either. If you think the good old U. S. A. is in a bad way more than temporarily, just try to figure out some other place you'd rather be.

"But, until times do loosen up, we've got to have a little help.

"So I'm asking *you* to give us a lift, just as I would give one to you if I stood in your shoes and you in mine.

"Now don't send me any money—that isn't the idea. Don't even send any to the Committee which signs this appeal.

"The best way to help us is to give as generously as you can to the Unemployment Emergency Committee *in your own town*, as well as to the established welfare, charity and relief organizations there.

"That's my story, the rest is up to you.

"I'll see it through—if *you* will!"

—Unemployed, 1931

THE PRESIDENT'S ORGANIZATION ON UNEMPLOYMENT RELIEF

Walter S. Gifford
Director

COMMITTEE ON MOBILIZATION OF RELIEF RESOURCES

Chairman

The President's Organization on Unemployment Relief is non-political and non-sectarian. Its purpose is to aid local welfare and relief agencies everywhere to provide for local needs. All facilities for the nation-wide program, including this advertisement, have been furnished to the Committee without cost.

FIGURE 12-1. *Advertisement for the President's Organization on Unemployment Relief* (Saturday Evening Post, October 24, 1931)

various as Jack Conroy's *The Disinherited* (1933, published first as a series of autobiographical sketches in H. L. Mencken's *American Mercury*), Frank Capra's *Meet John Doe* (1941), and Sidney Hillman and the CIO's vision of the "Keynesian Co-operative Commonwealth." Announcing this arrival, however, the ad from the President's Organization on Unemployment Relief violates several key conventions of mass advertising: associating consumption with status mobility, the democratic discourse of advertising, its texts and images, erased all class distinctions in favor of a homogeneously happy middle-class ideal. Perhaps more important, making production and the producing classes invisible, modern advertising also rigorously purged its seductive tableaux of any specific historical markers. To render its subjective pleasures that much finer, advertising substituted its own privatized, self-reflexive temporality for all references to public and collective historical experience. In this modernist chronotope, all consumers are equal, and each exists equally in the cathected "now" of consumption. Referring explicitly to the depression and "five or six million of us — out of jobs," this proletarian intruder bursts into the text of New Era prosperity and drags the messy facts of contemporary history into a sociocultural space normally reserved for the dreamwork of America's consumer-citizens, not for confrontations with class difference.

The cause of this contretemps lies perhaps in the ad's author, the President's Organization for Unemployment Relief. POUR was a quasi-governmental agency created by President Herbert Hoover in the late summer of 1931 and charged with the specific task of "cooperat[ing] with the public authorities to mobilize the national, state and local agencies of every kind which will have charge of the activities arising out of unemployment this winter" (Hoover, *State Papers* 609). Like Hoover's more general response to the depression, POUR embodied his commitment to a variant of enlightened liberalism. Recognizing the potential dangers of a society dominated by the aggressive, impersonal forces of capitalist markets but dedicated to the strict separation of state and civil society, Hoover looked to the "moral capacity for cooperation" (*State Papers* 7) as a way to preserve "the values of individualism" (*American Individualism* 8) in an increasingly competitive and corporate society. Denied an activist role in American society, the state could, however, apply its moral and intellectual authority to encourage cooperation and compassion as necessary civic virtues. Hoover was adamantly and famously opposed to direct federal relief on the grounds that, like other governmental initiatives, it might "stifle initiative and invention" and "cramp and cripple the mental and spiritual energies of our people" (*The New Day* 163). As he made clear in

a 1932 radio address, Hoover refused to yield in his belief that no "governmental action, no economic doctrine, no economic plan, can replace that
God-imposed duty of the individual man and woman to their neighbors"
("I Am" 356). Hoover thus saw relief for America's millions of unemployed
workers and their families as a private affair conducted among local community members. Using the bully pulpit of the White House and the
bureaucratic resources of Washington, the state could, however, apply its
technical and administrative expertise to encourage and coordinate the
scattered, often chaotic local efforts to meet the crisis of unemployment.
This was the role assigned to POUR in the autumn of 1931.

Though POUR was empowered to rationalize the nation's disorganized
and antiquated system of private relief, the real centerpiece of its effort lay
in its massive media blitz of radio, billboard, newspaper, and magazine
advertising. Using donated labor from the nation's leading ad agencies, free
advertising space in the major media, and the leadership of America's
corporate elite, POUR exemplified Hoover's cooperative ideal and communicated his moral imperative to voluntary and cooperative self-help on
a mass scale. The themes of Hoover's enlightened liberalism appear quite
explicitly in the POUR ad featuring a proletarian spokesman and his
doughty resolve (see figure 12–1). Asking for "a little help" from the *Saturday Evening Post*'s largely middle-class readers, the ad's working-class
hero grounds his appeal in communal solidarity ("I'm asking *you* to give
us a lift, just as I would give one to you") and emphatically directs his
audience to "local welfare and charity organizations," not to the state (represented as an innocent bystander to the business of social welfare by the
titles and signatures toward the bottom of the page). To persuade their
readers, other POUR ads relied more clearly on advertising's recombinant
logic and thus adapted Hoover's moral appeal to the familiar hedonistic
and privatized codes of mass consumption. One POUR ad translated the
unemployment crisis into a domestic crisis of "companionate marriage,"
a disruption of emotional intimacy between husband and wife that could
only be resolved by more consumer spending, even if "spending" in this
case meant charitable giving (see figure 12–2). It was POUR's overenthu-
siastic embrace of advertising and its discourses of consumption that
prompted Senator Edward Costigan's indignant outburst to Walter Gifford,
president of AT&T and director of POUR, at the Senate's 1931 hearings
on unemployment relief: "Is it your feeling that we, as a people, ought to
follow the practice of advertising ourselves into the thrill of great spiritual
experiences?" (quoted in Piven and Cloward 52).

Perhaps Costigan himself failed to grasp the power of New Era capital-

Tonight . . . say *this* to your wife . . . then look into her eyes!

"I gave a lot more than we had planned . . . Are you angry?"

IF you should tell her that you merely "contributed"—that you gave no more than you really felt obliged to—her eyes will tell you nothing. But deep down in her woman's heart, she will feel just a little disappointed—a tiny bit ashamed.

But tonight—*confess* to her that you have dug into the very bottom of your pocket—that you gave perhaps a little *more* than you could afford—that you opened not just your purse, but your heart as well.

In her eyes you'll see neither reproach nor anger. *Trust* her to understand.

Trust her to appreciate the generous spirit—the good fellowship and manly sympathy which prompted you to help give unhappy people the courage to face the coming winter with their heads held high with faith and hope.

It is true—the world *respects* the man who lives within his income. But the world *adores* the man who *gives* BEYOND his income.

No—when you tell her that you have given somewhat *more* than you had planned, you will see no censure in her eyes. But *love!*

> The President's Organization on Unemployment Relief appeals to you to give generously now in your own community. There is no national fund. Contribute through your local welfare and relief organizations, through your community chest, or through your special emergency relief committee. All facilities for the furtherance of this nation-wide relief program, including this advertisement, have been furnished the Committee without cost.

THE PRESIDENT'S ORGANIZATION ON UNEMPLOYMENT RELIEF

Committee on Mobilization of Relief Resources

Walter S. Gifford, *Director*

Owen D. Young, *Chairman*

FIGURE 12-2. *Advertisement for the President's Organization on Unemployment Relief* (Life, October 30, 1931)

ism's consumer revolution and its penetration into everyday life. More important, what escaped the senator's attention was the duplex, often explicitly allegorical, message of mass advertising. While ads set out to sell products, their equally prized objective was to sell consumption; while the POUR ads set out to encourage private relief, their textual strategies also set out to address middle-class readers made increasingly anxious by an economic and social crisis now entering its third year. Taken individually, the unemployed could often serve as the object of genuine pathos: in December 1931, the *New York Times* published a story about Mr. and Mrs. Wilifred Wild, a young couple who, after searching unsuccessfully for work, now chose "to starve [rather] than beg." The Wilds, so the *Times* reported, "had resigned themselves to dying together" (quoted in Shannon 36). More usually, the readers of such respectable organs as the *Saturday Evening Post, Time,* and *Life* encountered the unemployed as a nameless, anarchic mass, a mob made significant by its often violent, apparently irrational destruction of private property.

As Louis Adamic noted in early 1931, "Millions of jobless and work-eager people were not newsworthy in the eyes of the press in any big way—or at least the press did not become acutely cognizant of their existence and their plight—until the situation was dramatized or intensified with violence and bloodshed" (109). Corroborating Adamic's thesis, Mauritz Hallgren culled the nation's newspapers to compile a year's worth of front-page stories about the unemployed: in Detroit, five hundred unemployed men rioted in Cadillac Square; in Indiana Harbor, Indiana, fifteen hundred jobless men stormed the Fruit Growers Express Company demanding work (166–72). In his book *Seeds of Revolt* (1933), Hallgren's list runs for half a dozen pages. Emerging in the national media as ominous signifiers of national disaster, these images of the unemployed often stood at the center of unsettling and apocalyptic speculations, such as those George Leighton and Frank Tannenbaum published in *Harper's* and *Scribner's* and titled, respectively, "And If the Revolution Comes . . . ?" (1932) and "The Prospect of Violent Revolution in the United States" (1931). Startling newspaper photographs of U.S. regular army troops violently expelling the Bonus Expeditionary Force, a ragtag army of World War I veterans, from Washington, D.C., in 1932 only seemed to confirm the dark possibilities Leighton and Tannenbaum outlined. Except on rare occasions, the "unemployed" who greeted middle-class readers in the mass media did so on the condition that they represented agents of social disorder, made anonymous and doubly dangerous by their participation in "mob" politics.

It is within this repertoire of social disorder, mob violence, and moral degeneracy that the POUR ad assiduously works to construct its "representative" voice of the "Unemployed, 1931" and to construct the authority of the new social contract it offers. As the ad's proletarian spokesman labors to make clear, he is not in fact representative of the "Unemployed, 1931." Rather, he fashions his identity by noting his difference from those who ascribe "fault," who "beg," and who denigrate America by looking to "some other place." Taking up dominant images of the unemployed as an insubordinate mass, this worker clarifies his cooperative impulses by distinguishing himself from these other "dangerous classes." In this scenario, national unity in a time of crisis depends on the expulsion of deviant citizens, those potential un-Americans who might ruffle the (putatively) smooth relations of cooperation and exchange between classes. Despite this conclusion, the threatening remainder of cross-class cooperation still plays an important part in the contractual language of the ad's appeal; the conditional clause in "I'll see it through if *you* will" also implies that, conversely, "If you don't give, then I might see not see it through." Yet even as it reopens the threat of insubordination, the ad clarifies the relation between middle-class reader and the "unemployed" through its "representative" image of the worker in rough shirt and baggy trousers who happily tightens his own belt. The jobless worker happily enacts, as terms of his submission and proof of his good faith, his own fantastically staged self-discipline under the attentive gaze of the middle-class reader. Invoking class difference and the threat of class conflict to enact the necessary value of social discipline, this POUR ad implicitly acknowledges and confirms the power relations concealed by Hoover's moral discourse of voluntary cooperation and civic virtue.

To understand the popular currency of this solution to the "problem" of unemployment, we might look at the ways in which class difference and its potential threats are contextualized in the magazine fiction that surrounds the POUR ad. In particular, three stories in the same October issue of the *Saturday Evening Post* pursue analogous, "disciplinary" routes to the symbolic construction of a national-community. The plot of "Jeptha's Daughter" by Ben Ames Williams revolves around the failure of the Atlas Lumber Company, an allusion to the nation's economic crisis shared by Thomas McMorrow's "1931—Old Style," a story that centers on corruption in the construction industry. Likewise, Clarence B. Kelland's "Elephants and Go Carts" focuses on the efforts of Stephen Howland, a local banker, to rescue the fictional town of Chester from imminent economic ruin. In each of these stories, "traditional" values, such as community, family, and work, are threatened by internal subversion. In Williams's story, Dan Atlas, the rightful heir to the Atlas Lumber Company, refuses his legacy and abdicates his family responsibility to pursue a life of youthful pleasure lifted straight out of the previous decade's infamous melodramas of "flaming youth," such as F. Scott Fitzgerald's *This Side of Paradise* (1920) and Percy Marks's *The Plastic Age* (1924). "'That's the baby,'" Dan says as he introduces himself to the story's heroine and its readers. "'Say you're a smooth egg. Well, I'm going to bring you to a boil'" (38). The corruption of youth is matched in "1931—Old Style" by the corruption of George Hake, a building contractor who bribes, connives, and cheats his way through the business world only to abandon his trusty business partner, Harry Addicks, with a huge, overdue mortgage payment. Like the young banker who "tramples everybody who gets in his way" (86) in "Elephants and Go Carts," each of these characters represents an acquisitive individualism run rampant, a force that threatens their respective communities because it readily sacrifices the general good for the fruits of self-interest.

By supplying "low" doubles for these middle-class delinquents, each story plays out its conflicts between order and anarchy, authority and insubordination, community and self, in the more vivid terms of social difference. In "Jeptha's Daughter," the efficiency and productivity of the Atlas lumber camp are threatened by a bootlegging cook, Charlie Feese, a "gross" man who parodies Dan Atlas's prolificacy and whose name connotes the "dirty" pleasures he introduces by way of cheap whiskey into the once orderly lumber camp (42). Acting in a "traditionally" female role as the agent of moral health and domestication, the boss's daughter runs this disruptive character out of the camp, returns the temporarily drunken, unruly lumberjacks to the ways of clean living and hard work, and thus practices a dry run for her future reformation of young Dan Atlas. "1931— Old Style" draws its narrative of social disorder and discipline along even more traditional lines. As Harry Addicks struggles to recover from his partner's betrayal, the real conflict in the story settles into a nativist drama that conflates ethnicity, class, and social deviance. The subcontractor who employs scab labor and thus queers Harry's deal with the building trades is named Spinacchio; the mysterious Mr. Rothschild extracts usurious interest from an earlier loan to Harry and his partner; and, in the story's climactic scene, Harry punches out Mike Largo, a tough, bejeweled enforcer for the Electrical Contractors' Protective Alliance and a character the narrator simply refers to as "this sinister second-generation American" (100). The moral of these stories, as Stephen Howland phrases it in "Elephants and Go Carts," is that "in these times it is ration every dog and keep him good-natured so he won't start a general dog-fight" (12). The intrusion of "outsiders" like Charlie Feese and Mike Largo threatens to stir up an already volatile working class and thus to foment the dog-eat-dog conditions of social chaos. With these agents of difference expelled, the various incarnations of national community represented in the *Saturday Evening Post* might achieve the kind of cooperative order envisioned, for instance, by the narrator of "1931—Old Style." "This was in 1931," he tells his readers, "and work was scarce. The workmen were as disciplined as soldiers, responding instantly to commands, seeming incapable of self-assertion" (11).

Noting this shift is important because it points to the powerful but unstable role that social difference played in the representation and experience of crisis early in the depression. For all their philosophical disagreements, radicals, liberals, and readers of the *Saturday Evening Post* shared a common, usually ambivalent, appreciation of what this new arrival of the working classes held in store for American culture and society. Linked to the threat of social disorder, articulated in the POUR ads and the *Post* fiction, social difference could and soon would be mobilized along different narrative and ideological trajectories.

As the case of Edmund Wilson demonstrates, class difference played an enabling, even liberating, role in the political and cultural transformations of postwar modernism and its intellectual and artistic life. Even as *Axel's Castle* (1931) certified his reputation as America's finest appreciator of the literary avant garde in 1931, Wilson was moving from New York into the less familiar terrain of San Diego, Memphis, the auto factories of Detroit, Indian reservations in Arizona, and the backwoods of Kentucky. Wilson would later collect his sketches of local places and hard times in *The American Jitters* (1932), a book he described to Allen Tate as "a sort of fragmentary history of what is happening here—events during the Depression" (*Letters* 220). In October of that year, his travels led him to Lawrence, Massachusetts, a decaying textile town made legendary in U.S. labor history by its Wobblie-led textile strike of 1912. After recording the poverty and destitution of the town's working classes, caught up in yet another strike against their bosses, Wilson paused to adopt the imaginary perspective of the mill owners, foreigners like himself to the proletarian experience of American life. "You forget," he wrote, "that the people beyond have faces too—from here you cannot see their faces any more than they can see the faces here. You are aware only, in spite of feeble and diseased children, in spite of foolish broken-spirited men and slattern-looking stringy haired women, of the strong and rich human material of life that seems to persist on the wrong side of the social wall" (*Jitters* 275). Wilson cited as examples of this hidden but "rich human material" "handsome well-formed Portuguese girls," "pretty and plump French-Canadian women with civilized black eyes," and "German and Polish men, self-confident, accurate and energetic, who know as much about their factories as their masters" (*Jitters* 275–76). Moving beyond appearances, Wilson thought he had discovered an authentic culture, a way of life that somehow nurtured human dignity and pride, even in the teeth of social crisis and class warfare. Ironically, however, the factors that circumscribed the gaze of Lawrence's capitalist mill owners — class, birth, and culture — also created "the social wall" that separated Wilson, the cosmopolitan intellectual and blue-blooded liberal, from the authenticity he ascribed to Lawrence's immigrant working classes. Seeking to root the "faceless" existence of these marginalized Americans in the meticulously recorded details of everyday life, Wilson struggled in his writing to transact an emotional and moral alliance with these dispossessed people and, in the process, to transform his own intellectual identity as literary critic by bridging high culture and proletarian experience.

Like many radicalized intellectuals in the 1930s, Wilson experienced the social and economic crisis of the early 1930s not just as a crisis of political allegiance but also as a specifically vocational crisis. The breakup of American society challenged these intellectuals to forfeit their transcendent status and to reconnect the value and meaning of their work to new constituencies and new goals. Though they might remain literary critics, writers, and historians, radical intellectuals also began to investigate roles closer, at least in their modus operandi, to the new intellectual described by Louis Adamic as a "socio-political-cultural Darwin" setting out to explore the United States as a "Land Nobody Knew" (*My America* 44). The crisis of the "traditional intellectual," separated by class and culture from the "Land Nobody Knew," repeats itself as a central motif in Wilson's *American Jitters*. In Lawrence, capitalist owners and the intellectual tourist share the view from above "the social wall"; in "Still Meditations of a Progressive," the liberal intellectual, suspended aloft in an airplane, offers his anxious reflections on the distance encompassed by his airborne view of the landscape below; and, in "The First of May," Wilson abruptly zooms down from the panoptic view afforded by the top of the Empire State Building to a more empirical and intensely particularized account of one worker's suicide in the city's boroughs. In each of these cases, Wilson's jittery self-reflections on his own transcendent position produce scenes of disruption and dislocation, scenes that owe their sudden instabilities to the looming presence of the other and the intellectual's discomfiting encounter with class difference.

The crisis of transcendence supplies Wilson's writing with its major theme and dominant motifs in the early 1930s. For example, *Beppo and Beth*, a play he wrote in 1932 but did not publish until 1937, translates the terms of this crisis into a spatial and social opposition between the highrise, ultramodern apartment of Beppo, a moderately successful ad man, and the dirty, tough city streets below. "It's all so bleak and abstract," one of Beppo's houseguests comments as he gazes out from the apartment's balcony. "'It's as if people were realizing for the first time that the city is really a prison—though I d-don't know whether they're even so human as that—they're more like a lot of bugs that have just had the light turned off on them—they're still moving around in the darkness waiting for it to flash on again so they can keep flying against it. I've never known New York so ominous'" (212). Distance creates the illusion of autonomy, of the integrity of a space described by Beppo as "a little palace where my friends and Mimi [his daughter] and I could admire ourselves and make fun of the world" (284). When Luke Bostok, the financier and owner of Beppo's building, explains the "fictional" credit that created the Richelieu-Versailles, Wilson allegorically connects the transcendent pleasures of Beppo's "palace" and its residents to the speculative economy of New Era capitalism.

In the play's version of the 1929 crash, however, Mimi's love affair with Jack Payne, the local bootlegger and crime boss, sets off a series of transgressive intrusions by various representatives of the working-class dwellers in the streets below. Beppo's girlfriend, a second-generation immigrant and aspiring nightclub singer named June, shows up to baffle the reunion of Beppo and his estranged wife, Beth; the sound of gunfire interrupts things at several points as Al Gammel, a washed-up, cocaine-addicted thug attempts, incompetently, to assassinate Luke Bostok; and, finally, Jack and Mimi elope, forsaking Beppo and Beth to descend to the world outside. Connecting and confusing high and low realms, these intrusions destroy Beppo's illusions of safety and refuge. By the play's end, he and Beth are busy lighting out for the territories, hoping to recover in Mexico's exotic setting the kind of "natural" order and stability denied them in New York.

With its narrative of disruption, class transgression, and collapse, *Beppo and Beth* recapitulates the same motifs that define the situation of the radicalized intellectual in *American Jitters*. Both scenes of crisis in *American Jitters* and *Beppo and Beth* look back, however, to the earlier themes Wilson developed through his critical engagement with literary modernism. *Axel's Castle* scolds such modernists as Valéry, Proust, and Eliot for the self-conscious obscurity of their prose and poetry, but Wilson's real argument is about cultural politics, not literary form. Justly repelled by modern society, Wilson's modernists used difficult, esoteric art to fashion a transcendent refuge from history. The price of this transcendence was, according to Wilson, an abdication of cultural authority in the public sphere. While some modernists, such as Valéry, chose to ensconce themselves in the "Axel's Castle" of aesthetic "experiment," other modernists— most notably Rimbaud—set out to rediscover "the lost brutality and innocence of Europe" in "the non-Christian, non-middle-class life of the Orient, of Africa" (276). In either case, Wilson concludes that the cultural politics of modernism turn out either to comply with the antinomian definitions of art and society offered by capitalist culture or to be "a good deal of interesting social criticism . . . which does not aim at anything" (290). As Wilson described it in *American Jitters*, the security of "Axel's Castle," like the haven of the Richelieu-Versaille, had been demolished by the depression. But for those radical intellectuals who looked to class struggle as "the motor power of hope" that might direct their "creative imagination for the possibilities of human life" (290), Wilson offered the cautionary examples of Rimbaud and Beppo. Resolving their respective crises by fetishizing social difference as absolute otherness, each becomes a displaced person—as deluded as Axel, as inconsequential as any tourist. To trace the semantic figures of social difference as they emerge in the culture of the early 1930s is also to constellate texts like Wilson's into new relations, relations that also cut across the bias of elite and popular culture to conjoin very distinct sociocultural realms, such as those of mass advertising and literary production.

William Faulkner's 1931 novel, *Sanctuary*, occupies one particularly complex moment in such a constellation. We do not often think of Faulkner as a popular novelist, but *Sanctuary* gained him a significant public profile and a not insignificant financial boost after the commercial and critical failure of such novels as *The Sound and the Fury* (1929) and *As I Lay Dying* (1930). Within weeks of its publication, *Sanctuary* had sold almost five thousand copies, more than the combined sales of these earlier novels. Until 1948, it would remain Faulkner's only novel to stay consistently in print. In late 1931, *Sanctuary* also become the first of Faulkner's books to be reissued in several successive editions of the cheaper and more popular Modern Library editions.[1] More mediated signs of *Sanctuary*'s popular status would include, for instance, the rapid proliferation of the novel's many paratexts: interviews with its author; Corey Ford's 1932 *Van-*

ity Fair satire of Faulkner and his novel, titled *Popeye the Pooh*; and the nationwide release of a movie version of the novel, *The Story of Temple Drake*, by Paramount Pictures in 1933. Once established, the popular identification of Faulkner as "the author of *Sanctuary*" proved difficult to escape. Indeed, Faulkner grew so alarmed at this reception and the way it tended to make *Sanctuary* the exemplary text of his entire oeuvre that he quickly published his famous apologetic disavowal of the novel as the preface to the Modern Library edition. Instead of constituting a "problem," as it did for Faulkner and most of his later, postwar critics, the popular appropriation of *Sanctuary* belongs to the same structure of feeling as is outlined by Hoover's POUR ad, the *Saturday Evening Post*, and Edmund Wilson.

Contemporary reviewers of *Sanctuary* generally attributed its popularity to the new "cult of cruelty," a development in American literature that reflected both the moral failure of American culture and the decline of American society.[2] Responding to this influential articulation of the novel's significance, one veteran of the political and cultural battles of the early 1930s later suggested a more psychosocial explanation for the novel's popular reception and its relentless fascination with violence; *Sanctuary*, Malcolm Cowley explained in his 1946 introduction to *The Portable Faulkner*, "is an example of the Freudian method turned backwards, being full of sexual nightmares that are in reality social symbols" (15). The chief sexual nightmare in the novel is Popeye's vicious rape of Temple Drake with a corn cob, but as Cowley's comments indicate, this is a sexual transgression entangled in a violation of class boundaries.

Sanctuary divides its characters and settings into two discrete and opposite social spaces: modern, urban Memphis and rural Jefferson, the symbolic center of an agrarian culture and society that refers back to the postbellum South celebrated by Allen Tate and others in *I'll Take My Stand* (1930). In the novel's complicated structure of doubling and repetition, the gangsters and whores of Memphis stand in parodic, mocking relation to the Victorian proprieties of Jefferson; the black comedy of a gangster's funeral and Miss Reba's pet dog, named after her ex-husband, for example, submit the sanctified institutions of Jefferson to a comic, irreverent reinterpretation. The Old Frenchman place, where Temple is raped, is also the site where an agrarian economy, represented by the production of moonshine, intersects with an urban economy of distribution and consumption. As a setting inhabited by both Memphis criminals and the "yeoman" of Yoknapatawpha County, the Old Frenchman place enables and exacerbates the dangers of cross-class contact. Most significantly, the liminalities of the Old Frenchman place open Jefferson up to the intrusive presence of Popeye, a figure who belongs, intertextually, to the popular fiction and film genres of the period that metaphorically equated America's urban, immigrant working classes with crime and disorder.

Temple's rape, which occurs amid a confusing narrative rush of events and perspectives, is never actually presented in *Sanctuary*'s narrative discourse. This absence, in turn, shifts the novel's narrative focus from the motives behind actions to the effects, and chief among these effects is Temple's sudden transformation from an eminently conventional southern college woman to Popeye's gin-drinking, chain-smoking, consensual sex slave. In *Sanctuary*, sexual violence establishes a disquieting identity across the social differences of class; all of the characteristics attributed *to* the other—irrationality, anarchy, disorder—now reappear *within* characters who belong to the world of Jefferson. In Faulkner's "misogynous vision" (Guerard), this inversion centers on, but is not confined to, women. Horace Benbow sets out to rescue Temple from her abduction, but when he hears her tell the confusing, nightmarish tale of her rape, Faulkner's respectable, straight- laced lawyer suddenly discovers his own transgressive desires for Little Belle, his stepdaughter; thinking back on Temple's story in his hotel room, Horace imagines Little Belle's "small face [that] seemed to swoon in a voluptuous languor, blurring still more, fading, leaving upon his eye a soft and fading aftermath of invitation and voluptuous promise and secret affirmation like a scent itself" (234). The horror and repulsion in Faulkner's novel are driven by a nagging insecurity about the boundaries that distinguish Jefferson from Memphis and the decorous middle classes from a degraded working class.

As Horace's case demonstrates in Faulkner's vision of social crisis, Popeye's disruptive powers, once unleashed, are communicated throughout the social order, disturbing and then explicitly canceling the difference between Jefferson and Memphis and between agrarian community and urban society. To redress her victimization, Temple cooperates with Jefferson's legal authorities to convict an innocent man, Lee Goodwin, of her rape. Instead of neutralizing Popeye's crime, however, this action only escalates his initial disruption as an angry mob lynches Goodwin the night after his conviction. When Horace, who has defended Goodwin in court, arrives too late at the lynch scene, a voice in the crowd shouts out, "'Do to the lawyer what we did to him. What he did to her. Only we never used a cob. We made him wish he had used a cob'" (311). Horace escapes, only to return to Belle, his wife, and the stifling, demeaning routines of a marriage he had sought to escape at the beginning of the novel. Meanwhile, we last glimpse Temple as she sits on "a gray day, a gray summer, a gray year" (332) in Paris's Luxembourg Gardens and gazes across "the opposite semi-circle of trees where at somber intervals the dead tranquil queens in stained marble mused, and on into the sky lying prone and vanquished in the embrace of the season of rain and death" (333). *Sanctuary*'s terrifying vision of social crisis ends with only a kind of affectless immobility.

Seizing on the commercial popularity of Faulkner's novel, Hollywood quickly released its own sanitized version of *Sanctuary* in 1933. When Paramount Pictures erased Popeye and his rape from *The Story of Temple Drake*, it was left to one of the depression's greatest texts of social crisis, *King Kong*, to restore the horrific power of social difference to the silver screen. Besides narrating the disruptive intrusion of an outsider from "the other side of the social wall" into a stable and ordered social world, *King Kong* deploys other motifs common to Faulkner's apocalyptic narrative. Abduction is a key event in both, as is the unsettling alliance of women and monsters; both are stories about the fascination and danger of difference and its unexpected powers of inversion. Like *Sanctuary*, *King Kong* juxtaposes two antithetical settings, Kong's home in the jungles of Skull Island and his exile in Manhattan, and then presents its imaginary version of social crisis as the product of their violent collision. The point of this juxtaposition may not be, as Noel Carroll has recently argued, to draw a social Darwinist lesson about the timeless continuities between ancient and modern jungles. Rather, the point (in more purely Hollywood terms) is that *Kong*'s on-screen terror originates in its hero's spectacular power to transform New York City into a chaotic, apocalyptic mess, his ability to turn the city's ordered streets and vertiginous heights into a zone of pure, random terror. Thus, when Kong chooses the Empire State Building, only recently completed in 1931 as an art deco shrine to American modernity, to be the site of his last stand, he invites the movie's audience to momentarily reexperience the impersonal materiality of the city itself as mere contingency. *Kong*'s immediate and enduring popularity may rest with the ambivalent structure of this invitation; encouraged by the narrative and the camera to identify with Kong, the vengeful victim of modernity, and with the panicked masses who flee his wrath, the movie's viewer enjoys the thrill of freedom that accompanies destruction and the fearful terror that accompanies powerlessness. From this perspective, *Kong* offered its depression-era audience emancipation *from* and further subjection *to* the alien and inaccessible forces that might, amid bank failures, market crashes, and mass unemployment, seem to control their individual and collective destinies.

All of this said, *King Kong*'s most significant addition to our constellation of texts may be the way it questions the power to represent the crisis
of difference itself. *Kong* is, after all, a movie about making a movie. The
voyage to Skull Island is initiated by "that crazy fellow" Carl Denham, a
famous director of "jungle pictures," who pursues his "reckless" desire to
"make the greatest picture in the world." Keeping his knowledge of Kong's
existence a secret, Denham rescues Ann Darrow (Fay Wray) from depres-
sion-struck New York, sets sail, and begins to rehearse Ann for her future
encounter with Kong. Even before they meet Kong, Denham has already
planned out the plot and theme of his blockbuster movie. When he sees
Jack Driscoll (Frank Reicher), the ship's hard-boiled first mate, starting to
fall in love with Ann, Denham warns him, "'The beast was a tough guy
too. He could lick the world but when he saw beauty, she got him. He went
soft. He forgot his wisdom and the little guys licked him. Think it over
Jack.'" Denham's interest in Ann, like his commitment to the "romance"
plot of his movie, is purely commercial. As he tells a theatrical agent at
the beginning of *Kong*, "'The critics and the exhibitors all say, if this picture had love interest it would gross twice as much. All right, the public
wants a girl and this time I'm gonna give them what they want.'" After Ann
is abducted by Kong and then rescued by Jack from the primeval forests
of Skull Island, Denham uses the dream of "striking it rich" to convince
his shaken colleagues into shipping a gas-bombed Kong back to New York.
"'We came here to make a moving picture,'" he declares over the prostrate
body of Kong, "'and we've found something worth more than all the
movies in the world. The whole world'll pay to see this. We're millionaires,
boys. Why, in a few months it'll be up in lights on Broadway—Kong,
Eighth Wonder of the World.'"

It is Denham's grand, entrepreneurial ambition, not Kong's attraction
to Ann, that brings the primordial otherness of Skull Island straight into
the heart of an unsuspecting modern world. When he makes Kong into
Broadway's latest spectacle, however, Denham uses the "romance" plot
to sell Kong to the press and the public. After hearing about Ann's adventure on the island, a reporter murmurs, "'Beauty and the beast, huh.'"
Denham answers excitedly, "'That's it, play up that angle. Beauty and the
beast. Kong could have stayed safely where he was, but he couldn't stay
away from beauty. That's your story, boys.'" In the final scene of the movie, which repeats the earlier scene of his abduction from Skull Island, an
awed crowd gathers once again around the huge, prostrate body of a defeated Kong. A policeman turns to Denham and laconically reports, "'The
airplanes done it.'" Absorbed into the power of his own fiction and forget-

ting his earlier appeal to the ship's crew, Denham solemnly intones, "Oh no, it wasn't the airplanes; it was beauty killed the beast." Making sense of Kong's death this way, Denham once again represses his role in both Kong's and the city's destruction. But this final publicity release only conceals what the movie has already presented as its real plot: Denham's "reckless" desire, having discovered its monstrous embodiment in Kong, succeeds in communicating its destructive, antisocial effects to the city as a whole. Denham's "romance" plot, like Temple's various convoluted versions of her rape, turns out to be a convenient fiction, a story aimed not at uncovering but at repressing the truth of social crisis.

I have retold this story of affective disinvestment as a progressive deterioration in the hearty confidence of the POUR ad's worker and his promise of national and social unity. In the popular culture of the early 1930s, the representation of social difference increasingly introduces a profound ambivalence into narratives of social crisis and recovery. From Hoover's POUR ad to Kong's dislocation of narrative, truth, and self-identity, this ambivalence begins to serve as the site of an equally profound insecurity about the value and fate of the contemporary social order. Without the appearance of some alternative "romance," both Kong and Sanctuary can imagine only a cynical detachment and disavowal as the appropriate means to cope with a crumbling society.

For a brief moment in the early 1930s, Edmund Wilson was convinced that Marxism alone, the last "great political-intellectual movement of our time" ("Appeal" 238), could restore some sense of hope and desire to a people traumatized by the crisis of American capitalism. Though rejecting Marxism, John Dewey also wondered where "the glamour of imagination would next find its outlet" (294). Both of these intellectuals were confident, in their own ways, that a new "romance" was the necessary precondition to social recovery. Like Gramsci, they understood that a radical politics of social change had to proceed from the recognition that "every crisis is also a moment of reconstruction; that there is no destruction which is not, also, reconstruction; that historically nothing is dismantled without also attempting to put something new in its place" (Hall 164–65).

Within the destabilized terrain of popular culture in 1932, this work of reconstruction was already taking place. In October of that year, even the powerful Hearst chain, a beacon of conservative thought and opinion throughout the 1930s, greeted the creation of Hoover's Reconstruction Finance Corporation with rhetoric and images that counterposed the government's "select clientele" of big business and "the privileged class-es" against the misery and destitution of the nation's "ten million unem-ployed." Speaking for corporate capitalism a month before the 1932 pres-idential election, Henry Luce's glossy new magazine, *Fortune*, published its own account of the New Era's social and economic failure. Titled "No One Has Starved," in a parodic allusion to Hoover's own declaration on unemployment relief, the *Fortune* article invoked the U.S. Constitution to constellate its own images of unemployed Mexicans heading for the Rio Grande, hunger marchers in New York, Communist-inspired demonstra-tions, and the Bonus Expeditionary Force—and thus to rearticulate the meaning of the depression. The ironies of this collage were directed at the president; only six weeks earlier, he had ordered General Douglas Mac-Arthur to burn down the pathetic shantytown of the Bonus Expeditionary Force and scatter more than ten thousand unemployed veterans into the neighboring countryside. Here in the visual and textual fields of *Fortune* magazine, with their articulation of civil disobedience and constitutional rights, social difference was already entertaining new values, and novel forms of "imagined community" were already being assembled for popu-lar consumption (Anderson).

NOTES

1. On Faulkner's publishing history, see Blotner 684–86 and 743.
2. For this general approach, see Canby; Hartwick 160–66; Reynolds; and Hicks.

WORKS CITED

Adamic, Louis. *My America, 1928–1938.* New York: Harper and Brothers, 1938.
———. "The Papers Print the Riots." *Scribner's,* February 1932, 109–11.
Anderson, Benedict. *Imagined Communities: Reflections on the Origin and Spread of Nationalism.* London: Verso, 1983.
Blotner, Joseph. *Faulkner: A Biography.* New York: Random House, 1974.
Canby, Henry Seidel. "The Literature of Horror." *Saturday Review of Litera-ture,* October 20, 1934, 1, 221.
Carroll, Noel. "*King Kong*: Ape and Essence." *Planks of Reason: Essays on the Horror Film.* Ed. Barry Keith Grant. Metuchen, N.J.: Scarecrow Press, 1984. 215–44.

Cowley, Malcolm. Introduction. *The Portable Faulkner*. Ed. Malcolm Cowley. New York: Viking, 1946. 1–24.

Dewey, John. "The Collapse of a Romance." *New Republic*, April 27, 1932, 292–94.

Faulkner, William. *Sanctuary*. 1931. New York: Vintage, 1987.

Gramsci, Antonio. *Selections from the Prison Notebooks of Antonio Gramsci*. Trans. Quintin Hoare and Geoffery Nowell Smith. New York: International Publishers, 1971.

Guerad, Albert. "The Misogynous Vision as High Art: Faulkner's *Sanctuary*." *Southern Review* 12 (Fall 1976): 215–31.

Hall, Stuart. *The Hard Road to Renewal*. New York: Verso, 1988.

Hallgren, Mauritz. *Seeds of Revolt*. New York: Alfred A. Knopf, 1933.

Hartwick, Henry. *The Foreground of American Fiction*. New York: American Book, 1934.

Hicks, Granville. "The Crisis in Criticism." *New Masses*, February 1933, 3–5.

Hoover, Herbert. *American Individualism*. New York: Doubleday, Page, 1932.

——. "I Am Opposed to Any . . . Dole." *Survey Graphic*, January 1932, 146.

——. *The New Day: The Campaign Speeches of Herbert Hoover*. Palo Alto, Calif.: Stanford University Press, 1928.

——. *The State Papers and Other Writings of Herbert Hoover*. Vol. 1. Ed. William Starr Myers. New York: Doubleday, Doran, 1934.

Kelland, Clarence B. "Elephants and Go Carts." *Saturday Evening Post*, October 24, 1931, 12–13.

King Kong. Directed by Merian C. Cooper and Ernest B. Schoedsack. RKO Radio, 1933.

Lears, T. J. Jackson. "Some Versions of Fantasy: Toward a Cultural History of American Advertising, 1880–1930." *Prospects* 9 (1984): 349–405.

Leighton, George. "And If the Revolution Comes . . . ?" *Harper's*, September 1932, 466.

McMorrow, Thomas. "1931—Old Style." *Saturday Evening Post*, October 24, 1931, 11, 100–102.

"No One Has Starved." *Fortune*, September 1932, 11–22.

Piven, Frances Fox, and Richard A. Cloward. *Regulating the Poor: The Functions of Public Welfare*. New York: Pantheon, 1971.

Reynolds, Alan. "The Cult of Cruelty." *Bookman*, January–February 1932, 477–87.

Shannon, David A., ed. *The Great Depression*. New York: Prentice-Hall, 1960.

Tannenbaum, Frank. "The Prospect of Violent Revolution in the United States." *Scribner's*, October 1931, 521–25.

Terkel, Studs. *Hard Times: An Oral History of the Great Depression*. 1970. New York: Pantheon, 1986.

Williams, Ben Ames. "Jeptha's Daughter." *Saturday Evening Post*, October 24, 1931, 3, 38–42.

Wilson, Edmund. *The American Jitters: A Year of the Slump.* New York: Charles Scribner's Sons, 1932.

———. "An Appeal to Progressives." *New Republic,* January 14, 1931, 234–38.

———. *Axel's Castle.* New York: Charles Scribner's Sons, 1931.

———. *Beppo and Beth. This Room and This Gin and These Sandwiches.* By Wilson. New York: New Republic, 1937.

———. *Letters on Literature and Politics, 1912–1972.* Ed. Elena Wilson. New York: Farrar, Straus and Giroux, 1977.

13

POLITICAL

INCORRECTNESS:

THE 1930S

LEGACY FOR

LITERARY STUDIES

Repeating a familiar pronouncement, René Girard recently informed an interviewer for the French daily *Le Figaro* that "les dernier marxistes ont trouve refuge dans les universites americaines." One of the U.S. academics Girard presumably had in mind, Stanley Aronowitz, told the *Chronicle of Higher Education* that he "stopped describing himself as Marxist in the 1970s" and "recently discarded the socialist label" for "radical democrat" (Mooney 20). American professors' varied, dissonant preoccupation in the 1990s with a set of concerns often labeled "Marxism" reverberates historically. To students of American antecedents, such remarks recall the 1930s, a decade when American Marxists, many of them professed Communists, far from needing a cloistered collegiate "refuge" or engaging in serial relabeling, influenced American culture well beyond their actual numbers. As Edmund Wilson recalls the decade, "The eruption of Marxist issues out of the literary circle of the radicals into the fields of general criticism" dates to 1930, to Mike Gold's assault on Thornton Wilder in the pages of the *New Republic* (*Shores of Light* 539).

The literary cultures of the 1990s and the 1930s differ sharply, especially now that the nominally "Communist" Soviet empire, once the cynosure of progressive hope, has shattered. Nevertheless, professedly Marxist inquirers in each decade do share a set of common questions. How do prevailing hierarchies and the apportionment of state power, financial advantage, and other forms of institutional authority (churches, families, schools) condition what we say, write, perceive, imagine, perform, paint, and so on? How in turn do the words, ideas, and images of individual agents reinforce or undermine these arrangements? In a 1936 letter to John Dos Passos, Wilson described the extent to which Marxist "agitators made their influence felt" by raising "fundamental questions" (*Letters* 257). To work as a Marxist was thus to ask these "fundamental" materialist questions, to identify with a critical legacy—"the larger tradition of social concern," in Tillie Olsen's phrase (quoted in Rosenfelt 376), or "the heritage of free thought," in Richard Wright's words (352). Most strenuously promoted in the work of Marx and Engels, this legacy pervades a range of post-Enlightenment writers, such as William Blake, Thomas Paine, John Stuart Mill, Margaret Fuller, Henrik Ibsen, Max Weber, and W. E. B. Du Bois. Joseph Freeman, who served the Communist Party throughout the 1930s as its most donnish literary theorist, noted how much that decade became a time of testing for this legacy and how much the Communist Party–sponsored convergence—"the great popular movement for the preservation of nineteenth-century democratic ideals against the onslaught of fascism" (known as the Popular Front)—became its vehicle: "It took the turbulent thirties to alter attitudes toward history. . . . Revolution and counterrevolution, invasion and civil war, the collapse of the economic system and the dissolution of an entire culture centered . . . thoughts on the historic process" ("Biographical Films" 902). For this reason, because Popular Front leftism spoke so directly to the moment, even decidedly noncommunist critics acknowledged and drew on the prevailing "intellectual vitality" that Robert Warshow grudgingly and retrospectively ascribed to Marxists in the Communist Party (33). R. P. Blackmur, for example, observed sixty years ago that "the process of becoming a Communist is not the deep obliterating dye of religious conversion; it is the adoption of an additional view which modifies [and] ought to vitalize" the critic's mind (221). When vitalized by such "additional views," a Marxist or radical "critic's mind" takes as its point of departure the agnostic premise that Freeman enunciated in 1936, the recognition that no status quo—the "circumscribed experience" of a dominant class—is "eternal, natural, alone, real" ("Mask" 8).

The habits of perception and the program for inquiry that Freeman and other 1930s Marxists promoted rest on a too often utopian, more credibly skeptical egalitarianism. At its least utopian, this egalitarian agenda involves acting to reduce want and violence; to narrow the gap between the materially secure, comfortable inhabitants of the globe and those lacking the most minimal advantages; and (for academics and intellectuals) to include everyone in the pleasures and obligations by and for which we live. Marxism, with its critique of contingent and constructed social differences, promised the most persuasive approach to this egalitarian inclusiveness.

Richard Wright recalled succinctly, "I was a Communist because I was a Negro" (quoted in Fabre 230). For Wright and other Marxist writers of the 1930s, art and critique served a politics of inclusion, a set of positions that right-wing journalists now hasten to slander as "p.c." The narrator of Joseph Freeman's novel *Never Call Retreat*, published after he left the Communist Party, elaborated the distinctly "literary" appeal of this politics, of its more grandiose utopian manifestation, between the world wars:

> The fact is my father had begun calling himself a socialist. I doubt whether he belonged to any political party. . . . His views on the evils of the old order and the marvels of the new were abstract and, for the most part, I suspect, a tribute to the prevailing literary fashion. But my father was an eloquent man; when he denounced the evils of "child labor, imperialist exploitation, poverty, inequality, and war," my young heart trembled with a nameless fear and hatred of the prevailing world. On the other hand, his glowing pictures of the future classless society filled me with a wonderful sense of hope and longing, though if anyone had asked me what I longed for, I would have had a hard time explaining. (129)

"Explaining," as well as evoking such desire, constituted the literary Left's agenda as early as the 1920s and throughout the 1930s. As a means to the end Freeman's narrator longs for — "classlessness" — literary Marxists as early as the 1920s and throughout the 1930s sedulously pursued a political practice only recently sanctioned in mainstream academic criticism (and ratified by such successes as the *Heath Anthology*), the inclusion of neglected — especially African-American and Hispanic-American — voices and concerns.

Mike Gold — until recently widely dismissed as a Stalinist hack and Party hatchetman — insisted, for instance, on the common ground, "the hopeless melancholy of poverty," shared by Yiddish culture and "Negro spirituals" and claimed credit for his effort on behalf of the Party to integrate American letters "with Negro workers displaying for the first time . . . full humanity . . . tragic courage and simple, sober, self-respect": "No American author of any quality can find it in himself any longer to show the Negro as a strutting clown. The cliche has been shattered forever, outside of Holly-

wood and the *Saturday Evening Post*. And for this enormous new perception, this lifting to human dignity of the Negro people, to whom give thanks
but to 'Moscow-dominated, party-dictated' pioneers of proletarian literature
in the Thirties?" (*Hollow Men* 48). Gold's approach—speaking for "the
Other" when others may not yet be authorized to speak for themselves—
might meet with suspicion and even disparagement by today's academic
standards. Nevertheless, in its time it served to stimulate the sort of inclusiveness and reciprocity that academic critics have come to belatedly. In
Gold's writing, the tension between needing to include and fearing to oc-
clude neglected voices figured in these efforts. This tension surfaces in the
agon between a Europeanized, English-speaking villain and a Spanish-speak-
ing, indigent hero in Gold's 1920 *Liberator* story "Two Mexicos," which
evokes the prerevolutionary stress produced by the *latifundio* system. Gold's
objection, in his 1940 report from Puerto Rico on the policy of "producing
colonial subjects" by schooling inhabitants "in English, the tongue of the
master" (Folsom 61, 52–54) and his introduction to Langston Hughes's 1938
collection *A New Song* represent efforts to resolve this tension: "[Hughes]
has expressed the hopes, the dreams, and the awakening of the Negro
people. . . . but in choosing his theme, has been led on until he has also
become a voice crying for justice for all humanity." Therein lies all the moral
authority the Left has traditionally claimed and can ever credibly claim. It
resides in the central universalist tenet of Marxism: contingent class identity precedes allegedly innate ethnic, racial, and even gender difference. Most
emphasis on such differences consequently serves to exacerbate them on
behalf of the owning-governing classes. This vision disciplined the radical
criticism of the 1930s and provided it with a resonance and audience that
today's academic criticism often lacks. The power of this position brought
Richard Wright to Marxism and, briefly, to the Communist Party:

> It was not the economics of Communism . . . nor the excitement of
> underground politics that claimed me; my attention was caught by
> the similarity of the experiences of workers in other lands, by the
> possibility of uniting scattered yet kindred people into a whole. . . . My
> life as a Negro in America had made me feel . . . that the problem of
> unity was more important than bread, more important than physical
> living itself; for I felt that without a common bond uniting men, with-
> out a continuous current of shared thought and feeling circulating
> through the social system, like blood coursing through the body, there
> could be no living worthy of being called human. (302)

Now, of course, such sentiments would face deconstructionist suspicion, New Historicist unpacking, dismissal by empire-building identity politicians—all purporting speaking from the Left—as belonging to deluded, outmoded grand récits of liberal humanism. Such balkanizing, ethnic and sexual identity politics gainsay the egalitarian profession of many on the academic Left and stand in chastening contrast to Wright's remembrance of the 1930s. An op-ed piece by the labor historian Nelson Lichtenstein illustrates this first by quoting a rousing thirties slogan, "Black and white, unite, fight!" and then countering with a rhetorical question and a historical survey, "Could any idea seem more bitterly absurd today, when racial resentment and conflict drive so much of American politics, when the very meaning of equality, integration, and ethnic identity are so hotly contested? Communists and Socialists put this slogan on their banners during the big marches of the unemployed in the depths of the Great Depression." Only such an "absurd" unifying vision can make credible the legitimate and salutary sensitivity to the historically neglected that we profess. Denounced by snobs and bigots as "political correctness," this commitment can easily become mindless, as its enemies charge, when it lacks the integrationist impetus Wright described, the agenda thirties radicals pursued under the Popular Front rubric. According to Alan Wald, "The possibility of reaching a mass audience" and "the notion that radical politics could be transmitted to a large audience in the garb of liberal sentiments and idealized patriotism" underlay this agenda (101).

Whatever its limitations, such an approach reaches further than the cloistered mandarinism Girard mocked. This mandarinism enervates today's academic Marxists and divorces them from the often persuasive and sometimes inspiring civic Marxism of the 1930s, which rested on an unembarrassed passion for justice, sentiments widely seen today as vulgar or unwittingly complicit with hegemonists and oppressors. As T. V. Reed argues, "The Left needs strategically and ironically to play tradition and (post)modernity . . . against each other. . . . and politics here is about knowing those points where the immediate, purist pursuit of one's full cultural-political agenda undermines the very means of achieving any significant part of that agenda" (170). Reed shows how Ralph Ellison's rendering of the Brotherhood in *Invisible Man* provides a critique of the worst excesses of thirties Communist Party dogmatism, its pseudoscientific reading of history, and its failures to recognize how class affinities and ethnic or racial identities could not be contained in the taxonomically discrete boxes to which Communist practice invidiously assigned them. Reed argues that such self-defeating purism is neither inevitable nor exclusively academic in its tendency to "get in the way of the search for real political power by disempowering all those folks who alone could provide the sources for change" (82). Reed's critique of "purism" recalls the attack in Kenneth Burke's 1931 *Counter-Statement* on virtue and efficiency on both the right and left, along with the "menace" that "pure art" poses for emancipatory politics (Aaron 288–90). The pure art of the aesthete and the pure heart of the activist both produce orthodoxies—formulas of correctness—that stifle thinking and discourse, even when their advocates profess liberation. Resisting orthodoxy, Burke envisions "the ironist . . . essentially impure. . . . he must deprecate his own enthusiasms, and mistrust his own resentments" so that "to the slogan-minded, the ralliers around the flag, the marchers who convert a simple idea into action," he is an "outsider" who won't scoff at the activists but who will instead "observe them with nostalgia" and "must feel a kind of awe for their assurance" (102).

The ivory tower condition of most Left criticism and advocacy today, in contrast to its greater public diffusion in the 1930s, inhibits the stance Burke solicits. The recent chartering of Teachers for a Democratic Culture, with its dawning recognition of these impediments and the need to address "a wider public," moves contemporary academic radicals closer to their nonacademic precursors of the 1930s. Harvey Teres contrasts today's academic literary Marxism with our predecessors': "the dramatic politicization of theory and criticism during the past decade . . . has often been confined to the politics of criticism alone, as if this could be separated from the politics of the critic as citizen . . . largely without crucial references to political events, movements, causes, or constituencies outside the academy" (128). Consequently, professedly progressive criticism today sidesteps the questions that, according to Paula Rabinowitz, revolutionary writers in the 1930s directly confronted in ways we might do well to emulate: questions about "the political efficacy of intellectual labor" (25).

Such evasions have produced failure. The academic Marxism so widely accepted in the humanities provides no practical political leverage and appeals to no mass audience, so that self-congratulation for the purity of our motives and for the deftness of our theories constitutes the shrunken horizons of what many professed leftists regard as politics. In the work of many such academics, according to Henry Louis Gates Jr., "feel-good moralism" leads to "the routinized production of righteous indignation" as a "substitute for critical rigor" (199, 202). Unless scholars and critics who claim to speak from the Left set out to seize and maintain the rhetorical authority and the moral legitimacy traditionally the province of democratic egalitarianism, we face the consequence Antonio Gramsci foresaw over half a century ago, conditions that make "marxism itself . . . a 'prejudice' and 'superstition'" (87).

Resisting this consequence might involve some revision of the very name "Marxism," which retains hagiographic residue that Michel Foucault exposed in "What Is an Author?" Foucault named Marx a "founder of discursivity," who had created "the possibility for something other than [his] discourse, yet something belonging to what [he] founded" (114). Such hagiographic naming contradicts the skepticism toward all forms of transcendentalist mystifications that makes Marxism such a compelling heuristic. Turning Marx's and Engels's writing into Marxism, according to Foucault, transposes "the empirical characteristics of the author into a transcendental anonymity" (104).

In cultivating an antitranscendentalist worldliness, it may be important to recall that the circumstances of leftist criticism in the 1930s contrast sharply with current circumstances. The radical critique we loosely name Marxism flourished in the streets—entirely without the support of, usually in the face of widespread resistance from, the academic establishment. As Meridel Le Sueur observed, "In this crisis political and economic activity are no longer specialized and theoretic classroom sociology. They represent an accumulation of forces, a direction of energies and tendencies that show whether you are going to get enough to eat, get married, whether your child will be born alive or dead, or whether you are going to be thrown out in the streets tomorrow" (300). When Le Sueur was writing, the public gathered at union halls, city parks, and theaters and actually paid to hear, say, Mike Gold and Heywood Broun stage a communism-versus-socialism debate, and monthly magazines served as forums for radical critiques instead of the graduate seminars and little-read, institutionally subsidized quarterlies that serve nowadays. Because of the cloistered state of academic criticism, contemporary radical efforts to integrate humanitarian commitments into the humanities expend debilitating efforts straining against academic occupational hazards—pseudoscientific and aestheticist pretensions to Olympian objectivity or ivory tower purity as well as mercenary careerism masked as egalitarian critique. Frank Lentricchia proposes Burke as a model for overcoming these occupational hazards: "Burke's challenge to the Marxist intellectual is to stop making things easy for himself by talking into the mirror of the committed and to enter into a dialogue with the uncommitted. . . . to move inward into an examination of the rhetorical grounds of the dissemination of faith and simultaneously outward into critical scrutiny of the rhetorical structure of the dominant hegemony that inhibits the creation of new allegiances" (26).

Such inhibitions pose a greater constraint now than they did in the 1930s, when the careerist guild mentality that hobbles the professoriat and confines our discourse to authorized forms of sophistication was only emergent, not yet fully in force. Hence, our precursors could more easily risk enthusiasm to the point of ingenuousness in their passion for justice. As George Steiner, no friend of any on the Left, wrote of Bertolt Brecht, "Those who were wrong, hideously wrong, like the Bolsheviks, the Communards in France in 1871, the International Brigades in the Spanish Civil War, the millions who died proclaiming their fidelity to Stalin, were in a paradoxical, profoundly tragic way, less wrong than the clairvoyant, than the ironists and yuppies. . . . better to have been hallucinated by justice than to have been awakened to junk food" (114). Obviously a product of the 1990s, Steiner's revisionism belongs to a post–Cold War climate that should prove especially hospitable to the genealogical reclamation this collection pursues. Now that communism no longer poses a revolutionary alternative to the long-established, uneasily evolving political and economic organization of life in Western Europe and North America—a compelling new reason to hope that Stalinism will become a vexing historical problem and no longer a demonizing name for mass murder or a demagogic reproach to the integrity of nonviolent leftisms—we can study work by even the most diehard Communists without fearing that such attention constitutes an endorsement of the gulag.[1] Steiner's elegiac defense of Stalinists—an instance of the critical "nostalgia" Burke proposes—clears a space for us to examine and apply the thirties legacy unconstrained by the bias that Vivian Gornick sought to exorcise almost two decades ago:

> For thirty years now people have been writing about the communists with an oppressive distance between themselves and their subject, a distance that often masquerades as objectivity but in fact conveys only an emotional and intellectual atmosphere of "otherness"—as though something not quite recognizable, something vaguely nonhuman was being described. . . . This is the language of men who have assumed an intellectual opposition to the human falsifications inherent in the communist passion, and in the process are themselves committing human falsifications. Denouncing a monolithic political reality that is summed up in one armor-plated word . . . "Stalinism" . . . , they deny the teeming, contradictory life behind the word. (18–19)

Moreover, as Stephen Spender warns, scholars on the Left need to keep reminding listeners and readers that "it is not capitalism which triumphed" with the fall of the Soviet empire "so much as democracy which has been justified as putting brakes on the great and powerful and corrupt in the West. . . . the democratic West had escaped the disasters falling on the communist countries only because [of] institutionalized dissent" (20). But progressives fail as often as reactionaries and status quo supporters to heed and act on the dissolution of venerated boundaries, and, as a result, Left snobberies inhibit liberating openings and alliances as much as the avowedly reactionary "culture war" that Pat Buchanan and other influential Republicans pursued during the 1992 election campaigns. One progressive political scientist, for example, argues in a Popular Front vein against the neo-Victorian aversion to "people in trade" that keeps progressive academics from forging enabling alliances in our struggle—our Kulturkampf—to foster and illuminate a more inclusive heritage:

> Even in the politically explosive debate over multiculturalism, the business community's economic interests have gradually moved much closer to the interests of the former radicals of the 1960s than to the canon's more conservative defenders. . . . The concerns of the business community are less philosophical but no less compelling. Demographic trends make it quite clear that the domestic workforce . . . will include growing numbers of women, racial minorities, and recent immigrants. . . . the growing numbers of international competitors and customers will also be racially and culturally diverse. Under these circumstances, employees who are sensitive to issues of gender, racial, and cultural diversity are likely to be more valuable than those who are not. While the motivations of the academic and business communities . . . are quite different, their conclusions on educational goals are not. Those inside the academy who support multiculturalism primarily as a matter of principle are likely to find increasing support from a business community that supports it primarily as a matter of practicality. (Daly 11)

A measure of how much traditional right-left, capitalist-socialist boundaries continue to dissolve appears in a recent homecoming report by the Tiananmen movement leader Shen Tong, who found "progress toward a real market economy" and "the advent of cultural pluralism" in opposition to an entrenched once-revolutionary Maoist gerontocracy, "the decaying corpse of Marxist rule."

Obstacles to the consciousness-altering, egalitarian agenda many of us profess include our own reductive demonizing caricatures of obsolescing hierarchies—pseudorevolutionary, sentimentally post-1960s, exclusively verbal defiances of capitalists who, in places like China, share in some traditionally leftist goals—and the tenacious Cold War image Gornick indicts. Educated readers of the thirties Left writers who might provide an inspiring legacy persist in identifying this legacy entirely with Stalinist "artists in uniform" (to use Max Eastman's phrase) and with cookie-cutter proletarian literature.

Overcoming the second obstacle will entail reacquainting readers with old and new anthologies, such as the landmark *Proletarian Literature in the United States* and *Writing Red*, and such literary histories as Walter B. Rideout's *Radical Novel in the United States*, Daniel Aaron's *Writers on the Left*, Cary Nelson's *Repression and Recovery*, Paula Rabinowitz's *Labor and Desire*, and James Murphy's *The Proletarian Moment*. Such work illustrates the diversity of writing and the diversity of intellectual approaches, even within a frame of a shared egalitarian politics called progressivism, Marxism, or leftism. Perhaps these impressions will help us surmount the first, more intractable obstacle: the moralistic binaries that make much self-styled Left political criticism nothing more than self-congratulation and the resulting narrow emphasis on crucial diversities of native condition—ancestry (race, ethnicity), sex, parental economic condition. Attention to such circumstantial diversities often obscures the diversities that the literary Left of the 1930s seemed more committed to cultivating: diversities of temperament, style, subject matter, and even partisan affiliation. Like our thirties predecessors, we will want to avoid allowing doctrine, certitude, and indignation to impede efforts to "re-form the generic boundaries of writing itself" and—like Joseph Freeman—to recognize and even honor work "officially discredited" by whatever party we adhere to (Rabinowitz 2, 21). Even the alleged party-line enforcer Mike Gold, as he promoted the Communist Party's proletarian literature program, insisted, "There is nothing finished or dogmatic in proletarian thought. We cannot afford it. . . . It would be fatal for us to have fixed minds. Proletarian literature is taking many forms. There is not a standard model which all writers must imitate or even a standard set of thoughts" ("Proletarian" 74). Can we say the same for academic criticism today?

NOTE

1. There are exceptions to this glasnost. When my book *Left Letters: The Culture Wars of Mike Gold and Joseph Freeman* was published, a member of

the *Partisan Review* editorial board informed me that the editor would not even consider assigning someone to review a book that studied rather than excoriated Mike Gold.

WORKS CITED

Aaron, Daniel. *Writers on the Left: Episodes in American Literary Communism.* 1961. New York: Columbia University Press, 1992.

Blackmur, R. P. *The Double Agent: Essays in Craft and Elucidation.* New York: Arrow, 1935.

Bloom, James D. *Left Letters: The Culture Wars of Mike Gold and Joseph Freeman.* New York: Columbia University Press, 1992.

Burke, Kenneth. *Counter-Statement.* 1931. Berkeley: University of California Press, 1968.

Daly, William. "The Academy, the Economy, and the Liberal Arts." *Academe,* July–August 1992, 10–12.

Fabre, Michel. *The Unfinished Quest of Richard Wright.* Trans. Isabel Barzun. New York: William Morrow, 1973.

Folsom, Mike, ed. *Mike Gold: A Literary Anthology.* New York: International, 1972.

Foucault, Michel. "What Is an Author?" *The Foucault Reader.* Ed. Paul Rabinow; trans. Josue Harari. New York: Pantheon, 1984. 101–16.

Freeman, Joseph. "Biographical Films." *Theater Arts Monthly,* December 1941, 900–906.

———. "Mask, Image Truth." *Partisan Review,* July–August 1938, 3–17.

———. *Never Call Retreat.* New York: Farrar Rinehart, 1943.

Gates, Henry Louis, Jr. *Loose Canons: Notes on the Cultural Wars.* New York: Oxford University Press, 1992.

Girard, René. Interview with Vera Kornick. *Le Figaro,* May 21, 1992, 25.

Gold, Michael. *The Hollow Men.* New York: International Publishers, 1941.

———. Introduction. *A New Song.* By Langston Hughes. New York: International Workers Order, 1938. n.p.

———. "A Proletarian Novel?" *New Republic,* June 6, 1930, 74.

Gornick, Vivian. *The Romance of American Communism.* New York: Basic, 1977.

Gramsci, Antonio. "Marxism and Modern Culture." *The Modern Prince and Other Essays.* By Gramsci; trans. Louis Marx. New York: International Publishers, 1957. 82–89.

Hicks, Granville, Michael Gold, Isidor Schneider, Joseph North, Paul Peters, and Alan Calmer, eds. *Proletarian Literature in the United States.* New York: International Publishers, 1935.

Lentricchia, Frank. *Criticism and Social Change.* Chicago: University of Chicago Press, 1982.

Le Sueur, Meridel. "The Fetish of Being Outside." *Writing Red: An Anthology of American Women Writers, 1930–1940.* Ed. Charlotte Nekola and Paula Rabinowitz. New York: Feminist Press, 1987. 299–303.

Lichtenstein, Nelson. "Whatever Happened to the Working Class." *New York Times,* September 7, 1992, A19.

Mooney, Carolyn. "Down but Not Out: Socialist Scholars Gather to Redefine Political and Academic Assumptions in Post-Soviet Era." *Chronicle of Higher Education,* May 6, 1992, 19–21.

Murphy, James. *The Proletarian Moment: The Controversy over Leftism in Literature.* Urbana: University of Illinois Press, 1991.

Nelson, Cary. *Repression and Recovery: Modern American Poetry and the Politics of Cultural Memory.* Madison: University of Wisconsin Press, 1989.

Rabinowitz, Paula. *Labor and Desire: Women's Revolutionary Fiction in Depression America.* Chapel Hill: University of North Carolina Press, 1991.

Reed, T. V. *Fifteen Jugglers, Five Believers: Literary Politics and the Poetics of American Social Movements.* Berkeley: University of California Press, 1992.

Rideout, Walter B. *The Radical Novel in the United States, 1900–1954: Some Interrelations of Literature and Society.* 1956. New York: Columbia University Press, 1992.

Rosenfelt, Deborah. "From the Thirties: Tillie Olsen and the Radical Tradition." *Feminist Studies* 7 (Fall 1981): 370–406.

Shen Tong. "The Next Revolution." *New York Times,* September 2, 1992, A19.

Spender, Stephen. "Commentary." *The Value of Dissent.* Vol. 1. Colombo: Civil Rights Movement of Sri Lanka, 1992. 19–20.

Steiner, George. "Books: BB." *New Yorker,* September 10, 1990, 113–20.

Teachers for a Democratic Society. "University Professors Unite against Anti-PC Onslaught." *In These Times,* October 9–15, 1991, 17.

Teres, Harvey. "Remaking Marxist Criticism: PR's Eilotic Leftism, 1934–36." *American Literature* 64 (March 1992): 127–53.

Wald, Alan. *The Responsibility of Intellectuals: Selected Essays on Marxist Traditions in Cultural Commitment.* Atlantic Highlands, N.J.: Humanities Press, 1992.

Warshow, Robert. *The Immediate Experience: Movies, Comics, Theater, and Other Aspects of Popular Culture.* New York: Doubleday, 1963.

Wilson, Edmund. *Letters on Literature and Politics, 1912–1972.* Ed. Elena Wilson. New York: Farrar, Straus and Giroux, 1977.

———. *The Shores of Light.* New York: Vintage, 1961.

Wright, Richard. *Later Works: Black Boy (American Hunger) and The Outsider.* Ed. Arnold Rampersad. New York: Library of America, 1991.

CONTRIBUTORS

James D. Bloom is a professor of English at Muhlenberg College. His most recent book is *Left Letters: The Culture Wars of Mike Gold and Joseph Freeman*.

Constance Coiner is an associate professor of English at SUNY–Binghamton and a member of the editorial board of *Radical Teacher*. She is the author of *Better Red: The Writing and Resistance of Tillie Olsen and Meridel Le Sueur*.

Morris Dickstein teaches English and film at Queens College and at the Graduate Center of the City University of New York. His books include *Gates of Eden: American Culture in the Sixties* and *Double Agent: The Critic and Society*. He is working on a book on America in the 1930s.

Fred L. Gardaphè is an associate professor of English at Columbia College in Chicago. He is editor of *New Chicago Stories*, contributing editor of *Italian American Ways*, and cocontributing editor of *From the Margin: Writings in Italian Americana*. He is also cofounder and coeditor of the journal *Voices in Italian Americana*. His articles on Italian-American literature have appeared in many journals, and he has recently completed a book-length study entitled *Italian Signs, American Streets: Cultural Representation in the Italian/American Narrative*.

Lawrence F. Hanley is an assistant professor at the City College of New York. He has recently published an article on proletarian literature, "Cultural Work and Class Conflict: Rereading and Remaking *Proletarian Literature in the United States*," and is completing a manuscript of representations of class in American high and low culture of the 1930s.

Colette A. Hyman teaches history and women's studies at Winona State University. She has published articles on political theater and the labor movement and is completing a study of workers' theater and labor activism.

Sherry Lee Linkon is an associate professor of English and the coordinator of the American Studies Program at Youngstown State University. She has published articles on nineteenth- and twentieth-century American women writers and on feminist pedagogy.

WILLIAM J. MAXWELL is an assistant professor of English at the University of Illinois at Urbana-Champaign, where he teaches African-American and American literature. He is currently completing a study on the shifting relations among black writers, white writers, and Marxism on the cultural left in the United States between the two world wars.

JAMES A. MILLER is a professor of English and the director of the American Studies Program at Trinity College. He is currently working on a manuscript about African-American cultural politics during the 1930s.

BILL MULLEN in an associate professor of English at Youngstown State University. He has published articles on African-American literature and on Chinese and Chinese-American literature.

CARY NELSON is Jubilee Professor of Liberal Arts and Sciences at the University of Illinois at Urbana-Champaign. He is the author or editor of ten books, including *Repression and Recovery: Modern American Poetry and the Politics of Cultural Memory, 1910–1945* and the coedited collections *Marxism and the Interpretation of Culture* and *Cultural Studies*.

JESSICA KIMBALL PRINTZ is a doctoral candidate in the department of English at the University of Michigan. Her previous publication, "Marketable Bodies, Possessive Peacocks, and Text as Excess," a study of Grace Edwards-Yearwood's *In the Shadow of the Peacock*, appeared in *Callaloo*.

PAULA RABINOWITZ teaches English, American studies, women's studies, and cultural studies at the University of Minnesota. She is the coeditor, with Charlotte Nekola, of *Writing Red* and author of *Labor and Desire* and *They Must Be Represented: The Politics of Documentary*.

SUZANNE SOWINSKA is completing a book-length study of depression-era women writers. Prior to her return to academia, she worked as a union organizer for the clerical and technical division of the United Auto Workers and was also active in the feminist peace movement.

ALAN M. WALD is a professor of English at the University of Michigan. He has published several books on the 1930s, including *The New York Intellectuals*.

INDEX